Magic Digest

Fun Magic For Everyone

By George B. Anderson

DIGEST BOOKS, INC., NORTHFIELD, ILLINOIS

ISBN 0-695-80339-5   Library of Congress Catalog Card #77-187084

Table of Contents

DEDICATION

To Scott and the Two Mikes, three junior magicians who've inherited my love for magic, and to everyone, everywhere, who believes in miracles.

George B. Anderson

You Can Do Great Magic Tricks

Magic is a wonderful hobby, but getting started as an amateur magician has never been easy. The magicians' fraternity has been about as tough to break into as the Social Register.

You see, the method for accomplishing any good magic trick has always been a *secret,* and those on the inside don't want those on the outside to know how any trick is done. They shoo 'em away.

One way they do it is by selling the idea that the conjuring art is extremely difficult, possible of attainment only by a few born necromancers.

If a candidate for admission to the elect group is really determined, he goes to a magic shop where tricks are sold. The man behind the counter recognizes him as a rank beginner and sells him a few simple mechanical tricks, like the Ball and Vase, which has been a breakfast food premium for years.

The candidate practices the tricks he's bought and, at the first opportunity, performs them for an audience.

Much to his disappointment, nobody's mystified. They laugh at him.

"Old stuff," they say. "Kid stuff! Why, I got that stupid trick in a box of Crackerjack when I was six years old. *Everybody* knows that one."

Usually, the candidate is discouraged. Real magic is just—well, too much of a *mystery* for him to ever fathom. He gives up.

But if he's determined, he buys a magic book.

And unless he's been extremely lucky in his choice of a book, he's now fully convinced that magic *is* too complex for him. The book, written by a magician, assumes that he's *already* a conjurer and it's loaded with professional terminology that might as well be ancient Sanskrit as far as our would-be prestidigitator is concerned.

It says, "Get rid of the duplicate coin by your favorite method." *What* favorite method? It says, "Invite the spectator to remove any card from the deck, and force the five of spades on him." It says, "Finger-palm the ball." Huh? He reads on. "After the chosen card has been replaced somewhere near the middle of the deck, secretly bring it to the bottom by means of the Pass."

He wasn't easily discouraged, but now he gives up in disgust.

When I wrote *How to Be a Junior Magician,* I had a seven-year old boy and a six-year old girl try every trick in the manuscript. They couldn't do two of the tricks well, so those were eliminated before the book went to press.

Some of the tricks those youngsters did are being featured by professional magicians who make a living from magic.

Too complex? Too difficult? Nonsense!

Now, I don't claim that all magic tricks are ridiculously easy to learn. Far from it. Both of the books for professional magicians I've written require an advanced knowledge of magic. Our would-be hobbyist would be wasting his time and money if he bought them.

The book you now have in your hands is something else. It isn't for children and isn't for professional magicians, although both groups could get a lot out of it. This book is primarily for the person who enjoys magic and would like to be able to entertain people with it.

It's for the person who, for any of numerous reasons, is being called upon to make public appearances and wants to make those appearances different, impressive, memorable and enjoyable.

It's for the person who has no musical talent but wants to carry his weight in social gatherings.

It's for the salesman who needs a quick attention-getter and interest-arouser.

It's for the professional man who wants a hobby that's both relaxing and stimulating.

It's for all those people with a bit of "ham" in their makeup who want to exercise it but don't know how.

It's for those who want a hobby in which every member of the family can participate.

Most of all, it's for the person who thinks being able to do some knockout magic tricks would be a lot of fun.

In short, this is a magic book for everybody.

It assumes that you don't know anything about magic but want to learn. It gives you tricks you can learn to perform smoothly without any previous experience.

That means it does *not* cover a category known as "magicians' tricks," which are not aimed at an audience but at magicians, themselves. There are a lot of "magicians' tricks." Some aren't very entertaining, but all of them are extremely difficult. Being able to do one of them impresses the daylights out of seasoned professional magicians who realize that it took months, maybe even years, to learn. The average audience doesn't appreciate such tricks; they're too complicated and confusing.

Neither does it cover another category known as Stage Illusions. These are big, spectacular tricks in which a spangled girl assistant disappears in a flash from one cage and appears instantly in another, across the stage. Or the girl floats through the air without visible means of support. Or, as Jarrow, an expert illusion builder, wrote in describing Houdini's Vanishing Elephant Illusion, "Two assistants wheeled a raised platform out onto the stage and spun it around to show all four sides. Curtains hanging from a framework on the platform could be opened and closed. An elephant lumbered up onto the platform, the curtains were instantly reopened, the elephant had completely vanished, and eight assistants pushed the platform off-stage."

Big illusions are awesomely impressive, and not as difficult to learn as the "magicians' tricks." The trouble is, they cost a fortune—and what do you do with them after you buy them? Thurston, Dante, Blackstone and Nicola were the last of a long line of superb illusionists, at their peak when "the talkies"

dealt a crushing blow to live variety entertainment. Even in the few places where theaters remained available, rocketing costs of transporting and setting up such shows became prohibitive.

When economics demanded that emphasis be put on a different kind of magic, what for want of a better name we'll call the "club act" came into its own. It used smaller tricks, many of them mechanical, and still required a sizable performing area. Some of the apparatus looked as phoney as a three-dollar bill and much of it was cumbersome. It took some club-act performers longer to set up their equipment than to do their actual performances.

Gradually, a smaller, more intimate type of club act evolved, using common items that didn't look so much like gimmicked apparatus. This book will give you enough club act material so that you can do a creditable "act" whenever you like.

Currently the most popular of all magicians is the "close-up" performer. "Close-up" magic has come into its own, and the emphasis in this book is on it. In a night club, restaurant or bar, the close-up magician comes to your table upon request and performs excellent magic for you and your guests at close range, without dubious equipment. The so-called "magic" bartender" who dispenses drinks and magic in almost equal quantities falls into this group. If he's good, which he usually is, his income from magic usually exceeds his union wage as a bartender.

In many ways, close-up magic is the most mystifying of all. It's done right under your nose, with every-day objects that you can examine. It has an intimacy that no other type of legerdemain can approach. It makes every member of the audience a participant who remembers what he's seen and the magician who baffled him.

It has to be better magic, in most cases, than stage tricks. It can't depend on trick boxes, complicated stage lighting, trap doors and the assistance of five or six aides.

Most close-up tricks have to be simple. Done under such close scrutiny, there are too many points of vulnerability in a complicated trick. This doesn't mean that all close-up tricks are easy to do. Some require awesome skill. But there are hundreds of good close-up tricks that *are* easy to learn, with the proper instruction, and which are more mystifying than many of the big tricks that had to be viewed from afar.

For thousands of amateur magicians, close-up magic is certainly the most practical kind of performance, as well as the most satisfying. When you're asked to entertain at a party where you're a guest, it's somewhat impractical to set up a Sawing a Woman in Half illusion. Unskilled amateurs who take half an hour to set up a bulging suitcase of mechanical apparatus can bore the daylights out of an audience before they ever get around to doing their first trick.

Don Alan, who has appeared on most of the major TV variety shows can fascinate any group for a full hour using only a part of the contents of a slim, trim attache case. So can "Senator" Crandall of West Coast Magic Castle fame. John Thompson can entertain—and I mean entertain—an audience for any specified length of time with nothing but a deck of cards and his fine talent.

The most advanced of close-up magicians is the "Magicians' Magician." Dai Vernon is a classic example. Vernon is a flawless performer, a superb manipulator and an inventive genius. His original tricks are so perfect that he gets his kicks out of doing them for advanced amateurs and professional magicians, almost to the exclusion of general audiences. There are at least a dozen practitioners of the art of hocus-pocus who, given a choice, would never perform for any audience except one made up of skilled magicians.

A part of magic's fascination for everyone who does it is mystifying an audience. The "Magicians' Magician" has carried this phase to the ultimate. He baffles people who know almost everything there is to know about legerdemain. Some of his tricks require manipulative skill it has taken him a lifetime to acquire.

Like most magicians, he doesn't refer to what he's doing as "tricks." They're "effects." The professional magician seems to think there's a bad connotation in the word "trick," but tricks are what an audience wants to see and tricks are what you want to learn to do.

Most people who would like to do close-up magic don't do it because they're afraid to try it. They can't believe they could be skillful enough to fool any audience at such close range. And it's a pity they have that misconception.

Any person of normal intelligence can entertain and mystify with close-up magic if he acquires the right tricks and learns to perform them as they're meant to be done. The simpler any trick is, the better it's apt to be.

All of the tricks you're going to learn from this book are great, and they're simple. They've all been audience-tested under the most trying conditions. They don't require any phony-looking equipment. My six-year old grandson does some of them well enough to fool not only his classmates at school but his teachers.

What you learn from this book can give you a lifetime of pleasure.

It can make friends for you. It can give you unshakeable poise, even if you're the most bashful, self-conscious introvert.

It can improve your conversational ability.

With what you find within these pages, you can go into a group of strangers, focus attention upon yourself, and be on friendly terms with everyone within five minutes.

You can enjoy the immense satisfaction that comes from entertaining other people.

You can be happier. Magic is fun—fun to watch and fun to do. There's something so intriguing about it that those who take up its pursuit as a hobby never tire of it. There are always new tricks to learn and new audiences to entertain.

Youngsters would be hard-pressed to find another hobby anywhere nearly as rewarding. A well-known educator, Maurice Turner, in the introduction to my children's magic book, urged teachers to encourage the study of magic. "It develops self-confidence," he said, "as no other form of public appearance can."

He might have added that it improves the mental processes by stimulating a special kind of thinking that's valuable in every area. Nobody who understands magic accepts everything at face value. In politics and business, for example, he looks for "gimmicks," for subtle misdirection, for illusion—and sometimes finds them.

If you learn to do just one close-up trick well, you have a valuable asset that nobody can take away from you. You can get immediate attention with a good trick, and be remembered where others are quickly forgotten. With one good trick, you can *entertain* those around you, and an entertaining person is always welcome in any group.

When I was in my mid-twenties, I got a job as editor of the *Chicago Tribune* Syndicate Advertising Service, a copy and art service sold to newspapers throughout the United States. The *Tribune* Company was a huge organization, and the only people I knew in it were my immediate superior and less than a dozen copy writers and artists with whom I came into daily contact.

The *Tribune* had an annual weekend outing for its advertising department, and I was invited. My boss, who was on the entertainment committee, suggested that it might be nice for me to do a little magic at the big Saturday night dinner.

Within half an hour after I'd performed, I'd been introduced to all the key people in the organization and had been invited into so many congenial groups that I couldn't get around to all of them. Among other things, I was invited to the advertising director's home as a guest, and the advertising director was the top man in the organization.

Without the magic, it would have taken me five years to build the contacts I made in that one evening. A few months after my performance, I was made manager of the entire syndicate ad service operation.

Magic had paid my way through college. I developed a trick of driving automobiles blindfolded. Selling it as a newpaper exploitation stunt, I made enough money during 12 weeks of summer vacation to put me through a year of school. And after college, my first job was on the Sioux City *Tribune,* a newspaper for which I'd done the blindfold drive.

The first radio dramatic series I ever sold was "Easy Money," a rackets exposé in which an ex-magician turned rackets detective was the hero. A prospective buyer said, "I like the show, but could anyone really do that poker deal with a legitimate deck of cards?"

I had him send out for a deck of cards, did the trick and had the beginning of a new career. The show went on the air five days later, the first of five half-hour radio mystery series I wrote and packaged, and had a long run on NBC radio.

Magic has always been good to me, but if it had never done a thing for me, it's been such great fun that I'd hate to have missed it.

Don't read this book in the hope that it will make you a professional magician.

Heaven forbid!

If you'll accept my definition of a professional magician as one who makes a good living from the full-time performance of magic, you'll agree that there aren't many true professionals around. Some of them are superlative performers, but their market has serious limitations.

Before the "talkies" and television came along, nearly every town of over 25,000 population had at least one vaudeville theater that used a minimum of ten acts a week. Flourishing chautauquas and lyceum circuits were a lucrative market. Hundreds of magicians made an above-average living playing one-night stands in small towns. Others specialized in the night club and supper club field, where competition for acts was keen.

Only the night-spot market remains, and it's greatly diminished.

Try to make a list of active professional magicians whose names you can remember. I guarantee that it will be a short list, not because of any lack of talent but because the outlets for variety acts are gone.

And yet, the universal appeal of magic survives. While genuine professional magicians are few in number, the semi-professional and able amateur are thriving as never before.

Thousands of them attend at least one of the three major national magic conventions. Regional get-togethers are held every month in various sections of the country. Magic "lecturers" from all over the world appear in the key cities of the United States with what amounts to instruction for their substantial audiences of magic fans.

There are three major national magic magazines, as well as perhaps a dozen smaller ones specializing in specific areas of magic. Magic supply houses have healthy mail-order patronage.

No other hobby that I know of produces the steady flow of books that conjuring does. Magic, Inc., of Chicago publishes a magic book catalogue that is larger than the catalogues of many general publishers. The lay public never sees most of these books. They are written exclusively for the magic fraternity.

The semi-pro magician depends on another source of income for his livelihood, but augments it by selling his magical services outside of his regular working hours. He is often of top professional caliber. A tool and die cutter, for example, happens to be one of the greatest card manipulators in the world. He has written over a dozen books on card manipulation, has invented hundreds of tricks, and gives lessons to expert card manipulators. He could undoubtedly be a full-time professional, but magic is his hobby. While he makes money from it, he does it for fun.

The amateur ranges all the way from exceptionally good to incredibly bad. Magic is such an attractive, many-faceted hobby that it attracts its share of "nuts," people who go completely overboard on it. But it also draws a tremendous number of solid professional men.

It's unique in entertainment forms in that it's a contest between the performer and his audience. When somebody gets up to sing a song, play a musical instrument or do a dance, the audience hopes—sometimes in vain—that the performance will be good.

But whether a magician is performing for one person or a thousand, his audience hopes to catch him. He knows when he does it that any magic trick is a challenge to every spectator. And if he's done his home work, he knows that nobody is going to catch him. It's one man against a group, and the one man is sure he'll win. Knowing that the audience will do its darndest to fathom the secret of his trick without even coming close is the greatest confidence builder in the world.

The ad lib element of magic adds to the fun of performing, too. A part of the effect you get with a trick depends on audience reaction—and that may vary considerably. You have a story theme for each trick, but you change it to fit the situation. And since there's considerable audience participation, the verbal exchange between a performer and an audience can't be planned in advance. Nobody does magic for long without becoming a good ad libber.

And you don't do magic very long without learning a great deal about people. Everyone who's done magic for any length of time can spot the most cooperative volunteer assistant in any group. You can also spot the "wise guy" who thinks he knows all the answers and wants to air his brilliance. You soon learn how to handle him so that he doesn't have a chance. Remember, you're the performer and you can make up your own rules as you go along.

Nearly every magician has one or two pet "sucker" tricks for the benefit of such show-offs. These are tricks in which the performer deliberately makes it look like he's been caught—and then proves that he's in complete command.

Personally, I've never liked to embarrass *any* member of my audience, even an obnoxious show-off. Normally, when a know-it-all says, "Oh, I know how you do that one," I greet him as a brother magician and hand over the paraphernalia for the trick I'm doing. "Since you know the trick," I say, "I wonder if you'd do me a favor and finish it while I get the props ready for a particularly good trick I want to do next."

Some day, maybe, I'll run into somebody who'll be able to perform the trick with expertise—but in a good many years of using this ploy, it's never happened. After the fellow has fumbled ineptly for a few minutes, he's lost all his enthusiasm for trying to reveal the secret of further tricks.

I like this treatment much better than that employed by an excellent night club magician who asks in a wounded voice, "Look, pal, how would you like it if I came in where *you* were working and showed everybody how you use your swab and plunger?"

One way or another, the would-be heckler soon ceases to bother you. Actually, you reach a point where you enjoy baffling him—and the rest of the audience enjoys it, too.

Far more important than handling the heckler, you learn how to win an audience. You learn how to make people like your performance and you.

There are a lot of tricks in this book, and some will appeal to you more than others. Instead of grasping the rudiments of all of them, start by learning to do one of them well.

For some reason, beginners in magic usually try to learn as many tricks as they can in the shortest possible time. As a result, they fumble through trick after trick, not doing any one well enough to merit praise.

Start by learning to do one trick as well as you can. Fit it to your personality. If some of the moves involved in its performance seem awkward to you, alter them so that they become comfortable. Make that one trick a little gem. And once you have it where you can score with it, learn to do another one.

One real blockbuster trick, well done, will do more to establish your reputation as a magician than a dozen mediocre tricks.

Even some seasoned professionals have a tendency to emulate that Oriental performer, On Too Long. Magic is probably the most taxing entertainment there is for a spectator. He works hard throughout your performance, trying to figure out your secrets. Work him too hard and you either wear him out or leave him numb.

Some smart professionals who command high fees will tell you that they don't do over a dozen tricks. They do that dozen so well that audiences will pay to see them perform.

The brilliant Jimmy Renaux, who has been featured at Radio City Music Hall and in top supper clubs throughout the world does an act that runs six minutes —but it's a breath-taking six minutes that would be hard to top.

With all the brilliant, massive, expensive illusions that the late Harry Blackstone performed, he is best remembered for his Dancing Handkerchief trick, a simple trick done so magnificently that nobody who ever saw it will ever forget it.

Howard Thurston spent a fortune on the development of spectacular illusions, and his Floating Lady was a magic classic. But the thing that stands out in my recollection of Thurston is his bare-hand production of playing cards and subsequent scaling of them into the audience, even up into the second balcony of a large theater.

With all the astounding illusions in the Dante show, the highlight of his performance as far as I'm concerned was his version of a trick with a couple of pieces of sash cord, a trick you'll learn in this book.

In each of the three foregoing examples, the performer put the stamp of his personality on a simple trick and made it a great one.

Years ago when my thirst for magic knowledge was insatiable, Blackstone gave me a sharp reprimand. "It's stupid to try to learn every trick in the world, kid," he said. "Just plain stupid. Learn to perform one trick better than anyone else can do it and you'll have something."

With a good close-up trick, you're in a far better position than Jack Dempsey was when he was asked to contribute something to a large social gathering in which he found himself.

"Folks," the Manassa Mauler said, "I can't sing and I can't dance. And I'm not much of a public speaker. But just to show my heart's in the right place, I'll fight any man in the house."

The Ground Rules of Magic

Before you learn to do any tricks, you should acknowledge a few simple rules of the magic art. Not even being aware of these rules has caused many would-be magicians to fail in spite of having all the attributes needed for successful performance.

1. Decide on a style of performance and stick with it. You can't be a glib, wise-cracking comedian with one trick and a deep, dark mysterious swami with the next one. You can't alternate between pantomime and a barrage of patter. You can't work at a lightning-fast tempo on one trick and slow and easy on another.

At least, you can't be more than one personality within the confines of one act. The old-time magician who did a full-evening show used a number of different styles to give variety, but he did it in different segments of his show. Each segment had him following one style.

While a stage or club act can be effectively done in pantomime, the silent style is inappropriate for close-up magic. One extremely bashful introvert, trying to overcome his timidity through the hobby of magic, found that the only way in which he could work without being frightened and nervous was to put on a clown wig of the rustic bumpkin "Toby" type and act the part of a shy yokel. The character he portrayed was really funny, and the laughs he drew from his performance put him completely at ease.

Don Alan is the rapid-fire gag comedian when he does close-up tricks. Jay Marshall is the suave, sophisticated, cultured comedian. "Senator" Crandall is the cynical curmudgeon. Al Flosso is a Coney Island pitchman. Neil Foster, one of the world's greatest magic perfectionists, does a straight, unadorned, low-key performance that depends on sheer miracles for its effectiveness. Dai Vernon, another miracle man, works straight, too. Karrell Fox, one of the funniest men in magic, is W. C. Fields without makeup.

Each of these great close-up magicians has a natural style that fits his personality. The role he plays isn't forced, and he can concentrate on what he's doing without having to think about style.

The forced, artificial Mysterious Swami style affected by many beginners is sometimes pathetic and seldom impressive. A young man still in his teens, wearing the hirsute adornment of the late Alexander Herrmann and prattling ponderously about his occult abilities is simply ridiculous.

If you're a good conversationalist, develop an intimate, conversational style for your tricks. If you're a natural comedian, be a comedian while you're performing—but be the kind of comic you naturally are.

In other words, be yourself. But be yourself at your attractive best. When you bring out all the strong points of your personality and fit your tricks to that personality, you have Style.

The late Dr. Harlan Tarbell who started thousands on the magic hobby with his magic correspondence course, was a good story-teller, and he wove an interesting story around each close-up trick he did. He didn't try to be funny, because he knew he wasn't a comedian. He sold his audiences as much with his story plots as with the tricks they accompanied.

2. Make your personal appearance indicate the quality of your performance. I've seen touring performers of stature come in off the road looking like panhandlers—unshaven, covered with the grime accumulated in 600 miles of uninterrupted driving, dressed in old, almost shabby clothes. But when the time came for them to work, a transformation had taken place. They were immaculately dressed, scrubbed and barbered, full of vitality. They looked like Star Performers.

Appearance is even more important for an unknown close-up magician than it is for a well-known professional. First impressions are usually lasting—and even if your magic is good enough to overcome a sloppy appearance, why give yourself that extra work?

The commonest appearance offense in close-up magic stems from the performer's hands. The nature of what he's doing focuses attention on them, and attention at close range. Dirty fingernails immediately downgrade the close-up magician several notches, and dirty hands and frayed cuffs puts him in the also-ran category.

When the late Bert Allerton was doing close-up magic at the tables in the Pump Room of the Ambassador East hotel in Chicago, performing by request at tables occupied by celebrities from almost every field, he was invariably the best-groomed man in the famous room.

As a non-professional, you certainly want to be accepted on equal terms by those people you're entertaining, and you can't do it unless you're as well-groomed as they are.

3. Never do a trick in public unless you can do it well. This is a cardinal rule, one that shouldn't even have to be mentioned, but it's violated all the time. Ardent magic fans are always on the lookout for new tricks, and when they get one that appeals to them, they're eager to dazzle an audience with it. Much too often, they try to perform it before they're able to do the trick justice.

No matter how simple a trick is, practice it until you're absolutely sure of every phase of it and are at ease with it, unworried about anything possibly going wrong. Then do it for an intimate acquaintance, asking for criticism. Quite often you'll find that doing a trick for somebody is much different from doing it in front of a mirror. If you fluff a trick, drop it from your performance immediately and don't reinsert it until you're positive that the error won't occur again.

Many amateur magicians have far more tricks than they could possibly encompass in a full hour's performance. They seem to think that the number of tricks they can do is the yardstick of their magical status. Unfortunately, they can't do *any* of their vast array of tricks superbly well. They bumble their way through inept performances in the belief, the badly

mistaken belief, that quantity offsets poor quality.

The late Max Malini, one of the greatest close-up magicians who ever lived and certainly one of the most successful, seldom did more than ten tricks—but he did each of them so well that it was a gem.

Paul Braden, internationally famous as LePaul, the card manipulator, once said, "I buy practically every new sleight-of-hand trick that hits the market. But I don't buy them to *perform*. I buy them for my personal amusement and because they whet my mind. They keep me on my toes and alert to what's happening in the field of magic. But over the years, I don't think I've ever added more than one trick a year to my performing repertoire."

The late Gene Bernstein, a lawyer who served as international president of one of the great magic clubs, did a hypnotism routine and a trick with a pencil that raps out "spirit" signals. Those two things established his reputation among magicians as an able performer. If anyone else does the spirit rapping pencil as well as Gene did, nobody seems aware of it.

Most magicians, both amateur and professional, have achieved their reputations with one trick—a trick they perform so well that it's a blockbuster.

Remember the rule and accept it—if you can't do a trick well, don't do it in public.

4. Routine your tricks. Decide in advance what tricks you're going to do when you're called on to perform, and integrate them with each other so that you have a performance, not a series of unconnected items. It's easy to make one trick flow smoothly into another by what you say, your "patter." But it isn't easy to do on the spur of the moment, without planning.

Routine your tricks in logical sequence. A drama doesn't start with a climax and then dwindle away to nothing, and neither should your magic. Start with a "flash" trick, something quick and snappy that commands immediate attention. Then do several of your pet effects, but do them in ascending order, starting with the one that gets the least audience reaction and continuing with tricks that top it. And wind up your performance with your blockbuster, your pet trick, the one you think is the best thing in your repertoire.

In routining your performance, decide how much time you should allow and stick to it. A good, fast 15 minutes is usually plenty long—and is far better than a half-hour that limps to a close.

Quite often, the most effective performance consists of one excellent trick, done with a strong build-up.

If you're doing a 15- or 20-minute performance of close-up magic, some ardent magic fan in your audience will nearly always beg, "Let's see one more." The temptation to continue is almost overwhelming, if you have as much "ham" in your makeup as I do —but don't succumb to it. New magic fans often become such ardent devotees that they want to perform constantly, and even the greatest professional can't sustain interest for an unlimited amount of time.

5. Never, never, NEVER expose a trick under any circumstances. And this means *any* trick, whether or not it's in your repertoire.

When you reveal the secret of a trick you've just performed, you completely destroy the impact you've made. A trick is effective only so long as it mystifies. Make no exceptions to this rule. If you expose the secret of a good trick to one close friend, he's almost certain to pass the information along to others and the trick soon loses its worth. All the time and effort you've expended *making* it a good trick can be destroyed by exposure.

Tricks normally cost money—a great deal more than you're paying for those in this book. While you may be paying something for physical equipment, a substantial part of the price of a trick is charged for the secret or method of doing it. You've thrown that money away when you let anyone else in on the secret.

Actually, you do your audience a disservice when you reveal the secret of a trick. As a magician, you're selling illusion, and you destroy the illusion when you show how a trick is done.

On top of that, you reveal yourself as being grossly unprofessional when you expose. Magicians know the damage that exposure can do, and most of them are almost rabid on the subject. Aside from destroying your own tricks, let's assume that you know through your interest in magic how the Sawing a Woman in Half illusion is done. It's inconceivable that you'll do the trick yourself. Its bulk, its cost, the need for trained assistants and the staging requirements make such a trick completely impractical for you. But a professional magician who features the illusion is booked into your community.

Friends who know of your interest in magic will almost inevitably ask you if you know how it's done. Now, you can do one of three things. You can say you don't know; you can say, "Yes, but it's a violation of the magician's code of ethics to ever reveal the secret of a trick,"—or you can get a brief spotlight and show how well-informed you are by blabbing the modus operandi of the illusion.

If you take the third course, you spoil the pleasure of watching the highly mystifying illusion for your questioner. It's a little like revealing the solution of an exciting mystery novel to someone who's just starting to read it.

And you seriously damage the professional magician right in the pocketbook. He's working hard to keep magic a popular form of entertainment, which benefits you, and you're deliberately destroying him.

Mark Wilson of TV fame is a brilliant close-up magician as well as a stage illusionist, and he has a highly effective stock answer for the awed spectator who asks, "Say, how did you do that?"

"Quite well, I thought," Mark answers affably. "Don't you agree?"

If a magician doesn't deliberately expose tricks, he doesn't do it inadvertently, either. He *never* lets anyone examine his equipment either prior to or following his performance if there's the slightest chance that such inspection will disclose a secret. When he passes anything for examination, he's sure that it can be thoroughly scrutinized from every angle without giving the spectator any clue. And he doesn't expose by bungling.

6. Amateur or professional, you extend professional courtesy to other performers.

Magicians are a close-knit clan. They dig each other. They may have widely varying temperaments and personalities, but their mutual love of magic is enough to establish a bond. Teen-age boys and aging doctors, dentists, educators, lawyers, executives of giant corporations, men from all walks of life, meet on even terms at the magic society conventions. The oldsters give the youngsters sound advice, and the juvenile wand wielders often knock the elderly for a loop with magical innovations. There's no generation gap when magic fans get together.

When a magician visits another magician's community, he is given a royal welcome. If the visitor is booked in for a public appearance, the local magic fans see that the show is a resounding success. They turn out en masse and they applaud like mad, even if the performance doesn't merit it.

It's a strange thing. Magicians enjoy watching magic more than anyone else in the world. They may and often do know how every trick in a performer's routine is done, but they enjoy every second of it. They compare his techniques with their own. The secret of a trick is secondary. It's how the performer handles it that holds their interest.

Neil Foster has done the Zombie Floating Ball trick for years, and in his hands it's a magic classic. Lay audiences think it's a terrific trick, and they applaud it heartily. But their applause is nothing compared to that of magicians. Probably every magician, amateur or professional, who watches Neil do the floating ball trick knows how it's done. Many of them do it themselves.

But they don't do it like Neil does, and they know it. It's a difficult trick that requires muscular coordination, delicate timing and difficult manipulation. Knowing this, magicians see how beautifully Neil has solved every problem and what a masterpiece he's made of Zombie. They realize that they're witnessing an artistic triumph.

They used to flip in the same way over Blackstone's Dancing Handkerchief. They drooled over Cardini's flawless sleight-of-hand act, knowing every move of it but recognizing how great each move was.

Other magicians will be quick to help you, once

they see you have genuine respect for the craft. And it's up to you to help them. You don't knock another magician's performance. If there's something about it you don't like, you tell him, not the world at large. You don't try to top him when he's the performer of record. You don't bother him when he's busy setting up a performance. And you don't copy his pet, individualized tricks.

At least, you *shouldn't* do such a thing. Unfortunately, there are always a few eager copyists around. When a magician comes up with a trick that makes a big hit, they are quick to put the same trick into their own performances. Somehow, the imitators never seem to make the grade, but they're successful in one thing—they spoil the trick for its originator.

Years ago, an excellent magician named Tommy Martin dug an obscure trick out of the ancient book, T. Nelson Downes' *Art of Magic*. Tommy tore a small piece of tissue paper into bits, dipped them into a glass of water, squeezed the surplus moisture from them and put the sodden paper mass onto an open Oriental fan. He bounced the wet paper up and down on the fan, and slowly, that paper materialized into an egg. He lifted the egg from the fan and without any false moves cracked it against the rim of a tumbler and let the yolk and white fall inside the glass.

The trick has been around for years, but nobody had paid any attention to it. It made a reputation for Tommy Martin and got him top dates across the country. But within a year, every incompetent, fumbling imitator in the United States was doing the Egg on Fan trick—doing it with much less finesse than Martin. Bookers finally asked Tommy to drop the trick "because people have seen it too many times."

For some strange reason, piracy is tolerated in magic, maybe because the basic secrets of most good tricks date back to antiquity and are in the public domain. But an artist who deliberately copies another's painting or a writer who cribs another's words or a musician who plagiarizes another's tune is treated as a common thief. When another magician puts a stamp of his individuality on a trick, it is only common decency for other magicians to leave that trick alone—or, at the very least, to present it in an entirely different way.

The big magic supply houses such as Abbott's, of Colon, Mich., and Magic, Inc., of Chicago manufacture and sell specific tricks to anyone who wants to pay the price for them. Many of these tricks are sold with suggested "patter." If a trick is flashy and easy to do, hundreds of amateur magicians will buy the same trick and perform it in the same way to the accompaniment of the same memorized script.

A few years ago when I was producing a magic show, "Magic Ranch," on the ABC network, we had a spot in every half-hour show for a "junior magician." And every week, every youngster who auditioned for the spot wanted to do a catalogued trick, The Sucker Die Box. The ones who had anything fresh to offer were the exceptions—and, of course, it was the exceptions who were chosen.

It's not only professional discourtesy to copy another performer but it's rank stupidity. You are different in some way from every other human being in the world and if your magic is going to entertain anyone, you must get some individuality into it.

Since magic has existed as long as civilization and since so many amateur and professional magicians are doing so many tricks, it is virtually impossible for you to come up with anything that's really new. But you can give it a new slant, a new dress, a new approach that will make it your trick.

7. Accept prevailing performing conditions. If you're going to be doing close-up magic at a card table with a handful of people watching, it's idiotic to attempt big mechanical tricks that were meant for a stage. If you're doing a casual performance at a social gathering, you shouldn't do any tricks that require elaborate, time-consuming preparation. If you're going to perform in the middle of a circle, eliminate any tricks that have bad "angles," that can be detected from the side or from behind you. If you're going to do a trick to capture the interest of a prospective customer, it's incongruous to do one that requires an Oriental design box and two full-size billiard balls. Do a trick with a coin, a cigaret, a handkerchief, your billfold, a slip of paper or, at most, a deck of cards.

I have a special fondness for "mental telepathy" or mind-reading tricks because most of them can be performed under almost any conditions. You don't need a stage, your audience can be almost any size, people can surround you, and you can dispense with big, cumbersome equipment.

8. Don't embarrass anyone in your audience. I know, some magicians get big laughs by dragging a reluctant volunteer assistant from the audience and then making that person look like a moron. And I both detest and resent it. Sure, audiences will laugh when one of their number is made the fall guy for crude jokes, but I don't think anyone who professes to be an entertainer has any right to embarrass any member of his audience. Blackstone was the epitome of charm when working with an audience assistant, unless he happened to draw an obnoxious smart-alec who had to be cooled off. His graciousness and warm friendliness with audience volunteers made parts of his performance where he needed their help charming highlights of the show. With adults, the volunteer assistant often wound up with a little magical gift, and his technique with children made it obvious that he was crazy about them. He got plenty of laughs *with* them but never *at* them. He and his assistants shared in the joke, and if there had to be a fall-guy, it was Blackstone, not the volunteer.

15

9. Keep it clean. Following logically right on the heels of Rule 8, anything off-color or risqué in your performance will inevitably embarrass *somebody* in your audience. Magic doesn't need "blue" material, and even in this permissive age, a performer who resorts to double-entendre to get laughs in a field that has always been regarded as wholesome family entertainment lowers his standing with his audience. Even at a stag party, there are always a few people who resent dirty material, and they're usually very articulate about it. Religious jokes are always highly questionable, and so are jokes about minority groups. Good taste should be a paramount consideration when you do magic, and even when a bit is hilariously funny, if you're in doubt about its good taste, eliminate it.

10. Never do tricks with dangerous items in front of children. For example, one of the tricks you're going to learn in this book is the old Houdini trick in which you put a fresh packet of needles in your mouth along with some white thread, take a drink of water, let the audience examine the inside of your mouth, and then produce from between your lips the needles neatly threaded at even lengths along the white thread. It's a brilliant trick, but it's an adult trick. Tricks with knives and live flames fall into the same taboo list when children are present. The children should know they can't duplicate what the magician does, but they'll often try. A doctor once told me that every time a circus side show with a fire eater in it hit town, he could count on a few children being rushed in with serious mouth and lip burns.

11. Have a definite terminal point. Wind up your final trick in such a way that it's obviously a conclusion to your performance. If you've built to a climax with your final trick, you can ruin everything by ending the trick and saying weakly, "Well, I guess that's all." Back in the days of vaudeville, the great audience psychologists who were star performers spent more time on "A Finish" than on any other part of their routine. Work out a finish for your last trick that says, "This is it, folks!" without *your* having to say it.

The points we've covered in this chapter are more important from the standpoint of effect on your audience than the actual tricks you do.

Of course, you think right now that the tricks are the most important part of a magic performance. You think learning to do them is going to be a chore. You wonder if you'll be able to develop the talent to do them properly.

You'll discover as you progress from trick to trick that every item in this book has been carefully worked out, with every problem covered so that anyone who follows the instructions can learn to perform it well.

Before we continue, let's clear up a few common misconceptions.

You don't need lightning speed in your fingers to do some good sleight-of-hand tricks. Some manipulative moves are so difficult that they're not worth the time and effort, while others are easy. Speed isn't the basic essential of sleight-of-hand. Any fast movement attracts attention to itself, which is exactly what you want to avoid. The late Laurie Ireland taught me the great secret of what I regard as the best sleight-of-hand—that a broad movement covers a simultaneous smaller movement.

He illustrated his point with an extremely complicated manipulative move with a deck of cards. It was a sleight that simply couldn't be done indetectably with the deck held normally at waist level. He lifted the deck up to my eye level to show me the face of the bottom card of the deck. Then he let his hands drop back to waist level. It was a broad, fast movement—a completely natural one. And while his hands were dropping, his fingers performed the complicated move. It was indetectable.

Harry Blackstone carried the "broad movement covers a simultaneous smaller one" to the ultimate. In a fast and furious opening spectacle with the stage filled with pretty girls and assistants, he had to load a couple of live ducks into a pail that had just been shown empty. Other people on the show told him it was physically impossible for him to load the ducks into the pail without being seen.

His simple solution to the problem was to have the assistant who'd just handed him the pail trip and fall down as he stepped back. It worked. It was absolutely impossible for anyone to keep his eyes riveted on Blackstone while the assistant was taking that rather violent spill.

Another common misconception is that whenever anything vanishes, it goes up the magician's sleeve. Sleeving is a difficult manipulation for the highly advanced sleight-of-hand performer, and there aren't too many places where it can be used. Because so many spectators *think* a vanished object went up the magician's sleeve, most magicians seldom use it.

There's another wild myth that most tricks are done with mirrors. Very few tricks are done with mirrors, and most of those few are stage illusions. In close-up magic, the Mirror Glass, a tumbler divided down the middle with a mirror, is about the only prop I can think of, off-hand, that uses a mirror—and for close-up work, most magicians don't feel comfortable with it. It's too easy to detect.

Most lay audiences decide that Neil Foster's Zombie Floating Ball trick has to be done with an invisible black silk thread. Nothing could be farther from the truth. For one thing, any performer who could put the silver ball through the gyrations Zombie undergoes, manipulating it with a thread, would have to be super-human.

Some good tricks utilize a black nylon filament

thread or a human hair, but seldom is anything suspended in air from either.

I once asked the Laurie Ireland previously mentioned where it would be possible to buy a kind of thread that would be really invisible to the human eye.

"I have it in stock," he said. "Here, I'll show you." He ran a magic shop, and he hauled out a couple of tricks that I knew were operated by threads. He proceeded to do the tricks and, strain my eyes to the utmost, I couldn't see a sign of any thread.

And then he laughed at me. He had done the tricks with common white twine instead of black silk thread, but had worked out a progression of moves so that the twine was always hidden from the spectator's view.

There's another school of thought that dismisses any card trick with, "You're using a trick deck."

While it's true that many amazing card tricks can be done with a trick deck, the close-up performer seldom uses one. I discarded all but two trick deck card tricks many years ago, shortly after I quit doing magic professionally. My card repertoire today consists only of card tricks I can do in anyone's home, under any conditions, with a borrowed deck. Most of the casual performers I know follow the same practice. And there are card technicians who can do practically any trick with a borrowed deck that can be done with a trick deck, plus some that no trick deck ever devised could possibly accomplish.

If the audience has misconceptions about magic, so have magicians. The commonest, I think, is that any *new* trick is bound to be good. There is what amounts to a mania for new tricks.

The magic supply companies are hard-pressed to meet the demand for "something new," but since it's their business to sell their wares, they try to do it. They all have far superior tricks in stock, but a new trick is easier to sell, so they push it. And you can't blame them. Most of the new tricks utilize old principles, and all that's new about some of them is the name.

On the rare occasions when a new trick that's absolutely great comes along, practically every amateur and semi-pro in the country buys it and it's soon worked to death. A few years ago, a great little trick with a Coke bottle and a match or toothpick came along. It was called Anti-Gravico, and the immediate piracy of it was almost as sensational as the trick. Before long, every youngster who did any magic had it and it was so over-worked that smart magicians dropped it.

There's what amounts to almost an army of amateur and semi-pro magicians who seem to feel that you can't be any good unless you call yourself "The Great Soandso." Would that more of them deserved the title! A few of them show great originality and bill themselves as "The Amazing Sonandso" or "The Stupendous Soandso." Harry Cecil, a really competent close-up magician, got so fed up with it that he billed himself as "The World's Worst Magician."

There's another group of magicians that resents additions to the fold. This group tries to "put down" and discourage amateurs. Given its way, the entire magical body would consist of a few professionals.

They don't seem to realize that it's the enthusiastic amateurs who keep magic alive and prosperous.

If the game of golf were confined to the top professionals, how long would the game thrive? The big tournaments with their enormous purses would cease to exist. It's the amateurs in any sport or hobby who keep the professionals going.

Welcome to the fraternity. You're about to become an amateur magician. But don't say I didn't warn you. Once you learn to do a few good tricks, you're hooked for life.

The Ground Rules of Magic

1. Decide on a style of performance and stick with it.
2. Make your personal appearance indicate the quality of your performance.
3. Never do a trick in public unless you can do it well.
4. Routine your tricks.
5. Never, never, NEVER expose a trick under any circumstances.
6. Amateur or professional, you extend professional courtesy to other performers.
7. Accept prevailing performance conditions.
8. Don't embarrass anyone in your audience.
9. Keep it clean.
10. Never do tricks with dangerous items in front of children.
11. Have a definite terminal point.

Any Time, Anywhere

The most treasured tricks in magic are those that can be done anywhere, under any conditions, without advance preparation and, if necessary, with borrowed articles. They can be done at close range, with spectators breathing down your neck. The materials used to perform them can be thoroughly examined.

These are great reputation makers. People *know* that there can't be any skullduggery involved. There's nothing more embarrassing for a would-be magician than to be asked on the spur of the moment to do a trick that a member of the audience has seen him do, and to have to decline because the trick requires advance preparation. "I'm not ready" or "I don't have the special coins with me" is a horrible excuse that convinces the group you depend solely on mechanical equipment.

The first trick you're going to learn to do is priceless. It's called The Impossible Knot, and it involves much audience participation. I've seen groups at parties become so fascinated with it that they fooled with it for more than an hour, becoming more and more confused and mystified as time went on.

If you're only going to learn one trick, you can have more fun with this one than any I've ever discovered. It's a sleight-of-hand trick, and yet you'll be able to do it almost instantly. Don't be frightened because the basic setup looks complicated. It isn't, believe me.

THE IMPOSSIBLE KNOT

The only prop for this trick is a square of silk, either 24 inches or, preferably, 36. A man's square silk ascot tie works fine, and so does a babushka. It can be rolled into a compact little bundle. If you'll tuck it into the top of a pants' pocket, it will stay there without making any noticeable bulge, and won't interfere with the normal use of the pocket.

Doing the trick in someone's home, you can do it just as easily with a borrowed silk scarf, babushka or ascot as with your own. Nothing about the square of silk is tricked.

If you'll hold diagonal ends of the silk between the left thumb and forefinger and the right thumb and forefinger, it will hang down between the hands in a V. Twirl the V to make the silk form a loose rope. It will have a tendency to unroll from time to time dur-

ing the routine. Don't worry about it; just give it a few twirls so that it wraps around itself again.

Actually, you can do the trick just as well with a yard length of soft sash cord as with the silk. We're using the silk because you're going to learn to do a whole series of tricks with this same piece of silk, tricks that blend together. And the silk is much flashier than the piece of rope. However, if you think it would be easier for you to learn with soft sash cord, go ahead and learn with it. Sooner or later, however, you'll switch to the silk.

As soon as you've twirled the silk into a loose rope, you say words to this effect:

"Everybody remembers that ancient catch bet of tieing a knot in a handkerchief without letting go of either hand. As you undoubtedly recall, you won the

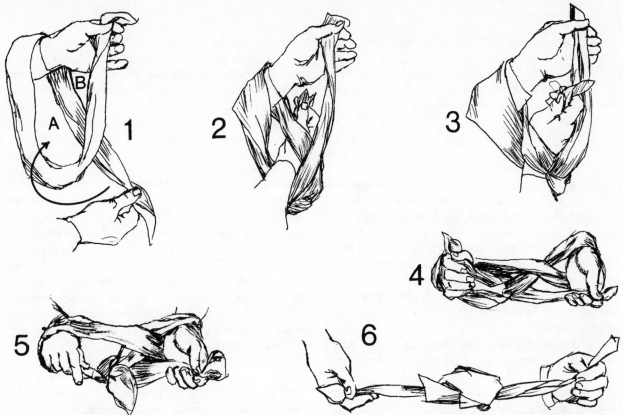

bet by folding your arms before you took hold of the ends of the handkerchief. There was, in effect, a knot already in your arms before you grasped the handkerchief, and you simply transferred it to the hank as you unfolded your arms."

You illustrate as you talk. With your arms folded and the silk either on a table top or being held by a spectator, you take the two opposite ends of it. Your right fingers, extending out over your left upper arm, take one end, and your left fingers, extending down under your right upper arm, take the other end. Now, if you unfold your arms and draw the hands apart, a knot will form in the silk.

"You won the bet," you continue, "but you had to resort to trickery to do it. The knot was already in existence when you grasped the ends of the handkerchief. That seemed downright deceitful to me, and I determined to find a way to tie a knot without letting go of either end without any trickery. After months of thought, experimentation, practice and self-denial, I finally succeeded. Watch!"

Hold the opposite ends of the twirled silk between the thumb and forefinger of each hand. There's a certain way you must drape the silk, and it sounds complex, but isn't. Hold the left end stationary. Now bring the end held by the right thumb and finger down and out over the left wrist, a little above the wrist watch. A U made up of about two-thirds of the silk hangs down behind your left arm on the near side. Your right fingers, still holding their end of the silk, come down on the far side of the arm, slightly shortening the hanging U as they reach the bottom. They come up *behind* the silken rope from the bottom of the U.

This U is now divided into two sections by the silk rope extending downward on the far side of your arm. Now bring the right fingers up behind the U and push them forward, out through Section A. They are now on the far side of the U. Now, move the right wrist to the right and bring the entire hand, still holding the silk, *back* through Section B. Draw the silk taut against the backs of your wrists. Looking down at your hands, they will look something like Drawing 4. The left end is wrapped around the right end, each end pulling back on itself.

A piece of the right end presses against the heel of the right palm. Now comes the sleight-of-hand. As you turn both wrists palm down, grip the end of the silk against the heel of the palm with the right third and little fingers. As the palms reach palm-down position, release the end of the silk rope that has been held by the right thumb and forefinger. You still have the end under control with the third and little fingers. As you slip the circlets of silk rope off your wrists and pull your hands apart, transfer the grip back to the thumb and forefinger.

As the hands pull apart, the knot forms in the silken rope much nearer to your left hand, which has remained stationary, than to the right. Both palms are now upward, there is a knot in the rope, and the release of the rope end by the right fingers to make the knot possible has been absolutely indetectable. You can't even see the move, yourself. You can't see it when somebody else is doing it, even when you know what to look for. It is almost automatic, your hands are palm down when it happens, there is no fumbling, and the broader move of turning the palms down and slipping the silken rope from your wrists completely covers it.

There's an optical illusion, with the knot appearing close to the left fingers, that any sneaky business must be done by them—and they remain fixed firmly to their end of the rope.

Repeat it for your audience several times, slowly and deliberately. And now comes the part of the trick that makes it a work of art.

"If you'll stop to think about it, you'll realize that it's physically impossible to tie a knot in anything without letting go of either end. It simply defies every physical law.

"Some people think that I do it by sleight-of-hand. In a way, I wish they were right, because anybody who could let go of the end of this silk for a split second, make a knot with it and regrasp it without being detected would have to be the world's greatest sleight-of-hand artist.

"If you're still skeptical, I'll *prove* to you that I never at any time let go of either end. Before I start to tie the knot, this time, please tie one end of the silken rope around my left thumb and the other end around my right thumb. Tie my thumbs firmly—tightly enough so that you know I couldn't possibly slip the knots off my thumbs and then slip them back on again."

When the two ends of the silken rope are tied around the two thumbs, as you've directed, you make the *identical* moves that you've made before: A U draped behind the left hand and wrist, up, out and over to the far side. Then pull the right end down and bring it up behind the now bisected U. Put it through the left side to the front and bring it back to the right through the right section. Pull the silken rope taut around your wrists.

"The knot is now formed," you tell your audience. "To guarantee that I resort to no trickery, please remove the ends from my thumbs and pull the rope from my wrists, yourself."

This is where the real beauty of the trick begins to show. The spectator who tied your thumbs now unties the ends and pulls the silken rope from your wrists. There's a knot in it!

Without the tiny sleight-of-hand move, if you pull the silken rope from your wrists and pull the ends apart, there is no knot. But if *somebody else* takes the ends and you slip your wrists out, *a knot automatically forms.*

"Almost anybody can do it," you continue. "The big thing is to slip the silken rope off your wrists quickly, in one fluid motion that doesn't upset anything. The wrist motion is everything. Here—I'll show you."

At this point, you direct a spectator how to drape the silken rope over his left wrist and hand. You put his hands through at the proper places. He slips the rope from his wrists and there's no knot.

"Your wrist movement wasn't quite right," you say. "Let's try it again." This time, when the right hand has gone through to the final position, you say, "Here, I'll help you." You grasp both the ends that he's holding.

"Turn your hands palms down simultaneously and pull them out of the rope in one quick, easy motion."

He pulls his hands out of the rope, the ends of which you're holding. You pull the ends apart and there's a knot!

"There! You see? Much better! As I told you, it's all in the wrist motion. Try it again if you like."

When others try it, they succeed or fail according to your wishes. If you take the ends and let them slip out their wrists, they have a knot. If *they* hold onto the ends and slip out their wrists, no knot forms.

While there's absolutely no logic to your statement that "It's all in the wrist motion," they see what they take as positive proof that it *is* the wrist motion that makes the difference.

Cynical, skeptical, hard-bitten people who are anything but gullible will work for a half hour at a time trying to master the "wrist move." They seem to be so close that they don't want to give up.

It can't be sleight-of-hand, they reason, because you formed the knot while the two ends of the silk rope were tied around your thumbs.

I've never seen *anyone* get caught with this trick. The head of a large national advertising agency once said to me, "Look, I know there's gotta be a trick to it. Hell, it's *impossible* to get a real knot in anything without letting go of either hand. But if there *is* a trick to it, I'll be eternally damned if I can see what it is —and I've gotta know. I'll pay you 50 bucks to teach me the secret."

I turned him down, but a New York magic shop proprietor finally taught him the trick—for $75.

And the agency head thought it was worth every penny. "In this business," he explained to me later, "you've gotta do a lot of horsing around with clients —after hours, at conventions, all the time. And the Impossible Knot knocks 'em for a loop. It's worth a fortune to me."

That New York magic shop proprietor might have given him some follow-up tricks for that kind of money, but he didn't. You, however, are going to get the full treatment.

THE INSTANT ONE-HAND KNOT

You drape the silken rope over your right hand, show it front and back, give it a little flip—and there's a knot in it.

There are two ways to do it, both are easy, and you can take your choice. The effect in either case is amazingly magical.

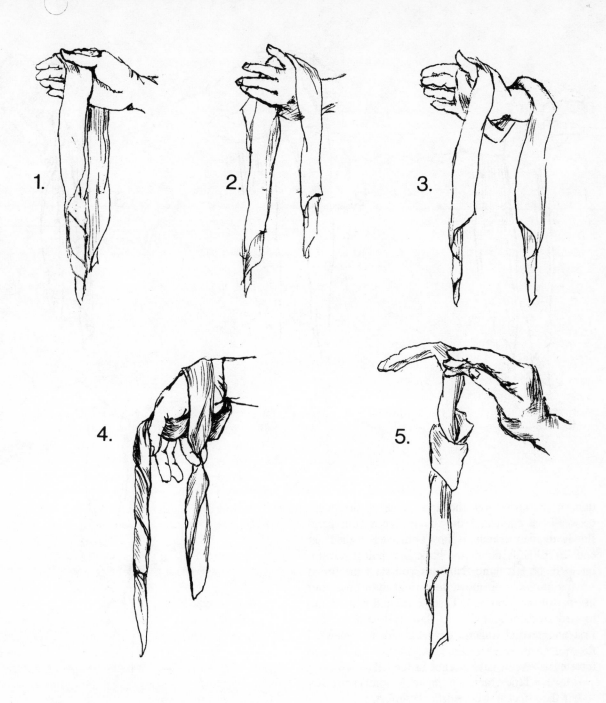

1.

2.

3.

4.

5.

Here again, you have an illustration of a broad movement masking a lesser simultaneous one.

Hold out your right hand, palm wide open, at a right angle to the floor. Drape the silk over the upper edge of the palm, well into the crotch created by the thumb. The palm faces your audience. Now, flip your hand over to the left, flipping over both ends of the silk with it. Retain a grip on the silk with your thumb, which is now at the bottom of the palm rather than the top. You have slowly and fairly shown that there's no knot in either side of the silk.

Now you make a broad up and down movement with the right hand, but this time you bring the hand back around with the palm facing you, *without* flipping either end of the silk. The two ends of the silk remain on the same sides as before the broad movement starts. Only the position of the palm has changed. The position of the silk is as in Figure 3.

As you move the hand up and down in a broad arc, you move your third and little fingers back toward the wrist and clip the short end of the silk between them. That's the whole move. Open your thumb grip, and make a downward throwing motion, holding tight with your third and little fingers to the end of the silk. It will drop from your hand with a knot in it.

In the other method, you start from the same posi-

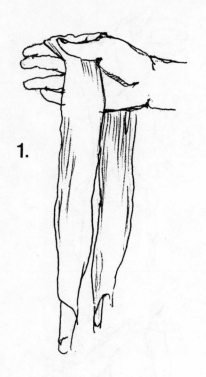

1.

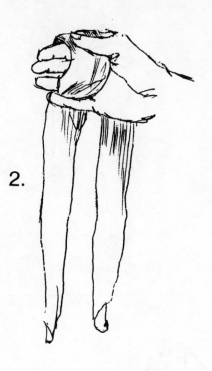

2.

3.

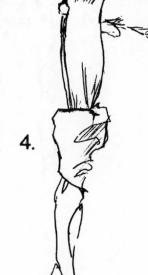

4.

tion, silk draped over the upper side of the palm, between the palm and the thumb. Turn your hand slowly and deliberately to show both sides. If the front end isn't slightly below the back end, pull it down a bit with the left hand. Now, as you start the broad waving motion, you move your right little finger out in *front* of the front end. Turn your hand with thumb toward the floor and clip the short end between your first and second fingers. Give the silk a downward throw, releasing everything except the thumb and forefinger. You'll have a knot in the silk.

It takes a little practice to make the knots smoothly —but the effect is well worth the effort.

THE SNAP KNOT

Before I learned to tie these knots, I used to "snap" a knot into the silk right after pulling it from my pocket, before I demonstrated the Impossible Knot. Nothing could be simpler.

The knot is already in the silk, close to one end. You tie a knot in one end and roll the silk from the other, so that the knotted end is on the outside of the ball of silk in the upper part of your pocket. You pull the silk from your pocket, grasping it at the knot by the right thumb and forefinger, letting the short end hang over the top edge of your palm, away from you. Your palm faces you. The NK (No Knot) end hangs free. Pick it up with the left thumb and fore-

finger and put it between the right first and second fingers, gripping it.

Now, release it with a snapping motion. Nothing happens. "In a case like that," you say, "we have to try it again." You place the NK end in the same position as previously. Move your right hand forward and make a snapping motion again, the same as before, EXCEPT that this time you release the end held between the thumb and forefinger. From all appearances, you have snapped a knot into the end of the silk. Quickly take the other end between the left thumb and forefinger and show it in all directions. Let someone untie the knot.

22

THE PHANTOM KNOT

You've already learned some sleight-of-hand, and now you're about to learn a beautiful move with a silk or rope that is useful in many tricks.

With the left hand palm down, put one end of your silken rope between the first and second fingers, at about the first joint. The silken rope hangs down toward the floor. Turn your left palm so that it's facing you, and the clipped end of the silk now protrudes from the back of your fingers, toward those who are watching. With great originality, we'll call this End A.

The right hand now brings End B (you're right, that's the other end) up across End A and nips it between the thumb and forefinger. Three or four inches of End A should extend from between the left first and second fingers. If the end is too short, simply pull it out away from your hand enough to get the desired length.

You should now be holding a loop of silken rope in your left hand, End B extending from the back of your hand from between the thumb and forefinger, End A extending from between the first and second fingers. As you look at it, End B is on top of and in front of End A.

Reach your right hand through the loop, away from you, and grasp End A as it hangs from the back of the left hand. Pull it down through the loop, toward you. As you do this, the left third and little fingers close over the part of the silken rope closest to them, an extension from End B. Pull End A tight, to form a knot. A small loop is formed as the knot tightens, by the part of the silk held by the left third and little fingers. The silken rope tightens *around* this little loop or bight. The instant the knot is tight, the left third and little fingers reopen. You have just tied what seems to be a perfectly normal knot into the silken rope. Hold End B in its position between left thumb and forefinger and take End A between right thumb and forefinger, exhibiting the knot. Extend the silken rope toward someone, asking the person to blow on the knot. The silken rope is held taut at this time. As the spectator blows, you apply a little extra pull to the silken rope. Don't make a deliberate tug. The extra tension should be so small as to be imperceptible. With it, the knot will seem to disintegrate and you will be holding a silken rope without a knot in it. The knot has vanished!

Tie this knot over and over again, until you can do it without thinking about it. Having a knot melt away to nothing is a good enough trick in itself, but it is just the beginning of what you can do once you've mastered this move. For example, you can do a trick that's a real stunner. I call it:

SILK THROUGH THE BODY

Have a spectator extend his arms and clasp his hands tightly together, toward you. Hold the silken rope in the starting position for the Phantom Knot. Let the loose end hang down between his arms and hands. Grasp End B between the right thumb and forefinger and bring it up to the left thumb and forefinger, exactly as in the Phantom Knot trick. Tie the Phantom Knot tightly around his arm. End A is now in your right hand. Bring it down beneath the spectator's arm and back up so that it is on the side of the spectator's arm away from you. Tie it and End B in two legitimate knots.

Caution the spectator to keep his hands tightly clasped so that there's no possibility of removing the silken rope from his arm without untieing the knots. Grip the last knot tied firmly between the right thumb and forefinger and give a small, quick tug. The silk comes completely free of his arm and may be examined. While there are only two knots in it, nobody ever notices the discrepancy.

The illusion is that the silken rope has passed right through his arm. When smoothly done, this trick never fails to bring exclamations of astonishment. This is one of those great tricks that you may repeat several times without anyone catching the secret.

24

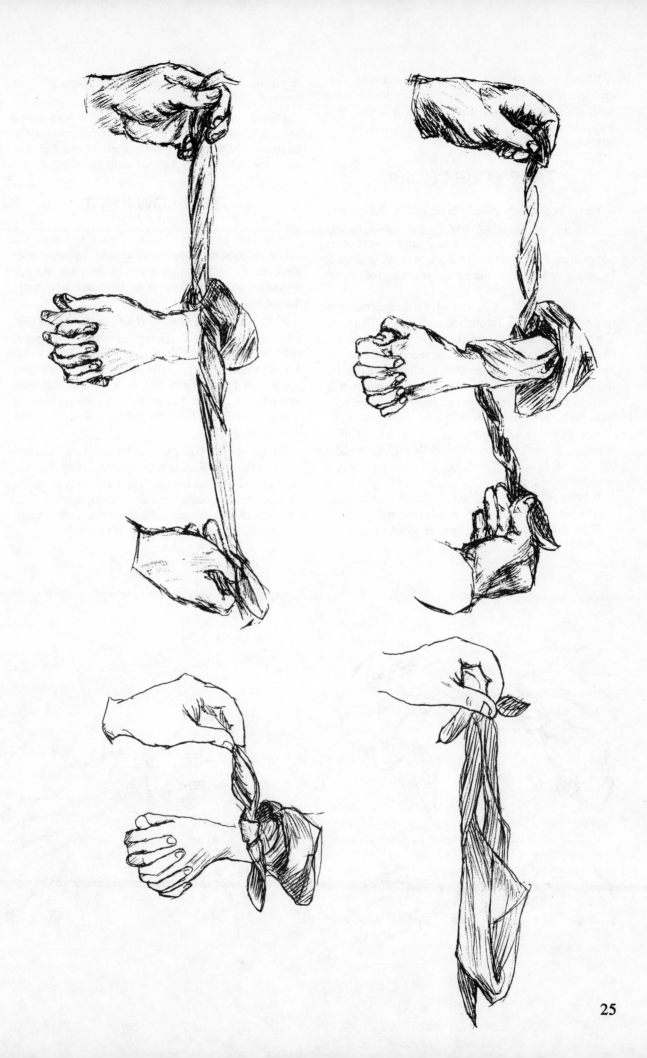

After you've removed the firmly tied silk from several spectators' wrists or arms, you can do the same trick all over again but with a different setting that makes it seem to be an entirely different phenomenon. We'll call this trick:

TAKE YOUR CHOICE

Have two cheap plastic bracelets or bangles of contrasting colors. They may be purchased at any ten-cent store. However, if two feminine spectators are wearing solid bracelets or if one is wearing several, by all means borrow the solid bracelets and forget about using your own.

Have a spectator hold one of the bracelets, drop one end of the silk through it and tie the Phantom Knot. Keep End A between your right thumb and forefinger. Have a spectator hold the second bracelet up against the first, the one that is already tied onto the silk. Bring End A down to the rings and put it through *both* of them, outward and away from you. Now tie a couple of knots with ends A and B.

For purposes of explanation, we'll call the first bracelet that was tied into the silk Bracelet One and the second Bracelet Two. Ask the spectator which bracelet he wants.

If he says bracelet One, simply give it a gentle tug. As it comes free of the silk, hand it to him.

If he says bracelet Two, grip bracelet One in the left hand, and hand him the silk, with Bracelet Two knotted onto it.

Do *not* repeat this one. Because the spectator doesn't know what you're going to do, he gets the impression that you can remove either bracelet and leave the other firmly knotted onto the silk.

THE BLOW KNOT

While you're doing tricks with the silken rope, it's always a good little throw-away trick to apparently tie a couple of tight, fair knots in the ends, have a spectator blow on them and they seem to untie themselves.

Keep your hands moving while you tie (?) the first knot. Actually you don't tie anything. You simply twist the ends around each other so that End A and End B wind up in opposite hands from where they started. Pull them tight, and then tie *one* legitimate knot. Let a spectator take the two ends and pull it tighter, while you hold the silk tightly right at the knot juncture.

At this point, you can exhibit the loop, and the knots in the ends appear to be tightly, firmly tied. Let the knotted portion have a little slack. Ask someone to blow on the knots, and as they do, apply a little pressure, pulling the two sides of the silk slightly apart. The knots (?) will twirl free as if by magic.

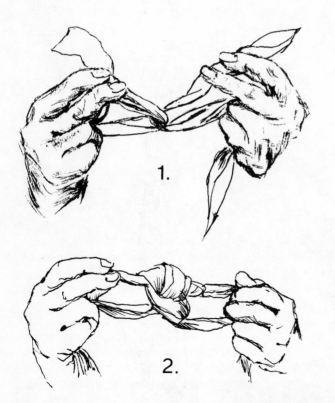

1.

2.

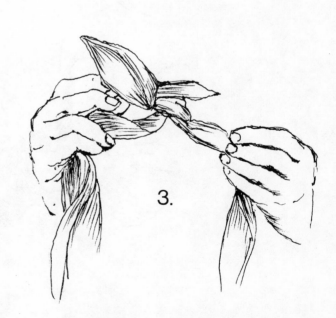

3.

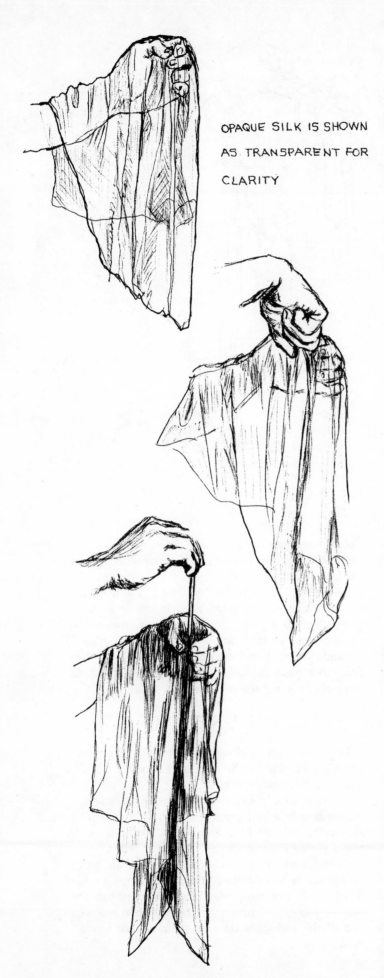

OPAQUE SILK IS SHOWN AS TRANSPARENT FOR CLARITY

TRIPLE CHOICE

You already have a good routine with the silken rope, but if you want another trick, let someone hold up a cane, yardstick, broomstick, or anything similar. Tie *three* silken ropes of contrasting colors onto the stick, using the Phantom Knot for each tie. Now, ask the spectator which one of the three silks he wants removed from the stick.

Whichever one he names, lift it away from the stick with a single tug. Quickly slide the other two off the end of the stick as if they were firmly knotted.

For an entirely different kind of trick with the silk, do the trick called:

PENETRATION

Cup your left hand into a loose fist and drape the silk over it. The move is perfectly fair, just what it seems to be. Now, while you're picking up a knife, a ball-point pen or a wand with the right hand, *open* the fist and then close it. This move forms an open channel of silk within your fist.

With your right forefinger, go through the motions of poking a little well into the left fist, so that a little bag of silk seems to be encased in it.

Drop the pen, wand or knife into the well and bring it out at the bottom. Everything looks completely fair from any angle. Drop it through several times, right under the spectator's nose. At the conclusion, whip the silk from your left fist and hand everything for examination.

"Some people," you admit at this point, "get the idea that there's something tricky about the piece of silk I use. And since I wouldn't want *you* to accuse me of flimflammery, I'll use a length of silk ribbon from now on. This piece of ribbon has virtually no bulk and it would be impossible to hide anything of any size behind it. Examine it, please."

While your spectators are inspecting a 36-inch length of quarter or half-inch ribbon, you either borrow a solid bracelet or get out one of the plastic ones that's part of your equipment. You're ready to do:

INSTANT OFF AND ON

Drape the ribbon across the upper edge of your left forefinger, so that about half of it hangs down on each side. Now, put your thumb beneath the ribbon that hangs across your palm and move it out and up, parallel with the forefinger and about two inches apart from it. Don't try to hide any part of this movement. Turn the hand so that the tips of the fingers and the tip of the thumb face your spectators.

"With the ribbon in this position," you say, "the only possible way to thread the bracelet onto it is to

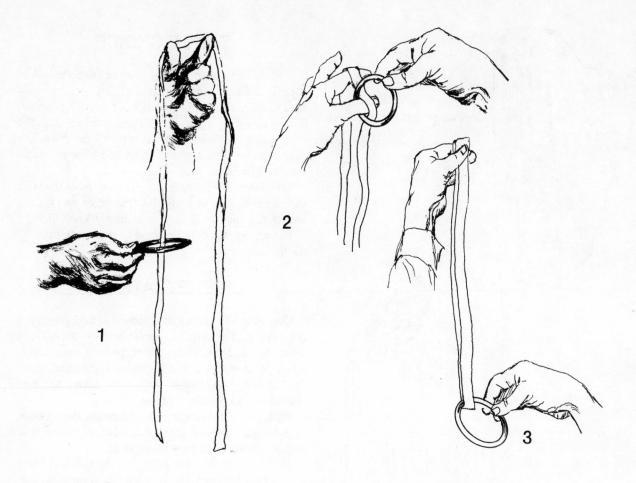

bring it down to one of the two ends." Demonstrate this, letting the bracelet come up over each end and then bringing it back free again.

"Putting the bracelet against the middle of the ribbon and bringing it down between the thumb and fingers, there's no way in the world to thread it into the ribbon." Demonstrate this, too, letting the spectators see exactly what happens.

"The only way to get the bracelet onto the ribbon from the center is to do it magically. I'll show you how."

At this point, turn the back of the hand toward the spectators and slightly cup your fingers. Drop your thumb out from under the ribbon so that the ribbon is simply hanging from the edge of the forefinger. With your right hand, bring the bracelet down behind the fingers exactly as you did before.

Put the thumb across the left edge of the bracelet and under the ribbon, as illustrated in Figure 2. Bring the thumb back out to about its original starting position, with a loop of ribbon over its back.

Now, pull the bracelet downwards until it is below the hand and the two ends of the ribbon are gripped in the left hand. The bracelet is threaded onto the ribbon.

Spectators will swear that the two ends of the ribbon were never out of sight, and yet pressure of the bracelet downward against the center of the ribbon has apparently threaded it.

"If you'll think about it," you say, "you'll realize that this is absolutely impossible. It just never happened. Very few people in this world are masters of the technique of threading a bracelet onto a ribbon without putting it on from one end or the other. I'm going to explain the technique to you right now." At this point, you get ready to do:

PIN-A-RIBBON

Lay the length of ribbon in a straight line across the table top. Put the bracelet on top of the ribbon, a little to the right of center.

"Now, a simple way to *attach* the bracelet to the ribbon is with a safety pin." You pull up a loop of ribbon through the bracelet and pin it with a small safety pin to the end that extends to the right.

"The bracelet is now *attached* to the ribbon, but it isn't really threaded onto it, and there's nothing magical about it. Common sense keeps repeating that the only way to get the bracelet *onto* the ribbon is to put one of the two ends through it, which we haven't done."

"There's a simple little sleight-of-hand move that's needed to accomplish the impossible, and the Magicians' Union insists that I cover my hands with a handkerchief while I do it. But don't worry—I'll leave both ends of the ribbon in plain sight at all times."

You throw a handkerchief or the silk you've previously been using over the center of the ribbon and the bracelet. Now, you put your thumb through the little loop that was formed when the ribbon was pinned. Touch your left forefinger firmly to the tip of the thumb. The loop of ribbon is loose within the circle thus formed. Remove the right hand from beneath the handkerchief.

Grasp the right end of the ribbon between your right thumb and forefinger, and start to hand it to one of the spectators. The left end of the ribbon will have gone through the circle made by your left thumb and forefinger. Pull away the handkerchief with your left hand. The movements with left and right hand are almost simultaneous, but the left hand removes the handkerchief *after* the right hand has started its movement. It pulls the handkerchief to the *left,* the thumb and forefinger still encircling the loop of ribbon until the ribbon is entirely free of the hand.

With the right hand, give the end of the ribbon to a spectator. Tell him to hold the left end in the other hand while a second spectator releases the safety pin. When the safety pin is removed, everyone sees that the bracelet is now threaded onto the ribbon.

A trick could hardly be easier to do, yet the effect is completely baffling. Again, spectators will swear that the ends of the ribbon were never out of sight.

"So now," you smile and shake your head ruefully, "you're sure there's something tricky about the ribbon. Maybe I can convince you there isn't by using a piece of rope."

The ideal rope for all rope tricks is soft sash cord. If the cord is stiff, you must work the stiffness out of it before you use it. Magic supply houses stock a soft sash cord that is just right. Have a 36-inch length

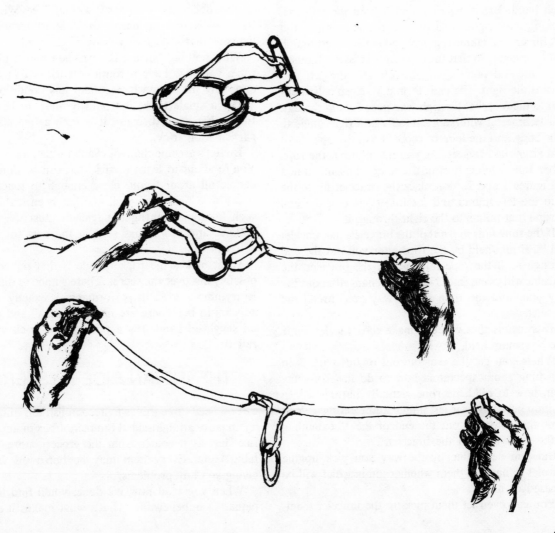

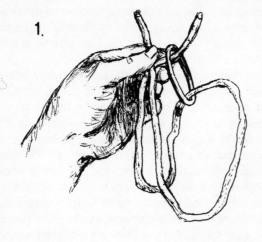

1.

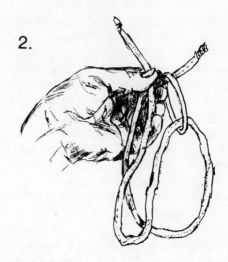

2.

of it and you're all set to do a trick that falls into the same classic category as the Impossible Knot. This is the:

IMPOSSIBLE PENETRATION

Thread the borrowed solid bracelet or your own plastic one onto the length of rope, with an end in each hand. Bring the right end behind the left one, moving your right hand over to the left thumb and forefinger, and taking the right end between left thumb and forefinger, so that the rope ends cross each other, the right end pointing to the left and the left end toward the right. The ends form a V. Even call attention to the fact that the right end goes *behind* the left.

The bracelet will hang naturally at a right angle to your body and the loop of rope. Grasp the bottom of it in your right fingers. As you lift the ring, the rope either falls behind it or in front of it, as illustrated in Figures 1 and 2. You place the bracelet up to the V in the left thumb and forefinger, putting the end of rope that points to the right through it.

If the rope falls in *front* of the bracelet, the bracelet will be firmly held by the rope after you put the end through it. If the rope falls *behind* the bracelet, the bracelet will come free. Nothing is changed about the way you hold the rope or the way you thread the bracelet.

This means that you can make the bracelet come free or remain held, at will.

Where you get the real fun out of this trick is in "teaching" your spectators how to do it. You show them how to hold the rope, actually putting it into position between their left thumb and forefinger. You show them how to put the end of the V extending to the right through the bracelet.

But you determine by the way you pick up the bracelet to hand to them whether the bracelet will be released or not.

You can even let them pick up the bracelet them-selves. Watch and see whether the rope falls to the front or to the rear of the bracelet. Once you see which way it falls, say, "I can mentally will you to release the bracelet or keep it threaded on the rope. This time (rope behind ring) I've decided I want the bracelet to come free."

A spectator who tries it on his own will get varying results. Sometimes the bracelet will remain threaded on the rope and sometimes it will fall free. What baffles him is that he hasn't the faintest idea *why* it happens that way. Every move is identical.

With nothing but a silk, a ribbon and a piece of rope, you now have a routine of tricks that can be done any time, anywhere, under any conditions.

For a single trick, it would be hard to beat The Impossible Knot, because it is such a fine audience participation trick.

But let's assume that you want a little more variety. You're about to learn a trick that can be done with people all around you, close enough to touch you. It is also a fine stage trick and has been featured as such by some top-flight magicians. Just the secret, without any props, has sold in the past for a ten-dollar price.

What makes the trick unique is that nobody can possibly discover the secret. There's none to discover! Everything used in its performance is exactly what it appears to be. There are no "gimmicks" and there's no sleight-of-hand. It's a phenomenal trick and we call it:

THE INDIAN RICE MYSTERY

You need three things to accomplish this miracle— a jam jar or straight-sided tumbler, a box of uncooked rice, just as it comes from the grocery store, and a table knife. Every item may be borrowed without giving you any problems.

When you read how it's done, you'll find the explanation unbelievable. That's what makes it such a terrific trick; people who see it can't believe that there's no trickery about it, either.

The effect is simple. You pour a quantity of loose, uncooked rice into an empty jar. Then you plunge a common table knife into the rice. When you lift the handle of the knife, the jam jar and rice cling to the knife blade, suspended without visible means of support. You can handle it with complete freedom. And yet, when you offer it to a member of the audience, the jar and loose rice won't cling to the knife blade at all. Dipping the blade into the jar has no more effect than if it were dipped into a jar of water.

A jam jar that turns inward at the top is preferable. Any container that is larger at the top than at the bottom won't work. Although a straight-sided glass will work, once you're familiar with the trick and have the knack of it, a container that is narrower at the top than at the bottom is preferable.

Most stage magicians use an ornate brass bowl or vase. A clear-glass container is greatly to be preferred, in my opinion, because it shows the absence of trickery.

Many of the little glasses in which commercial preserves, jellies and jams are packed are ideal for the trick.

To start with, open the box of rice grains and sift a few of them through your fingers. If anyone likes, you may let him examine the rice to his heart's content.

Once your audience is satisfied that there's nothing

tricky about the rice, pour enough of it into the jam jar to fill it to overflowing. Rap the bottom of the jar sharply against a solid table top a couple of times, ostensibly to get rid of the surplus rice at the top, but actually to pack the rice down in the jar as solidly as possible. Brush off any rice that extends above the lip of the jar.

Now, make a crunching, stabbing motion with the knife, downward into the rice, a number of times. The purpose of this movement is to pack the rice even harder. With repeated thrusts, you can feel the rice packing more firmly into the jar.

When the rice is firm enough, grip the handle of the knife firmly and shove the blade straight down, firmly and solidly. It should now be wedged into the rice as firmly as if it were buried in solid cement.

You'll need to do a little experimenting to get the proper "feel" of the rice and knife blade, but once you get it, you'll have it for good. The problem most magicians have the first time they try it is purely psychological. They don't see how the trick could possibly work and don't expect it to work. If they persist, they find that their disbelief was ungrounded. The knife blade will pick up the jar and the rice as if everything were one solid unit.

Now, if you put the jam jar onto your left palm to hand to someone else to try it, grip the bottom firmly, and give the knife blade a slight back-and-forth twisting motion, the knife will not only come free but will unpack the solid rice.

A spectator who now lowers the blade into the jar will get absolutely no resistance. The blade won't cling at all. The rice can be poured back into its original container and everything can be minutely examined.

Impossible? Indeed it is—but it works.

I use a story about life in ancient India, where rice was the staff of life. When a young man and young woman became engaged, they went to a Shaman or Hindu mystic to learn whether or not the marriage would be successful.

The Shaman used a crystal jar to symbolize the prospective bride, and a silver knife to represent the groom. Since rice represented life, rice was poured into the jar. Now, if the prospective groom partook of the rice (insertion of the knife blade) the two people, the bride and groom, should become as one. They and their lives should adhere in one solid unit.

When such a thing happened, the young couple felt that a miracle had happened and that their marriage would be divinely blessed.

Of course, an unscrupulous suitor who had been spurned by the young lady often went to the Shaman and bribed him. In such a case, the knife blade never clung to the jar and the marriage was considered to be doomed.

A friend who learned the trick from me tells the

story about a bride who knew nothing about cookery and whose husband loved rice pudding. The bride looked first for some instructions on how to cook rice. The cookbook made the erroneous assumption that everybody knows you boil rice. All it said was, "When you insert a knife-blade into the rice and a few grains of it cling to the knife, it is ready to eat." The bride jabbed a knife blade into a jar of raw, hard rice—and not a few grains but *all* of it clung to the blade. She poured some canned pudding sauce over the top and served it to her husband with the knife handle extending from the top. He removed the knife handle and never believed her story that hard, uncooked rice grains had clung to the blade. "For that matter," my friend continues, "I'll confess that I don't believe her story, either. Do you?"

Don't be discouraged if this trick doesn't work the first time you try it. I don't know *anybody* who has been lucky enough to do it the first time. As I recall, it took me almost an hour to get the knack. My six-year old grandson caught the feel of it in about half an hour.

The trick is worth learning because it can be done under any conditions and is an unexplainable miracle to every audience. When you're at a party and do the trick with borrowed rice, one of the host's table knives and a suitable jar or glass from the kitchen, you have a blockbuster.

BURNED AND RESTORED
BORROWED BILL

The finale of this trick depends on whether or not you're carrying any equipment. What's needed is so small that people who like the trick always have it with them. If you find yourself without the equipment, you can still do a version of the trick—and whatever version you use, you'll give your audience plenty to think about.

The basic ingredients are a letter envelope, preferably of the size used for social correspondence, not the long envelope used in business, and a borrowed bill of any denomination from a dollar to a thousand.

An old-time circus sideshow magician, Bluey-Bluey, is generally credited with the trick's invention.

I know that a magician in a traveling carnival side-show taught it to me, and he had many variations.

My handling varies considerably from Bluey-Bluey's. I agree with him, however, that cheap envelopes are best for the trick, particularly when you start with an unprepared envelope.

At the outset, you should use a prepared envelope. On the back of the envelope, a little more than half-way down, type the following:

TO WHOM IT MAY CONCERN,

Anywhere,
U.S.A.

Note that the "To Whom It May Concern" is underlined. There's a reason. Make about an inch slit in the underlining with a razor blade, putting something inside the envelope so that the blade doesn't cut through the other thickness of the envelope. The slit should be on the back or address side, directly in line with the point of the flap on the other side, but at least half an inch below the V opening on the back.

This envelope can be casually shown, front and back, without the slightest chance of anyone discovering the slit. The envelope may either be in your inside jacket pocket or on the table, flap side up.

Announce that you want to borrow a bill of any denomination from a dollar to a thousand. You promise that you'll return it.

Tell the person who offers you a bill that in order to make sure you return his bill and not a counterfeit, he should copy the serial number. See that he does this, and have someone else verify that he's copied it correctly.

Take the bill from him and roll it into a tube which will be somewhat shorter than a cigarette. Once it is in tube form, flatten it by running your fingers along it.

Once the bill is folded, either pick up the envelope from the table with your left hand or reach into the inside coat pocket and remove it. Show it casually, front and back, but don't call any particular attention to it.

Now, if you hold the envelope in the left hand in position to insert the bill, either end pointing downward, into the envelope, you'll find that your left thumb is on the open or flap side of the envelope and your fingers are on the back, covering the slit without any maneuvering or artificial movement.

The flap of the envelope is open. The right hand inserts the rolled-up bill, held only by the thumb and forefinger. You push the bottom end of the bill through the slit, to the outside of the address side. Ideally, it should extend out about half-way, a little less if anything.

Remove your right fingers and hold the open side of the envelope toward the audience, showing the top part of the bill extending from the V opening. Moisten

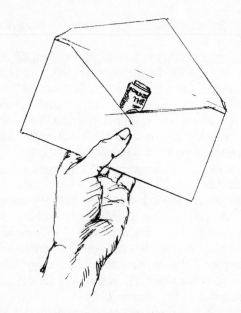

the flap of the envelope and show that the bill is still there before sealing the flap with your right thumb and fingers.

At this point, remove a packet of paper matches from your pocket with your right hand. Tear out a match, close the packet and place it under your left thumb in position so that if the envelope were still open, the match packet would completely cover the part of the bill that's still inside the envelope.

Strike the match against the striking surface of the packet and hold the flame to the far corner of the envelope until the paper ignites. While this is happening, you have bent the half of the bill that protrudes through the envelope upward with your left fingers. You press them firmly against the bottom half of the bill that is now folded back up in line with the top end that's inside the envelope. As the flame creeps closer to your left hand, grasp the envelope at the top between your right thumb and fingers and *slide* it out from behind the packet of matches. The matches completely mask the folded borrowed bill that is now in your left hand, pressed firmly behind the packet.

All eyes are on the burning envelope as your left hand drops naturally to the left-hand pants pocket, where it leaves the matches.

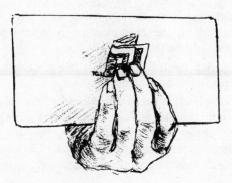

You hold the burning envelope in your right fingers as long as is reasonably feasible without burning yourself, and then drop the remains into an ashtray.

The borrowed bill has apparently been burned. Actually, it just went to your left pants pocket, in your left hand.

You now have to bring back the borrowed bill in some way. One of my favorites is extremely simple.

I bought a cheap, cloth coin purse of the snap variety at a ten-cent store. It had a seam at the bottom, which I carefully opened with a razor blade to make a one-inch opening. Then I put two small safety pins through both sides of the cloth at the top, one on either side of the snap and sealed them shut with gummed stickers. I then wrapped a small rubber band tightly around the snap.

When I use this "finish" for the trick, I have this purse, prepared in this manner, in my left-hand pants pocket. When I insert the match packet into the pocket, I quickly shove the bill into the slit at the bottom of the purse, and just as quickly remove the purse from the pocket, smoothing out any possible wrinkle in the slit as I do it.

I hold the purse up, going directly to the person who loaned me the bill, and say, "I promised to return your bill to you. This is an extremely difficult trick and things sometimes go wrong, so I always carry a coin purse in my pocket with another bill in it. To be sure that I don't inadvertently spend the money, I keep the purse rather securely closed." I then tear the paper seals from the ends of the safety pins, try to unsnap the opening and discover (?) that I must first remove the rubber band.

Once the rubber band is off, I hold the purse out to the spectator, gripping it by the bottom between the left thumb and fingers, and invite him to open it and remove the bill. I tell him that I want him to open out the bill and check the serial number so that he can verify the fact that it is really the bill he loaned me. While I'm saying this, I casually put the purse back where it came from. There's not the slightest interest in the purse at this point. All eyes are on the spectator as he checks the serial number on the bill.

At one time, I used a piece of mechanical equipment called the Brema Bill Tube for the reproduction of the bill. It's a brass tube with a cap that screws on and then has a bolt going through both itself and the tube, the bolt being firmly screwed on, too. It's a superbly made piece of mechanical equipment and the method of getting the bill into the tube defies detection.

However, to my way of thinking, it's completely foreign to anything anybody would ever carry in his pocket. I think the audience immediately recognizes it for what it is—a trick device. To my way of thinking, the simple coin purse is immeasurably better. If you want to be a perfectionist, you can have a duplicate coin purse in your left pants pocket, without any slit in its bottom. You've dropped the safety pins and the rubber band onto the table before you put the purse back into your pocket. If anyone asks to see the purse, you can hand him the unslitted duplicate.

Now, here's a little confession. I've carried the undoctored duplicate purse in my pocket for years, whenever I've done the "set" version of the trick. And I've never once had anyone ask to inspect the purse. The impact of seeing a bill burned and then seeing that the reproduced bill bears the exact serial number of the borrowed bill completely overshadows the purse. To deliberately reach into your pocket and toss the purse out for examination as an afterthought would, in my opinion, be a grievous error. You'd be calling attention to something that could start a new train of thought and, at the least, something that would detract from the interest of the restored bill.

A lawyer to whom I taught the trick has a fine way of reproducing the bill that's also subtle advertising for him. He puts a quarter-inch of rubber cement around the back edges of two of his business cards. He then puts a piece of paper, larger than the cards, between the two facing backs of the cards. He moves the paper gently upward from the bottom just enough so that the two rubber-cemented surfaces along the bottom edges come into contact and form a firm seal. The two cards, with the paper still between them, are in his pants pocket, open edge up. He puts the folded bill, opened out to its original length, into the opening and pulls out the paper. The instant the surfaces on the three sides that were protected by the paper come in contact with each other, they form a firm seal, aided by a pressure of the fingers wherever they haven't made contact.

He hands this double business card to the person who loaned him the bill, and the spectator usually has quite a time getting the bill out from between the sealed cards.

Now, let's consider doing the trick when you're completely unprepared.

You borrow an unprepared envelope. You show the address side, then turn it over and show the flap side. You insert your right thumb into the envelope and pull it open to let one or two spectators see that there's nothing concealed inside. Your left fingers are on the address side, left thumb on the flap side. Your right thumb is inside the envelope. With your right thumb-nail and ball of the thumb and pressure from the left fingers, you deliberately tear a ragged slit into the back of the envelope, in the same position as the razor-blade slit in the prepared envelope. A cheap envelope is definitely superior, because the tear makes no noise.

After you've made the tear, you remove your right thumb from inside the envelope and show it again, front and back, the envelope held naturally in the left

hand, the fingers on the address side covering the jagged slit.

When you've sealed the envelope, with half of the bill extending outside of the address side, you light a match and, holding the envelope in front of you, flap side facing your audience, put the match behind the envelope so that the spectators see the bill is still in the envelope. The shadow of the bill will show, but not a trace of the slit will be visible. After showing the shadow of the bill by means of the flame, I sometimes "accidentally" let the envelope catch fire.

With the bill in the left hand, I approach the owner and say, "As you can see, I had a little mishap. Do you have another bill I might borrow?" I thrust my left hand boldly into his left coat pocket, unfold the bill and remove it. "This one will be satisfactory. Will you please copy the serial number on it?" He quickly discovers that it is his original bill.

With a small group of spectators, I sometimes take the ash tray containing the ashes of the burned envelope up to the owner of the bill, put it on the floor in front of him and tell him if he'll stir around in the ashes, he'll find his bill. I'm standing beside him as I say this. When he leans forward to pick up the ash tray, his posterior lifts sufficiently from his chair so that if I drop the folded bill, he is sitting on it when he resumes his natural position. I then move away from him. When he says that the bill isn't in the ash tray, I reply, "No wonder. You're sitting on it." He gets up and discovers the bill on the chair. For some reason, he thinks it would have been absolutely impossible for anyone to put it there. He checks the serial number and verifies it.

DOLLAR BILL IN CIGARETTE

Here's a carefully prepared trick that has been a favorite of mine for years. It's the Bluey-Bluey "burning a bill" trick with the added wallop of reproducing the bill from a lighted cigarette.

There are mechanical and sleight-of-hand versions, and I see no reason for you to learn them. This version is extremely simple.

To start your preparation, you get two brand new dollar bills at the bank, in sequence. Getting them presents no problem. You'll find that you can erase the final digit in the serial number with a typewriter eraser. Indeed, the eraser on many common lead pencils will do the job effectively.

Erase the final digit on both bills thoroughly, so that not a trace of it remains.

Now, roll the open, untipped end of a cigaret between your thumb and forefinger so that some of the tobacco comes out. Pull it out onto the table. Continue until the cigaret is almost a shell. Then roll one of the bills into a tight, firm, compact tube, insert it

into the cigarette shell and stuff tobacco back in on top of it. A pair of tweezers helps this operation. When you've reinserted as much tobacco as you can, trim the loose strands at the open end with a pair of scissors. I use a premium length cigarette because you can get more tobacco back into it. I mark the top of the filter with a pencil dot, so that I can spot the doctored cigarette quickly and put it into the open side of a partly used pack. That's the advance preparation.

When you want to perform the trick, you have the pack with the prepared cigarette in your pocket.

You say words to this effect. "I'm not going to ask anyone to lend me a dollar bill for this trick for two reasons. First, people seem reluctant to trust a magician with their money. Secondly, I insist on an absolutely new, crisp dollar bill untouched by human hands, for reasons which will become apparent to you. So I'm going to use a dollar bill of my own."

You hold up the other bill with the last digit removed from the serial number. "As you can see it's brand new, unused. So that there can't be any possibility of any substitution, I'll ask this gentleman to copy down the serial number." You hand him the bill, a pencil and a slip of paper.

You take back the bill, roll it up into a tube, flatten the tube, and proceed as in the Bluey-Bluey "burning a bill" trick. While the envelope is burning, you say, "There's an old Turkish belief that if you light a cigarette containing Latakia tobacco from a burning bill, the bill will materialize again. Silly, isn't it?"

You reach into your pocket with your left hand for the pack of cigarettes, leaving the bill from the envelope behind.

You bring your hand back into sight with the pack of cigarettes, remove the one with the dot at the top of the filter, put it between your lips, and light it from the envelope flame. The burning envelope is then dropped into the ash tray.

"Now," you continue, "you'll see why I insist on a brand new dollar bill. Believe it or not, I'm smoking money, not tobacco." You walk up to the man who copied the serial number, the cigarette between your lips. You ask him to take it from your mouth and break it open. He does, and discovers the rolled-up bill. You direct him to open it and check the serial number, and call attention that you never touched it.

He checks the serial number and attests that it is the same as the bill that went into the envelope.

Applause, applause!

Fishing for Money

Ask five or six people in your audience to remove dollar bills from their pockets. Stop in front of one of the volunteers and have him copy the serial number on his bill. Take it from him and fold it a certain way, telling the other volunteers to watch closely and fold their bills the same way.

While your back is turned, another spectator gathers up the folded bills in a hat and shakes them up or stirs them up in any way he chooses.

You turn around and pick up a toy fishpole with a plastic worm at the end of the line. While the spectator holds the hat, you dip the end of the line into it and lift it up. The worm is holding a bill, and the spectator acknowledges that it's his. The serial number tallies.

You file down the edge of a Shick injector razor blade so that it will no longer cut, and you have this palmed in your right hand when you approach the spectator who has copied the serial number of his bill. You fold the bill around the blade.

The plastic worm has one of the little Alnico magnets imbedded in it. When you lift the fishing rod and a bill is clinging to the worm's mouth, you advance to the spectator, pull away the bill and open it, retaining the blade in your fingers.

THE GREAT COAT TRICK

This is one of those any time, anywhere tricks that never fails to stun an audience.

The only necessity in the way of props is two pieces of rope, five feet long. Preferably, this should be the soft sash cord you'll be using in other tricks. Also, if there's a wooden coat hanger of the type that has a wooden cross-bar and wire, between which you hang slacks, so much the better. The wooden cross-bar on this type of coat hanger swings free at one end but can be slipped into a metal curve that holds it in place when you hang pants from it.

If there doesn't happen to be one of these coat hangers handy, don't worry. You can use a magic wand, a ruler, a wooden spoon with long handle, or even a piece of broomstick.

You hang the two pieces of rope, side by side, across the hanger cross-bar, the wand, the ruler or whatever you're using. They hang down side by side, and you adjust them so that the four ends are even.

"We'll tie the two ropes together," you say, "to guarantee against any skullduggery." You tie one simple knot in the two hanging ropes, tieing one to the other as if each were a single strand of rope instead of two strands. The two strands of the right-hand rope are brought over in front of and across the left-hand two strands, brought around behind, up through the opening between the two ropes at the top, and forward. The knot is pulled tight. Actually, if the stick from which the ropes are hanging were to be removed at this point, the two ropes would come apart. They aren't really tied together at all. You do not, of course, point out this fact.

What you do is borrow someone's sports jacket or suit coat. If you're using the coat hanger, put it on the hanger and have the gentleman who was wearing it thread one set of ropes down through the left sleeve and the other set down through the right sleeve.

You're holding either the coat by the neck or holding the end of the hanger. The back of the coat faces the audience, with two ends of rope hanging from each sleeve. If people are watching from behind you or on the sides, don't worry. They can't discover a thing.

Ask the owner of the coat to hold the ropes extending from one sleeve, and get another spectator to hold those extending from the other sleeve. Have them stand well apart so that the sleeves of the coat are

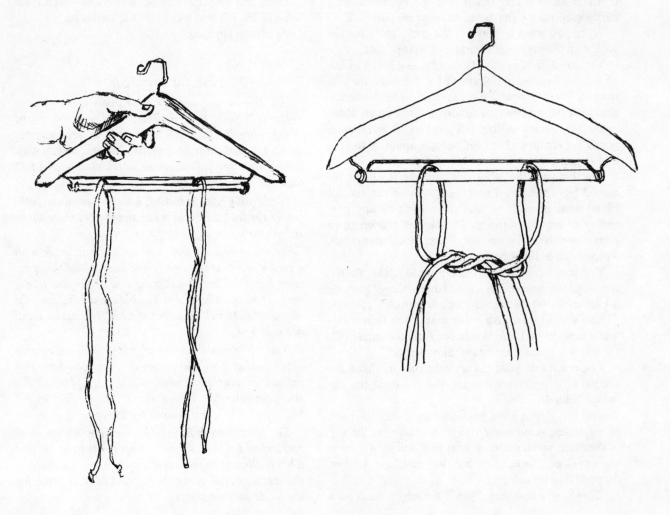

extended outward, parallel to the floor. Now ask each man to hand you either of the two ends of the rope he's holding. Take a rope end from each man, tie the two into a single knot, and hand each man the end of the knotted rope that now extends toward him.

Caution the men to grip the rope ends firmly, walk back behind the coat. If you're using the coat hanger, hang the hook over your right thumb and with the left hand, slip the two loops of rope off the end of the wooden cross-bar. If you're using a stick, simply remove it.

Now, ask your two assistants to pull gently but firmly on the ropes. You suddenly walk away, holding the coat, now free of the ropes, which are stretched taut between the two men, without any knot in them.

The effect of this trick is really spectacular, and has to be seen to be appreciated. On top of that, it's extremely easy to do. What more could you ask?

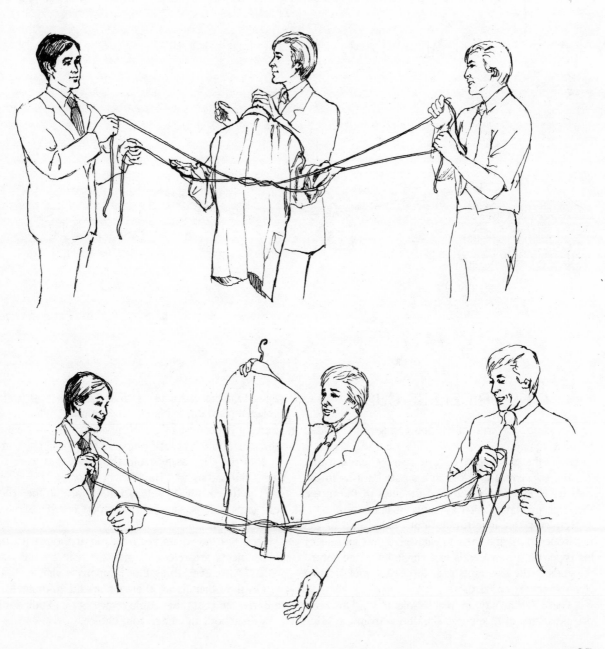

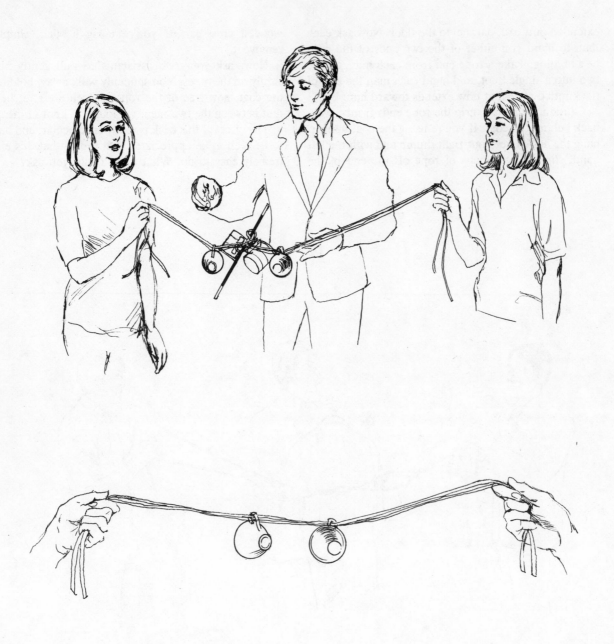

THE PRICELESS CUPS

The same trick with different dressing has an added perplexing feature.

Drape the two lengths of rope over a stick or wand. Tie the two ropes together in a single knot as in the coat trick. Have two men hold the ends of the ropes, the stick or wand half-way between them.

You now thread a tin cup onto either end of the two ropes. Ask the men to each give you an end of his rope, tie the two ends in a single knot and return the ends to the assistants as before. Now pick up two cheap crockery coffee cups.

"These," you say in mock solemnity, "are two priceless cups of rare porcelain, dating from the Ming

dynasty. One estimate of their value is 500 dollars apiece. (PAUSE) That's one estimate. They're extremely delicate; I might even say fragile—so handle them carefully." Thread one onto each of the two ends.

Pull the stick away from the ropes that were tied around it and shout, "Pull!"

The tin cups will clatter to the floor and the crockery cups will be securely threaded on the two outstretched ropes.

This has the advantage over the previous trick that two objects are released and two held by the same ropes. Also, everything that happens is visible.

On the other hand, there's something about using a borrowed coat that people remember and talk about. Try them both and make your choice.

THE SPONGE BALLS

Dozens of tricks and routines with sponge balls have been marketed by professional magicians. The average amateur is uncomfortable with most of them because all sponge ball tricks demand being able to place a sponge ball into the left hand from the right and make it disappear. Most written descriptions of how to do this well are confusing, and many of them completely overlook important elements that make sponge ball tricks effective.

We'll start with a simple sponge ball trick that has a most startling effect.

But, of course, we should start with some sponge balls. Where do you get them?

Well, you can buy them from a magic supply house or you can buy a sponge rubber or nylon bath sponge for little money. A pair of sharp scissors will cut it into 1½-inch cubes without any difficulty. Now, if you'll nip away the corners, you'll find that you can trim one of these cubes into a 1¼-inch ball without any difficulty. The 1¼-inch size is big enough to be plainly visible to your audience and yet small enough to handle without any problems.

You start by tossing two sponge balls out onto the table top. Pick up one of them in your right hand by nipping the top of it between the ball of the right thumb and the flesh between the first and second joints of the right forefinger. Lift your right hand from the table with the ball, with the second, third and little fingers raised up at almost a right angle to the thumb and forefinger, which are parallel to the floor. The ball is plainly visible to everyone.

Without changing the position of any of the right fingers even slightly, press the ball against the palm of the left hand. Now, bring the left fingers up and close them on it, keeping your tight grip of the ball with the right thumb and forefinger. As your left fingers close over the ball, let the right second, third and little fingers that have been pointing upward relax downward against the back of the left fist. Your right hand pulls away from the left fist and these fingers fall naturally against the forefinger. You extend the left fist as if it contained the ball.

Your right hand has pulled away from the left, the ball in it completely concealed by the back of the hand. It moves *immediately* in a continuous motion to the sponge ball remaining on the table, grips this ball tightly against the ball already in the hand, picks it up, and holds the two balls squeezed together as one, between the thumb and the first and second fingers. Show it openly, *at once,* without any fumbling. To all

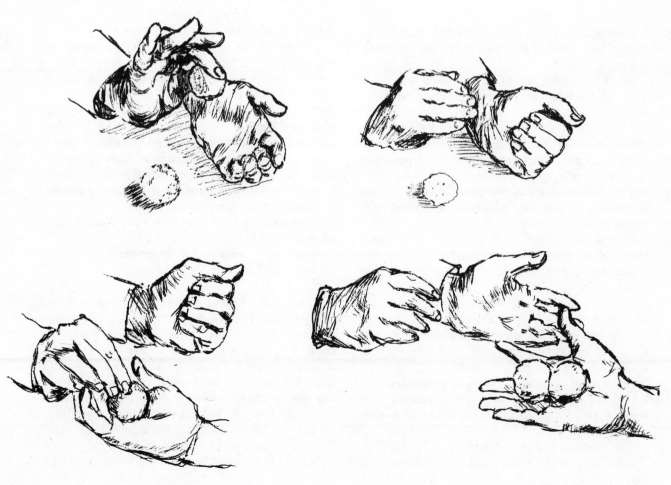

39

easier. The instant you have a ball hidden in your right hand, you pick up the pencil, which gives you a natural reason to have your hand closed around it. The ball compresses enough so that the hand gripping the pencil looks perfectly natural.

There comes a final stage in most sponge-ball routines when you have to get rid of an extra ball of which your audience is unaware. It's hidden in your right hand, which is wrapped around the pencil.

What could be more natural than to stick the pencil into your inside coat pocket? And of course, the extra unwanted ball goes right along with it.

You've just completed the startling little trick where the spectator opens his fist and finds that he's holding two sponge balls instead of one. You put the two balls onto the table. Unbeknownst to the audience, you have a third sponge ball wedged between your coat collar and your shirt collar.

At this point, you introduce an opaque plastic cup. If you're working completely impromptu, you can use a borrowed coffee cup. Whichever you're using, you tap it with the pencil.

"Getting a ball to go from the fist to this cup is much more difficult," you observe, "because the cup is so much less porous than the human skin." You put down the pencil and very openly invert the cup by gripping it with the fingers inside and the thumb on the outside as you turn it mouth down. You turn the mouth down in this way because that's exactly the way you'll do it when there's trickery involved.

The right hand is obviously empty. You pick up one of the two sponge balls on the table in the approved grip for the placement in the left fist, nipped between thumb and forefinger. You put the ball onto the left palm, close your left fingers over it and remove your right hand (which still contains the ball). You quickly pick up the pencil and say, "Watch! I'm about to show you some real misdirection." You lift the left fist to the level of your head, and tap the left elbow with the pencil. The right hand wrapped naturally around the pencil contains the ball.

"And now," you ask, "where do you think the ball is? Is it still in my left fist or is it under the cup?"

Whatever the answer, you open your fist and turn the cup mouth up with the left hand.

"Neither place. You have to watch these magicians. Remember, I told you there was going to be some misdirection? Well, while I tapped my left elbow with the pencil, you watched the pencil instead of my left fist and I was able to put the sponge ball under the collar of my coat." You openly reach your left fingers under the coat collar and remove the sponge ball that was planted there, putting it down beside the other one on the table. As you're putting it down, you drop the pencil to the table and put the fingers of your right hand inside the cup. The sponge ball that was in your right hand is between them and the inside surface of

appearances, it is one ball. One of the beauties of sponge ball tricks is that two balls may be openly gripped as one.

Don't make a big deal of the fact that it is only one ball. The spectators *see* it as one, without your telling them.

Move to a spectator and say, "I'll ask you to hold this second ball tightly in your left fist. Really squeeze it, because these things are tricky and you never can tell when they'll jump up at you."

Place the two balls as one onto his left palm, still in a tight grip, and bring his fingers up around them as you release your hold.

Extend your left fist, palm upward, so that it's near his. If he's turned his hand palm down, have him turn it back up so that its position matches that of your clenched fist.

Now, with a pencil, tap your fist lightly and do the same with his. "Tap, tap. And now, when I open my fist, the ball has vanished. Do you suppose the same thing has happened with yours? No? You still feel the ball? All right, open your hand."

As he opens his hand, expecting to see only one ball, the two balls that have been tightly compressed almost leap up from his palm. The effect is beautiful—real magic.

The repeated use of the pencil as a "pointer" or "tapper" also makes sponge ball manipulation much

the cup, completely concealed. You turn the cup mouth down, leaving the ball under it.

"Let's try it again, and this time, try to be more observant." You repeat the move of seeming to put a ball into the left hand, reaching immediately for the pencil, which you grasp with your fingers around it. "Last time," you say, "I didn't tap the cup. This time, I will." You tap your left fist with the pencil, and then tap the cup. Your left hand opens to show itself empty, reaches out and picks up the cup, revealing the sponge ball beneath it. You toss the ball into the mouth-up cup.

"We'll try it again," you say. You take the pencil in the left hand as your right hand grips the cup just as it did before, turning it mouth down and leaving its hidden sponge ball with the one already there.

You lay down the pencil, pick up the remaining sponge ball in the accepted manner, go through the move of leaving it in the left fist, tap the fist and the inverted cup, and ask a spectator to lift the cup.

As he's doing it, you put the pencil into your inside coat pocket, leaving the extra sponge ball with it.

Numerous books have been written about sponge ball manipulation. Magic shops sell all kinds of sponge ball tricks, some good and some impractical.

The best sponge ball routine for practical use is, in my opinion, the one originated by Don Alan and sold by Magic, Inc., Jay and Frances Marshall's excellent magic supply house at 5052 Lincoln avenue in Chicago. It is too advanced for a beginner, but after you've acquired some proficiency in the manipulation of sponge balls, I'd highly recommend it. Don did it on his first television show, which I produced, and it made a reputation for him.

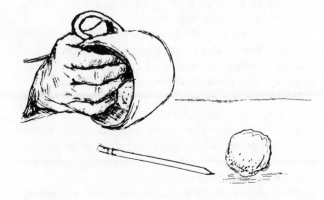

41

THE VANISHING COAT HANGER

This trick is so simple it's almost silly when you know the secret. And yet, Don Alan did it on my "Magic Ranch" television show which ran on the ABC network. It completely mystified the audience.

He wrapped a full-size coat hanger in a double sheet of newspaper. There was no question but what the coat hanger was there, thanks to the awkward shape of the newspaper-wrapped package.

Suddenly, he crushed the awkward package into a ball of wadded newspaper. The coat hanger had vanished.

Here's how he did it. He put a wire coat hanger on on old board and pounded nails into the board at the three inside angles of the wire coat hanger, leaving the nails protruding an inch.

Then he took a spool of soft solder and wrapped it tightly around the three nails, bringing up a piece and forming the hook part of a hanger and wrapping the other loose end around the bottom of the hook part, so that, to all appearances, it was just another coat hanger. He removed it from the nail form and gave it whatever finishing touches were necessary to make it a convincing duplicate of a legitimate wire

coat hanger. It was this soft solder form that was carefully wrapped in newspaper.

The paper could be wadded into a ball with no difficulty whatsoever. Indeed, the only trick was to keep the coat hanger from collapsing *before* he was ready to make it vanish.

In performing this trick, I recommend that you have the soft soldering wire fake coat hanger sandwiched between two genuine ones. Rap the top one sharply on the table top, put it down, pick up the middle, now the top one, and wrap it in a sheet of newspaper. When the hanger has vanished, the two remaining ones will stand rigid examination. Anyone who tries to crumple one inside a sheet of paper will be faced with an impossibility. If you want a no-skill trick for a breather, this could be it.

Now, we'll try one that *does* require some skill, but is worth every bit of time you spend on it. Many first-rate wonder workers will tell you it's their favorite close-up impromptu trick.

What you're going to get is not the complete routine they use, but one you can do. At least, you can do it well after you've become familiar with it. And whatever you do, do *not* perform this trick for friends until you've mastered it. It's far too good to be "given away" by inept handling.

Once you've smoothed out the basics I'm about to give you, there's almost no limit to how much farther you can develop the routine. Experiment, and try to come up with some developments of your own.

Whenever you do any "standard" trick, try to add something to it, a new twist, a different ending, a laugh—something. The easiest thing to change is the standard "patter," and unless you do, you become a carbon copy of every other magician who's using the "words that came with the trick."

It's a dice trick, in this case, and there are plenty

of amusing stories about dice. Use them. If you don't know any, you'll find some in *Gambler's Digest*. Since I gathered the anecdotes for that book, I'm not going to repeat them in this one.

The "Paddle Move" described in this trick is described in detail in The Paddle Trick in the Impromptu Close-Up routine. I suggest you turn to it and read it before you try this trick.

It's called:

PARADISE DICE ROUTINE

It's paradise for an amateur magician when he finds a routine that's easy to do and baffles his audiences. Bruce Elliott, author of *The Best in Magic, Classic Secrets of Magic* and *Magic as a Hobby,* presented the grand-daddy of dice routines to the magic fraternity back in 1948, when he was publishing *The Phoenix* magazine. Bruce is an able writer who knows magic as few people do, and he's responsible for many great tricks. It was only natural that he recognized a sure winner in Dr. Sack's Spotted Sorcery routine. No routine since then could be called completely original; they've all drawn on the Sack idea, the conception of using the "Paddle Move" or a variation of it in showing the top and bottom of a pair of dice. Dr. Sack also made excellent use of the fact that the top and bottom spots on a die will always total 7; if an ace is up, a 6 will be on the bottom, if a 2 is up, a five will be on the bottom, etc.

Don't use dice that are too large for you to handle. The dice used at casino crap tables are much too big for most people. Since this is a close-up routine, the dice don't have to be big. Dice a half-inch square or less are fine. Sometimes when I've been teaching this routine and the student has had difficulty in doing the turn-over move, I've started him with dice about a quarter-inch square. Once the student mastered the move, he had no difficulty in moving up to half-inch dice.

The basic sleight of hand move is similar to the paddle move. You hold a pair of dice between your right thumb and forefinger, thumb on one side and forefinger on the other. Your hand is palm down. The ball of the forefinger covers one side of the dice and the ball of the thumb covers the opposite side. You are looking down at the top of the dice.

Now, if you turn your right hand over to the right to bring it palm up, you will show the bottom side of the dice. This movement of turning over the hand is the natural way to show the bottoms.

But let's get to the basic move. While you turn over the right hand to bring it palm up, your thumb and forefinger roll the dice over a quarter turn to your right. What appears to be the bottom side is actually the surface that was originally against your right forefinger. The surface that was under your right thumb

at the starting point replaces what was originally the top surface.

You should grasp the similarity to the paddle move immediately. The illusion is identical. As your hand turns to the right, so do your thumb and forefinger, revolving the dice a quarter-turn.

You do not need to make a wide, fast move. If you turn your hand over smoothly and naturally, the turn of the dice will be invisible.

When you turn your hand back palm down, you naturally turn it to the left. If your right thumb and forefinger turn the dice a quarter-turn to the left during the turn-over of the hand, the dice will be back to their original starting position. The left-turn hides the left quarter-turn of the dice just as well as the right turn of the hand covers the right-turn of the dice.

Either movement should be absolutely indetectable. You shouldn't be able to see the dice turning an extra quarter-turn, yourself, as you look at your right hand.

Experiment with the position of the thumb and forefinger on the pair of dice. The main pressure on the cubes should be at the spot where they touch each other—the line where they join. Determine where

your thumb and forefinger should be on the opposite sides of the dice for the quarter-turn move to be natural and easy.

You start your routine by telling a spectator to roll the two dice out onto the table while your back is turned, add the top and bottom of each die together and then add the two totals together. You instruct him to pick up the dice before you turn to face him. When you turn around, you say, "The total you arrived at is 14. Isn't that correct? Of course it is, and my knowing the total is no mystery. You see, no matter what numbers are rolled, the total of the top and bottom sides of two dice will always add to 14."

You take the dice and demonstrate.

Then you pick up the dice with a 5 and 4 on top, a 4 and 5 under your forefinger, a 3 and 2 under your thumb and a 2 and 3 on the bottom. All you have to do is pick up the dice with a 5 and 4 on top and turn them so that a 3 and 2 will be under your thumb. The other numbers will fall into place.

"With 9 on top, there will always be 5 on the bottom side," you explain, showing the top of the dice first with the two held in the proper position for the turn-over move. You turn the hand over naturally to the right, *without* making any move, bringing it palm up and showing the 2 and 3 on the bottom. You turn the hand back palm down and continue, "But with a 5 and 4 on top, a total of nine, if you look at the bottom and see another 5 and 4 there, a total of 9, you have a right to be suspicious." You turn your hand over, palm up again, this time making the turn-over move, and a 9 total, a 5 and 4, is on the bottom. You continue. "With 9 on the bottom, you should have 5 on top." You turn the hand back down without making the turn-over move and show a 3 and 2 on top. "Now, some people accuse me of having a 3 and 2 on the top and a 3 and 2 on the bottom." As you say this, you turn your hand to the right to bring it palm up, but this time you make the turn-over move in reverse, to the left, bringing the 2 and 3 under your thumb to what was originally the bottom side. You turn the hand back palm down, reversing the move, and you've shown a 2 and 3 on both the top and bottom. You now have a 3 and 2 on top and 4 and 5 on the bottom. "Of course, that isn't so," you continue. "With 5 on top, there *must* be 9 on the bottom." You turn the hand palm up again and show 9 on the bottom. "Of course, some people also accuse me of having 9 on the bottom and 9 on the top." You turn the hand over, making the turn-over move and show a 9 on the top. "Of course, that's all wrong. With a 9 on the bottom, you should have a 5 on the top. To get it, I just rub the top of the dice lightly." You bring your left forefinger over the dice, which conceals them momentarily as you make a rubbing motion. While you "rub" with the left forefinger, you make the turn-over with your right thumb and fore-finger. Now, when you pull your left forefinger away, you have a 3 and 2 on top.

They will be slightly out of adjustment. Square them up, openly and deliberately. "The 2 is closest to me," you point out, "and the 3 is closest to you—3 at the front and 2 at the rear. Watch closely."

You make a brief little up-and-down shaking motion with your right thumb and forefinger, not more than five or six inches, making the turn-over move as you do it. This motion is brisk. While you're making it, you make the turn-over move to the right and the two and three that were under your thumb are now on top. Repeat this move several times, apparently making the 2 and 3 change places.

You toss the dice to the table and roll them a couple of times. Then you pick them up between right thumb and forefinger again, 3 and 2 on top, ace and 4 under your thumb, and 6 and 3 under your forefinger.

"Actually," you continue, "what most people forget is that there's always more than one way to arrive at the total of 14. "For example, with 5 on top, I can get 9 on the bottom with either 6 and 3," you turn your hand palm up, making the turn-over move to show the 6 and 3, and then turn your hand palm down again, reversing the move, "or 5 and 4." As you say, "5 and 4," you turn your hand palm up, without making the turn-over move, and show the 5 and 4. "You can have either 5 and 4 or 6 and 3," you continue, turning your hand palm down to show the 3 and 2 on top and then turning it palm up, making the turn-over move, to show the 6 and 3. You hold the 6 and 3 palm up as you continue, "Of course, the same thing applies to the tops of the dice as to the bottoms, just so the total comes to 14. Instead of 3 and 2 on top, what else could I have to make 14?"

When the spectator answers, "4 and 1," you turn your hand slowly and deliberately palm down without making the turn-over move. An ace and 4 are now on top. You nod your head. "There you are," you say, and toss the dice to the table. As the spectators examine the dice, reach into your side coat pocket where you have three more dice of the same size. Grasp them against the palm of your hand with the third and little fingers curled over them, holding them in place. The thumb, forefinger and middle finger are open, relaxed. Reach for the dice on the table and scoop them up. "No, the dice aren't crooked," you tell your audience. "The secret is that while you thought I only used two dice, I used quite a few." You roll all the dice out of your palm onto the table. "But don't tell anybody, please. It's too good a trick to give away."

Getting the extra dice into your hand is the simplest thing in the world, because the people who have been watching the trick inevitably give the two dice on the table a thorough examination.

And while you accept your applause, say a Thank You to Dr. Sack, who first came up with the idea.

With Dessert and Coffee

Few tricks are especially appropriate for the dinner table. Unless you're being paid to do a professional performance at the dinner table, any trick should be done without extraneous props. There's something ridiculous about a dinner guest, asked to do a trick, pulling a set of linking rings from his pocket, or reaching under the table and bringing out some magic boxes. Unless you have a trick that fits the scene, it's much better to say, "Wait 'til we get away from the dinner table."

If you're the only person seated at one side of a square table, it's much, much easier to perform than if you're closely sandwiched between two other guests. These two people can actually look behind your hands, and they can certainly see your lap. It's well under such circumstances to remember the cardinal rule, "If you don't think you can get away with it, don't do it."

It took me a long time to discover an absurdly simple solution to the problem. If I'm sandwiched between two guests and am asked to do a trick, I immediately say, "Perhaps I'd better change places with the host or hostess (who are normally seated at the head and foot of the table) so that everyone can see what I'm doing and so I'll have more room."

Seated at a side of the table where I'm not hemmed in by other guests, I have two favorite dinner table tricks that never fail to impress. I like them because they're done with items that are on the table, are completely impromptu, and happen to be strong tricks.

The first is:

THE VANISHING SPOON

You can start by remarking that almost everyone knows the old illusion of bending a spoon in which you grasp a spoon in your right fist, the point of the spoon bowl touching the table cloth and the handle extending straight up through the fist. You press down with your fist, pretending to bend the bowl, letting the handle slide back toward your body from your fist as the bowl of the spoon flattens part way toward the tablecloth. This must be done quickly for there to be any illusion at all.

"But the trick I'm going to do is the no-nonsense bending of a spoon practically double," you announce. So saying, you wrap the fingers of both hands around the spoon. The thumbs of your two fists touch each other, and the spoon is completely concealed by your hands. You are holding it as you would naturally hold it if you were going to try to bend it in half. Your fists are about six inches above the table top.

You look earnestly at the hostess and say, "Sometimes, certain kinds of silverware are difficult to bend back into their original shape." While you're saying this, your fists drop naturally to the table. The first

knuckles of the fingers of both hands are actually resting on the edge of the table. You lean slightly forward and ask, "Would you mind if the spoon happens to be permanently bent?"

Your two thumbs are all that are holding the spoon in place from the side closest to you. While you're asking the question, you simply release the pressure of the thumbs enough for the spoon to drop silently and automatically into your lap.

There has been absolutely no visible movement of your hands. The spoon was completely concealed and, to all appearances, is still between your fists. The minute you release it, while you're asking the question, your hands move out about a foot toward the center of the table, lifting to a point about a foot above its surface. You hold the hands as if they actually clenched the spoon. You now lean forward, rising slightly from your chair, as you slam the fists down onto the table cloth. Don't open them until they actually hit the cloth. At this point, you've let the spoon slide off your lap and drop to the floor. If it clatters, fine. If it doesn't, it makes no difference. Spread your fingers apart and then turn over your hands, showing the palms. And remark, "I decided at the last minute not to risk damaging one of your spoons, so I knocked it through the table instead of bending it. That never seems to damage the spoon." You lean over to the floor and retrieve it, putting it back on the table. "You see, it isn't any worse for the experience."

This is a ridiculously easy trick to do. If you hold the spoon between your fists so that it's completely covered and if you let it slip from the fists without any movement of the hands, nobody can possibly see

how it's done. Once the spoon is on your lap, continue to hold the fists in a rigid line, as if they still contained it. The trick is all done before anyone knows what's happening.

If you're going to do one trick at the dinner table, this is a hard one to beat.

Another "through the table top" trick that is even more spectacular but a little bit more difficult to do smoothly is:

HEADS OR TAILS

While this trick is slightly more complicated than the trick in which you knock a spoon through the table top, the misdirection is so perfect that dinner guests are completely baffled.

You remove a penny, nickel or dime from your pocket and lay it on the tablecloth.

Now you pick up one of the salt shakers, and if it's a tall one, so much the better. You put it squarely in front of you and drape your napkin over it so that the top of the shaker sticks up somewhere near the middle of the napkin. You form your right thumb and forefinger in a circle around the top of the protrusion in the napkin and bring them down to the top of the table, forming a tight-fitting cloth shroud over the salt shaker. The form of the shaker should be plainly visible through the napkin. You are gripping the shaker firmly through the cloth with your encircling thumb and forefinger.

"Now, I'm going to put the salt shaker over the coin," you announce, "and I'll place the coin beneath it with either heads or tails up. The reason I cover the shaker with my napkin is so that you can't possibly see how I place the coin. No matter how I place it, something strange will happen."

You move the covered shaker over above the coin and reach under the napkin with your left hand, either turning the coin over or leaving it as it is. You pull your left hand away, letting it drop to your lap, and bring the base of the shaker atop the coin, still gripping it through the cloth. You know whether the coin is heads or tails up.

You ask a spectator to call either heads or tails. If the coin is heads up and the spectator calls head, you say, "I was able to control your impulses. I put the coin heads up and willed you to call heads."

If the spectator says, "Tails," you say, "Sorry, you're wrong. No matter how many times you try, you won't be able to call the coin right."

Whichever approach you take, you lift the salt cellar and napkin away from the coin, pulling the right hand back toward the edge of the table. You look at the coin and get everyone else to look at it, confirming that what you said was right.

"We'll try it again," you continue, and go through

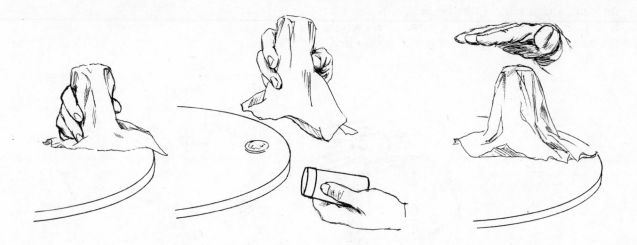

the same movements of turning the coin and placing the salt shaker over it as before.

This time, as you pull the shaker and napkin away, you let the side of your right hand rest against the edge of the table. An imperceptible lessening of pressure by the thumb and forefinger allow the salt shaker to drop to your lap. You look at the coin, along with everyone else. You have a fifty-fifty chance of being right with the placement of the coin. If you *were* right, you say, "You see, you can't win. If I could do it a third time, I'm sure you'd be convinced."

If you missed, you say, "Well, accidents will occasionally happen, but I'll bet any amount of money you can't cross me up again."

Your left hand is on your lap. The right, holding the shell form of the salt shaker carefully, brings the empty form carefully over the coin. The left hand reaches under the napkin edge as before, then goes back to the lap, where it picks up the shaker. Your thumb and forefinger, holding the empty napkin form, move down to the table top, and to all appearances the shaker is again on top of the coin.

You ask the spectator to call heads or tails. Whichever he calls, you immediately lift your right hand from the table top and slam it down on top of the napkin form, flattening it to the table. At the same time, your left hand raps the shaker against the underside of the table and immediately pulls it out and puts it on the table.

Don't worry about the shell formed by the napkin collapsing prematurely. I've even done the trick many times with paper napkins.

Really, all you need to learn to do is to hold the "shell" form exactly as you held it while it contained the shaker. As for letting the shaker drop to your lap, it almost takes care of itself. The slightest release of pressure by the thumb and forefinger allows it to drop.

You *have* to move the napkin and shaker back toward yourself to let people see the face of the coin, so there's nothing peculiar about the move. And, since they don't know what's going to happen, spectators look at the coin, not your hand containing the napkin-covered shaker. To convince myself of this, I did the "drop" of the shaker badly several times, and not once did anyone at the table have the faintest idea of what had happened.

This is a spectacular table trick that you can do well with, at the most, ten minutes of practice. Once you can shape the napkin so it holds its form and once you can move the hand back toward yourself and release the shaker without being self-conscious, you have it made.

Two good tricks are normally enough for the dinner table. But what if you're sandwiched between two people and don't want to be presumptious enough to ask the host to change places with you? The simplest "out" is to do:

THE COIN AND GLASS ILLUSION

This is not really a magic trick in the truest sense, but give it enough buildup and it will be highly effective.

"Magic is illusion," you say. "It isn't what you see but what you *think* you see that counts. If I were to tell you that I was going to balance a half-dollar on the rim of a water glass, you wouldn't think much of it. Actually, it's an extremely difficult thing to do, but you wouldn't be much impressed. However, if I were to tell you that I was going to balance the *edge* of a half-dollar on the rim of a tumbler, you'd think I was talking about an impossibility—and, of course, impossibilities are a magician's stock in trade. Does anyone have a half-dollar? Thank you."

If nobody at the table has a half-dollar, the little trick can be done with a quarter, although it's more difficult. And, strangely, the larger coin makes the trick seem more impossible. You put two forks across the coin, letting their upper tines hold them in place, like this:

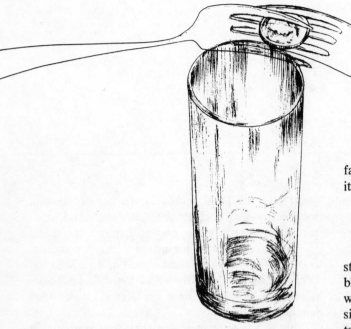

Then you rest the edge of the coin farthest from the tines of the forks on the lip of the glass, moving the fork handles outward or inward gently until you have a balance.

The coin will bob gently up and down without losing its apparently precarious balance. Even when you see it, it's unbelievable.

One time, I did this little balancing trick in a restaurant and the proprietor happened to walk by my table. He took the water glass, coin and forks up to the front window and had me rebalance the unit in the center of his window display. There were crowds gathered around that window all the rest of the day, and a good many people came inside to ask the proprietor the secret of the little illusion. An occasional draft made the coin bob up and down from time to time. The restaurant owner was so pleased that he insisted on entertaining my wife and me at dinner the following evening. That simple little trick, which isn't really a trick at all, became the pride of his life. He put a glass, coin and forks in his window every three or four months from then on, and he said that it was the greatest eye-catcher he'd ever had.

I hesitated to include the next trick, because beginners always convince themselves of its difficulty. It *does* take a little practice, but it's really quite simple. A traveling man or "drummer" who called on my

father showed it to me when I was a youngster, and it's been a favorite trick of mine ever since. I call it:

SILVER THROUGH GLASS

All you need is a water tumbler, and a quarter. A stemmed goblet won't work. A heavy cut-glass tumbler is difficult to handle, but any ordinary water glass works fine. You can do the trick with people at both sides, behind you, anywhere. And it's a fine dinner table trick.

To avoid a psychological block, hold a quarter in your right fingers and toss it quickly into your left hand. Look at your hands while you do it. Try to throw it so it hits your left forefinger and second and third fingers, which then close on it. Is that difficult? Is it any great problem requiring exceptional skill? Of course not.

All right, you pick up a tumbler with your left hand, so that the mouth of the glass is against your palm and the solid bottom is at the end away from your palm. The open mouth of the glass is against your palm. If you turn the bottom of the glass toward your right hand, so that the tumbler is parallel to the floor, your thumb extends along the top edge, pointing away from you and slightly to the right. Your little finger is on the bottom of the glass, extended straight out, in line with the length of the tumbler. Your first, second and third fingers curl over the far side of the glass.

Actually, you grip the tumbler between your thumb and little finger. You can lift the three fingers clear of the side of the tumbler and it won't affect your grip at all. They *rest* against the far side of the glass; they don't grip it.

Now, you hold a quarter flat between your thumb on one side and your first and second fingers on the other side. You hold it so that one edge clicks against the bottom of the tumbler. You pull back your hand and the coin about a foot to the right several times,

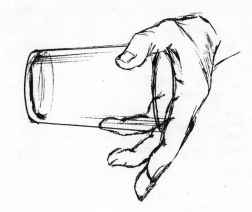

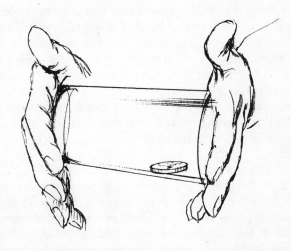

bringing it in toward the glass and rapping it sharply against the bottom.

You pull back the hand again, exactly as before. Only this time, instead of rapping the coin against the bottom of the glass, you throw it sharply to your left hand. Your first, second and third fingers open to catch it.

If they *do* catch it, the coin automatically falls into the glass. You press your right palm firmly against the bottom of the glass and open *all* your fingers so that the glass is held firmly between the two palms. Shake the coin gently, and let everyone at the table see that it is now inside the tumbler.

The movement of the coin through the air is so fast that the human eye can't see it. The effect is well worth the effort required to learn to do it smoothly.

The big secret is to *watch your hands* when you make the throw. And forget about the glass. Ignore it completely. You're throwing the coin into the slightly cupped first, second and third fingers.

If you'll only believe what you read here, you'll soon have a beautiful trick that's effective at the dinner table, for close-up work, and even on the stage. Do not think you have to throw the coin with lightning speed or terrific force. A quick toss is impossible to follow with the eye.

While I've done magic for years, I've never regarded myself as a sleight-of-hand artist. The really first-rate manipulative magicians spend hours, days and months on intricate sleight-of-hand moves. I've never had the time for consistent, rigorous practice, and I've always felt that there were enough fine tricks around that didn't require intricate manipulation.

I *never* practice the Silver Through Glass trick. And because I don't, I've had the coin wedge between the base of my first, second and third left-hand fingers and the rim of the glass on a few occasions. It hasn't caused the slightest problem. If you start shaking the glass the instant your right hand presses against the bottom of it, you can release the coin from where it's

wedged, it will start rattling and nobody will know that it *was* trapped between your fingers and the rim of the glass.

If you miss your fingers altogether now and then, the coin simply drops to the floor. If anything, failure of the coin to penetrate (?) the glass now and then seems to help rather than hurt the effect. Perhaps it's somewhat like the professional acrobat who deliberately misses his big trick on the first attempt in order to build up its difficulty in his audience's estimation.

It's a sleight-of-hand trick and you can do it!

Now I'm going to teach you a beautiful sleight-of-hand trick in which the sleight-of-hand is that you move your thumb a couple of inches along the surface of a lead pencil. That's all.

BORROWED RING ON PENCIL

While most tricks that require equipment shouldn't be done at the dinner table, you can certainly be excused for having a lead pencil in your coat pocket.

That's your sole equipment. It should, incidentally, be a full-length pencil, not a short one.

Borrow a ring from one of the women at the table, preferably a wedding band. The pencil lays across your right hand, eraser end just touching your little finger, pointed end extending out at a right angle to your forefinger. Your palm is open, and the pencil is across your fingers, not your palm. The right thumb rests on the pencil from the top, closer to the eraser end than to the pointed end. You borrow the ring, take it in your left fingers and lay it on top of the pencil, holding it in place with your thumb. This is all very open.

At this point, you say that you want someone to hold both ends of the pencil tightly. You transfer the pencil and ring to your left hand. It is turned palm down and you put it into the hand point first. The instant the two forefingers touch, you pull back the right thumb, with the ring beneath it, to the right, far enough for the ring to slip over the eraser end of the pencil. The move is completely hidden by the hands. You tilt the point of the pencil downward to the left and the ring slides down into your left fist, which you close around the pencil and ring as your right hand pulls away.

Without calling attention to the right hand, you let everyone see that it's empty. Now, you have one of the guests grip both ends of the pencil, one in either hand. You say, "I have the ring in my left fist and I'm going to attempt to get it onto the pencil while you're holding both ends." You pull your hand away sharply, giving a spinning motion to the ring as your fingers withdraw. If the ring starts spinning on the pencil as your hand moves away, people seem to think they actually saw the ring go onto the pencil.

It's a little trick, but the famous Max Malini used to make a similar trick a highlight of his performance.

It's a perfect example of the broad movement of putting the pencil and ring into the left fist covering the small movement of the thumb as it pulls the ring or rather slides it back over the eraser end.

When I first started doing the trick, I used to slide the ring back down again, keeping it pressed against my right thumb. And I found that this was not only unnecessary but complicated the performance of the trick. Tilting the pencil slightly point downward once it is in the left hand and letting the ring slide down into the left fist of its own momentum before the left hand and the right separate is not only simpler but more convincing. The movement of the right thumb to bring the ring under the left fingers takes too long and is too easy to catch.

The trick as I've described it is ridiculously simple and extremely effective. Many professional magicians do a similar trick with a special mechanical ring known as the Jardine Ellis ring. Some beautiful effects can be accomplished with the Ellis ring and whole manuscripts have been written describing a variety of approaches to its use—but I think using a borrowed finger ring makes the trick more mystifying, more personal and more memorable.

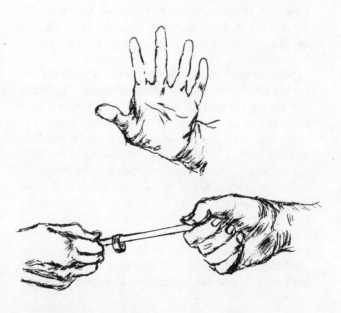

Quick Trick

Before you get ready to perform, write the numeral, 9, on the inside of your left forearm with soft toilet soap. It will be invisible.

To do your trick, toss a packet of paper matches to someone and ask him to tear out part of one row —any number just so there's at least one match left in the row. When he has done this, ask him to count the remaining matches. If he has a two-digit total, he is to tear out the number of matches that would represent each digit. For example, with 15 matches, he would tear out one and five, a total of six.

When he has done this, he is to count the number of matches remaining in the packet, without revealing the number. You pick up one of the discarded matches, light it and burn a small piece of paper to ashes. You roll up your left sleeve and rub the ashes gently against the inside of your forearm. A black "9" will appear on your forearm, distinctly outlines.

The spectator acknowledges that there were nine matches left in the packet. If he has followed instructions correctly, his final number will always be 9.

WOOFLE DUST AND ICE

This isn't really a trick, but it's an entertaining diversion. Dip into a water glass with a spoon and remove a cube of ice. Put it on a saucer.

Now, drape a piece of common string across the top of the surface of the ice. Say, "I'd never attempt this but I noticed some woofle dust." You pick up a salt shaker and point to it. "This woofle dust has a remarkable magnetic property."

Sprinkle a generous quantity of salt over the ice and string. "You can't see it happening, but the magnetism is beginning to build up." Press *down* with the taut ends of the string so that the string presses against the upper surface of the ice cube. "I think I can already feel the magnetic pull." You relax your hold on the string so that it's no longer taut, lift it upward, and the ice will come up with it.

All there is to it is that salt melts ice, which is a commonly known phenomenon. The downward pressure of the string imbeds it into the ice cube.

KNIFE PENETRATION

In the "Any Time, Anywhere" classification, you learned a trick called "Penetration" in which you used a silk and a magic wand. It can be done equally well at the dinner table with a napkin and a table knife.

THE NUMEROLOGY TRICK

This is more entertainment than mystification. For some reason, the public is always interested in astrol-ogy, numerology, and kindred subjects, even when they don't believe there's any logical ground for belief in them.

You say, "I've been doing considerable reading about numerology, and whether you believe in it or not, you can't argue against the preciseness of mathematical science. Numbers are constant; they don't change and they always have the same meaning."

At the top of a sheet of paper, you write:

1 2 3 4 5 6 7 9

"I've omitted Number Eight because it happens to be my numerological number, and it's a well-known fact that a student of numerology can't impart any satisfactory information about his own particular number to another."

You look at one of the guests. "Unless your numerological number is eight, give me your favorite number, the one you think is lucky for you—one of the digits at the top of this paper."

Whatever digit the person gives, come up with a little character analysis and fortune telling, being careful to keep it flattering and pleasant. Whatever you see in the person's future is always good. The chances are that you're well acquainted with the people at the dinner table, so you can give a good reading. You don't say that a person is stubborn; he has great determination. He isn't irresponsible; he's happy, carefree and optimistic. He isn't stingy; he has a keen sense of the value of money.

It doesn't make much difference what you say; everyone at the table will be interested. Try to keep it amusing, pleasing to the subject, and not too long.

"Now," you say, "there's one infallible way to learn whether or not six (or whatever number the person selected) *is* truly your lucky number."

Let's say the chosen number was six. Whatever it was, mentally multiply it by nine, in this case, 54. Instruct the subject, "Here's a pencil. Your numero-quotient is 54. Multiply the number I've written at the top of this sheet of paper by 54." Here's what happens:

$$
\begin{array}{r}
1\ 2\ 3\ 4\ 5\ 6\ 7\ 9 \\
\text{x}\ 5\ 4 \\
\hline
4\ 9\ 3\ 8\ 2\ 7\ 1\ 6 \\
6\ 1\ 7\ 2\ 8\ 3\ 9\ 5 \\
\hline
6\ 6\ 6\ 6\ 6\ 6\ 6\ 6 \\
\end{array}
$$

The subject shows the result of his multiplication. You nod your head sagely. "There's no doubt about it. Six is unquestionably your lucky number. If I were you I'd never do anything without giving great consideration to the Number Six and how it might influence the outcome."

Remember, multiply whatever number is chosen

by 9. That's the "numero-quotient" (whatever *that* is) to discover whether their favorite digit really is lucky. The result is always a whole string of their "lucky digit,"—unless they multiply or add incorrectly.

THE MAGIC SQUARE

That brings up another little mathematical diversion that may result in your being regarded as a mathematical genius.

A grade school math teacher showed me a magic square formula years ago, when she discovered I was interested in magic. Fortunately, I wrote it down. I've probably copied it a dozen times over the years, and I always keep this little block pasted in the front of my pocket memo pad:

B	1	12	7
11	8	B—1	2
5	10	3	B+2
4	B+1	6	9

Total: 24 to 100
"B" is selected total minus 20

With it, you can make a magic square totaling anywhere from 24 to 100. "B" is the basic number. You arrive at it by subtracting 20 from whatever number your audience chooses for the magic square. For example, if they pick 25, "B" would be 5. B + 1 would be 6, B — 1 would be 4, and B + 2 would be 7.

If your copy of the formula is glued to the left inside front cover of your pocket memo pad, you're in business. If there isn't a sheet of blank paper on the first right-hand page of the book, tear one out and put this blank page on top of the first page. Let's say they give you the number 30. You quickly make a magic square on the blank sheet as follows:

10	1	12	7
11	8	9	2
5	10	3	12
4	11	6	9

Every row will add to 30 horizontally, as will every vertical row. Both diagonals add to 30. The upper left four squares add to 30, and so do the four at the upper right. The same is true of the bottom two rows. The bottom middle four boxes add to 30, and so do the top middle four. The top two middle numbers and the bottom two middle numbers total 30, and so do the four numbers at the four corners of the square.

Altogether, you have 22 combinations that add to 30.

People will often want you to form a second magic square that adds up to a different total. Don't do it! What is interesting at the outset soon becomes tiresome—and a close scrutiny of several magic squares will show your spectators that the numbers in 12 of the squares are always the same.

Your "patter" can run something like this:

"From the beginning of time, the Magic Square has always been a mystic symbol. Early-day seers prepared Magic Squares for Emperors and Generals, who thought possession of such a square gave them supernatural powers. Sometimes, the seer spent months preparing a magic square that totaled the number the VIP desired.

"These ancient seers knew little about either mathematics or magic. I don't know much about mathematics, but I know enough about magic to turn out a magic square in less than a minute. 'Magic squares while you wait' is my trademark. Unfortunately, there doesn't seem to be the demand for them today that there was during the early centuries when superstition was prevalent. Some people still believe that a magic square adding up to their current age will bring a year of good luck. Give me any number from 24 to 100 and I'll make one for you."

When you hand the square to the person who gave you the number say something to the effect that "If you believe in the ancient Cabala, possession of this talisman will bring you health, wealth and happiness throughout the coming 365 days."

B	1	12	7
11	8	B-1	2
5	10	3	B+2
4	B+1	6	9

FOR ANY TOTAL
FROM 24 TO 100
"B" = TOTAL MINUS 20

At the Card Table

Probably no form of magic is as popular *with the people who do them* as card tricks. Unfortunately, a long series of card tricks almost has to become repetitious. You can divine and reproduce a chosen card, you can make a card vanish, you can make one card change to another. You can do Four Ace tricks. You can do a Poker Deal. If you're a manipulative expert, you can do fancy card fans and flourishes. And after that, regrettably, the *effect* of what you do begins to acquire a sameness.

I've often seen a good magician make the mistake of performing two card tricks that, to the viewer, were almost identical. Because the two tricks employed different *methods,* the magician thought he wasn't repeating.

There are card magic "nuts" who make pests and bores of themselves by doing one repetitious card trick after another, hour after hour, *ad nauseum,* ad boredom.

I happen to *know* hundreds of card tricks, but the ones I do for lay audiences come from a select group of not more than 25. It's a rare occasion when I do more than four or five.

I try to pick tricks that are real dazzlers and that are decidedly different from each other.

I don't use trick decks. If a trick can't be done with the cards that are in use at the card table, I forget it.

Some of my favorite card tricks require a little manipulative ability—but not much. Hefty volumes exist that do nothing but explain the techniques of complicated card sleights. If you can bring a chosen card to the top or bottom of the deck without the knowledge of your viewers, if you can force the spectator to take the card you want him to take, if you

can do a convincing false shuffle and can lift two cards from the top of the deck as one, you can do more card tricks than any audience wants to see.

I'm going to teach you the simplest way to handle the things I've mentioned, but first, I'm going to teach you some knockout card tricks that require no manipulative ability at all. The first is absurdly simple to do, and the effect is startling. It's called:

MATHEMATICAL ACES

Pick up the cards and say, "I'm going to show you a card trick that never fails to mystify me, every time I do it. Now, ordinarily, I don't like mathematical card tricks, but this is quite different." You fan the deck toward yourself and start running through the cards. "Frankly, I'm going to set up the deck in a very special order."

As you fan through the deck, you move cards at random from one place to another. During the course of this, you pull out the four Aces and put them on top of the deck, but you move enough *other* cards so that what you're doing isn't apparent.

Once you have the four Aces on top of the deck, you put the deck on the table. "Now, this is what baffles me. I know the cards are set up in a certain order and so do you. But I want you to cut the deck into four piles. Some of them can be thick piles and some as few as six or seven cards. The only restriction is that once you make a cut, you can't change it. That, you see, would alter the special arrangement. I won't influence your choice of where to cut in any way."

The spectator cuts the deck into four piles. He may

cut from the top and he may drop piles of cards from the bottom of the deck. However he chooses to cut, all you have to do is keep track of the top of the deck, the pile that has the four Aces on top of it.

"The mathematical formula for this trick is three under and three across," you explain, as you pick up any pile except the top one that has the four Aces on it.

"Three under and three across," you repeat. You deal off three cards from the top of the pile to the bottom, openly and cleanly. Then you deal a card from the top of the pile onto each of the three other piles—three across. You pick up a second pile and repeat the process. You do the same thing with the third pile. Lastly, you pick up the pile that was originally the top of the deck. It now has three indifferent cards on top of the four Aces. You deal exactly as you did with the three other piles—three under and three across. In other words, the three indifferent cards are dealt one by one from the top to the bottom of the pile. Then three cards are dealt from the top of the pile onto the top of the three other piles.

"I don't pretend to know why this works," you admit. "If you had cut one less card or one more card into any pile, you would have changed the entire outcome of the trick. But you cut as your fancy dictated. Now, would you please turn over the top card on each of the four piles."

The spectator turns over the four top cards, and, of course, reveals the four Aces.

After you've learned to do either of the two false

Quick Trick

A card trick that's so ridiculously simple it started as a gag, has astonishingly, mystified hundreds of people.

You look at the bottom of the deck, as unobtrusively as possible, and shuffle the card you see there to the top, remembering it. You lay the deck on your outstretched left palm and ask a spectator to cut it into two piles. Then you very deliberately look at the card cut to—let's say it's the six of hearts, and pronounce, "By looking at this card you cut to, I know that the top card is the nine of spades," the card you shuffled to the top. The spectator turns over the top card and sees that it is the nine of spades.

You immediately complete the cut, which puts the six of hearts you just looked at on top of the deck. Then you ask the spectator to cut two piles again. You look at the card on the bottom half of the deck and declare, "By looking at this card, I know that the top card is the six of hearts."

You can continue indefinitely, identifying the top card by looking at the card cut to. The strange thing is that most spectators don't have the faintest idea how you do it. More often than not, you're accused of using a marked deck.

shuffles I'll teach you, you can shuffle the cards before you offer them for cutting into four piles. But even *without* the false shuffle, you have a trick that's a stunner.

You toss the four Aces to one side, face up, and gather up the rest of the deck, putting it into your left hand as if in readiness to deal from it. Thumb three cards off slightly to the right, maybe about a quarter of an inch. Put your left little finger under the right edge of the bottom card of the three and push them back even with the top of the deck. If you now square them up with the rest of the cards, gripping the deck firmly at the right side with the fingers, you'll find that your left little finger automatically holds a break between those top three cards and the remainder of the deck, at the back, the end facing your body. You are now ready to do:

"YOUR CHOICE" FOUR ACES

The deck, with a break between the top three cards and the others, is in your left hand. Turn the four Aces face down with your right hand and pick them up, fingers at the front end and thumb at the rear end, and prepare to put them on top of the face-down deck. Bring them against the top of the deck without releasing them, as if you were depositing them. Your right thumb presses against the three cards above the break, gripping them right along with the Aces. If you push your thumb slightly forward, toward the front of the deck, the three indifferent cards are pressed firmly against the fingers of your right hand at the outer end. All seven cards will lift. You'll actually find it impossible to lift only the original four.

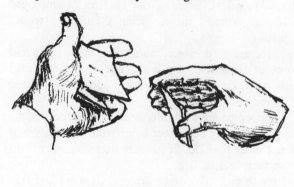

You say, "Oh, just a minute. Before I put the Aces back on top of the deck, perhaps we should see what order they're in."

You're holding the seven cards in a squared block between your right fingers at the outer end and right thumb at the inner end. Put the deck that was in your left hand onto the table and put the seven cards into your left hand, the backs facing the audience. You're now holding them on edge, by the sides, in the left hand, with the thumb holding the top side and the fingers the bottom side.

You keep the pile neatly squared and carefully take off the front card, turning it to face the audience. "The Ace of Hearts," you announce as you show it, and then slide it in at the back or bottom of the pile. "The Ace of Diamonds." You repeat the process with the second Ace from the top. "The Ace of Clubs." The third Ace is shown and goes to the bottom. "And that leaves the Ace of Spades." You turn it and show it to the audience, then put it back on the *front* of the cards you're holding in the left hand instead of on the back as you did with the other aces.

"We have the Ace of Spades on top," you say, as you replace the card there, "and," turning the pile face up, "the Ace of Clubs on the bottom."

You deposit the seven cards as four on top of the deck, holding the deck in your left hand.

"We'll put the four Aces face down in a row," you explain, dealing the Ace of Spades with your hands

up high enough so that everyone can see it. As you deal it off, your left hand comes closer to the table top, and you deal the next three cards face down without exposing their faces, so that you have a row of four face-down cards.

"The Four Aces," you say, pointing to the dealt cards. "And we'll put three indifferent cards on top of each one." You deal off the next three cards in a packet onto the Ace of Spades. Actually, these three cards are the other three Aces. Then you deal three more cards onto the next card in the row. After you've covered the Ace of Spades, you deal rather carelessly, so that the spectators can see the three-card piles don't contain any special cards.

"Now we have four four-card piles," you continue, "with an Ace at the bottom of each pile. Would you please move any two of the four piles toward yourself, forward."

If one of the two piles the spectator moves forward is the Ace of Spades pile, you continue, "Now please cover one of the two piles with your right hand."

You're playing Magician's Choice. Had neither of the piles the spectator moved forward been the Ace of Spades pile, you would have said, "Put them together and put them back on top of the deck. Now cover either of the two remaining piles with your right hand."

If the spectator covers the Ace of Spades pile, you pick up the remaining pile and put it on top of the deck. If he covers the other pile, tell him to put it on the deck.

In either case, you say, "You had an absolutely free choice of the four piles, and this is the pile you wound up with. Will you please turn it face up."

He turns it over and sees that it contains the four Aces.

The Magician's Choice idea comes in handy many times. I'm going to give you a card trick right now that depends on it and nothing else. The trick should be done only once before a group. If you repeat it, you'll get into trouble—but done once, it's a dandy. When you do it the first time you'll wonder why it fools anybody—but you'll find that it certainly does. The trick takes more nerve than anything else. I call it:

CHOICE PREDICTION

Let a spectator shuffle the cards. Take back the deck and in so doing, spot the bottom card. Be very casual about it. Let's say it's the seven of Clubs. Write "seven of Clubs" on a slip of paper, fold it, and toss it onto the table.

"Cut the deck into two piles," you direct, "and pick up either one." If he picks up the half with the seven of Clubs on the bottom, say, "Cut it into three piles." If he picks up the other half, direct him, "Put it aside and cut the remaining part of the deck into three piles."

Keep track of the pile that has the seven of Clubs on the bottom. "Push forward any two of the three piles," you direct. If he pushes the two piles that do *not* contain the seven of Clubs forward, pick them up and put them with the discarded half of the deck. Tell him to turn over his pile which was freely cut and look at the bottom card.

If he pushes forward the seven of Clubs pile, along with another, have him cover one pile with each hand and then lift either his right or left hand. If he lifts his right hand and it was on the seven of Clubs pile, say, "You had a free choice and this is the third of the cards you cut and chose." Have him turn the pile face up.

If he lifts the hand that is *not* over the seven of Clubs, tell him, "That leaves you with one pile, a pile you freely cut from the deck. Turn it over."

Whatever he does, you leave him looking at the seven of Clubs and tell him to open the slip containing your prediction.

Don't take my word for it that anything this simple could be a good trick. Try it!

MIRASKILL, By Stewart James

This creation of Stewart James is one of the greatest card tricks ever invented. It's both simple and baffling.

You have the cards shuffled, and fan them to your audience, showing that they're not in any set order. Say, "I'm going to write a prediction," and put the deck into the card case. You want two red cards at the top of the deck and two black cards at the bottom, or vice versa. You should never have to rearrange more than two cards to get this result.

"I'm going to write a prediction," you announce, and pick up a slip of paper and pencil. You put the piece of paper on the back of the card case, see that it's too flimsy to write on, and shove the deck into the case to give it solidity. You write on the slip, "You will have two cards less than I do."

Fold the slip without showing it, and put it on the table. You're holding the card case, flap toward yourself.

"Here's what's going to happen," you announce. "You'll deal off two cards at a time from the deck, face up. If both cards are red, they go into the red pile. If both cards are black, they go into the black pile. If you deal off a red and a black card, they go into the discard pile. Now, tell me which color you want for yourself, red or black." You're holding the card case in your hands, flap toward your body.

If the spectator chooses red, pull out the deck *minus* the two red cards at the top. If he chooses black, leave the two black cards on the bottom be-

hind. Toss the cards to him and say, "Shuffle the deck again before you start dealing. Shuffle as much as you like. Cut, too. Whenever you think the cards are thoroughly mixed, start dealing. A pair of reds go into the red pile, a pair of blacks go into the black pile, and one of each puts the pair of cards into the discard pile."

He deals off the cards, counts the number in the red and black piles, and then opens your prediction slip, which proves to be correct.

Put the cards back into the case and write another prediction. This time you write, "We will both have the same number of cards in our piles."

Hand him the card case, have him remove the deck, shuffle to his heart's content, and deal out the pairs. Again, your prediction will prove correct. You've given him a free choice of color both times and have never touched the cards once he starts dealing. He shuffles and cuts, for both deal-throughs.

If there's a better card trick around, I don't know where you'll find it, and you don't have to worry about any complicated sleight of hand.

MENTAL CARD SANDWICH

This is another easy one to do, with an entirely different effect. It gives you an unusual production of a chosen card that people will remember.

Let anyone shuffle the deck and remove five cards from it, face down. You fan the five cards toward the spectator, without looking at them yourself.

"I want you to think of any one card in this fan of five," you say. "You've thought of one? Good! Remove it from the fan and show it to someone else for verification; then replace it where it was. Don't let me see what it is. Just put it back where you got it, face down."

Now, it has to be either the top card of the five face-down ones, second from the top, third from the top, fourth, or the bottom card. All you need to do is keep track of it.

You toss the five card fan face down on the table, pick up the balance of the deck and fan it as evenly as possible. Now, you insert one of the cards from the fan of five face down between two cards in the deck, jutting out for about three-fourths of its length from the front end of the deck. It is inserted just deep enough to hold it firmly. You pick up the *second* of the five cards and insert it in the same front end of the deck, with one indifferent card between it and the first one. The *third* card you insert is the card the spectator removed to show to somebody. You don't know what it is and don't need to. All you care about is making it the *middle* card of the original five as they go back into the deck. After it's in place, protruding for three-fourths of its length out in front of the indifferent cards on either side of it, put a fourth card

next to it, one indifferent card intervening. Do the same with the fifth and last card. Now, close the fan carefully so that the five cards stay in place. They protrude from the top of the deck, and there's a card between each two that is level with the top edge of the deck.

Turn the deck so the backs face the audience and hold it in the left hand, thumb on the bottom long edge, the other four fingers on the top long edge.

"We now have a five-decker card sandwich," you announce. "If I push the cards through the deck, only four emerge at the other end." You push the five cards gently but firmly down level with the deck and as you do so, four cards move out at the opposite end. "If we push them into the deck again," you say, "only three come out." Now, we push the three cards through, and only two emerge. We push the two in, and one lone card comes out. What is the card you originally thought of?"

He names it, and you slowly turn the deck so that the protruding card faces him. It's the card he 'mentally' selected!

The trick is self-working. But practice it a few times, please, before you do it. You have to get the "feel" of pushing the cards back and forth. It's easy to do, but know you can do it.

HOW TO FORCE A CARD

Before you go any farther into card magic, you should learn how to make a spectator take the card you want him to select.

Most professional magicians are very, very good at the "classic" force. It's the one where you have the card you want taken about half-way down in the deck, under control. You fan cards slowly from the left hand to the right, timing it so that as the spectator reaches out for a card, he almost automatically gets the card you want him to take.

It requires skill to do the classic force well—and the skill comes only with practice, lots of practice. At this stage, you'd be much too nervous about it to execute it at all well.

And you don't need to. There are much simpler ways to force a card, ways that can't miss (which the classic force can). The late Theodore Annemann, one of magic's greatest inventors, once wrote a book for expert magicians, *202 Methods of Forcing*. In that book, he showed his readers over two hundreds ways to force a spectator to take the right card.

The first 'force' you're going to learn is so ridiculously simple that you won't believe it could fool anybody. I saw a top-flight performer use it on Johnny Carson's "Tonight" TV show, and it was never questioned. It baffled everybody.

Have the card you want taken on the top of the deck, face down. Tell the spectator to cut the deck

HANDKERCHIEF IS ACTUALLY OPAQUE ←

into two face-down piles. He will normally put the original top part of the deck to the right of the bottom part.

Say, "We'll complete the cut but will keep track of it." Pick up the bottom pile and put it atop the original top pile, crossways.

Do *not* have the spectator look at the top card beneath the crossways pile immediately. Keep talking, or have the spectator do some little thing in connection with the trick. *Then* say, "I want you to lift the crossways pile and look at the card you cut to, the top card of the bottom pile."

He looks at what was originally the top card of the deck, and you know what it is. Once he's looked at it, you're all set.

Here's one of my favorite forces. Have the card you want taken on top of the deck. Put the deck on your left palm, face down, and throw an *opaque* handkerchief over it. Never use a handkerchief that can be seen through. Now, as you throw the handkerchief over the deck, as soon as it is hidden, turn it over, face up, on your palm. Nothing could be simpler. Let the handkerchief drop onto the face-up deck. Hold out your palm and tell the spectator to lift a pile of cards from the deck, gripping them through the handkerchief. "Just lift off any number you choose."

As he lifts off a pile of cards, turn the remainder of the deck face down again on your palm. Take the handkerchief and cards from him with your right

hand, hold out your left palm and direct him to take the card he cut to. As soon as he takes it, put the deck together and hand it to him, telling him to shuffle his card back into the pack. You know the card he looks at, because it was originally the top card.

An even simpler force is one in which you overhand-shuffle the bottom card to the top. You know what it is. How? You looked at it as you started your overhand shuffle. Once it's on top of the deck, you have a spectator cut off any number of cards he likes.

"Mark your cut," you instruct him, "by placing the cards you cut off face-up on the face-down deck." He puts the block of cards face-up on top of the others, as instructed.

"At this point," you tell him, "not even you know the card you cut to." As you say this, you pick up the faced deck from above with your right hand and put it, top cards still face up, on your left palm.

You now turn your left palm face down as you ribbon-spread the deck across the table.

"Look at the first face-down card," you instruct the spectator, "remember it, and put the deck together in proper face-down order, shuffling your chosen card into it."

When you turn over your left palm to ribbon-spread the deck, the first face-down card in the spread automatically becomes the card that was on the top of the deck when you directed the spectator to cut.

There may be a simpler card force, but I doubt if

58

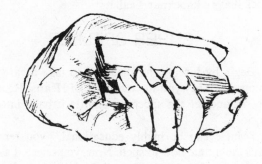

you'll ever find a cleaner one. Your movement in spreading the deck is perfectly natural, and yet you've automatically forced the top card of the deck.

While that's one of my favorite forces, I use it only in certain tricks. The one I employ most consistently uses the "Little Finger Control," and that's something you might as well learn right now.

Hold the deck face down in dealing position in the left hand. Pull the bottom half of the deck out from under, with your right thumb on one side of the rear end and your right first and second fingers on the other side. You pull out these cards as if you were going to cut them to the top, which is exactly what you're going to do. Glimpse the bottom card of this group as you pull it out and back.

Now, slap the pile of cards on top of those remaining in the left hand—EXCEPT that some of the flesh between the tip and first joint of your left little finger rests on top of the cards in the left hand. It is near the rear end of the deck, on the right side. Drop the cards in the right hand onto those in the left, squaring them and gripping them with the first, second and third fingers of the left hand, which are naturally along the right side of the now-complete deck.

You'll see that there is about a quarter-inch break between the face of the original bottom card and the back of the card just below it, at the right rear end of the pack. The left fingers curled up around the side of the deck conceal the break from the side, there *is* no break at the front, and the rear of the deck faces your body. The break is concealed from everyone except you.

Move the left thumb out to the left front edge of the

deck and riffle downward with it, letting cards pop up as they pass from under the thumb. It's an easy, natural way to riffle. Start riffling slowly from top to bottom, saying, "Say stop at any time." If you get too close to the bottom, start riffling again from the top and repeat the request.

The instant the spectator says, "Stop," quit riffling and hold the front left edge of the deck open with the left thumb at that point. Reach over to the left palm with the right hand so that the thumb will hold the narrow edge of the cards from the rear end and the four fingers will hold it from the front. You make a move as if you were going to remove all the cards above the break made by the left thumb with the riffle.

As you grasp all cards above the break with the right thumb, you move it slightly forward, the smallest fraction of an inch, and press against the front edge with your right fingers. If you lift the right hand now, you will be holding all the cards that were originally above the left little finger break. As the right fingers curl down onto the front of the deck and get ready to lift cards, release the riffle break that's been held with the left thumb.

Bring the front end of the deck up, faces of the

A Message From the Flame

An interesting way of revealing a chosen card depends on a paper match.

You must, of course, force the spectator to take a specific card, which may be accomplished by any of several methods explained in this book.

Write the name of a card on the head of a paper match with a pencil. The size of the match head requires that the card's designation be abbreviated. The Ace of Hearts becomes AH. The six of Spades becomes 6S, etc. Unless the match has a white head, the pencil lettering on the head will not be noticeable. At any rate, you don't call attention to it, and there's no reason for the spectator to be looking for such a thing until it's too late.

You have a card selected (forced), then reach into your pocket and remove a paper pack of matches. You take one out, light it and let it burn long enough so that the head is thoroughly charred.

When you blow it out, the name of the card will appear in solid black against the whitish charcoal.

One magician prints the names of every card in a suit on the front row of a packet of matches, with K, Q and J on the first three matches in the second row. He carries four packs of matches, one marked with each suit and carried in either the left or right pants pocket or coat pocket.

He offers a completely free choice of card, then reaches into the proper pocket, tears out the match with the abbreviation matching the card, and lights it.

cards away from you and toward the spectator. "Remember the card you stopped at," you order, and drop the cards back onto the deck.

If all you need is knowledge of the card the spectator selected, you may hand the deck to him at this point and tell him to shuffle it. If you need to keep the card under control, it's easy to do.

If you want to bring the card to the bottom of the deck, retain the left little finger break at the right rear end when you drop the cards back onto the deck. Then simply cut the deck, lifting off all cards above the break and putting them onto the table, then putting the cards remaining in the left hand on top of those on the table. The selected card is on the bottom of the deck.

If you want to bring the selected card to the top of the deck, simply take all cards above the little-finger break into your right hand in position for an overhand shuffle and shuffle them off, letting the last card in the right hand drop to the top of the deck. It is the chosen card.

The 'force' move should look as if you riffle the front edge of the deck with your left thumb until the spectator orders you to stop, and then lift up the cards above that point to let him see the card he stopped at. Keep your head turned to one side as you lift off the cards, so that it's obvious you aren't trying to get a glimpse of the face of the card. Indeed, it appears that you are trying *not* to see it.

Practice this routine several dozen times before you try it on anyone. Here's all there is to it:

1. Cut 'force' card from bottom to middle of deck, holding left little finger break below it.

2. Riffle front left edge of deck with left thumb until spectator says "Stop."

3. Bring right hand to top of deck, grasping cards above little-finger break between right thumb at rear and right fingers at front. Release riffle break held by left thumb as fingers lift cards from deck.

4. Show 'chosen' card to spectator without looking at it yourself, then drop it and cards above it back on top of deck, either maintaining control with left little finger or offering deck to spectator to shuffle.

So it may take you an hour to learn to do this 'force' smoothly. Believe me, it's worth it. You can do dozens of sleight of hand card tricks with this force and control, and nothing else. Learn it, and you'll use it as long as you do card tricks.

Once you can 'force' a card—and you can certainly do it in one of the first two ways I showed you, even before you've become proficient with the thumb riffle force—you're equipped to do a Card Spelling trick that's a knockout. I call it:

SUPER-SPELLER

Begin by forcing the spectator to take a card you know. Let's say you force the five of Hearts. Remember it, and let the spectator shuffle it back into the deck.

"Magic can be highly educational," you remark. "It's taught me how to spell. Now, you selected a card at random and shuffled it back into the deck. Do you have any idea where it is in the deck right now? You don't? I'll let you in on a little secret. Neither do I.

"I'm a great believer in telepathic waves, and I sometimes use them to find a chosen card. Give me the deck, please. I'm going to fan the cards from left to right, face up, and I want you to be looking for your chosen card as I do it—but don't give me any clues. Don't say a word. Just look. And don't tip me off when you see it by saying, 'I've seen it.' Let me go right on through the deck."

You begin fanning cards slowly from the left hand to the right, face up, not changing their position in the deck. Be looking for that five of Hearts. When you come to it, spell to yourself silently, "F-I-V-E-O-F-H-E-A-R-T-S," moving one card from the left under

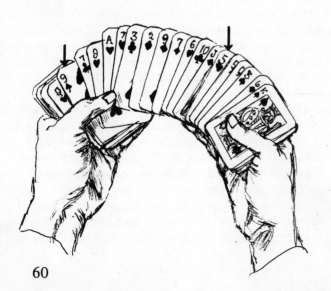

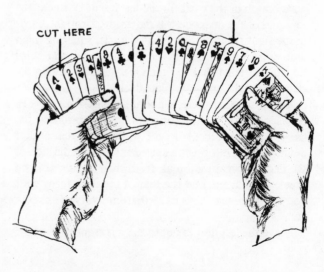

60

the five of Hearts with each letter after the first one, which is assigned to the chosen card, itself. When you reach the "S", keep right on fanning cards from left to right, but note the card immediately after the "S" and start spelling it silently, a letter for each card. Let's say it's the nine of Spades. Spell it out, one card for each letter. When you've spelled the final S, toss the balance of the cards in the left hand, face up, atop the face-up deck.

If the chosen card is too near the top of the deck, start spelling it when you come to it, anyway. When you reach the end of the deck, go back to the first face-up card on top of the face-up deck and continue spelling from where you left off. Spell the additional card, as before. And when you've completed silently spelling both cards, drop the balance of the deck in the left hand on top of the face-up cards in the right hand.

You have set up the cards, deliberately and openly, without the spectator having the faintest idea of what's happened.

You tell him at this point, "I didn't seem to get any telepathic waves from you, so I guess I'll have to find your card by spelling. I'll give you the deck and ask you to spell the name of your card, a letter at a time, out loud. You deal off one card for each letter. And you spell the "of." For example, if your card were the nine of Spades—that didn't happen to be the one you selected, did it?—Good—Deal off cards like this. N-I-N-E-O-F-S-P-A-D-E-S."

You turn the card on the final S face up, and it's the nine of Spades, which comes as a startler. Gather up the dealt cards from the table and put them on the *bottom* of the face-down deck. Hand the deck to the spectator and say, "I want you to spell out the name of your card exactly as I did with the nine of Spades, a card for each letter."

He does as instructed, and finds he's holding the five of Hearts as he spells the final S.

This is a superb trick, and there's an old axiom that you should always quit while you're ahead, but I have a follow-up spelling trick that I sometimes use because it has such an unexpected twist at the finish. It's only slightly more difficult to do than Super-Speller. I call it:

SAFETY CHECK SPELLER

"You did that very well," you compliment the spectator as you're shuffling the deck after completing Super-Speller. "You'd be surprised how many people can't spell out their cards simply because they don't know how to spell. A magician has to be prepared for people who can't even spell platitudinarianism, let alone the name of a card. Here."

You fan the deck toward him, face down, and give him a free choice of a card, widening the break

slightly where he removes the card. "Look at any card, remember it, and put it back where you got it."

As he reinserts the card in the fan, your fingers pull the card above it in the face-down fan over on top of it. Now, your left little finger, from beneath the spread of cards and hidden by it, comes up and makes a break between those two cards and the part of the deck that's on top of them, just as you held a break *below* the force card in the riffle force. Your left and right hands square up the deck. Your right hand reaches up from beneath and grips the deck preparatory to an overhand shuffle, thumb at the inner end and fingers at the outer end. They pick up the deck in a tight grip, and the break at the right rear inner end is transferred to the right thumb. You simply shuffle off all cards to the break and throw the balance of the deck on top of them in a block, squaring the cards up neatly. The deck is in your left hand and you thumb off the top card, turning it face up.

"You see, your card isn't the top card," you remark. You thumb the top card, now the chosen card,

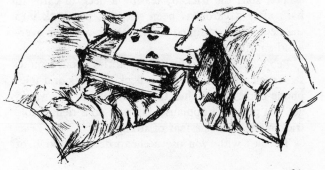

a fraction of an inch to the right, put the face-up card face up onto it and grip the two cards, top one face up and second one face down, between the right thumb and forefingers as you turn the balance of the deck face up. "And the bottom card isn't the one you selected, either." Apparently, the face-up card is put back on the now face-up deck so that it is face down. Actually, the selected card is now face up, on top of the deck, although viewers have no idea that this is so. You show the bottom card of the deck and start fanning the bottom cards, at the same time lifting the deck enough to get a quick glimpse of the face-up card on top of the deck, the selected card. Let's say it's the six of Spades.

"Let's see if your card is anywhere near the bottom," you say. "If it is, you obviously couldn't spell it from the top of the deck." You fan cards from the left side of the face-up deck to the right hand, spelling "S-I-X-O-F-S-P-A-D-E" as you run them. "Obviously," you remark, "if I put these cards on top of the deck, your card won't be close to the top." Move the packet of ten cards in the right hand to the top of the deck, on top of the reversed six of Spades. Fan a few more cards from the bottom and ask, "Is your chosen card anywhere near the bottom now?" Upon being told that it isn't, turn the deck face down, hand it to the spectator and tell him to spell out the name of his chosen card aloud, just as before, dealing off a card for each letter.

He gets ready to spell the final "S", and there is the six of Spades, staring at him face up from the face-down deck.

You smile. "When you get a person who has trouble with spelling, you play it safe," you say. "You make sure that he won't miss his card."

It's a nice surprise ending for any card spelling trick. Not only does the spectator spell to his card, but his card is reversed in the deck.

Next, I'm going to teach you a card trick that you never follow with further card effects, for the simple reason that you can't possibly top it. I do it only when I'm particularly anxious to make an impression on my audience, not because it's difficult but because you destroy a deck of cards every time you do it.

THE TORN DECK MIRACLE

You start the trick by tearing a deck of cards in half, after a card has been selected, put back into the deck and controlled to the top by a cut or overhand shuffle.

People have heard legendary stories about famous strong men who could tear a deck of cards or a telephone book in half. Just tearing a deck in two would get you plenty of applause, but you do a remarkable trick along with the feat of strength.

To start with, you use a cheap deck, the kind of cards that are offered as a "special" by cut-rate drug stores at 29¢ or some such price. Do *not* use plastic-coated cards. You have a perfect excuse for using cheap cards in the fact that you destroy a deck every time you do the trick.

You probably face a psychological block, just as I did when I first tackled the trick. You don't believe you could tear a deck of cards in half. You couldn't, unless you held the deck in the proper grip. You wrap your left fingers around half of the deck, thumb on one side, fingers on the other. Then you wrap your right hand around the other end so that the hands can twist in opposite directions against the deck. And as you start the tear, you have the long edge of the deck beveled so that you're tearing only a few thicknesses of card at the outset. It takes some experimentation to arrive at the grip that works best for you.

Until you get the right grip and learn how to apply the pressure, you resort to some simple trickery that makes tearing the deck easy.

You spread the deck out on a cookie sheet and put it into a 300 degree oven for anywhere from an hour and a half to two hours. I've never had a deck get browned from the heat, but I always look into the oven occasionally to see that such a thing doesn't happen.

With a "baked" deck, tearing the cards in half is child's play. The first few times you perform this trick, use such a deck, by all means. It will give you confidence. And after awhile, you'll discover that you no longer need to give the cards the heat treatment.

A card has been freely chosen from such a deck and you've shuffled or cut it to the top. Now you tear

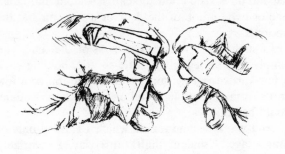

the deck in half, giving the feat a big buildup and making it look much more difficult than it really is.

Next, you put one of the torn halves on the table and overhand shuffle the other, shuffling the top piece of card to the bottom and then back to the top. You do the same thing with other half-deck.

Now, dealing "seconds" is ordinarily a difficult card maneuver, calling for long practice and considerable dexterity. But dealing seconds from a torn half-deck is no problem at all. The pieces are just half the length of a regular card. You hold the half-length packet in your left hand. The entire packet is against your palm. It doesn't extend out at either the top or the bottom. Your thumb is on top, against the chosen card, or half of it.

You turn the hand so that the back of it faces the audience, pull the top piece of card well down from the upper edge with your left thumb, and start dealing off pieces, apparently from the top.

If you want to be neat, have a sheet of newspaper on the table and let the pieces of card drop onto it. This will save a lot of cleaning up at the conclusion of the trick. Move your hands over in front of a spectator and ask him to say "Stop" at any time as you deal off pieces of card.

When he calls "Stop," you lower your left palm so that it's palm up, parallel to the floor, and very deliberately deal off the top piece of card with your left thumb and forefinger, handing the piece to him to hold.

You now pick up the other torn half of the deck and repeat the process with another spectator. When he calls "Stop," you very cleanly and openly hand him the top piece of card from the torn deck.

You remark, "If you two happened to stop me so that the two pieces you hold are halves of the same card, it would be a miracle, wouldn't it? Would you please fit the two halves of your cards together, without letting anybody else see them? They're halves of the same card, and they fit perfectly? Well, that *is* a miracle, isn't it? I congratulate you.

"But now, if the two halves you hold, which match, should happen to be halves of the card another spectator selected and shuffled back into the deck before

I tore it in half, that would be absolutely incredible, wouldn't it?

"That would be carrying the idea of miracles beyond the realm of belief into pure fantasy." You look at the person who originally selected the card. "What was the card you chose and then shuffled back into the deck before it was torn in half and then shuffled again?" He names the card. You take the two halves from the other two spectators and hold them up together so that everyone can see them.

If you can't flip any audience out of its skull with this one, give up. But, of course, you can. This one trick will make a reputation for you as a top card magician.

FALSE SHUFFLES

Before we continue with more card tricks, it's high time for you to learn something about false shuffling.

There are rare occasions in card magic when you're working with a stacked deck and want to give the impression of thoroughly shuffling the cards without disturbing the order of them. You can do this with a "lace-through" riffle shuffle in which the bottom half of the deck is interlaced into the top half and then pulled right on through in the course of squaring the deck and cutting. It isn't quite as difficult as it sounds, but difficult enough to discourage most beginners.

A much simpler false shuffle that leaves every card in its original position is done as follows.

You remove about half the cards with your right hand, fingers along the front end of the deck, thumb at the back end. The left hand takes a similar position on the bottom half of the deck. The cards form a V in front of you, open end facing the audience, pointed end facing you. With the thumbs, you riffle the rear right end of the bottom half into the rear left end of the top half, holding back a few cards with the right thumb so that the top three or four cards are all from the top half. Each half deck is gripped tightly by the fingers at the front end and thumbs at the rear end.

Now, if you make a move as if to complete the shuffle, moving the *front* ends of the cards together

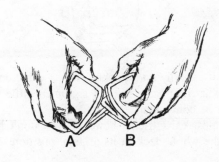

A   B

as if to complete the interlacing throughout the length of the cards, your fingers will almost completely mask the deck from the spectators. As you pull the two front ends together, you automatically pull the two rear ends *apart* so that they're no longer interlaced. The original top half of the deck is moved to the left, over on top of the original bottom half, and the two hands pick the deck up from the table, squaring up what looks like a now thoroughly shuffled pack.

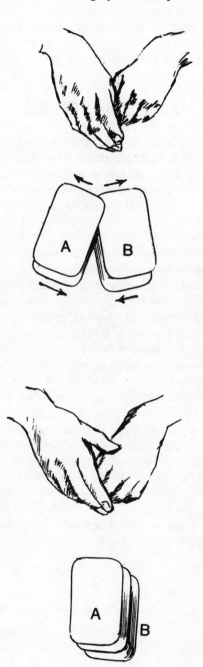

Do it casually and quickly, just as you'd do it if it were what it appears to be, a legitimate riffle shuffle. It will be convincing.

In most card tricks, however, you don't have to keep the whole deck in its original position. All you need to do is keep a few top cards, seldom more than one or two, on top of the deck or a few cards at the bottom.

In such cases, which exist most of the time, you simply make a legitimate riffle shuffle, holding back a few cards from the top to fall on the top or a few cards from the bottom to fall on the bottom. Nothing could be easier.

And yet, for some reason which I can lay only to long usage, I seldom shuffle this way. I invariably bring the card or cards I want to control to the top of the deck and then do the "Injog" overhand shuffle. When it's completed, the cards I want to control are still at the top. If the trick calls for them to be at the bottom, I simply continue the overhand shuffle, running them singly from my right hand to the left, putting them on the bottom and shuffling the rest of the deck on top of them.

The injog shuffle is one of the most useful moves in card magic. You bring a chosen card to the top of the deck by the little finger control and a cut to the break or an overhand shuffle to the break. That puts the card on top of the deck.

The beautiful thing about the injog shuffle is that you can now continue shuffling overhand indefinitely and still control the card, bringing it back to the top whenever you like.

Here's how it works:

You hold the deck in your left hand, chosen card or cards on top. Now, pull out somewhat less than half of the deck from the bottom, with your right thumb at one end and fingers at the other. Shuffle them off onto the chosen card.

But if you're going to shuffle them off onto the chosen card, how do you keep control of it? Easy.

As you shuffle off the first card from those in the right hand onto the chosen card, you move your right hand in a little closer to your body. The first card you shuffle off extends inward toward your body, past the inner end of the deck, as much as an inch. Now you shuffle the balance of the cards in your right hand sloppily on top of the injogged card. When you've run out of cards, pick up all the cards beneath the injogged card and throw them in a packet on top. That's the simplest way.

But there's another way that looks better. Pick up the entire deck in your right thumb and forefingers, making a break at the inner end, toward your body, with the right thumb. The outer edges are squared. Overhand shuffle to the break and drop the balance of the cards on top.

It reads—and sounds—much more difficult than it is in actual practice. I've done it so often over the years that I don't even have to think about it. You'll be surprised at how quickly you can master it.

I particularly like it because it is almost clumsy. It's a "slop" shuffle that gives the appearance of be-

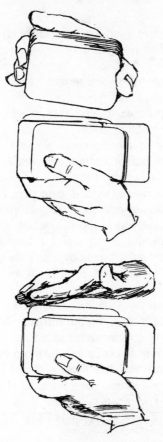

ing inexpertly and haphazardly done. It's particularly valuable when you're doing "Poker Deals" and have to maintain the top 25 cards in their correct position. All you need to do is take a little less than half of the deck in the right hand, injog the first card onto the stack of five poker hands, and shuffle off the rest haphazardly. Then pick up the whole deck, overhand shuffle cards from the right hand to left to the break your right thumb holds at the injog and drop the balance, which includes the 25-card stack, on top.

When you're performing card tricks before an audience of men, they inevitably ask for a Poker demonstration. Here's one of the simplest and best there is, that can be done with a borrowed deck. You have to know one thing—how to do the injog shuffle so as to maintain the top 25 cards in order. The rest is self-working.

SIMPLEX POKER DEAL

"Yes, I know how the card sharps deal crookedly in poker games," you admit, "but when people ask me to do it, they never seem to know the difference between the old-time card hustler's technique and that used by the modern card mechanic, as he calls himself. When I ask which they want, old-time poker deal or modern, they usually give me a blank look.

"So I'll demonstrate both methods. The old-time card sharp depended almost entirely on the bottom deal—dealing cards off the bottom of the deck instead of the top.

"In gathering up the cards to shuffle, he brought a good hand to the bottom. Strangely, nobody else in the game ever seemed to notice. Maybe it was so obvious that the other players couldn't believe there was a reason for it. To show you how this old-timer operated, I'll bring the four Aces to the bottom of the deck right now."

You fan the deck, faces of the cards toward yourself. You move the four Aces to the bottom of the deck, but you do something else of even more importance. You bring the four Kings to the top of the deck. You don't mention the Kings, and you move cards around casually with the excuse of hunting for the Aces. Don't move the last Ace to the bottom until the four Kings are on the top.

Square the deck, turn it face up, and fan off the four bottom cards, to show the spectators that the four Aces are on the bottom. Then turn the deck face down and start to deal.

"The old-timer dealt out five hands of poker, dealing from the top of the deck until he came to his own hand. He thumbed the top card slightly off the deck, just as he'd done for the other four cards, but the second finger of his right hand went into an open space between the first and second fingers of the left hand which were curled around the side of the deck. Actually, the deck was held between the thumb on the left side and the forefinger at the outer right end. As he reached his right hand for the card and the second finger went into the opening to the bottom of the deck, the left second, third and little fingers uncurled, permitting the right-hand second finger to pivot the bottom card out from the bottom. The thumb of the left hand drew back the top card as the right thumb and second finger pulled the bottom card away and dealt it to the table in front of him."

You deal off the bottom card deliberately and without trying to hide what you're doing. Indeed, you explain it. Don't worry if you're clumsy at it. You deal four face-down cards to each hand, dealing from the bottom to yourself.

"The old-timer had one psychological advantage. If anyone sensed something funny about the way he dealt cards to himself, the suspicion was allayed when

he dealt the last round of cards. Since he already had the four Aces in front of himself, he dealt his last card very openly and deliberately from the top of the deck."

You turn your hand face up. "As you can see, he had four Aces and an indifferent card."

You put the other four hands back on top of the deck, still face down, as you continue, "The modern card mechanic sneers at the idea of using such a crude technique. The bottom-deal is an extremely difficult thing to do indetectably, and the one thing the card mechanic wants to avoid is any possibility of getting caught cheating."

You throw your own hand face down on top of the deck. At this point, you either give the cards the overhand injog shuffle, shuffling only the bottom half of the deck as previously described, and bringing the original top-stock of 25 cards back to the top, or you use the V riffle shuffle. Don't make a big deal of the shuffle. Don't even say that you're doing it—just do it.

Square up the deck in your left hand, and with the right thumb and first two fingers at the inner ends, pull out roughly half of the cards, from the bottom, slap them onto the table, and drop the remaining cards on top. This false cut doesn't disturb the order of a single card.

Whatever you do, don't announce that you're going to cut the cards. Just make the false cut, as briskly as you'd cut the cards in an actual game. Pick up the deck immediately and get ready to deal.

"Once the cards are shuffled and cut," you continue, "the modern card mechanic deals the five hands openly and cleanly, without the slightest trickery that anyone could detect."

You deal five hands of five cards each, dealing off the card to your own hand slowly and deliberately, so that everyone can see it comes from the top of the deck.

"I think you'll agree that nobody in the game could accuse the modern card mechanic of crooked dealing. But he still has the four aces."

As you say this, you flip up your own hand. It contains not four Aces but four Kings, which should come as a complete surprise to your viewers.

"Darn it, I missed," you say, "but even so, I still have the winning hand." Spread each of the other four hands slightly as you throw them back on top of the deck, picking up three face-down cards from each one and turning it to your spectators, to show that no other hand has four of a kind. The four face-down hands are put back on top of the deck, not disturbing the order of cards in any hand. Your own four-King hand is put on top of the deck last.

Repeat the false-shuffle and false-cut as you continue, "The modern card mechanic doesn't give his victims a fighting chance. They can't catch him, because there's nothing to catch."

You deal five hands of five cards each again. And this time, when you turn up your own hand, you have the four Aces.

"That's better," you comment. "I was beginning to think I was slipping."

Gather up the cards, give them a legitimate shuffle and go into another trick.

There are many more complicated poker deals. Most of them call for a rather complex advance stacking. Quite a few of them require the dealer to second-deal and bottom-deal without detection. They're good, but they're for experts, and the poker demonstration I've just taught you is short, entertaining, and sure-fire. The only skill it requires is a false shuffle—but that's something that anybody who's going to do card tricks with a borrowed deck must be able to do, anyway.

In case you think it's difficult, we'll move on to a card trick that's anything but difficult. It's so simple, in fact, that its success never fails to amaze me. And yet, easy as it is, it's been around since the beginning of this century and has been included in expensive volumes of card magic many times. It's known as:

THE PIANO TRICK

The trick can be done at any time, with a borrowed deck, and it depends on what you say, not what you do.

The spectator is asked to place his hands, palms down, on the table top, just as they'd be if he were about to play the piano.

You deal off two cards and place them between his left hand little and third fingers. They stand on edge, held up by the fingers.

"Two cards, even," you say. You deal off two more cards and put them in the next opening until the four openings in the left hand contain eight cards, two between each two fingers.

"All even," you point out. You continue dealing off two cards at a time until three of the spaces in between the right thumb and fingers are filled. "All even," you say, "except for the last one." You put

one card between the right third and little fingers. "One card, odd."

Now you remove a pair of cards from the left fingers, laying them down on the table, side by side. "Two cards, even," you repeat. You take a second pair and put one on top of each of the first two, so that two piles are started. "Two more, even." You repeat this process until only the odd single card is left between the spectator's fingers. "Two even piles," you point out, "and one odd card. Cover either of the two even piles with your empty hand."

Whichever pile he covers, add the odd card to the other pile, saying, "And if I add an odd card to the other even pile, it becomes odd. I now have an odd pile and you have an even pile. Watch closely. If I move one card from my odd pile to your even pile, the situation will be reversed." You snap your forefinger against the packet of cards in front of you. "Did you feel that? One card went from my odd pile to your even pile. You should now have an odd number and I should have an even number. See if I'm right."

The spectator counts his cards and discovers he has seven, an odd number. You deal off pairs from your pile onto the deck, "Even, even, even, even." You have shown that your supposedly odd pile has become even.

That's all there is to it. You wouldn't think it would fool anybody, but it does. What you say while you're doing the trick is all-important.

THINK STOP

Here's a quick, dumbfounding card trick that it would be hard to beat. In its original version, as revealed in Jean Hugard and Fred Braue's fine book, *Expert Card Technique*, some tricky shuffling was involved and there was always a chance of failure. I've re-routined the trick so that the tricky shuffling and the control of a chosen card is eliminated—and so that you always succeed!

You let the spectator shuffle the deck, think of a card, remove that card from the deck and place it face down on the table, apart from the deck.

"This is a trick in mental telepathy," you announce. "I'm going to replace the card you thought of in the deck in a position that you can't possibly know. The importance of your being unaware of the card's location will become apparent to you as the trick progresses. I don't want to see the card you thought of, so I'll hold the deck behind my back and let you hand the card to me there."

With the deck in one hand, you take the card behind your back in the other and turn to face the spectator.

"I'm going to insert the card in the deck, but you won't know where." You thumb off five cards from the top and replace the "thought of" card, putting the other five cards on top of it so that it is now the sixth card down from the top. You square the deck and bring it around to the front.

You start dealing off cards from the deck to the

Master Location

The magician removed a deck of cards from its case and handed the cards to a spectator. "Shuffle to your heart's content," he said. "Any kind of a shuffle, even several kinds of shuffles. And I want you to note that I'll never have the deck in my hands from this point on. When you think you've mixed the cards enough, spread the deck out onto the table and touch one card. Move it out of the spread toward you. No, clear out, in front of you."

At this point, the magician put the tip of his forefinger to the card and moved it forward. There wasn't the slightest chance of his being able to peek at the face of the card. He turned his back to the spectator.

"While my back is turned," he instructed, "look at the face of the card and remember what it is. Show it to someone else, if you like. Then put it back into the spread, anywhere you like. Gather up the cards and shuffle again. Cut the cards a couple of times, too, if you like. Do you, yourself, have any idea where your chosen card is? No? Good!"

He turned around and instructed the spectator to deal the cards slowly from the top of the deck into a face-down pile. When the spectator had dealt about a dozen cards, the magician said sharply, "Stop." He pointed to the top card of the pile. "That should be your card. Turn it over."

The spectator turned it over, and acknowledged that the card was the one he originally pulled from the spread.

The magician who originated this sold it to other magicians for $25.

The secret was simple. Before performing, he put a little gob of red lipstick on the flap of the card case. The deck was red-backed. When he pulled the deck from the card case, he got the lipstick smear onto his right forefinger.

Then, when the spectator touched a card, he put his forefinger on it and shoved it right in front of the spectator. In so doing, he left a little red smear on the back of the card. If you knew it was there, it was ridiculously easy to spot. If you didn't know of its presence, you'd never have found it.

When the spectator dealt the cards face-down off the deck, the magician simply waited to see the card with the smear in the design.

He fooled some of the greatest card magicians in the world with it.

table top, one by one, very slowly and deliberately. As you deal off the fourth face-down card, say quickly, rather impatiently, "Just say stop at any time. Stop!"

You deal off the fifth card, just as slowly and deliberately as the other four.

Almost always, the spectator will say "Stop" as you deal off the sixth card. Sometimes, the "Stop" will come while you're dealing the fifth card. Less often, it will come as you're preparing to deal the seventh card.

When any of these things happen, you have a miracle. The sixth card is the chosen card. If "Stop" was called as you were dealing the fifth card, you move your hands slowly to the top of the deck and dramatically turn over the top card. If "Stop" came while you were dealing the sixth card or as you're preparing to deal the seventh, turn over the top card of the pile that's been dealt.

If the spectator doesn't say "Stop" at the right time, you probably aren't dealing slowly enough or didn't put enough impatience in your voice when you told him to say "Stop" at any time. But don't be discouraged. The trick is still going to work. Continue to deal, the seventh card going on top of the face-down chosen card. Keep track of how many cards are on top of it when the spectator finally says "Stop." There are seldom more than four or five, but you know how many.

At the call of "Stop" you turn the next card face up and put it on the table.

You put the pile of cards that have been dealt off back on top of the deck in a block, putting the deck behind your back as you say, "This card you stopped me at will serve as a locater card. With the deck behind my back, I'm going to insert it face up somewhere in the deck. Wherever I insert it, this face up card will find the card you originally thought of. The card you thought of will be directly beneath the face-up card."

You know the position of the "thought of" card. Let's say it's four down from the top of the deck, with three cards on top of it. You simply pick up the face-up card from the table, thumb off three cards (or whatever the proper number may be) insert the face-up card directly on top of the chosen card, replace the others and cut the deck, bringing the face-up card and the one beneath it to somewhere near the center of the deck. Bring the deck back to the front and ribbon-spread it on the table, so that the face-up card is revealed.

"Now, for the first time," you say, "tell us the name of the card you thought of."

The spectator complies. You tell him to remove the card directly beneath the face-up "locater" card and turn it face up. It is, naturally, the chosen card.

You can't realize what a great card trick this is until you try it. It's quick, direct—and seemingly impossible. When it works without the locater card, which is most of the time, nobody can come up with any possible explanation.

Locater Cards I

Some magicians who don't want to be bothered with sleight of hand or aren't capable of doing it use "locater" cards in their card tricks. If a chosen card is replaced directly beneath (or above) the "locater" card, it is easy to keep under control.

Probably the best "locater" card is one whose outer left and inner right corners have been slightly trimmed, seldom more than an eighth of an inch. A certain type of nail clipper will do a good trimming job, but a pair of manicure scissors are more often used.

Wherever this card is in the deck, if you hold the cards in your left hand and riffle the corners with your left thumb, there will be a distinct "click" and noticeable feel when you riffle to the card with the short corner. If you break the deck at this point and have a chosen card replaced, putting the cards on top of the break back and squaring the deck, you will have no difficulty locating the selected card. You simply riffle again with your thumb.

With a borrowed deck, the same result can be achieved by breaking the outer left and inner right corners of a card.

THE TWELVE-CARD COUNT

This is a trick I've been doing for years, because of its impact on any audience. Most magicians shy away from it, particularly beginners, because it requires some audacious sleight of hand and because of an inherent weakness if the spectator selects the number "Two."

While the trick has never given me any trouble, I recognize the average person's fears about it and have worked out a version for you that eliminates the problems.

"This is a highly educational trick," you announce, "called the Twelve-Card Count." You remove two common letter envelopes from your pocket and drop them onto the table. There's nothing gimmicked about them. They're just what they appear to be.

Next, you direct a spectator to shuffle the cards and deal 12 cards face down onto the palm of both your right and left hands. Caution him to deal carefully, making sure that there are exactly 12 cards in each pile.

At this point, you make a daring announcement. "I want to call your attention to the fact that my two

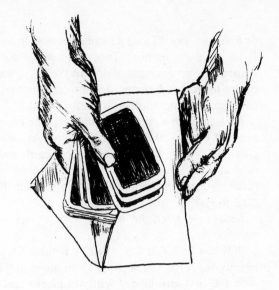

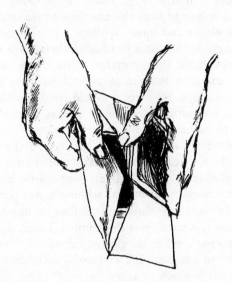

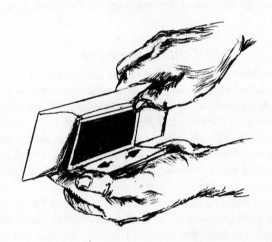

hands will never come together while they contain packets of cards. Both piles of 12 will be put into envelopes and the envelopes will be initialed so that you know beyond any shadow of doubt that no substitution takes place."

You drop the left-hand pile of 12 to the table top, openly and cleanly, and pick up one of the two envelopes between the left fingers. You open it out to show that it's empty. Now you hold it in your left hand, flap side toward your body, fan the pile in your right hand slightly and say, "The 12 cards in the right hand go into this envelope."

You put the cards into the envelope. Well, not quite. You've slightly fanned the backs of the cards. *Nine* of them go into the envelope and the top three, now squared are on the *back* of the envelope, the flap side, gripped by your left thumb. You tuck in the flap with your right fingers, and remove the envelope and the three cards behind it by gripping everything in the right hand. Your left hand picks up its pile of 12. "I want somebody to initial this envelope," you say, and lay the envelope, address side up, on top of the pile in your left palm as you reach into your pocket with your right hand for a pen or pencil.

You hand this to a spectator and direct him to initial the envelope and then hold it.

Unbeknownst to your audience, three cards have been added to the left hand pile. Pick up the second envelope with your right hand, drop the cards into it, tuck in the flap and ask a second spectator to initial this envelope. He keeps the envelope.

"Now, bear in mind," you say to this second spectator, "that both sets of 12 cards each were already in envelopes, completely out of my control, before I ask you to determine the outcome of this trick. Also, remember that my two hands never came together while they contained piles of 12 cards each. Now, the object of this trick is to magically transmit cards from one envelope to another. The number is never determined until the envelopes are out of my possession. And I'm going to tell you in advance exactly what's going to happen. I'll ask you for a number. If you give the number Two, for example, two cards will magically transmit themselves from his envelope to yours. Understood? All right, give me any number from One to Five, quickly, please."

If you insist upon haste, the spectator will blurt, "Three," 19 times out of 20. If he gives either One

69

or Five, you say, "I said a number *from* One *to* Five." If he gives the number Two, you say, "I used that number for an example, didn't I? We don't want the others to think I influenced you to choose that number. Please name another, quickly."

He's left with a choice of number Three or number Four. If he says "Four," which seldom happens, you continue, "Now, I can transfer these cards invisibly, or I can do it visibly, so that you actually see the cards go through the air. How do you want the first card to go?"

Sooner or later, he has to want to see one go visibly.

"Of course," you say, "there's nothing very mysterious about the visible way." You move to the man with the first envelope. "Will you please reach into your envelope and remove one card? Thank you."

Cutting the Aces

A Seattle magician who knows little sleight of hand has acquired a reputation as a card manipulator by his apparently skillful "cutting" to the four Aces.

He puts a downward bend in the deck as he holds it between thumb at one end and fingers at the other. The bend isn't necessary, actually, because any deck of cards that's "broken in" will already have a bend in it, one way or the other.

"So that you can see what I'm doing, that I'm actually cutting to the Aces and not switching cards on you," this magician tells his viewers, "I'll ask you to remove the four Aces from the deck. Now put them back, but face up, *so that you'll know immediately whether or not I cut to an Ace. Try to put them apart from each other, not all bunched together. Now, give the cards a shuffle if you like."*

He takes the shuffled deck and quickly cuts to the four Aces.

There's actually nothing to it. Since the four Aces have a bend in them just the opposite of the remaining cards, you can hardly keep from cutting at an Ace if you cut with the thumb at one long side of the deck and the fingers at the other. There will be a distinct "break" at every Ace.

If you want to control a chosen card to the bottom of the deck, hold the deck on the left hand and lift off a block of cards with the right. Now, bridge the cards remaining in the left hand by squeezing the thumb on one side and the fingers at the other side together rather sharply. Don't hold the bend; just make it quickly and then relax your grip.

Have the chosen card replaced on top of the cards in the left hand and toss the cards in the right hand on top, squaring the deck. Cut the cards at the inner end, where there will be a pronounced break. You will automatically cut the chosen card to the bottom.

You take the card, walk over to the man with the second envelope, and drop the card inside the flap.

"Not much magic," you smile, "but you'll have to admit that the card moved from one envelope to the other visibly. For the purpose of magic, the invisible way is much more impressive."

You return to the side of the man with the first envelope and snap your forefinger smartly against it. "Two! That's invisible. Did you feel it?"

If he says "No," you show concern. "You're not feeling very well, are you?" You snap the envelope again. "Three! Did you feel that?" If he says no, be alarmed. "Why, you're feeling terrible." Snap the envelope a fourth time. 'Four!" Four cards should now have moved from this envelope to the other one —one visibly and three invisibly.

"I told you that this is an educational card trick." You nod to the first spectator. "You started with 12 cards and four have transmitted themselves to the other envelope. How many should you have left?"

You nod with satisfaction as he says "Eight." You move to the man with the second envelope. "And you should now have how many?" He says, "Sixteen."

"I like to do educational tricks," you observe. "Will you gentlemen please count your cards and see whether or not your mental arithmetic was correct?"

They count their cards and confirm the number.

If the spectator gives the number Three, the trick is better but you lose the gag routine with the "visible" transfer of one card. It's well worth sacrificing, since the result is much cleaner.

If you don't mind learning a sleight-of-hand move that must be done smoothly, I recommend an older method that dispenses with the envelopes. The first pile of 12 cards is dealt onto your left hand. You spread the cards and count, making sure there are 12. In closing the spread, you insert your left little finger between the top three and the balance, holding a break at the rear right end.

The second 12 cards are dealt onto your right palm. You change your grip on them, holding them by the thumb at the rear end and fingers at the front end, backs of the cards toward your arched palm. Be careful to keep the back of the hand toward the spectators so as to avoid exposing the face of the bottom card. With the cards in this position, you advance toward the first spectator. You move your right hand toward him, in a pointing gesture, asking, "Do you have a handkerchief we may use for this experiment?" The right hand is fairly close to the left as you start to ask this question, and is slightly above it. As you move the right hand in the gesture toward the spectator, your right thumb picks up the left-hand three cards above the break, adding them to the bottom of the 12 it already holds. The move must be made casually, without hesitation. And it must be made without looking at your hands. As you extend the right-hand pile to be wrapped in the handkerchief, your left hand has moved away, out to the left.

The move seems more daring than it really is. Not once have I ever been caught at it. It does away with the use of the envelopes which, for some reason, I think improves the trick.

Most professional magicians who do the trick count the cards in the pile that decreases in number. They first false-count the pile as 12. After they've snapped the cards for the transmission of the first one, they false-count again, showing 11 left. Another false count shows ten left, and a third count, legitimate, shows nine left.

Some of them, unfortunately, don't do a convincing false count. Their technique is smooth, but their attitude convinces a viewer that something fishy is going on.

And, of course, all that counting slows down the trick. I think it's not only unnecessary but, after the first count, a bore. If I were you, I wouldn't bother learning to false count cards—at least, for this trick.

THE GOLDEN MIRACLE

This trick, with some variations, is one of the greatest card tricks ever conceived by man. The first version of it I ever ran across appeared in an old book, *The Art of Magic,* by T. Nelson Downs.

For your use, I've simplified it to the point where you can perform it without any difficulty, without lessening its strength in any way.

You start by allowing a spectator to shuffle the deck, which you then take from him and put into your left hand in normal dealing position. You arch your left palm so that the deck is held slightly away from it, fingers on the right side, thumb on the left.

"I want you to select a card from this deck," you say, "in the fairest possible manner—in a way that eliminates any possibility of my having influenced your choice and in a way which leaves me no possible way of discovering the chosen card's identity."

You remove a pencil from your pocket. You push the blunt end against the inner end of the cards, pushing out a packet several inches from the outer end. "Push out a packet of cards from anywhere in the deck, in this manner. Nothing could be fairer, nor could anything be left more completely to chance."

Have the spectator do as directed. Now, turn the outer end of the pack toward him. "Turn up the corner of the top card of those you pushed out," you direct, "just enough to learn the card's identity. Then push the little protruding block of cards back into the deck, and square it evenly, so that every card is in line."

You are holding the deck while he pushes out the block of cards with the blunt end of the pencil. You move the now protruding block of cards around so that it points to him. As he looks at the top card of the protruding block, *you* look at the face of the card directly above the break made by the pencil. It is the card directly above the card he's looking at. It's staring you right in the face. If it isn't, you tilt the deck enough so that it is.

As soon as the spectator has seen his card, let him push the block of which it's top card back into the deck and square the cards, which he puts down on the table.

"To do this trick," you continue, "I use five cards picked at random and a $25 gold piece."

You pick up the deck and start fanning the cards face up toward yourself, looking for the key card, the one you glimpsed above the break. As you fan face-up cards from left to right, the card immediately to the right of the key card will be the card he looked at. With the cards face up, it is immediately *above* the key card. If the cards were face down, it would be immediately *below* it. You remove the selected card and the two cards on either side of it, five cards in all. The chosen card is in the middle. These five cards aren't revealed to the audience. They are turned face down and dealt face down into a row—five face-down cards extending from left to right across the table, not more than two inches space between any two of them.

At this point, you remove a penny from your pocket. "And now I need the $25 gold piece," you say. "I always carry it with me because no other metal has the effect of gold on cards." You hold the penny gingerly between the right thumb and forefinger, forefinger on top, thumb beneath. You hold it so that it's about nine or ten inches above the center card of the five.

"I want you to hold this $25 gold piece exactly as I'm holding it," you continue, "thumb underneath, forefinger on top. Take it, please."

Don't extend the coin to the spectator. Make him reach to where you're holding it. Hold it steady, and insist that he grip it *exactly* as you've been holding it.

"Now, drop it," you say, rather sharply, as if you expected him to let go of it immediately. And as he releases it, you continue, "so that it lights on the back of any one of these five cards."

If you've handled it as directed, he will invariably drop the penny onto the center card, in which case your miracle is completed. Turn up each of the four

cards that don't have a penny covering them, saying, "This isn't your card and neither is this or this. What card *did* you look at?"

When he answers, tell him to turn over the card on which he placed the coin. He does, and it's the one he originally selected.

But let's say you draw a spectator who refuses to drop the coin on the center card. Pick up the other four cards and put them face-down in your left hand, in an order so that the chosen card, the one that was third in line, will be the top one of the face-down packet of four. Thumb this top card a tiny fraction of an inch to the right, place the card that was under the coin directly on top of it, and square up the packet, retaining a break under the top two face-down cards and moving them over to the right of the remainder, well-squared, about half their width. You do this in one continuous motion. You pick up the card, put it on top of the others and move it (with the one beneath it) half its width to the right. Your left thumb holds the two cards firmly squared, face down.

You snap your right finger against its extended surface. "This," you say, "is the one card of the five that attracted the $25 gold piece." It is face down. You put your right fingers on the under side and your thumb on top, as if to draw it away. But you start turning it over face-up *before* you draw it away. As the two hands turn over to reveal the face side, your left thumb pulls the top card back even with the others and your right hand pulls away with the chosen card.

You hand it to the spectator. The move simply couldn't be cleaner or less suspicious. You have shown both the back and front of the card. It is now a single card, and there are four indifferent cards left in the other hand. You toss them onto the table, face up, so that the audience may see there are no duplicates.

A wealthy Chicagoan who was fascinated by magic

and who had seen me do the trick four or five times over a period of years once offered me $100 to teach him the secret.

I refused to teach him the trick, because at that time, the denouement called for use of a murderously difficult sleight known as The Mexican Turnover. I knew he wouldn't be able to do it, particularly on a smooth table top. It involves flipping a card face up by putting another card under its edge, and switching the card in the fingers for the one face down on the table in the process of making the flip. It's never been a normal, natural way of turning a card face up, and it worked much better on a felt surface than on a smooth one. I had spent many hours on it before I felt confident enough to use it in this trick. Now, thanks to the turnover substitution in the hands, you don't need to worry about it.

And, as good as the move is, you should almost *never* have to use it. If you hold the penny according to instructions and guide the spectator as directed, he should drop the penny onto the third card in the row of five, 99 times out of a hundred.

The turn-over move is simply insurance for that one time out of a hundred when you need it.

Properly executed, I'd rate this as one of the great close-up card tricks of all time.

YOU DO AS I DO

Here's another great card trick, and it's almost ridiculously easy to do. Unlike several other tricks which achieve the same end result but which require expert manipulation, you don't have to know anything about sleight-of-hand to do it.

"This card trick is called You Do as I Do," you announce. "You take one deck of cards and I take another deck with contrasting backs. We both shuffle our decks, first a riffle shuffle and then an overhand shuffle. Then we exchange decks, so we both know that the other fellow hasn't arranged the cards in any special order."

At the completion of the riffle shuffle, you note and remember the bottom card of the deck you hand to the spectator.

That's all you have to do.

"Now," you continue, putting the deck he's just handed you onto the table, "I want you to cut your deck into three piles, exactly as I do." You pick up

all but about the bottom one-third of the deck, leaving it behind. You drop about another third of the deck beside it and leave the top remaining third of the deck to the right of the middle pile. Be sure that the spectator does the same thing.

"And the next thing we do," you continue, "is to look at the top card of our center pile and remember it."

You lift the top card of the center pile as if to look at it and remember it, then put it back down. You don't remember it. You wouldn't even need to look at it except for the overall effect you're trying to create.

"Next," you continue, "we put the pile of cards on the left (which was originally the bottom pile) on top of the center pile, and we put this double packet on top of the remaining pile." Again, see that the spectator follows instructions. If he does, he will have placed the original bottom card, the one you glimpsed and remembered, on top of the card he looked at.

"We exchange packs again," you continue. "I want you to remove your card from my deck and lay it face down on the table, while I remove my card from your deck and do the same."

You fan his deck toward yourself and look for the face-up original bottom card. The card immediately above and to the right of it as the cards face you will be the spectator's selected card. Remove it without exposing it, as you say, "I've found my card. Oh, I see you've found yours, too."

The two cards are side by side, face down on the table. "I called this trick You Do as I Do," you continue. "I didn't tell you that I expected you to do *exactly* as I did, because I thought that might scare you. What I actually wanted you to do was shuffle just as I did, cut the cards into three piles exactly as I did, look at the top card of the center pile and have it be the same card I looked at. That would be doing EXACTLY as I do, but I've found that if I tell people in advance what I expect of them, they get the idea I'm asking the impossible. Actually, it's only impossible when you *think* it is. Turn your card and mine both face up, please."

He turns the two cards over, and they're identical.

I taught this trick to one of the clumsiest men I know, a fellow who can't even shuffle a deck of cards without spilling some of them, and he's achieved quite a reputation as an expert card magician in his immediate circle.

THIS BOTTOM CARD   GOES ON THIS CARD

Cardology

The "Strip-Out" card sleight, properly done, is a beautiful move that brings a number of cards, inserted in different parts of the deck, to either the top or the bottom.

The cards to be stripped, let's say the four Aces, are shoved partly into the deck from the front end, extending above the rest of the cards for about half their length. It is apparent that the cards are widely separated.

The left hand holds the deck by the sides. The fingers of the right hand shove the extending cards on into the deck, the right forefinger pushing the left corner downward and to the left. This moves the left corner of the Aces slightly to the left of the rest of the deck. The right forefinger continues to move the cards down into the deck after the rest of the fingers are flush with the deck's outer end, moving this projecting corner about half an inch down from the top. If the cards, at a slight angle, are now squared, the four Aces will protrude about half an inch from the rear of the deck. If these projecting corners are now gripped firmly between the left thumb at one side and fingers at the other and the deck moved forward with the right hand, the Aces will "strip" from the deck, which is thrown on top of them. The four Aces are now at the bottom. To bring them to the top rather than the bottom, the projecting rear corners are grasped by the right thumb and fingers at the corners and stripped to the top.

YOU, CARD MANIPULATOR

If you'd like to get credit for being an expert card manipulator without putting in the hours of practice necessary to acquire that ability, here's your dish.

Have a spectator remove the four Aces from the deck. Pick them up with your right thumb at the left-hand bottom edge and your right first and second fingers at the right bottom edge. Now, squeeze the fingers together enough to put a decided bend in the lower end of the packet of aces. Hold that crimp or bend while you instruct the spectator to shuffle the balance of the pack.

Take the shuffled pack from him and insert the four aces at varying intervals, putting each ace in from the front end, holding it at the middle of the top end. Insert the four cards quickly and haphazardly, convincing the audience beyond any question that they haven't been put in any particular spot in the deck. They're widely separated.

Give the deck an overhand shuffle and a cut, doing it briskly. Put the deck onto your left palm. Now, if you'll cut off cards with your fingers at the front, thumb at the rear, you'll find that you can almost automatically cut to the four aces. Just let your right thumb pick up all the cards above each of the four little breaks at the rear end of the pack. As you locate each Ace, pick it off the pile with the thumb and fingers at the rear end and give it a crimp in the opposite direction from the one you used originally, so that the Ace will be flat when you toss it aside. You crimped it, produced it, took the crimp out of it and threw it aside, with each of the four.

If you want to make the trick even easier to do, crimp the inner end of the balance of the deck in the opposite direction as you take the shuffled deck from the spectator.

IN YOUR HAT

You can invent plenty of new tricks with what you already know about card magic. For example, let's take that business of crimping a card.

Have a deck shuffled by a spectator and divided into two halves. Pick up one half and toss it into a hat. The spectator has three or four people remove cards from the remaining half. You give him the hat and tell him to have the selected cards dropped into it. You instruct him to shake up the cards. He can even stir them around with his hand if he likes.

He now holds the hat up above your eye level and you reach into it with your right hand. One after another, you produce the cards that had been drawn from the other half of the deck. And you don't fumble around. You do it quickly.

How? When you tossed the first half of the deck

74

into the hat, you gave it a terrific crimp, a decided bend along the entire length of the packet.

Regardless of how much the cards are shaken up, the flat cards that were dropped into the hat by the spectators will stand out to your touch like beacons in a fog.

When you remove the balance of the cards from the hat, you, of course, crimp them in a reverse direction, making them flat again.

Pretty sneaky, huh?

THE CARD ON THE CEILING

The magically immortal Matt Schulien, Chicago restaurateur, made the Card on the Ceiling trick famous. Almost anywhere you go, somebody in the group is certain to have seen the trick performed and to mention it. This is *not* Matt Schulien's method of doing the trick, but a much simpler one.

Fan the cards, and have one selected. "After you've looked at it and marked it for future identification," you tell a spectator, "put it back into the deck exactly where you got it."

As he puts the card back into the deck, face down, put the tip of your left little finger on top of the lower right-hand corner. The move is completely concealed by the fanned cards.

Close the fan, keeping the left little finger-tip in position so that it forms anywhere from an eighth to a quarter of an inch break at the right rear corner, directly above the chosen card. Square up the cards, holding the break, and give the deck a cut.

You cut at the break, putting all the cards above the break onto the table and throwing the balance on top. This brings the chosen card to the top of the face-down deck, without any difficult sleight of hand. If you like, you can give the deck a riffle shuffle, being sure to keep the top card of the deck at the top when the shuffle is completed.

In your inner coat pocket is an envelope containing a toy magnet and a tiny open salve tin about half full of library paste. You remove it, reach in with your right fingers to remove the magnet, and in doing so, get a little blob of library paste on your second finger tip, which you immediately transfer under cover of the envelope to the under-side of the magnet. You don't need much of the paste, just a blob the size of a pin-head.

Remove the magnet and replace the envelope in your pocket, saying, "The next step is to magnetize the deck. Only one card, the one that has been handled by you, will respond to the magnetism." You lay the magnet on top of the deck, moving it slightly in the process so that the top card picks up the blob of paste.

You pick up the deck, magnet still on top, by grasping the two inner corners between your right thumb and right second finger. Remove the magnet with your left hand and toss it into your pocket.

Immediately with the removal of the magnet, you throw the deck toward the ceiling, keeping it flat. A little twist to the right as you make the throw will help to keep the deck flat.

If you've made the throw so that the deck hits the ceiling flat, the chosen card will stick to the ceiling when the deck falls.

You should practice the toss of the deck to the ceil-

ing before you perform the trick for spectators. Ted Annemann discovered that a little spin would help a flat contact. While you're getting the knack of the throw, a rubber band around the deck will save you a lot of time that would otherwise be spent in picking up cards.

Jay Marshall and Gene Keeney invented a method which many find preferable. Instead of the library paste, you snip off about an inch of cellophane sticky tape and make a ring of it, sticky side out. This is stuck to a button on your coat or vest. When you've brought the chosen card to the top of the deck, you simply hold the deck in front of the button and move the tape ring from the button to the top card.

Reputations have been made with several versions of this trick.

AL BAKER'S IMPOSSIBLE CARD LOCATION

The late Al Baker was one of the most beloved men in magic—and a charming performer of the old school. He invented many tricks, and while others have taken credit for this one, Al's subtle handling made it his.

You examine a borrowed deck of cards, give it an overhand shuffle and then a riffle shuffle, and hand it to a spectator.

The spectator is instructed to deal off cards alternately from the top of the deck into two face-down

Cardology

The "side-slip" is a card sleight which slips a chosen card out of the side of the deck into the face-down palm of the right hand. Usually, the right hand is then brought over the top of the deck to square it, depositing the side-slipped card. The move is most often used as a substitute for "the pass," to bring a chosen card to the top of the deck.

The deck is fanned for the selection of a card. As the card is replaced, the left fingers move directly beneath its face. The deck is squared by closing the fan from right to left with the right hand. While this is being done, the left fingers move the chosen card to the right. It extends from the right side of the deck at least half the card's width, covered by the palm-down right hand. While the deck is being squared, the right side of the right hand's heel and the little finger grip the right front and back corners of the card. The hand, gripping the card, moves slightly to the right, bringing the card clear of the deck, and then moves to the left, depositing the card on top of the deck as the fingers square the cards.

piles until he feels the urge to stop. You may turn your back to him during the process. When he tells you he's stopped, instruct him to look at the top card remaining on the deck, remember it, and put either of the two dealt-off piles on top of it. The remaining dealt-off pile is to be placed on the bottom of the deck and the deck given a cut.

You now face him, take the deck and fan it toward yourself. You pull out a card, tossing it onto the table face up, saying, "That's the color of your card." You toss out another face-up card, saying, "That's the suit." Then you remove a card and place it face-down on the table. "And that's your card," you declare. He names his card, turns over the face-down pasteboard and admits you're correct.

It's extremely simple, which is one of the things that makes it so good. When you examine the deck, you notice the two bottom cards and remember them. You overhand shuffle them to the top and then do a riffle shuffle, leaving them in place. Now, when the spectator deals off face-down cards into two piles, the two cards you know will be at the bottom of the two piles. When he stops dealing and looks at the top card remaining on the deck, replaces it and puts either of the dealt piles on top and the other on the bottom of the deck, one of the key cards is directly above the chosen card and the other is at the bottom of the deck. He cuts the deck and hands it to you. As you fan the cards face toward yourself, look for a key card. The first of the two you come to will be directly to the left of the chosen card. In other words, with the deck face up, the chosen card will be directly above it.

SHEER NERVE

Annemann did one card location that was so nervy, magicians couldn't believe it—but he always got away with it. He had a spectator remove a card and remember it. Then, his head turned away, he took the face down card in his right hand, deck in left hand, and put both hands behind his back, saying, "I'm going to put your card into the deck while the cards are behind my back, so that you know I can't look at any of the other cards or put it in any particular spot."

With the deck behind his back, he very deliberately put the chosen card on top of the deck and pulled an indifferent card out about an inch from the middle of the pack. Then he brought his hands to the front, observing, "It's not quite at the middle of the deck." He quickly shoved the protruding card square with the rest of the pack. The selected card was, of course, on top.

He did numerous tricks with this daring substitute for the pass. One simple one was to have the spectator deal four piles of cards from the top of the deck, as

many cards in each pile as he chose. Then, picking up each pile and apparently weighing it in his hand, he would declare that the chosen card was in one of the four piles. He carelessly fanned that pile, cutting it and handing to the spectator to acknowledge whether or not he had been correct. The card is, of course, always at the bottom of the first pile. In fanning and cutting the pile, Annemann glimpsed the chosen card.

When the spectator acknowledged the correctness of his selection, Annemann told him to form a mental picture of his card, and then, in dramatic fashion, told him what it was.

Another variation, used at a card table, was to ask a spectator to hold his right hand under the card table, about six inches beneath the table top. "Now," he said, "move to the center. I'll show you." Deck in his right hand, he deliberately put both hands under the table, grasped the spectator's wrist with his left hand, and moved the hands to about the center of the table. He deliberately thumbed off the top card of the deck, holding it against the under-side of the table top with his left protruding forefinger, the spectator's wrist being held with the other fingers.

He held the deck in his right hand and slammed it down firmly on top of the table, giving it a grinding motion. At the same time, he release his left-fore-finger hold on the chosen card on the under-side of the table, and let it drop into the spectator's hand.

It doesn't sound sensational, but if you're the spectator, you're absolutely dumbfounded when that chosen card lights on your face-up palm.

ANOTHER "THINK OF A CARD"

This trick depends on your power of observation, but you'll be delighted with its simplicity and you'll be amazed at how easy it is to accomplish.

Let a spectator shuffle the deck, and then have him deal four piles of eight cards each onto the table. Give him a free choice of one of the eight-piles.

"I want you to think of one of the cards in this pile," you tell him, as you show him the faces of the cards.

You then gather up all the cards and proceed to reveal the card he mentally chose.

When you show him the faces of the eight-card pile he picks, you fan the top four cards in your right hand and the bottom four cards in your left hand, with the hands at least a foot apart. Following this procedure, it's extremely simple to tell which pile contains the card of his mental choice. You ask him to concentrate on the card, and you know that the hand to which he directs his gaze contains the mentally selected pasteboard.

You look at the faces of the four cards, too, as you gather up the balance of the cards, and you remember their order from left to right, face up, which means that you have the order from the top down when the cards are returned to the face-down deck. Remember the order of the cards as a four-digit number 6379. If there's a picture card, shift it to the end, as: 493J.

You put the deck behind your back, remove the four cards in order, square them up and say, "With the deck behind my back, I'm going to put one card into my pocket." You quickly put the four cards as one into your right pants pocket, leaving the right hand in the pocket and putting the deck onto the table.

"Now," you ask, "what's the name of the card you mentally selected?"

When the spectator tells you, you know immediately whether it was the first, second, third or fourth card. You count to the correct number in your pocket, remove the card and throw it face-up onto the table.

Close-Up Honor Roll

Hundreds of expert magicians specialize in close-up magic, and all those who make a living from intimate magic are superior performers.

"Bests" in any category are a matter of opinion. MAGIC DIGEST *likes them all, but the following 25, listed alphabetically and not in order of rating, are our nominations for the close-up Hall of Fame:*

Don Alan	Ken Krenzel
Bruce Cervon	Charles Miller
Matt Corin	Pat Page
Persi Diaconis	Johnny Paul
Bud Dietrich	Del Ray
Derek Dingle	Alvin Schneider
Alex Elmsley	Bill Simon
Jimmy Grippo	Mike Skinner
Daniel Gros	John Thompson
Heba Haba	Eddie Tulloch
Bro. John Hamman	Dai Vernon
Larry Jennings	Ron Wilson
Peter Kane	

The superlative performance of any one of them is a memorable experience for any audience.

FOLLOW-UP CARD IN POCKET

You're now all set to do a great follow-up trick. Have the spectator shuffle the deck again and deal out four face-down cards, counting "One, two, three, four" as he does so.

Tell him that you're about to turn your back and that while your back is turned he is to look at one card of the four and remember its position in the line. When he says he has done this, you turn to face him again, gather up the four cards and put them into your pocket, under the three cards that are already there. You now pull out the three cards, one at a time, that were already in your pocket, putting them onto the table face down.

"If I've done this trick correctly," you observe, "the card you looked at is still in my pocket. Assume that it is, and lay out the other three cards in their proper position. For example, if Card Number One was the one you looked at, leave a blank at one and lay out the other three. If Card Number Two was your choice, leave a blank space at Number Two."

When he has laid out the cards with a blank space, you simply count to the right card of the four in your pocket, remove it and toss it face-up onto the table.

This is one trick that can be repeated without giving the secret away.

COUNTDOWN

Here's a card trick that's incredibly simple, and yet it has great impact. You write a prediction on the face of one of the cards in the deck and then hand the face-down deck to a spectator. He is instructed to deal cards face down into a pile from the top of the deck until he feels like stopping. At that time, he is given a choice of the top card on the deck or the top card on the pile. Whichever he chooses, he puts it on top of the pile after looking at its face. He puts the balance of the deck on top of the pile and cuts several times.

Have him spread the deck face up to find the card with the prediction written on its face. Leave it face up on the table and put all the cards that were above it on the bottom of the deck, in order. He counts to the number written on the prediction card and turns over the card he originally looked at.

How? Fan the deck toward yourself and look for a low spot card that has plenty of room on the face for a prediction. Make a quick count as to how far it is from the bottom of the deck. Let's say it's the ninth card up from the bottom. Write on it, "Your card will be the ninth card."

Whatever the number of cards the prediction card is from the bottom of the deck is the number at which the chosen card will be located. It's automatic.

DOUBLE REVERSE

Here's a trick that will get you credit for being a card manipulator.

Have a spectator shuffle the deck and cut it into approximately equal halves. He gives you either half and retains the other. Then, while your back is turned, he removes any card from his half and shows it to the other spectators.

While your back is turned, you turn the bottom card of your pile face up and remember it, putting it back on the bottom so that it's reversed from the other cards in the pile. You remove any card from your pile and hold it face down as you turn around to face the spectator. Before you turn around, you turn over your pile of cards so that it is face up except for the reversed card, which is now on top, back up.

"Insert your card anywhere in my pile, face down," you instruct the spectator, holding the cards well squared. "I'll do the same with your pile," you continue, shoving the card you removed from your pile into his.

As you're doing this, your left hand containing your pile drops to your side and you turn it over so that the card you originally reversed is now on the bottom.

Don't make a big deal of this. Simply let your hand drop to your side and have the packet facing the correct way when you bring the hand back up. Even if spectators watch your left hand, it's virtually impossible for them to see anything happening.

You now lift about half of the spectator's pile with your right hand, drop your pile onto it and put the balance on top. Let him cut the cards any number of times he chooses.

Both you and the spectator now name the cards you chose—only you name the card you originally reversed on the bottom of your pile.

Tell him to spread the cards—and the two selected cards will be face-up in the face-down deck!

The fact that the spectator does so much of the handling of the deck makes this trick particularly mystifying.

STABBING A CARD

Perhaps you've seen a magician have a card selected and returned to the deck, the deck wrapped in newspaper and then stabbed through the paper with a table knife or letter opener. When the paper is torn away, the magician shows that the knife has located the chosen card.

There are numerous ways of doing this effective trick, most of them difficult. The method I'm giving you here requires no advance preparation and no special equipment. It doesn't even require you to do the "pass," that move that brings a chosen card to the top of the deck.

You give a spectator a free selection of a card. While he's showing it to the others, you turn your back, lift about half of the deck from your left palm with your right thumb at the rear and fingers at the front end of the card, and squeeze hard enough to give the cards a substantial bend, so that they look like this:

You immediately drop the cards back on top of the deck and turn to face the spectator. You tell him to replace the card in the deck and you lift off all the bent cards. This is extremely easy to do, since the bend gives you a natural opening to grip the upper cards.

The chosen card is dropped onto the bottom half of the deck and you immediately put the cards you've lifted back down on top of it, squaring the pack. If there are people at side angle viewpoints, put your left thumb on top of the top card and press down, lightly, until you start to wrap the deck in a quarter-page piece of newspaper. Wrap the deck neatly. Hold the package from the top, in the left hand, thumb at inner end, fingers at outer end. A slight pressure from the top by the fingers will widen the arc above the chosen card.

Put the blade of the knife, which is parallel with the deck, into the side of the packet, midway between ends. If the blade doesn't find the break immediately, move it enough to find the right spot. As soon as the knife is inserted in the opening, release the pressure from the top and hold the deck with thumb on top, fingers on the bottom, pressing firmly to keep the knife from falling out (and to destroy the break). As soon as the paper is torn away, lift the knife and all the cards above it, asking the spectator to remove the card that was under the blade. It is, naturally, the card he previously selected.

ANOTHER CARD STABBING

A similar effect may be done with a sharp pocket knife. A card is looked at and returned to the deck, with your left little finger-tip holding its location at the rear right end of the deck. You divide the cards at the break and give them a riffle shuffle, making sure that the chosen card is the last one released from your left fingers so that it becomes the top card.

Now, you put your right palm on top of the deck and begin strewing the cards around on top of the table. At least, you appear to be mixing them up. Actually, your right palm remains firmly on top of the chosen card throughout the mixing process.

Still mixing the cards, you pick up a sheet of newspaper with your left hand and cover the cards, pulling back your right hand as the paper begins to rest on top of the pasteboards. Your right hand keeps the chosen card next to the palm until you've moved it slightly away from the rest of the spread, at which time, you lift the hand and bring it on out above the paper. You know where the chosen card is.

Your right hand picks up the open pocket knife and moves it slowly above the sheet of newspaper. Suddenly, your fist jabs downward. You lift it quickly, and it brings the newspaper along with it. You tear the paper away and show the chosen card impaled on the knife.

It's a dramatic trick and never fails to impress an audience when it's well done.

RESTORING A TORN CARD

You need duplicate cards for this one. If you buy two cheap decks, you'll have enough cards to do the trick 52 times—and it's a honey of a trick.

You pick two cards up from your kit of paraphernalia, holding them as one, pressed firmly together and completely aligned. Let's say that they're two Queens of Hearts. You grip them firmly in your left fingers at the left end—and I mean, firmly, so that they won't slip out of alignment. The card(s) is (are) facing your audience. You now fold it back toward

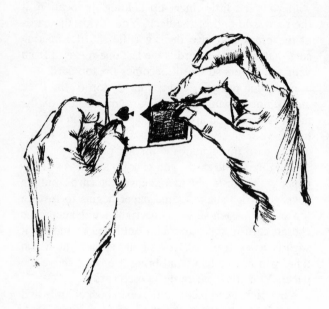

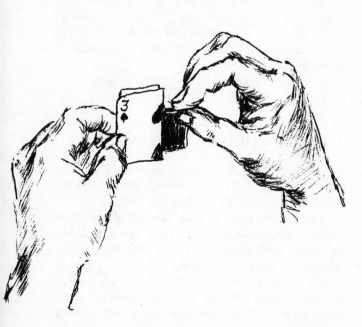

yourself, folding it in half and making a crease with your right thumb and forefinger. You move the *front* card back, holding the rear fold under your left thumb along with what was already there. You deliberately tear the front right-half off the card and put it on top of the left half. You now fold everything in half again, back toward your body, releasing only the front two pieces of card. You tear *them* off but put them at the *back* of the packet.

You next show the packet from all sides, held by the left thumb and forefinger. "We now have four pieces of card," you point out. "You saw me tear them. If there's any doubt that the card is quartered—" You pick up the two front pieces, one at a time, and deposit them at the back.

You now have a complete Queen of Hearts, folded in quarters, with four pieces of another queen behind them.

"Cup your hands around the pieces," you order a spectator, and start to deposit what he thinks are four pieces of card into his hands. As you reach forward to do this, your left thumb pulls the loose pieces back and down, while your fingers push the front folded card up and forward. As the folded card touches the spectator's palm, your right hand claps his other hand on top of the folded card and you walk away, the torn pieces palmed in your left hand. You reach into your left coat pocket for a pencil, leaving the pieces of card behind as you remove the pencil.

"This pencil will serve as a magic wand," you comment. You advance to the spectator again, tap the back of his hand with the pencil four times, say "Four pieces, four taps," and tell him to open his hands.

He unfolds the card and finds that it is restored.

It's possible to do this trick by having a card selected from the deck, forcing the spectator to take a specific card, the duplicate of which is face down on top of the deck. You put the chosen card on top of the deck and do a double-lift, lifting the two cards as one, after which you proceed with the tearing. I've always felt that this was totally unnecessary. Actually, it clutters the trick—and makes the whole business much more difficult.

SIMULCAST

Fan the cards casually toward yourself, remarking that there must be no joker in the pack for this trick to work. All you do is note and remember the second card from the top. Let's say it's the King of Diamonds.

Now, ask the spectator to cut the cards into two piles. You pick up the top pile, with the King of Diamonds second from the top, and shuffle it, leaving the top two cards intact. He shuffles the other half.

Now you trade packets, "so that each of us has shuffled the other one's cards." Each of you looks at the top card of his packet and puts it back on top, remembering it. Only you don't remember yours. You remember the King of Diamonds.

Now, each of you cuts his pile of cards into two piles and tries to predict whether the bottom pile is odd or even. You count your bottom pile and he counts his. Whether his pile is odd or even, have him throw the bottom pile on top of the top pile. If his bottom pile was odd, say, "That's a good sign. Mine was odd, too, so if I put one card from my pile into yours, they'll both be even."

Cardology

The "double-lift" is one of the most useful moves in card magic. Most commonly, it is the lifting off the deck of two cards as one. Adept card manipulators perform triple and quadruple lifts with ease.

One of the basic uses of the double-lift is to show that a previously selected card is not on top of the deck when, actually, it is. Two cards are lifted as one, the face of the second card shown, and the two cards, squarely aligned, placed back face down on the deck.

One of the most convincing double-lifts is done as follows: the deck is held in the left hand as for dealing, thumb on top, fingers curled over the right side. The left little finger riffles downward from the top, releasing two cards, and the flesh of this finger forms a tiny break between them and the balance of the deck. The left thumb-tip goes to the outer left end of the pack and pushes slightly back toward the body, which grips the two cards firmly between the thumb and the heel of the hand. The thumb then moves to the right, moving the two squared cards on a pivot at the heel of the hand. The right fingers turn the card over (cards, in reality), show the face and turn the card(s) back down, squaring it (them) with the deck.

A simpler but less convincing method is to riffle off the two top cards at the left outer end with the left thumb as you reach downward with the right hand, fingers at the outer end, thumb at the inner end, and lift the two cards up from the deck, show the face, and replace them, face-down.

Once he's returned the bottom pile to the top, with you making sure it's even, you put his pile on top of yours, square the deck, give it a false shuffle if you can do it convincingly, and tell him that you must both have a like number of cards for a Simulcast so he's to deal the deck into two face-down piles, dealing into the piles alternately. He picks up either pile and you pick up the other one.

"Neither of us has any idea which pile our card is in," you say. "I chose the King of Diamonds and I don't know what card you selected, but we'll deal cards face up from our packets, one at a time, simultaneously. If we're really synchronized, when my King of Diamonds shows up, your card should show up in the other pile."

You deal cards face up in unison, and his card always turns up simultaneously with the King of Diamonds—or whatever the second card from the top of the deck was.

This is the type of card trick I do *not* like, because of all the dealing and counting involved, but I have an amateur magician friend who gives it a big buildup and makes a feature trick of it.

The only mathematical card trick I ever really enjoyed doing was one called The Chicago Card Trick, and I can't for the life of me remember the formula. I quit doing it when I realized it was really a location of a card, and there were so many other card locations that were quicker and more dramatic. But here's a direct, no-nonsense trick that's really to my liking.

DUBLO-CATION

Have the cards shuffled by a spectator. Take the deck from him and announce that you're going to remove two very special, particular cards from it. Fan the deck toward yourself, noting the top and bottom cards. Let's say they're the Queen of Spades and the three of Hearts. Look through the deck and remove the mates of those two cards, the Queen of Clubs and the three of Diamonds. Put them face down on the table without letting anyone see what they are.

"Playing cards are romantic," you state. "Every card, given a little encouragement will find its proper mate. You don't know the identity of these two cards, but I want you to insert them part way into the deck, lengthwise, from the side of the deck, so that there'll be no question about where you insert them."

As soon as the spectator has inserted the cards lengthwise into the side of the deck, you pick up the cards. Slowly and deliberately, push the packet of cards above the insertion to the right, gripping them with your right fingers. Your left thumb holds the two inserted cards in place on top of the other half of the deck. Announce, "Perhaps we should have the cards face up in the face-down deck, to leave no doubt about where and what they are."

You turn your left hand over and slide the pair of sideways cards face up onto the cards in the right hand, turn the left hand back down again and deposit its cards on top of the face up cards. You put the deck on the table and ask the spectator to spread the deck to the two face-up cards.

"You had a completely free choice of where you put them into the deck," you say. "Please spread the cards and remove the two face-down cards directly above and below them. Wouldn't it be a miracle if you placed the Queen of Clubs and the three of Diamonds between the Queen of Spades and the Three of Hearts? It certainly would! Turn the two face-down cards over, please."

Now, that's what I call a good, simple, direct card trick.

The Jinx

The late Ted Annemann, brilliant magical inventor, published a magic magazine, The Jinx, *for a number of years. Every issue was eagerly awaited by magic fans throughout the world, not only for the sensational tricks it contained but for Annemann's biting editorial comment. He was merciless with anyone in the field of magic who, in his opinion, was doing any disservice to the conjuring art.*

Some of his feuds continued for months—and he was always willing to publish his antagonist's answer to his charges. Usually, however, he answered the answer with scathing criticism that topped his original attack.

His critical reviews of magic performances were unique at the time in that they were genuinely critical. Previous reviews in magic journals, usually written by close friends of the performers, had been puffery that sometimes had little justification.

Accused of hurting the cause of magic with his vitriolic reviews, Annemann replied, "Nothing hurts magic as much as a bad public performance. A lousy magician who gets bookings on the strength of fake reviews hurts magic more than the most flagrant exposer of our secrets."

WANT MORE CARD TRICKS?

There are hundreds and hundreds of them. Actually, there are hundreds of *books* devoted exclusively to card tricks, not to mention the myriad manuscripts on separate card tricks that can be bought from the magical supply houses.

If you want to learn more card tricks, they're certainly available. But let's learn first to do the ones outlined in this book, huh? They'll give you a better card repertoire than many magicians of long standing can offer.

Also, there will be other card tricks in other parts of this book, particularly in the section devoted to mental telepathy, in the section devoted to a club or stage act, and in the close-up routine.

If you reach the point where you want to specialize in card magic, you'll need to learn considerable sleight of hand, and some of it is far from easy. If you're determined to be a card manipulator, I'd strongly recommend that you buy Hugard's *Expert Card Technique,* the card section of Hilliard's *Greater Magic,* and the classic *Erdnase at the Card Table.*

Hugard and Braue's *Royal Road to Card Magic* is excellent because it teaches you progressively, as this book does. *Basic Card Technique* by Anthony Norman and *Close-Up Card Magic* by Harry Lorayne are currently among the most popular card magic books.

Even with these books, your task won't be easy. While you can get the basic idea of most card sleights from books, most of the expert card manipulators I happen to know have had personal instruction from another expert card manipulator. If you're fortunate enough to live in the vicinity of a great teacher, your path to card expertise will be much smoother than otherwise.

I hope you don't decide to go in for the hundreds of mathematical card tricks that require repeated counting of cards. Such tricks bore me to distraction —and the average layman finds it hard to stay awake through them. Actually, I think only the people who do them really enjoy them.

As far as I'm concerned, you already have all the good card tricks you'll ever need—and the ones you have are better than good; they're super. So let's move along.

At a Party

You, too, can be the life of the party—with magic. Of course, it must be the right kind of magic. And the right kind of magic for parties usually offers audience involvement. Tricks in which everybody feels a sense of participation are the ideal ones for party performance.

The Impossible Knot which, hopefully, you've already learned, is a perfect party trick, because everyone can share in it. One magician I know passes out half a dozen 36-inch lengths of soft sash cord when he does the trick. He gives the other guests the impression that he's going to teach them how to tie the Impossible Knot, and has them going through the motions along with him. Of course, they wind up with no knot, while he has one.

An interlude of Oregami, the Oriental art of paper folding, is excellent party fare. While not strictly magic, it goes well *with* magic, and you can teach everyone how to fold a simple Oregami figure.

So-called "mental" magic is terrific for parties. The idea of mind-reading or mental telepathy is intriguing to everyone, and you can inject a slight element of fortune telling into your routine for added interest. I've discovered that nearly everyone believes he has a superior sixth sense, and tricks in which you apparently read someone else's mind hold an audience spellbound. Mental magic will be covered in a later section of this book, with enough tricks so that you can do a whole routine of allegedly telepathic demonstrations.

While it would logically come under the Mental Magic classification, the Telephone Card Trick is such a fine party trick that we'll cover it here.

It's the trick in which an audience decides on any card in a deck of playing cards and one of the group is delegated to call your assistant on the phone and ask him to name the card. He does it, without fail.

THE TELEPHONE CARD TRICK

Some versions of this trick have sold for as much as $25, and some have employed complicated, expensive apparatus. One method that sold for $10 consisted of two printed cards, identical in content. Each card contained the names of 52 people, and each of the 52 names was the code signal for a specific card in the deck. The magician carried one card, and his assistant carried the other.

When the audience had selected a card, the magician had to sneak a look at his code card and find the name identified with that particular pasteboard. With a printed list of 52 names, doing this surreptitiously was a pretty good trick in itself.

The magician then instructed a member of the audience to dial the number where the assistant was waiting for a call and ask for "Percival Johnson" or whatever the right name for the card in question happened to be. The assistant had his card in front of him on the telephone table and ran down its length to the name and card combination. He then gave the caller the name of the correct card.

The idea was sound, but the operation was cumbersome. I've simplified it for you to the point where printed lists are unnecessary.

There are only 13 cards in each suit and only four suits. In this simplified method, the last name of the person the spectator is told to ask for identifies the suit, as follows:

Cummings (Clubs)   Dutton (Diamonds)
Stevens (Spades)   Hanson (Hearts)

In other words, the initial letter of the last name immediately identifies the suit.

For the denomination of the card, you use the first name. You eliminate the letter "I", and identify the card as follows:

1. Al	6. Frank	10. Kenneth
2. Bert	7. George	11. Leonard
3. Charles	8. Harry	12. Myron
4. Dave	9. John	13. Nelson
5. Elmer		

You don't even have to memorize the first names. *Any* first name beginning with the right letter gives your assistant the information he needs. If you're working with a female assistant, you could use the names Alice, Bertha, Clara, Doris, Ellen, Florence, Grace, Harriet, Julia, Kate, Lila, Millicent and Nora.

When you use this method, the trick is *all* audience participation. You call attention to the fact that you play no part in it at all.

You announce, "I want the group to arrive at any one of the 52 cards in the deck without my taking part in the selection." You hand a deck of cards to any one of the guests and tell him to shuffle it. When he's complied, you tell him to fan the deck in front of any other guest and let that guest remove any one card. This card is made known to the others in the group.

No method of picking a card could be fairer, you point out. Up to this time, you have *not* explained what the trick is to be. Once the card is selected and you know its identity, you tell the person who took the card from the deck that he or she is to go to the telephone. You write down a telephone number and a name on a slip of paper. You say, "My telepathic assistant or medium is waiting at this number. Dial it and ask for him. When you have him on the line, ask What card am I thinking of? Don't say anything else. Just What card am I thinking of? And he'll try to read your mind over the phone."

The assistant is waiting. The spectator dials the number, and your "medium" answers. "Is this John Hanson?" the spectator asks. Upon receiving an affirmative, he asks, "What card am I thinking of?" and gets an answer, "The Nine of Hearts."

Occasionally, the spectator will simply ask, "Mr. Hanson?" In that event, your assistant asks, "Which Mr. Hanson?"

Obviously, you can't repeat the trick. But it's a honey.

If you believe as I do that simplicity is a highly desirable virtue in any trick, then you'll probably prefer another method I'm going to give you.

In this section on card tricks, you learned several methods of forcing a particular card on a spectator. Either the "crossed cut" or the "under the handkerchief" method is fine for this particular trick.

You have it understood with your assistant that whenever he receives a call and the person asks, "What card am I thinking of?" he is to answer "The two of Clubs." If he receives a second call on the same evening, his answer is to be "The five of Hearts," and if he receives a third call, his answer is to be "The eight of Spades."

You let someone shuffle the cards and then fan them to the audience so they can see the cards are all different and are not set in any particular order.

"My assistant, Mr. ....," and you give his right name, before a card is chosen, "is waiting at the telephone at this number." You give his correct number. If somebody checks in the phone book, he'll find that the name and number are legitimate.

While you're fanning the cards to show that they're well mixed, you look for the two of Clubs. In closing the face-up fan, you simply break the deck to the left of the two of Clubs and reassemble the cards so that it is at the top of the face-down deck. You're now ready to do either the cross-cut or Under the Handkerchief force of that card.

"Don't show me the card," you instruct the spectator, "and don't let me know what it is. Show it to the others, if you like, while my back is turned. Then go to the phone, dial the number I've given you, ask for my assistant and ask him what card you selected."

The rest is absurdly simple. And you can repeat with a second and third spectator. The volunteer card-choosers ask for the same person, at the same number, every time.

To make memorization as simple as the trick, you can do it three times. You start with a deuce, the low card in a suit, and add three each time. Your first card is a deuce, your second is a five and your third is an eight. To keep the suits in proper order in your mind, the spectators CHOOSE a card. The suits run in the order of the consonants in the word "Choose," Clubs, Hearts and Spades.

While the spectator is at the phone asking for the first card, you study the deck—and bring the five of Hearts to the top, in readiness for a repeat.

Both of the methods I've given you have their strong points. Both are easy to do—and the effect on your audience is identical to what it would be if you were using a complicated, expensive, difficult method.

"Ask for the Wizard" is one of the most baffling methods, if your assistant at the other end of the phone line is alerted to your call. He picks up the phone and says slowly, "Clubs, Hearts, Diamonds, Spades." You wait to say Hello until he mentions the proper suit. Then you say, "I'd like to speak to the wizard." He says, "Ace, two, three, four, five, six, etc.," going through the cards in a suit until he reaches the proper one, at which point you say, "Hello, Wizard." You hand the phone to a spectator, who asks him for the name of the selected card.

While this is Mental Magic, it is strictly a party trick. It's impractical and necessarily slow for a stage trick. It's weak for a trick at casual, spur of the moment gatherings because you can't be sure your assistant will be at home. For what it is, it's hard to beat.

SWINDLES

There's a kind of trick which I call "Swindles" that is perfect for party use. The Swindles include such things as the Shell Game, Three-Card Monte, the Australian Belt and the Thirty-One Swindle. They're actually con games that are seldom practiced any more but are legendary. And they have audience participation to the ultimate degree.

Unfortunately, the best known is Three-Card Monte. It is also the most difficult to do, unless you resort to mechanical cards. The three-card monte "throw" as practiced by the old-time expert monte cardsharps was a thing of beauty—and not something easily learned.

Since you can't do Swindles and ignore Three-Card Monte, we'll start with a "gag" version of it. You carry the three cards for it in an envelope, which you empty onto the table.

"GAG" THREE-CARD MONTE

One of the three cards comes from a goofy deck that is sold by most novelty shops. It's a fun deck to have, in which all the Spades and Clubs are red and all the Diamonds and Hearts are black. The decks I have bear the brand name, "Enardoe," and list Edward O. Drane & Co., Chicago, Ill., as the source.

You use one card from such a deck, the Queen of Spades. It is sandwiched between the King of Diamonds and the King of Clubs, both of which are normal, legitimate cards. You fan them very openly.

"All you have to do," you say, "is keep track of the Queen of Hearts. Forget about the Kings. Just keep your eyes on the red Queen, in the middle." You turn your hand so that the cards are face down. You do it slowly and deliberately. Viewers can be positive that there's been no manipulation.

"We put the red Queen face down on the table," you continue, removing the middle card and letting the spectators get a flash of its red pip. "We put a King on each side of it." You put the two Kings face down on the table, the red Queen between them. "Now is where the tricky part comes in. Watch closely. We make the red King and the red Queen change places." You deliberately and slowly transpose the King of Diamonds and the red Queen of Spades.

"And now, I'll bet you any amount of money that you can't find the Queen of Hearts in this spread. I'll do better than that." You toss your wallet onto the table. "If you can pick up the Queen of Hearts from this spread on your first try, I'll give you everything in my wallet. You don't risk a penny of your own and I risk every dollar I have with me."

The spectator inevitably turns up the red Queen of Spades, and looks triumphant.

"You see," you nod, "you lose. You didn't find the Queen of Hearts for the excellent reason that there IS no Queen of Hearts here, and never was."

Don't explain. The light will dawn, there'll be a double take, and you'll get a terrific laugh.

You put the red Queen of Spades back into the envelope and take a legitimate Queen of Hearts from the deck, adding it to the King of Diamonds and King of Clubs on the table, in preparation for:

THE "GLIDE" FIND THE LADY

"That was a flim-flam," you admit cheerfully, "but now we'll do it with honest cards. The cards are honest but I'm not. Two kings and a queen, and the object is to find the lady."

You drop the face-up King of Diamonds onto the face-up King of Clubs, with the face-up Queen of Hearts on top of the kings. You pick up the three cards openly and gingerly, letting everyone see that the Queen is the face card. You turn them face down and take them into the left hand from above, thumb on the right edge, fingers on the left edge, curled under the packet.

You reach with your right forefinger and thumb to slide out the bottom card. As you do this, your left third finger slides or glides the bottom card back half an inch toward your body. The protrusion at the inner end is hidden by your left hand. The right fingers make a move as if sliding out the bottom card from the front of the deck. Actually, they are sliding out the *middle* card.

The right fingers put down the King of Clubs as you say, "First, the Queen of Hearts." You reach under the packet of two cards just as you did before, this time taking the Queen of Hearts. "Then the King of Diamonds," you say, putting down the Queen of Hearts. "And lastly, the King of Clubs." You let the spectators get a flash of the King of Clubs as you put it down.

"Now, watch closely. We move the Queen of Hearts to the right end and the King of Clubs to the left end." You deliberately transpose the two cards. "And now, find the lady—the Queen."

If you've done the glide move easily and naturally, they will pick up the card on the right end, sure that it's the Queen of Hearts. Actually, the Queen is in the middle and has been from the start.

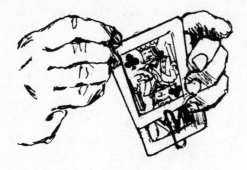

Continue, "I'll try to make it easier for you. This time, we'll put a paper clip on the inner end of the Queen of Hearts." You do so. You pick up either of the kings and hold it face down in the left hand, just as you held the three cards when you did the glide move. "We'll put the paper-clipped queen of Hearts in the middle." You put it beneath the King that's already in your left hand. "And we'll put the other King on the bottom." You slide the remaining King onto the bottom, from the front, but you slide the rear end *into* the paper clip, along with the Queen of Hearts. This is no problem. It's more difficult to keep the rear end from going into the paper clip than it is to insert it.

Now, reach with your right fingers for the bottom card, just as before, and just as before, glide the bottom card back half an inch with your left third finger. It takes the paper clip back right along with it. Pull out what is actually the second card from the bottom, the Queen of Hearts, now free of the paper clip. "A King," you say as you lay the card down, "then the Queen of Hearts." You pull out the card that is now on the bottom, the King with a paper clip on it. "And the last King." Again, you give the spectators a flash of the last King as you lay it down.

You shrug your shoulders. "This time, of course, I have no chance of fooling you. But the old Three-Card Monte man let his victims win occasionally, to keep them betting. Naturally, you know which one is the Queen this time. The one with the paper clip on it. Right?"

You pick it up and turn it over. "Wrong! The Queen is over here."

You pick up either of the Kings and hold it face up in your left hand. Then you put the Queen of Hearts on top of it, fanned to the right, also face up. Your thumb is on top of both cards and your fingers are beneath them.

With your right hand, you put a paper clip on the right side of the face-up Queen, about half-way down its length. You put it on only about half-way, so that about half of the clip protrudes from the right side of the card.

Then you turn your left hand face down, shoving the fingers forward and pulling the thumb back. This is done while you're turning over the cards. By the time the two cards are face down, the paper clip is on the King instead of on the Queen. As the hand comes to a rest, palm down, you drop both cards side by side onto the table. Your right hand puts the other King in line with them, and you ask the spectator to pick the Queen.

You then dispense with the paper clip and put the two Kings face down onto your palm, putting the Queen of hearts face down beneath them, very openly. You slowly turn the hand palm down, which leaves the Queen of Hearts facing the spectators, face up. The three cards are neatly squared.

Now, the left third finger pulls back the bottom King, in the glide movement. The Queen of Hearts and the King just beneath it are lifted as one card and moved, still face up, beneath the remaining face-up King. You square up the three cards, make the glide move with the third little finger again, and again move two cards as one from top to bottom. To the spectators, it seems that the Queen of Hearts is now sandwiched between the two face-up Aces. Actually, it is the bottom card. You turn your hand over, fan the cards, and put them out in a face-down row. After the spectators have picked the middle card as the Queen of Hearts, you may pick the cards up face-up again, leaving the face-up Queen on top. You make the glide movement again, apparently putting the Queen at the bottom but actually moving the top two face-up cards to the bottom. You turn the cards face down. The spectators should think the Queen is the top face-down card. Actually, it is in the middle.

You haven't done any of the real Three-Card

Monte moves, but, as far as your audience is concerned, you've given a convincing demonstration of the swindle. At this point, you put away the cards and get ready for the Australian Belt Swindle.

THE AUSTRALIAN BELT

"Not many people in this country have been fortunate enough to see the old Australian Belt come-on. It was a closely guarded secret of the old-time Australian swindler and is still prevalent in the Australian Bush. Very few crooked American gamblers ever learned to do it, mainly because it is so difficult and requires so many hours of practice."

The Australian sharper customarily used a four-foot thong of soft leather, tied together into a circle. You *can* use a four-foot length of soft string, but you greatly simplify things for yourself if you get a 48-inch length of ball-chain, tiny brass balls held together in a chain of the type sometimes found on light fixtures. There is a little clip for such chain. If you put the two ends of the chain into the two ends of the clip, you will have a circle of chain that is just the right weight and flexibility to make the trick easy.

"The idea of the Belt Swindle," you explain as you toss the circle of chain onto the table, "was that the con-man would lay the belt out in a pattern, usually with a Figure Eight in the middle. If a victim stuck his finger in either loop, the swindler would bet either that he could pull the chain free of the finger without dislodging it or that the finger would hold the chain."

"Actually," you explain, "if you put your finger in one loop of the Figure Eight, the chain will hold. If you put it in the other loop, the chain will come free. The swindler actually was betting that you couldn't pick the right loop." You proceed to demonstrate.

You lay the chain out in a long loop, a couple of inches wide. Your right hand goes out to the right end of the loop, close to the end but on the far side. Pick up the chain at this point by putting the fingers beneath it, the thumb on top. You lift the chain a couple of inches, your finger tips pointing away from you. Now you move the hand to the left and slightly forward until you reach the left end of the loop. Your hand has turned over slightly in making this move, and you stop when your fingertips are just inside the left end of the loop. You make the move in a wide arc, so that an additional loop forms. Without this extra loop, you wouldn't be able to form the Figure Eight.

The loop at the right end as you look at it will be much smaller than the one at the left end. Put the thumb and forefinger of each hand into one of the loops and pull them to equal size. You'll have a Figure Eight inside the rectangle. Now, with thumb and forefinger, pinch the sides of the rectangle together so that you have a double-strand Figure Eight.

If anyone puts a finger in the left loop and you pull one strand of the right hand, the finger will catch the loop. But if anyone puts a finger in the right-hand loop and you pull one strand of the left end, the entire loop will come free.

You demonstrate this several times. Now for the

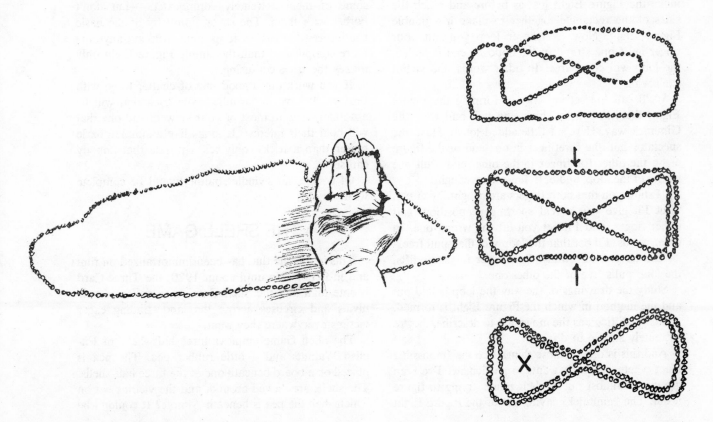

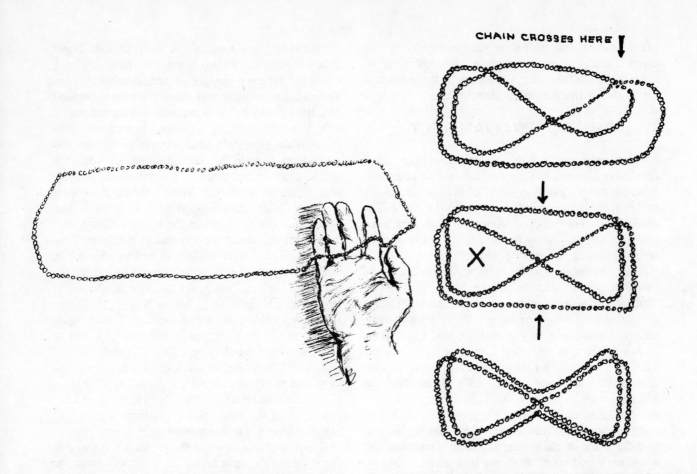

CHAIN CROSSES HERE

monkey business. You form the double Figure Eight again, apparently the same as before. Only this time, your fingers go under the right end of the loop on the side *closest* to you instead of away from you. You make the Figure Eight just as before and pinch the sides of the rectangle together to make it a double Figure Eight. Now, whichever loop you put your finger in, if one strand of the opposite end is pulled, the loop will come free. In other words, the victim can't win.

We'll call the second way of forming the Figure Eight, the way where either end will pull free, the Gimmick way. Here's a little added touch. Have the spectator put one forefinger in one end of the figure eight, the other forefinger in the other end. Pull one strand of the loop, and both fingers are caught.

"I show you that both fingers are caught," you say. "But I'll give you a real sporting proposition. Lift either finger, and I'll bet you lift the wrong one. In other words, I'll bet that the loop will then pull free."

You have a sure thing. Whichever finger he lifts, the loop pulls free of the other one.

Study the drawings of the way the loop is laid out and the method in which the Figure Eight is formed. Actually, difficult as the moves are to describe, they're extremely simple to do.

And this is one of those things like the Impossible Knot where everyone wants to participate. I've seen groups go almost out of their minds trying to figure it out. The "gimmick" laying out of the Figure Eight

is the same as the straight method—except that you grasp the loop on the side nearest you instead of the far side.

There are many variations to the old Belt Trick, some of them extremely complicated — but don't bother with them. The sheer simplicity of the basic routine is what makes it so good. Making anything more complicated than the simple Figure Eight only makes the trick confusing.

If you work out a good line of chatter to go with this, you'll have a "swindle" type trick that will be absolutely new to most of your viewers and one that will hold their interest. It looks like a simple puzzle rather than a trick—only it's a puzzle that nobody can solve.

Of course, no swindle routine would be complete without:

THE SHELL GAME

This is the one that has been immortalized on film and in fiction. Up until about 1920, the Three-Card Monte man and the Shell Game man followed carnivals and circuses across the land, finding eager victims everywhere they went.

The Shell Game employs three half-shells of English Walnuts and a little rubber pea. The pea is placed on a board beneath one of the three half-shells. The shells are moved around, and the victims bet on which shell the pea is beneath. Simple? It couldn't be

88

simpler. And neither could the victim who bets he can find the pea under a certain shell.

In the method you're going to learn, there is nothing wrong with either the shells or the pea. You split three English Walnuts in half, being careful not to break the shell. You removed the nut kernel and with a sharp knife, cut away the rough inside of the jagged lip. Get it smooth. All three half-shells are smoothed off this way on the inside. If you can't get them smooth enough to suit yourself, you can mold plastic wood putty inside each shell so that it forms a smooth surface. Let it harden.

The pea is not a real one. It is cut out of a piece of fine-grained, spongy rubber of the kind used in kneeling pads and bases for heavy objects. You should cut a little square of such rubber with a pair of scissors and then snip it so that it's perfectly round and no larger than a common pea. A soft rubber makeup sponge is excellent.

Put this pea beneath one of the shells. Grip the shell with the thumb at the rear and the forefinger at the front, slightly off-center to the right. The second finger is curled in, its side against the right side of the thumb and its nail touching the table top. Lift a shell with the fingers in this position. Put it down on top of the pea. Now, you'll find that if you move the shell slightly forward along the surface, the pea will automatically roll out the rear side of the shell into the space between the thumb and second finger. If you move the shell backward, the pea will go back under the shell.

Done on a table cloth, a felt surface, a rug or a few thicknesses of newspaper, the minute opening required for the pea to enter and exit will be made in the surface the shell rests upon, not by any perceptible lifting of the shell.

The sleight of hand is practically automatic. Move a shell slightly forward and the pea comes out from under, into perfect "palming" position between the thumb and second finger. As you remove the hand from the shell, the forefinger naturally drops down from above so that it rests naturally on the top edge of the thumb and second finger. The little pea is completely hidden.

Now, if you move the hand to another of the three shells and grasp it in the same way as the first one,

the pea will be in perfect position to roll under it when you move it slightly back toward yourself.

The little rubber pea, itself, is compressible, and the surface it rests upon has a "give." You can actually let a victim press down with his forefinger on the shell that has the pea beneath it. You move the shell slightly forward. The pea rolls into palming position and, his finger still pressed firmly down on the top of the shell, the victim is none the wiser. He is positive that the pea is still under the shell.

You can work out a great variety of moves and combinations. The pea is always under your control. One of the prettiest moves of all should be saved for your finale.

In this, you let the victim put the pea under any one of the three shells. You hand him a little juice glass or a glass of the kind that Kraft cheese spreads are sold in, and allow him to invert it over the shell. You put the other two shells on either side of the inverted glass, slightly forward. You move the glass forward, and the pea rolls between your thumb and second finger, just as smoothly and easily as if the glass weren't there. You move the other two shells slightly back, letting the pea roll under one of them. When it's under the glass, the shell always bounces as the pea comes out. Give the glass a jerky additional move forward to cover this, or at least account for it.

You can work out a fascinating routine, tailored to fit each situation. You're doing sleight of hand, and yet it's easy. You have everything under control.

I've never seen an audience that didn't find the shell game fascinating. It looks so ridiculously simple, and yet the viewer simply can't fathom the mystery.

The late Laurie Ireland was once hired to do the shell game to amuse visitors at a trade convention. Dressed as an old-time con-man, he kept up a running fire of chatter. His audience grew and grew. Finally, with a jam of several hundred people packed around him, he realized that new people were joining the group constantly but nobody was leaving. He did the shell game for a full hour—and finally, the people who had hired him told him to take a break. Nobody, they said, was paying any attention to the bar or any of the other diversions that were being offered. How I happen to know the story is true is that I happened

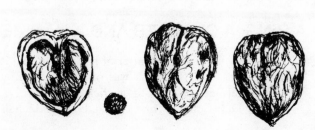

to be there and was lucky enough to get right up in the front row as the crowd formed.

There's another old Australian con game that was introduced to magicians in this country by the late Percy Abbott, the Aussie magician who founded the Abbott Magic Company. It's called:

THIRTY-ONE

Thirty-One is a swindle in which the victim thinks he has a sure thing and consequently bets his shirt.

The con man lays out twenty-four playing cards, a row of four sixes, a second row of four fives, then four fours, four threes, four deuces and four Aces. The cards are face up, the six row at the top and the Ace row at the bottom.

"All you have to do," the con man explains, "is hit the number 31 without going over. I turn down a card—let's say a six, and you turn down another, let's say a five, which makes a total of 11. We keep adding as we turn down cards. If you go over 31, you go broke. If you hit 31, you win. I'll show you how it works."

He plays a few games for fun, to explain the game. Some of the time, he wins—and some of the time, the customers win. But when they start playing for money, he *always* wins.

He has a shill working with him who approaches an interested spectator and whispers, "I know how it works. And I know how to beat it. All you have to do is hit the numbers 17 and 24 on your turn. Whoever hits 24 is bound to win. The highest number this fellow can possibly turn after you hit 24 is 30—with a six."

The potential victim thinks that over and watches the game awhile longer. He sees it's quite true. The player who hits 24 is bound to win. And he sees that the operator of the game, who makes the first move every time, can't possibly keep him from hitting 17. If he hits 17, the operator can't keep him from hitting 24.

You illustrate this with the cards as you explain it. "Finally," you say, "the victim decided to teach the operator a lesson. He offered to bet $50 on a hand of 31. Any one of you can play the part of the victim."

You get a volunteer, and for your first move, turn an Ace face down. Regardless of what card he turns, you turn down a second Ace. You turn down a third Ace on your third play. You let him arrive at 17 and 24 without any argument. And when he finally arrives at 24, you have turned down all four Aces previously. You now turn down a six, making 30. Since the Aces are all turned down, there is no card that he can turn without going "bust."

It's not really a trick but it's an interesting story that fits right in with your swindle routine. People

are always surprised when they see that there's no place for the victim to go except "bust."

The four Swindles you've just learned give you ideal party diversion. They're completely different from the usual run of party tricks, and they certainly don't require any big or elaborate props.

You could add a logical trick in the Poker Deal demonstration you learned in the card trick section, but remember that old Oriental magician, On Too Long. Don't be like him. It's hard to beat that advice, "Quit while you're ahead."

If you don't want to do Swindles, here's a little trick that women always seem to like. It's called:

A RING, A QUARTER AND A HANKIE

You may use either a quarter or half-dollar, and it may be borrowed. The trick was originally done by professional magicians with a trick coin called a "Folding Half Dollar." The magician borrowed a half dollar and switched it for his trick one. In this version, you use all unprepared materials.

You borrow a quarter or half-dollar and hold it up between your left thumb and first two fingers, thumb at the rear, fingers in front. A good part of the coin extends above your finger tips.

You throw a handkerchief over your hand, the center of it atop the top edge of the coin. You grasp the coin through the cloth with your right thumb and forefinger and move it slightly back toward yourself, cloth and all, getting a fold of cloth behind the coin with your left thumb, so that there are two thicknesses of linen between it and the coin. You hold this extra fold of cloth firmly in place. Now, you lift up the front corners of the handkerchief with your right hand, lifting them well above the coin so that everyone can see the coin is still there.

Now comes the secret of the trick. You've been holding the coin in your left fingers from beneath it. As you drop the front corners of the handkerchief, you let your left hand turn down so that all four corners of the handkerchief drop down in front of it, the back corners dropping from over the back of your left arm. You haven't changed your grip on the coin at all, but you are now holding it from above, not below. It is actually *outside* the handkerchief, at the back of it, but that fold of cloth makes it appear to be inside and beneath the handkerchief. If you give

the cloth a couple of twists, the coin will not only be completely wrapped in cloth but won't be in any danger of dropping free.

At this point, you ask one of the ladies present to lend you her wedding ring. You tell her to thread the four ends of the handkerchief through it and bring it down to the bottom so that it firmly traps the coin. With the ring pulled down to the center of the handkerchief, the coin is firmly trapped. To all appearances, the only way in the world to get the ring off would be to pull it back up over the four ends. The coin, being larger than the opening of the ring, keeps it from coming off the center.

The handkerchief can be handled freely. Have four spectators take the four corners of the handkerchief and pull them out fairly taut. From above, everyone sees a little well in the center of the handkerchief. The quarter or half-dollar is apparently in the well and the borrowed ring is on the under-side of the cloth, stopped from falling by the coin.

You reach beneath the handkerchief with both hands, pulling the coin free of the folds that are wrapped around it. Grip the top part of the little well firmly with the other hand, the left hand. Once you have the coin, the rings comes free, too. Put the coin into your right palm, turn the hand palm down, and clip the ring between the back of the first and second fingers. Bring the hand quickly from beneath the handkerchief to the top, shout "Pull," and release the coin from the palm as you display the ring, which has come free. You take your hand away and the coin has apparently pulled up out of the well with the ring's release of it.

It's easy, simple and mystifying. You can follow it with the Ring on Pencil trick, if you like!

AFTER-DINNER MINTS

A variation of the Miraskill card trick that you learned in the card section is a nice touch at a party, and one that the hostess usually finds particularly attractive.

You take a box of the flat, circular, pastel-colored after-dinner mints sold by most candy stores to the party. You have asked for two dozen red-colored cinnamon mint patties and two dozen white peppermint patties. Before you take the box to the party, you remove two of the red mints and put the cover back on the box.

Now, at the party, you dump the mints onto a clean, freshly laundered white handkerchief and gather up the four corners so that a bag is formed. You shake the bag up and down vigorously. Three candy plates are put on the table and one of the women is asked to put her glove on her right hand. As she is being blindfolded, she is asked whether she prefers the red cinnamon or the white peppermint patties. If she

names the red ones, you write a prediction, "You will have two less patties than I have." If she says white, you make the prediction, "Two more."

Three guests are designated to hold the plates. One is for red candies, one for white, and one for "mixed." The woman wearing the glove is asked to reach into the handkerchief bag and remove two mints at a time. She won't know whether they're two red, two white or one of each. Whoever is holding the designated plate holds it beneath her hand and she is asked to drop them. This continues until the handkerchief bag is empty. Her blindfold is removed. She counts the number of candies in the "red" plate and the number in the "white" plate. She is instructed to open your prediction, reads it, and it is correct. The candies are then passed to the guests.

At a children's party, wrapped toffee kisses of two different colors may be used, and the trick is always a hit.

FIND THE BODY

Don't look down your nose at this party trick because it uses a confederate. It's easy, it's mystifying, and it's the right kind of trick for a party. Your confederate can be given instructions right at the party, only a few minutes before you perform, and he'll do a good job.

You cut the crude form of a man from a piece of paper and then jab a hole in the chest at approximately the point where the heart would be.

"This," you announce, "is a murder victim. Now, a killer can't be convicted of murder without the presence of the victim's body—the corpus delicti. The police can be positive a person has been killed, but they can't prove it until they find the body, or at least, traces of it.

"Finding the corpus delicti is one of the most difficult and most important jobs a detective has. I'm going to be escorted out of the room by one of you, who will keep me under close watch and see to it that I can't spy or listen. You will then hide the body on somebody's person in this room. Once the body is hidden, call me and my guard back and I'll try to identify the person who's concealing the corpus delicti."

You're taken from the room and then brought back in. You walk around the room, apparently in deep concentration. Suddenly you stop, advance toward one of the guests, and say dramatically, "I arrest you for concealing the corpus delicti."

Without asking any questions, you have picked the guilty party.

How? When you get directly in front of the person who has the paper doll, your confederate sniffs. Not loud. Just a quick little intake of air through his nostrils—a sniff. You continue to walk around the room, apparently in deep concentration. You turn suddenly and walk back to the person you were next to when the sniff came. You point an accusing finger and make your declaration.

Don't make your pronouncement immediately following the little sniff. Wait awhile. People who think there must be a confederate giving a signal will be completely baffled.

It's hard to believe until you've tried it, but that little sniff is the best signal there is. Nobody notices it, and yet it is clearly recognizable to you.

On occasion, I've repeated this three or four times with different "tests," such as finding the person who's holding my watch, the person who picked up a coin from the table and stuck it in his pocket, and the woman who is holding one of the men's cigaret lighter. I've used the same signal for every test, and nobody has ever had the faintest clue.

Don't feel you're ruining your magical standing by using a confederate. Thurston, Blackstone and Dante all used assistants, didn't they? And they weren't slouches.

MacDonald Birch, a highly successful magician who for years featured The Vanishing Shetland Pony in his stage show, had one of the nerviest party tricks I've ever seen. It was so mystifying that I wanted to learn it, and he showed me the secret.

He was at a party in Sioux City, Iowa, where he was appearing, and he wasn't prepared to do any tricks, but the guests were insistent that he perform. He finally agreed, "but later, not now."

When he got ready, he took a handkerchief from his pocket and had it examined. Then he had two people hold the four corners of it, stretched out between them. He took off his coat, rolled up his shirt sleeves above the elbows, let a guest examine both his hands and then put them, unquestionably empty, under the handkerchief. Almost instantly, he pulled his hands out from under the stretched handkerchief and deposited a full size grapefruit on it. And I mean, that grapefruit was big. It was the cleanest bare-hand production I'd ever seen. With no coat, and sleeves rolled up above the elbow.

The secret was ridiculously simple. He rummaged around the kitchen and found something to produce —a grapefruit. Then he got one of the guests aside and had him stick the grapefruit under his coat, hold-ing it there with pressure from his elbow. He instructed the man what he was to do.

When he got ready to do the trick, he had one of the women take two ends of the handkerchief and brought her over in front of his "plant." Birch held the other two ends so that the handkerchief was stretched out flat and said to the man, "I want you to hold the other two ends, thumbs on top, fingers beneath." The man reached up from beneath, the grapefruit clutched in his left fingers beneath the handkerchief. Birch stepped back, had his hands examined, put them under the handkerchief and took the grapefruit from his confederate.

His one trick stunned everyone except the man who'd acted as his confederate.

Beginner's Trick

The first trick most junior magicians learn is that of restoring a broken toothpick or wooden match. It's easy, but it's effective.

A wooden match or toothpick is worked into the hem along one corner of the handkerchief, and the cloth smoothed out so that the preparation is not discernible.

The young magician removes the prepared handkerchief from his pocket, spreads it out onto the table top and places a wooden match or toothpick at about the center of the cloth square. He then folds over the corners to the center, with the prepared corner going first. The smaller square thus formed is folded over again twice, first from the top and then from right to left. The magician now picks up the folded handkerchief firmly at any edge, which permits the loose match or toothpick to drop to an inner edge. He grips the duplicate in the hem, its form clearly visible, and asks a spectator to break it into several pieces, through the cloth. The snap of the wood is audible, and the feel of the breaking wood is unmistakable.

The young magician now puts the folded handkerchief back on top of the table and slowly unfolds it, revealing the restored match or toothpick. He flips it onto the table for examination as he puts the handkerchief back into his pocket.

This simple trick has been the start of many a magic career.

Ice Breakers

You might be surprised how many people use magic in business.

Doctors, of course, have used it for years as a form of therapy. The story is, and I have no reason to believe it untrue, that Cardini, the wonderful card manipulator, learned the basic principles of his craft in a hospital bed. A psychiatrist once told me that when a certain type of patient had no interest in life, he had often promoted magic as a hobby and that it had worked wonders.

When I was running a country weekly newspaper in Nebraska, a lawyer wanted to discredit the damaging testimony of the plaintiff's star witness. He performed a simple magic trick in which misdirection was the key, and then asked the witness to describe the trick. The plaintiff's lawyer objected strenuously, but the judge said the question must be answered. The witness's description of what he had just seen bore no resemblance to what had actually happened, and the plaintiff's case fell apart.

I've known three dentists who built large practices with children because they kept their patients' minds occupied with little magic tricks.

Salesmen, of course, use magic more than any other group. A salesman who can do some good tricks has a tremendous advantage over his competitors. Many salesmen have to walk in "cold" and attract immediate attention and interest on the part of new potential customers. Magic does the job for them. It's quick, it's startling, it's different, and it breaks the ice.

My father ran a jewelry and optical store. He was never a magic fan and couldn't do a single trick, himself, but the two salesmen who called on him who did

magic were the two he always remembered—and they got the bulk of his business.

One of these salesmen sold, among other things, clocks. Dad told the story many times about the first time Steve called on him.

"He pulled a heavy cardboard contraption out of his sample case," he said, "and it was folded flat—just three pieces of heavy cardboard hinged together. All you could have hidden in it was a piece of paper.

"But Steve opened it up and showed it to me from all sides. I wondered what the hell he was doing. Well, he folded it into an upright triangle, reached into it from the top and damned if he didn't pull out a big clock. He started selling me that clock. Ordinarily, I'da have bought three or four of 'em, but doggoned if I didn't buy a dozen! Darndest thing I ever saw, the way that big, solid clock just came outta nowhere."

I once saw Steve sell Dad some fountain pens. He must have done half a dozen tricks with the pen he was pushing, and I wanted one, myself, before he got through. During the course of his tricks, he threw in a lot of salesmanship, and that pen became the most remarkable pen ever marketed.

A fellow in the office supply business once won a prize for selling more check protectors than any other salesman in the country. He told me how he did it. The check protector hung from a hook inside his suit coat, and a thin catgut loop extended from it to a point just over his necktie.

"I want to show you something remarkable," he said to his prospective customer, and whipped a heavy silk handkerchief from his pocket. He showed both sides of it and then held it in front of himself by the two upper corners. He hooked his left thumb into the catgut loop as he walked up to the man's desk, reached out and spread the silk handkerchief on top of the desk. Only it didn't spread. Strangely, there was something bulky beneath it. He slowly pulled the handkerchief away and there, right on the prospect's desk, sat the check protector.

A wallpaper salesman of my acquaintance rubber-cemented wallpaper patterns to thin cards, about the size of a playing card. He pulls this packet of cards from his pocket, holds it in his left hand, the pattern on the front card facing the customer. He passes his right hand over the packet, and the pattern changes. It changes again and again!

He is simply doing a manipulative card trick called The Color Change. Every time he passes his hand over the face of the packet, his left forefinger pushes the rear card into his right palm. His right hand makes a little flourish and drops the palmed card onto the face of the pack.

It's no great shakes of a trick, but he does it well and he gets immediate attention. He says he used to talk about the wide choice of patterns he had but that nobody paid much attention. "Now," he grins, "they tell *me* what a wonderful range of patterns I have."

A hefty book could be written about specific salesmen and the tricks they are currently using in their selling.

One of the cutest ice breakers that is often used at conventions is a commercial product, the Hole-Tite Pencil. It's a pencil with a loop of cord extending from one end. The salesman loops the cord through a button-hole of your coat. Then you try to take it off. You can't do it. The pencil is simply too long to permit you to unloop it. You don't get it off until the salesman who looped it on shows you how. The pencils can be bought in quantities from magical supply houses.

Performing at trade shows and conventions has become a thriving business for the club and close-up magicians who've pursued it.

The sales manager of a large, wealthy, highly successful company confided in me, "Our competitors spend more and more money on their trade-show booths. Most of them give away expensive premiums. We simply hire a good close-up magician, and we invariably steal the show. We've found a good performer who knows how to tie his magic in with our line, and he does a fine selling job for us while he's drawing the crowds and entertaining them. We invariably win, with a much smaller expenditure than that of our competition."

Mark Wilson, an excellent performer, a polished gentleman and an intelligent young man, has made a study of commercial magic applications, and has come up with trade show and convention ideas that qualify

Making George Turn Over

Hold a dollar bill with George Washington's picture facing you. Fold it down from the top to half its width. Now, fold over a third of the bill from right to left. Then fold the two thicknesses over again from right to left.

Now, you release the end that is at the right, taking it in your right fingers. Let the end that's at the left unfold to your left fingers. Open up the folded-over width and Washington's portrait will now be upside down.

Properly done, it appears that you fold down the upper half of the bill, give the length a couple of folds and then unfold it just as you folded it in the first place.

as sensational. The pulling power and salesmanship of his promotions are so unquestionable that he can just about take his pick of clients.

Karrell Fox, the wonderfully funny Detroit magician, has produced numerous sales promotions that depend on magic, among them being a number of touring units called The Magic World of Ford.

Chicago seems to be a mecca for so-called "Industrial" magicians, and they all do well, working for the same sponsors at the same trade shows and conventions, year after year.

Yes, magic is a great selling tool—and one of its big values is as an ice breaker.

This application calls for a special kind of trick. It must be quick and effective, without seeming to be elaborate or pretentious. It shouldn't employ obvious props or gadgets. If it is amusing, so much the better.

Every salesman who uses Ice Breakers must work out his own application of them to what he's selling, his personality, and the immediate selling situation. Almost any trick can, with a little thought, be twisted around to illustrate almost any point.

An Ice Breaker that I stumbled across eight or nine years ago is seldom performed, is quick, is highly mystifying, and is one you can do. Not only can you do it but you can do it at any time, right in a man's office. It requires a dollar bill, a couple of paper clips and a rubber band. You wouldn't even have to carry your own paper clips and rubber band because these are items to be found in every office. I call the trick

CLIPPED FOR A SNAPPY BUCK

This trick was originated, I understand, by Bill Bowman. You fold a dollar bill lengthwise in half. It retains its original length but is now only half its original width. The original upper and lower edges of the bill are face to face, toward your body. You slip a rubber band onto the bill and fold over about a third of its length to the right, so that the rubber band

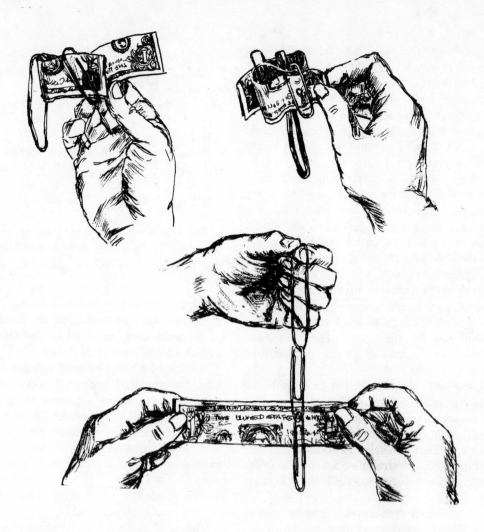

is covered by the fold. You hold this fold in place with a paper clip, which is pushed on from the front, the folded side, so that the rubber band is now clipped inside the fold. The clip is not in contact with the rubber band. One important thing—the long end of the paper clip should be on the side you're looking at, the upper side. The short end of the clip is on the bottom.

You now turn the folded bill over from right to left and fold the free end from left to right. You put a second paper clip onto this end from the top, folded edge. This second clip goes over two folded edges, free of the third. Again, the long side of the clip must be on top.

At this point, you have the spectator grip the loose end of the rubber band. You grip the two ends of the folded bill, one end between thumb and forefinger of each hand.

Pull the two ends apart briskly. For some baffling reason, the rubber band and the paper clips link together, so fast that the human eye can't see it happen. Release the end of the bill that's between your right thumb and forefinger until the bill is free of the rubber band, and then grip it again as quickly as possible, holding it stretched its full length between the two thumbs and forefingers. The spectator is hold-

ing the rubber band, and the two paper clips are linked together on it.

The effect is unexplainable. How did the paper clips get onto the rubber band, and how did they become linked together? If you follow instructions on folding the bill and putting on the clips and rubber band correctly, the trick works itself.

A friend of mine who sells a high-priced, quality line tells a little story about a customer who simply wouldn't pay for quality merchandise. He wanted to hold onto his money, every penny of it, so much that he clipped every dollar bill to a rubber band and had the rubber bands on his key ring.

My friend folds and clips a bill as he talks. "Time after time," he says, "this customer bought cheap, shoddy, unsatisfactory merchandise, convincing himself that he was getting a bargain because the price was so low. He refused to admit that quality is more important than price. And do you know what happened to him?" At this point, he has the customer hold onto the free end of the rubber band. "Every time," he continues, pulling the ends of the bill apart, "he got clipped."

The customer is looking at the rubber band he's holding, two paper clips hanging from it.

Another salesman, a young fellow, says to the prospect, "I just saw the darndest thing. A fellow showed me a trick." He does the trick. "I asked him how the trick worked, and he *didn't know*. He could do it, but he didn't know how. He said, 'What do I care how it works, as long as I get results?' Well, a lot of our customers can't see how we can give the values we do, but they don't care, either, because they know they're getting what they want. We *do* know how we do it, though. We can give you top value because—" and he goes into his sales pitch.

The next trick is one that requires advance preparation, but you can prepare it in quantity, and you can carry enough of the props for six or seven performances without making any noticeable bulge in your pocket. It's well worth the effort. I call it:

KEEP IT BRIEF

Clip about a dozen pieces of newsprint from any newspaper, using the column lines for a guide. Clip strips about 15 inches long and one column wide. Try to clip columns that contain solid body type. Pieces of paper that contain part of display ads aren't good. You coat both sides of these strips with rubber cement. Put a thin coat of rubber cement on one side

and let it dry, which will happen rather quickly. Now, dust the coated side with talcum powder. Don't worry about the powder showing. Put it on thick, so that every bit of the coated surface is powdered.

Then, put a coat of rubber cement on the other side of each strip. Let it dry and powder it. Fold the strips in half, so that each folded paper is 7½ inches long. With one of these folded strips in your coat pocket, you're all set for one performance. Most people who do the trick keep a half-dozen papers in their inside upper coat pocket.

The effect of the trick is simply this. You open out a strip and refold it. You are holding both loose ends of the strip in your left hand. Now, with a pair of scissors, you cut off a piece across the folded edge. Drop the lower end from your left hand. The paper has obviously been cut, but the lower end hangs down, still attached. The strip still has a fold in it and is shorter by the length of the piece that was cut, but it's still intact.

You can keep folding and keep cutting until the strip is down to practically nothing. You cut across both the upper and lower sides of the folded edge, *not* between them. One cutting edge of the scissors is below the folded edge and the other one above. If you cut at an angle, the paper will drop open with an

angular fold. You see, the pressure of the scissor blades welds the cut edges together, thanks to the rubber cement.

By the time you're ready to perform, the surplus powder should have dropped off. If it hasn't, blow it off before you put the strips in your pocket. Properly prepared, neither the rubber cement nor the talc give any phony appearance to the paper.

You can't *pull* on the two ends after a cut has been made. The paper will pull apart at the cut. But if you let one end drop after each cut and then fold it back up, you won't need to worry about the halves coming apart.

Here's the approach that one salesman uses:

"Our sales manager asked the salesmen in our company to get together and prepare an ideal sales presentation. We were pretty proud of it, so we had it printed and showed him a copy. He didn't even read it. 'It's too long,' he said, and snipped part of it out. We reworked it and took it back to him. 'It's still too long,' he told us, and cut out some more. That happened time after time (illustrating with numerous cuts) and finally our masterpiece was down to a couple of paragraphs. 'Cut it some more,' he said. We told him we didn't see how we could, and he said, 'Do you know what the perfect sales presentation is for our product? I've used it for years and I'll tell you. Here it is. I defy you to find as good a value as you can get from us, anywhere else in the world.' "

Another salesman uses a routine about involved, tricky contracts with lots of fine print. He tells how *his* company kept shortening and simplifying its contract, cutting away a piece of the strip from time to time as he talks. Finally, he concludes, his company arrived at what customers regard as a perfect contract. It says, simply, Satisfaction or Your Money Back.

While this is a "quickie" and is small, it is, with the right presentation, an excellent club or stage trick. It's visible from a distance and is so uncomplicated that a sizable audience can see it. It's also a trick the performer doesn't have to worry about, since it works automatically.

Coins are ideal for Ice Breaker tricks. My problem has always been that I'm simply not a good coin manipulator. A good coin trick, however, is always convincing, and it's natural for anyone to have some coins in his pocket. I've sometimes used a silly little coin trick that *should* be glaringly obvious to the spectator but never is. I call it:

MATCHING PENNIES

The only requirement is that you have 27 pennies in your pocket. The 27 isn't a "must." It could be 32 or, possibly 19. The point is that you should have more pennies than the average person ever carries.

For the purposes of illustration, we'll stick with 27.

You ask the spectator if he has any pennies in his pocket. In this era of sales tax, he will nearly always say "Yes."

You touch your fingers lightly against the outside of his pants pocket.

"I have exactly as many pennies as you have," you announce, "plus three, and enough left over to make exactly 27."

He takes his pennies from his pocket and counts them. Let's say there are seven. You count out seven pennies. "Plus three," you say, counting out three more. "But I said I'd have enough left over to make exactly 27. There are now ten. So I should have how many more? Seventeen. Right? Count them."

You hand him the 17 pennies and he counts them. Your prediction was correct.

What you've actually predicted is that you'll have 27 pennies—a reasonable assumption, since you *know* that's the number. It's the way you state it that makes the trick—"as many as you have, plus three, and enough left over to make exactly 27."

I know—you don't think it will fool anybody. All right, just try it and see.

SYMPATHETIC COINS

Karrell Fox has had a cute little coin trick for years, and it's a baffler. He lays a row of quarters or half dollars across his left palm, about six in all. Every other coin is heads up and every other one is tails up. He calls attention to this and stacks the coins, without any monkey business. They are alternately heads and tails. He picks up the stack from above with his right thumb on the edge toward his body, his fingers on the edge away from himself. Now he drops the coins very

deliberately onto his left palm, one at a time. The right hand is maybe four or five inches above the left palm. The coins are now all heads or all tails up, whichever Karrell wants them to be.

Strangely, the trick is absolutely undetectable. He drops one coin by releasing it from the thumb and fingers simultaneously. Pressure on both edges is taken away at the same time. If the coin is heads up, that's the way it lands on the left palm. He drops the *next* coin by releasing pressure from the thumb only. The fingers don't release their pressure a bit. The coin turns completely over in dropping—but the turnover can't be seen. It's impossible to detect. You don't have to do it fast. Indeed, you can do it very deliberately. You can watch another person doing it for hours and never catch the turnover of a single coin. It's so easy that it hasn't been done much. If it required a complicated mechanical box and involved covering the coins with a handkerchief, it would probably be done much more often. Actually, it's simplicity is the thing that makes it so good.

A KNOTTY PROBLEM

Howard Thurston used to like this trick as a close-up Ice Breaker. Since his time, a mechanical method involving use of a mechanical reel has been widely sold. It's beautiful, and the mechanical operation is extremely clever, but for your purposes, I think the old, no-gadget method is better.

You remove your dark-colored silk handkerchief from your outer breast pocket and twirl it into a silken rope. You hold one end of the rope in your left fingertips and with your right hand, you tie a big, loose knot in the silk, tying it from the bottom end. You now take the top end from your left hand into the right thumb and fingertips and extend your hand, with the silken rope out toward the spectator. The lower end of the silken rope curls upward as if it were alive and the knot unties itself—visibly!

Here we are, at last—a trick that's done with a black thread. Today, it's done with a length of black nylon or silk. One end of the thread is tied or affixed

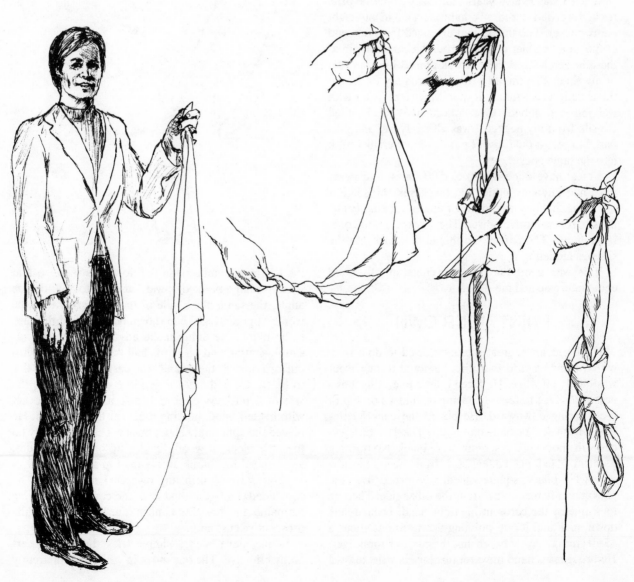

to one corner of the silk handkerchief. A small, unnoticeable weight may be attached to the other end, although I never bother with it.

You pull the silk from your pocket and twirl the ends so that it forms a loose rope. The right end is the one that has the black thread attached. It drops to the floor, unnoticed. You release the right end and hold the left end between your left thumb and forefinger, the fingers at about chest level. You step firmly on the black thread where it rests on the floor. Now, with your right hand, you tie a big, loose knot in the silken rope, from the bottom. You have to lower your left hand to make this possible, because you tie the thread into the knot right along with the lower end of the silk handkerchief. You can't avoid its going through. If you get a knot, the thread will be a part of it.

Now, if you lift the upper end of the silken rope, the knot will rise up and untie itself. Gather up the silk and put it back into your pocket, maneuvering so that the thread goes with it.

When I was twelve years old, this was my favorite trick. I carried a red silk handkerchief in my right pants pocket. The thread that extended from one end of the handkerchief was tied around a common pin at the other end—and the pin was pinned into the sole of my shoe. The thread extended from my pocket to the shoetip at all times. It didn't interfere at all with walking, and nobody ever noticed it. When I pulled the silk from my pocket, I was all ready, set and prepared to go. At the finish, I put the handkerchief back into the same pocket.

I must have done that trick 500 times, and never once had anybody notice the black silk thread. For one thing, nobody would ever think of looking *below* the silk for its motive power. They'd expect it to come from *above*. The part of the thread that was with the silk was hidden by it.

If it was good enough for Thurston, it's good enough for you and me.

PRINT YOUR OWN

Hugh Hogan, a great salesman, used to do a trick with a business card that didn't amount to much but was highly effective. He faced a little pile of his business cards face to face, 12 facing up and 12 on top of these facing downward. He pulled the packet carelessly from his pocket and said, "The last business cards the home office sent me were blank. No printing on them." He fanned a few cards from the top to show they were blank, squared them up, turned over the packet and fanned a few from the other side. Then he took one of the cards in his right hand, printed side down, and held it out, pointing downward at about a 45-degree angle, between his thumb and forefinger. He brought his hand upward, turning his wrist toward

the left as his hand made the upward sweep, so that when his hand pointed upward at close to a 90-degree angle, the same blank side of the card still faced the front. Apparently, he had shown both sides of the card to be blank. He didn't make anything of it. He was simply stating that his cards had been delivered without printing on them, and was casually showing this to be so. He had cut a little piece of plywood to the size of a business card and took it from his pocket with his left hand, holding it out on the left palm. He placed the apparently blank business card carefully on the little block of wood, lined it up on all four sides, and rubbed his thumb across the top surface.

"So I have to print my own as I need them," he concluded, and he turned over the card, now bearing his name and business connection, handing it to the prospective customer.

It may have been a simple trick, but it was certainly effective. The one move in which he apparently showed both sides of the card was a variation of the old Paddle Move that many children learn when they get their first magic set. The right palm faces the spectator both when the hand points downward and when it points upward, but that incongruity goes unnoticed.

Actually, the casual and convincing way in which he fanned the packet of cards from both sides had the customer believing the cards were blank on both sides before he ever exhibited a single card and did the paddle move.

He did another trick with a business card that I've never quite understood—but I know it works. He folded a card in half and slipped a rubber band over one end so that the band hung down from inside the fold. For purposes of identification, I call the trick

THE INDESTRUCTIBLE RUBBER BAND

Hugh carried a small, dull, loose pair of kindergarten scissors in his side coat pocket, just for this trick. He snapped the rubber band a couple of times to show that it was actually inside the folded card. Then he took out his loose, dull scissors and inserted one blade under the folded card, between it and the part of the rubber band that extended outside the

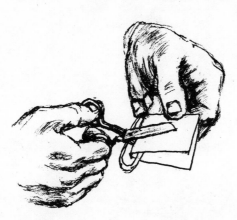

fold. The other blade was on the top side of the folded card, at right angles to the rubber band. Two thicknesses of card were between the blades, with one thickness of rubber band between them.

He cut the card in half, right down the middle, all the way from the fold to the two ends. There was no question about it. The card had been cut in two. There was also no question about the rubber band being between the two folded sections—but the rubber band *hadn't been cut!* It was intact.

Now, the scissors *had* to come together over the band in the cutting process. And yet, the band was unsevered.

"Just cut slowly and carefully," he told me, "and the trick will work. Most office desk scissors are old

and loose. When I see a pair like that, I use them rather than my own. But if you use a tight, sharp pair of scissors, you'll cut the band."

Having used the rubber band in this trick, he did another with it, a trick called:

THE JUMPING BAND

He put the rubber band around the first two fingers of his right hand, and it mysteriously jumped to the third and little fingers. The late Dr. Harlan Tarbell taught the trick to many youngsters in his magic course.

It's easy but startling. You put the band around your first two fingers and snap it a few times with your left fingers. Then, as you start to close the right hand into a fist, back toward spectators, the left thumb and forefinger pull out a piece of the band at the back. The left fingers put the band over the outer ends of

all four fingers of the closing fist, giving it another snap as they do it. The right thumb nips the band tightly at the point where it comes around the fore-finger toward the palm.

At this point, if you open your right fist and release the thumb pressure, you'll discover that the band is now on your third and little fingers.

Close your fist again, first reaching down behind the palm with your right thumb and hooking it through the band. You'll find it a simple matter to put the band over all four fingertips with the thumb, without using the left hand. Now, if you open the fist a second time, the band will jump back to the first two fingers.

Hugh always crisscrossed a second rubber band over the tips of all four fingers. For some reason, that outer band made the trick seem impossible, although it didn't interfere with the movement of the jumping band in any way.

THE RUBBER PENCIL

This is a little "throw-away" that anyone can do with a little practice—and nobody can do without some experimentation. You hold the pencil loosely between the tips of the thumb and second finger, thumb tip upward, against the bottom side of the pencil. A common error that most beginners make is to hold the pencil about midway from tip to eraser. It should be held with the eraser end to your right, about one-third of the length in. The big secret is to move your whole arm up and down, not just your hand.

Held in this way, loosely, if you give the hand a gentle up-and-down motion, the pencil will "wiggle." You can wave it up and down in such a way that it will appear to be bending, as if made of rubber. The illusion is the same as that of "bending a half-dollar" in which you nip a half-dollar between the thumbs and fingers of both ends. If you bend the *hands,* the coin appears to be bending.

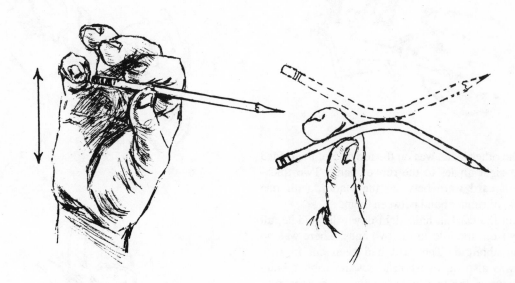

You're a Mindreader!

In my first book of mental magic for professional magicians, I wrote, "Do a straight magic act and you're fighting your audience. The layman who isn't trying to catch you, trying to figure out your tricks, must be that guy in the eighth row who's sound asleep. The straight magic act is entertainment, sure, but it's also a battle of wits between the performer and spectators.

"When you get into mental magic, however, you're in another world. Even when you tell your audience that you're resorting to trickery (and let's not go quite that far) nobody wants to believe you. The bulk of your spectators want to believe in spite of the evidence."

Your approach to mental magic must be decidedly different. You do *not* carefully show both your hands empty. To do so would be to create the impression that you're doing tricks. And you're not trying to sell that idea. You want your audience to believe that you're reading minds — that you're doing mental telepathy.

As you progress in mental magic, you will actually come closer and closer to genuine telepathy. My theory is that everyone is born with a sixth sense, an extra-sensory perception, but that the sixth sense is exercised so little that it soon atrophies.

Most magicians who do mental magic believe in ESP. They do tricks, but they operate in the mindreading field, and their ESP sharpens. There's an advanced form of mental magic called Contact Mindreading that comes close to genuine telepathy. Five or six performers have become so proficient at it that their performances *are* genuine telepathy. There's no other way to explain what they do.

Magic, Inc., publisher of *It Must Be Mindreading,* says of it, "Positively the greatest book on mental magic ever published." I took the approach throughout the book that you, as a mental magician, should do things that would draw from your audience the conclusion, "It must be mindreading."

The mental magician who uses special devices that give the impression of being "equipment," the type of thing that stage magicians often use, destroys the illusion he's trying to create.

Now, if you were capable of genuine mindreading, you would never ask anyone to write anything. And since you're *not* a real mindreader, you need to get information — and information that's been written down on a slip of paper is possible to acquire.

Most of the younger generation has never seen the "Question Answering Act," which in its heyday was one of the biggest money-makers in magic. Such performers as Anna Eva Fay, Alexander, Rajah Raboid, Dr. X and numerous others made fortunes with it. A theater that could book in a question-answering act was almost certain to do capacity business.

Back when the Question Answering Act was the hottest thing in mental magic, all mental magicians had spectators write their questions on slips of paper. The writing was either done with the paper on a file board that took a carbon impression of the written words, or the questions were collected by assistants, after which information could be conveyed to the "mindreader."

One fairly plausible excuse for writing down the questions was, "Unless you write down your question, you may hear me answer someone else's question and forget your own."

I felt that asking spectators to write out their questions was stretching their credulity, but I had to know what their questions were. I handled the problem by announcing, "Think of your question. Don't write it down! In order to fix a mental picture of your question firmly in mind, I will ask you to write down a word or phrase connected with the question and then concentrate on it. Pick a word or phrase that makes a mental picture of your question to you. Maybe one word won't convey the proper mental picture. That's quite all right. Use three or four words. Just be sure that your phrase gives you a good mental picture of your question. You know from your school day experience that writing down information is the surest way to fix it in your mind. My experience has been that writing down information is also the best way to fix a question in a person's mind with sufficient clarity that the idea of the question can be mentally projected."

Once you know the "word or phrase," it's easy to pump enough to get the gist of the question.

How do you do it? I'll give you some examples. A young lady who isn't wearing a wedding ring and looks like a native-born resident of this country writes on her slip, "Viet Nam." Nothing more. I say to her hesitantly, "Your question concerns not only yourself but someone else. Is it a man?" She nods her head. "This man is outside the continental limits of the United States. Is that correct?" She says "Yes." Had she said No, I'd have continued, "But there's a possibility that he may have to take a trip outside this country. Is that right?" But she said Yes, so I continue, "He seems to be employed in some branch of government service. Is that correct?" I get a nod. "My thought waves don't tell me for sure when he'll return to the United States, but I see a possibility that it may be sooner than expected. He seems to be in—Viet Nam. Is that correct?"

Her "Yes" is almost a sure bet to bring spontaneous applause. I continue, "You have a deep personal interest in this man and the length of time he stays in Viet Nam is important in the determination of your question. Let me say that he will be there no longer than is necessary and all you can do is wait."

I ask the girl what her question was, and she replies, "Will my fiancee be back from Viet Nam in time for us to be married by Christmas?"

Another questioner, not wearing a wedding ring, writes "Oil well" on her slip. That's not much to work on. My first thought is that she wants to know about an investment, but I proceed with caution. "I get a picture of something entirely foreign to my own experience. I see some huge derricks. Does that mean anything to you?" She says Yes, so I continue. "Does this line of work concern you personally or someone in whom you're interested?" Someone I'm interested in." she acknowledges.

"I thought so," I nod. "It's a man. He's something of a gambler, the type who'll take chances to make money. As I see it, your interest is financial." She surprises me by saying "no." "Maybe you don't understand me," I continue. "Your interest is financial in that you want him to make money. Is that correct?" She nods. "He seems to be quite close to you," I continue. "My fiancee," she answers.

"My dear young lady," I continue, "oil is always a gamble, but the returns sometimes make the risk worthwhile. Frankly, if I could tell you whether or not your sweetheart's oil well will be successful, I'd be a millionaire. Unfortunately, I'm a telepathist, not a divining rod." I learn later that her question was, "Will Bert's oil well come in?"

But how did I get the words, "Oil well"? Easily, as you'll learn later.

When you're not doing a question-answering act, you still need to have information written. So what's your excuse?

For "later verification." I sometimes say, "This is to prevent your changing your mind during the course of this test. That sometimes happens, and when it does, thought transference is almost impossible."

The interest in mental magic is tremendous, except for children. The current crop of teen-agers is as much interested in ESP as are its elders. Most good mental magic is impromptu and can be done under almost any conditions. Props are few, and what you use is nearly always small—small enough to be carried in the pockets or a brief case.

We'll start with a simple audience participation trick that isn't really a trick; at least, you don't use trick devices or any sleight of hand. It's called:

THE SEX INDICATOR

A multimillionaire manufacturer of my acquaintance is so fascinated with the Sex Indicator that he had a jeweler make one up for him in gold chain, with a tiny crystal ball on one end. He regards it as one of the miracles of all time and hauls it out on the slightest provocation.

You won't need any gold chain or small crystal ball. A 24-inch length of string with a brass nut or weight tied to one end of it will be quite as effective as anything a jeweler could make up for you.

In days of laxer regulation of advertising claims, mail-order swindlers got rich selling the little gadget as a sex indicator, getting a dollar for a piece of string and a fishline sinker. The instructions solemnly stated that when the free end of the string is held over any person or thing, the weight will swing back and forth if the object is male, in a circle if it's female. Farmers all over the United States sent in their dollars for Sex Indicators to use in selecting eggs for hatching. The idea was that they could avoid getting too many roosters by eliminating eggs over which the pendulum swung back and forth.

I've talked to farmers in the present supposedly enlightened age who swear by the Sex Indicator, the secret of which has been passed down to them by their parents.

Tie a little weight onto one end of a two-foot length of string. Hold the other end of the string between your thumb and forefinger, so that the weight is an inch or two above another person's palm. Don't try to make the pendulum swing. Just concentrate on the thought that if the surface closest to the weight is male, the pendulum will swing back and forth; if it's female, the weight will swing in a circle.

I find the little gadget a good opening for a series of mental tricks because it explains something about mental telepathy. Thought creates a physical reaction. You don't realize that you're moving the pendulum, but thinking about it causes you to do so.

The physical reaction to thought is a common thing. When you say, "I could tell he was being untruthful," how can you tell? By the liar's physical reaction, of course—perhaps by a shiftiness of the eyes, a squirming, a generally uncomfortable look that can't be hidden.

The polygraph or lie detector is based on the physical reaction to thought, and the polygraph is a telepathic machine that reveals what a subject is thinking, in spite of what he says.

Physical reaction to thought is the basis of Contact Mindreading, an intriguing subject on which I've

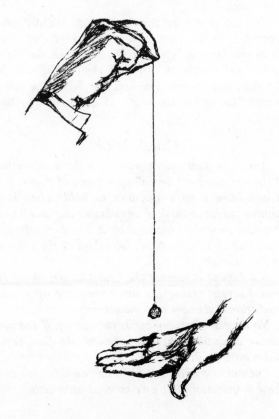

written another book. The Sex Indicator is the easiest possible method of demonstrating it.

Get several members of the group to try it. When you get them to use it, you are also demonstrating what I call a "mental force." The simplest explanation of this is that you force someone to do something by the power of suggestion.

If you were to tell your subject that the pendulum always swings in a straight line over a female surface and in a circle over a male surface, it would perform in that manner.

I've never seen a group that wasn't fascinated by the simple little device. The man who has the gold-chain Sex Indicator refuses to listen to my simple explanation of it. He prefers to regard his little toy as something deep, dark and mysterious. He doesn't do any other tricks, but he has a barrel of fun with the Sex Indicator.

Obviously, you can't get caught on this trick, because there's nothing to catch. Similar in that respect is a trick that was a favorite of the late "Dr. Q.," a pseudo-telepathist who was highly successful. I call it:

THINK OF A FINGER!

This is a little mind-reading trick based on somewhat the same principle as the Sex Indicator. Some people can do it successfully right from their introduction to it. Some get the knack or "feel" in half an hour, while others need hours of practice. And over the years, I've found four or five professional magicians who sincerely wanted to learn the trick and simply couldn't do it, no matter how diligently they tried. When it works, it has terrific impact because the only explanation as far as your audience is concerned is, "It must be mindreading."

You ask a subject to hold out his right palm, fingers extended and wide apart. You instruct him that he is to think of any one of the five fingers, really concentrating on it. Tell him that it would be the easiest thing in the world for him to fool you by not concentrating on one finger or by trying to mislead you. "But this is an experiment in mental telepathy," you add, "and we're trying to see if you can convey a thought to me."

Emphasize that he is to concentrate on one finger to the exclusion of everything else. Then touch your right forefinger tip to the tip of each of his five fingers, in turn. Press your own finger tip lightly against each one.

If he's really concentrating on one finger, the "feel" of that finger will be entirely different from the others. It will offer more resistance to your light pressure. It will seem to be firmer.

Try it. If it doesn't work, simply shrug it off with a "Well, I guess you're not getting through to me," and go on to something else. A failure in mental magic

is entirely different from one in other kinds of magic. It often strengthens the believability of what you're doing. Al Baker who originated the trick, taught it to Dr. Q, who had difficulty learning it, but eventually made it a pet trick.

I ran into one interesting case of a brash young salesman who never once "divined" the right finger in practice. In spite of repeated failures, he tried the trick at a cocktail party—and it worked, the first time! He tells me that he's done it dozens of times since then and it's never failed.

"Dr. Q.," who used a good many mechanical devices in his stage performance, made a big thing of this simple little test, building it up as "positive proof" of his telepathic ability.

But you undoubtedly want something less "iffy," and we're here to oblige. I've used the next one ever since I was 12 years old, and it's never failed for the simple reason that it can't. I call it:

MENTAL CHOICE

Run through a borrowed pack of cards, faces toward yourself, and move the four sevens to the top of the deck. Then run off seven indifferent cards into your right hand, quickly, without calling attention to how many there are. Square them up and put the squared pile on the table. Take off the four sevens in another block, squared up, and put it on the table beside the pile of seven cards.

Now, on a slip of paper, write, "You will pick the seven Pile."

You're all set.

"We'll start with an easy test of telepathy, in which I will you to make a certain choice," you say. "I would have a fifty-fifty chance of being right, with nothing but luck. However, I'm not going to depend on luck, and I guarantee that I'll be right. I've predicted on this slip of paper which of the two piles of cards you'll select, and the one you touch is the one we'll use. I'll perform the test just once, knowing that I won't need to do it more than once to prove that I can do it. Touch a finger to either pile and I guarantee that it will be the one I predicted."

Let's say, the spectator touches the pile of Seven-spots. Tell him to turn them face up. "All sevens," you remark, as you turn over the other pile, fan it

carelessly and put it back on top of the deck. "The other pile, as you can see, is a mixture of various cards, without rhyme or reason. Now, read my prediction."

He reads it aloud. You've succeeded.

But let's say he touched the pile of indifferent cards. "Count the number of cards in the pile you selected," you direct him. When he's done that, you count the pile of Sevens, face down, showing that there are only four cards in it. You toss the four cards back onto the deck. "The pile you picked contained seven cards and the other pile contained four," you continue. "Open my prediction and read it aloud."

If ever there was a mental magic trick that can't fail, this is it. Needless to say, you do *not* repeat this trick.

An ideal follow-up is:

ONE CHANCE IN TEN

"I had a fifty-fifty chance of being right on that prediction," you say, "so now let's progress to the more difficult tests. In this one, there's a ninety percent chance of error—but I'm not worried. We use all the cards from Ace through ten, one of each. I don't include any face cards, because I don't want you to think I'm influencing your choice. Not much!"

You remove an Ace, a deuce, the three of Hearts, a four, a five, a six, a seven, an eight, a nine and a ten from the deck. Pay no attention to suit, except for the three of Hearts.

"I'm going to put these cards out in a row, in a very special order."

You lay down the deuce, face up. Slightly overlapping it to the right, you put the four-spot. Next to it, overlapping, goes the six, and then the eight-spot. Next comes the three of Hearts, followed by the Ace, five, seven, nine and ten. When the pile is turned face down. the cards, in order, will be two,

Quick Trick

Announce that you're going to make a prediction. Write the number "Seven" on a piece of paper, fold it and hand it to a spectator to hold. Then have another spectator think of any number and add 9 to it. Have him multiply his total by 2. He then subtracts 4 and divides by 2. Now, he subtracts the number he first thought of.

Ask him to announce the figure he arrives at. He says, "Seven." Have the other spectator open your prediction and show it to the others.

No matter what number is thought of, if the procedure as outlined here is followed, the final result will always be 7.

The only way you can go wrong on this trick is to draw a spectator who isn't good at arithmetic.

four, six, eight, three, Ace, five, seven, nine and ten. All even cards up to the ten are above the three-spot and all odd cards are below it, with the ten-spot at the bottom of the pile.

"I want you to think of any one of these ten cards," you say, prior to assembling the cards in a face-down packet. "You have a perfectly free choice, but once you've thought of a card, don't change your mind. And concentrate hard on the card you choose. Keep a mental picture of it in your mind.

"Now I'll gather up the ten cards and put them back into the deck in a very special way, behind my back, so that you can't possibly know what I'm doing."

With the balance of the deck in one hand, the pile of ten cards in the other, you slip the bottom card of the pile, the ten-spot, into your hip pocket.

Then you count down four cards from the top of the pile without disturbing their order, and turn the fifth card, the three of Hearts, face up. You replace the other four cards on top of it, put the whole pile on top of the deck and cut the deck, bringing them to about the middle. You square the deck and bring it around to the front.

"I gave you a free choice, one card out of ten," you continue. "I've rearranged the deck. And now, for the first time, what is the card you thought of?"

If the spectator says, "The ten-spot," you turn your back to him again and direct him to reach into your hip pocket where he will find one card. He is to remove it from your pocket and show it. While he's doing this, with your back turned to him, it's a simple matter to fan the cards slightly and turn over the three of Hearts so it faces the same way as the balance of the deck.

The ten-spot is seldom chosen, however. The commonest choice is the three of Hearts. If he names the three of Hearts, you spread the face-down deck and show the three of Hearts face-up. You have a real miracle.

If he names any other card of the ten, you say, "When I put the cards behind my back, I reversed one card in the deck to serve as a locater. Let's see what it is."

You spread the deck. "A three-spot."

With the face-down deck spread from left to right, the cards above and to the right of the face-up trey are the eight, the six, the four and the deuce, in that order. The cards immediately to the left of the trey are the Ace, five, seven and nine, in that order.

If the card he has named is the Ace, you know that it's the card immediately to the left of the locater card, and you let him remove it and turn it over. If he names the eight, you know that it's immediately above the trey. You break the deck at the trey and show that it located the eight.

If he names the six or five, you know that it is two cards above or below the face-up trey. You say, "The locater card is a three-spot, so we count one, two, three." You start your three-count with the locater card, itself, which makes the three count come on the second card in whichever direction you're counting. You turn this card over and show that the locater card has found it.

If he names the four or seven, you start your three count with the card *next* to the three-spot, and turn over the card that comes on the count of three.

If he names the deuce or nine, you count three and turn up the *next* card.

Some people protest that the trick involves too much memorization, which simply isn't true. Simply remember that the two, four, six and eight go in order on one side of the three of Hearts, and the one (Ace), five, seven and nine on the other side. The ten-spot is a loner. When you spread the cards face down on the table, you can certainly remember the location of the four cards on each side and govern the use of the locater card accordingly.

Done with the proper buildup, the trick is a stunner —and it's easy. Again, do *not* repeat it.

I performed this trick last night before a little group that contained an avid amateur magician. Later in the evening, he said to me, "I wish I was advanced enough at sleight of hand to do that mental trick with the ten cards. One trick as good as that is all you need to knock 'em right off their seats."

Sleight of hand? There's not one manipulative move.

And now I'm going to give you a "think of a card" trick that's so good I hate to part with it, for fear

that some reader will do it injustice. It's the ultimate in mindreading with cards. It's a brash trick that calls for daring on the magician's part—but so is nearly every good mindreading trick. Done with assurance, it's absolutely untoppable. I call it:

THE HOAX "THINK OF A CARD"

You *never* do this trick for one person. Preferably, you do it for a group of a dozen or more people.

One person in the group is going to know how the trick works. Not even that one person will know quite how you achieve what happens. But for all the other spectators, the effect will be simply stupendous.

When I first started performing this effect, it was as a part of a more complicated presentation called "A Trick for Eddie Clever." I had never met Eddie Clever, but his monthly presentation of new tricks in *The Linking Ring* magazine had given me great pleasure for many years. When I learned that he was suffering from a serious ailment, I decided to market a new trick, with the proceeds going to him.

Frances Ireland Marshall of the magic supply house that is now called Magic, Inc., published the trick without charge. I sent a half-page ad to the three leading magic magazines with instructions to run it in their first available issue and send the bill to me.

Lip Reading

Mental magicians have often used lip reading to great advantage and to the complete mystification of their audiences. Any deaf person who has taken a course in lip reading will tell you that it's possible to "catch" almost everything that's said in a room by watching lip movements.

A young couple who did a mindreading act in a carnival show baffled other magicians by the young woman's ability to answer questions whispered to the young man. It was obvious that none of the usual methods were in operation.

It turned out that the feminine member of the team had taught lip reading for several years in a school for the deaf—and she was amazingly good at it.

Few magicians want to take the trouble to learn the art, but it is often glaringly apparent what card a person took from the deck when he whispers the name of it to another person. One magician who has concentrated on lip reading in relation to playing cards says, "Actually, you learn to distinguish 17 words— the cards from Ace to King and the four suits. Jack and King are the most difficult to distinguish by lip reading. The suits are easy." He has a person think of any card in the deck and whisper his selection to another spectator for future verification. In divining the card, he does a little "fishing" if he's in doubt.

The ad made it clear that the entire proceeds from the sale of the trick would go to Mr. Clever.

Not one of the magazines ever billed me, and all three of them ran it more than once. A number of magic supply houses bought stocks of the trick at the full retail price. Every penny went to Eddie Clever. Magicians all over the country bought A Trick for Eddie Clever; and one professional wrote me that while he thought the trick was a superb value, he regretted to see such a fine trick so widely circulated. "It's one of those things," he said, "that should be privately held by only a select few."

The Hoax Think of a Card was the climax of A Trick for Eddie Clever. Performers of mental magic will tell you that it's worth far more than the cost of this book.

Much mental magic is audacious, and Hoax is no exception. The trick is uncluttered with equipment or rigamarole. It is direct and simple. An ad for it could state, without misrepresentation.

A spectator, not a confederate, is asked to shuffle a borrowed deck of cards to his heart's content. He hands the deck to the magician who never, at any time, looks at the face of a single card. The magician, without any fumbling or manipulation, fans the face-down deck in as even a fan as he can make. He says to the spectator, "I'm going to have you look at this evenly-fanned deck of cards. Don't ask any questions. Don't say a word. Just follow instructions. Think of any card you see in the fan. Concentrate on it and don't forget its name."

The magician holds the fanned deck up for the spectator's inspection. He then puts the deck behind his back, removes one card and puts it face down on the table. The balance of the deck is put aside. The spectator is asked for the first time to name his thought-of-card. He does. The magician invites him to turn over the face down card on the table. It is the card which the spectator had just named!

It would be hard to find anything which would be more startling to an audience. And you can do it!

How? When you're handed the face-down deck, you fan it from right to left instead of in the usual way, from left to right. To make the evenest possible fan, I usually hold the front edge of the deck between the thumb and left fingers, the rear edge with my right thumb and fingers, and flex the deck as I fan. If you've ever made a card "rosette" you have fanned cards with this motion. A clean deck fans more evenly than a dirty one. All you have to do is fan the deck evenly.

Why fan the deck from right to left instead of from left to right? Because when a deck of cards is fanned in such a way, every card in the deck will be blank except for the face card on the bottom of the deck. The spectator will only see one card—the bottom one.

When you put the deck behind your back, it is the bottom card, of course, that you remove and put face down on the table.

I usually begin the trick by saying to the spectator, "You and I are going to perform an experiment in mental telepathy. If it's to be successful, your part in the experiment is actually far more important than mine. Don't worry about it. If you follow instructions explicitly, we'll perform the most amazing test of telepathy this audience has ever seen."

I always congratulate the assisting spectator at the conclusion of the trick. "You were great!" I say. And to the rest of the audience, "You don't realize it, but the success of this test depended far more on him than on me. How about a hand for him?"

In 25 years of doing this trick, I have only once had the assisting spectator blow the whistle on me. And here's exactly what happened.

The uncooperative spectator blurted, "But I only saw one card! The rest of the cards were blank."

I smiled. "You *thought* you saw just one card, which is exactly what I intended. Actually, you saw

52 cards." I handed the deck to another spectator "See how many blank cards you can find in the deck."

The spectator's lack of cooperation didn't hurt the trick a bit. The audience felt that if I could make my subject see only one card in an evenly fanned pack of 52, my telepathic powers must be rather remarkable.

That spectator was an exception. The volunteer assistant normally gets a big kick out of being on the inside. He feels important. He knows how the trick was done and nobody else does. If he keeps his information a secret, he keeps everyone else mystified. If he blabs, they know just as much as he does, and he isn't about to have that happen.

When I first began doing the trick, I tried to pick a good-natured, easy-going type of assistant. After a few performances, I took them as they came.

And even the assistant, who knows he only saw one card, wonders *how* you were able to fan the cards evenly and still have only one card face visible to him.

This trick is so good that I want to caution you not to abuse it. Don't do it at a bridge table with only three people as your audience. Use it when you have a fairly large group that you want to impress.

For a small group, even for one person, here's a simple little trick that depends on the Magician's Choice I've previously mentioned. I call it:

THREE-WAY PREDICTION

On a slip of paper, print the letter "C". Next to it, draw a small triangle. And to the right of the triangle, print the numeral "7". Fold the slip and have it in readiness.

You toss the folded paper onto the table, saying that it contains a prediction. On another sheet of paper, you print a row of five letters:

A B C D E

Say to the subject, "I want you to draw a circle around any one of these letters.

Usually, the circle will be drawn around the "C." Fine! If it isn't, there's no real problem. You call on Magician's Choice. Say it's drawn around the "B." Say to the spectator, "Now draw a circle around

another letter." If it's the "C," you say, "You've narrowed your choice down to two letters." You print A, B and C beneath the first line and tell him to put an X through either one. If he puts the X through the C, you say, "So your final choice is C." If he puts it through the B, you say, "That leaves the C."

If he should draw his first circle around a letter other than the C and his second circle around, say, the D, you say, "That leaves A C E," printing the three letters on a second line. "Now put an X on one of them." If the X isn't put on the middle letter, say, "That narrows it down to two letters," printing the two remaining letters on a third line. "Put a check mark beneath either of them."

Whatever the spectator does, you contrive to wind up with the letter C.

Then you say, "Now beneath the letter C, I want you to draw any simple geometrical figure—a parallelogram, hexagon, triangle, tetrahedron, octagon, or whatever you choose."

The triangle is nearly always the choice. If it isn't, have him make a second geometrical figure beside the first, "So we'll have a choice." Seldom are as many as three figures required to get a triangle. If you need as many as three, go into the circle, X and check mark routine.

Then you say, "Now write down any numeral, one through nine." Seven is the commonest choice. If seven isn't chosen, ask for a second numeral. If you get any two that add to seven, have them added together. If you get a 9 and 2 or an 8 and 1, have the smaller subtracted from the larger. If you get numbers that won't work out to 7, keep going. I've never had more than five numerals without getting a seven. With five, a 7 included, you go into the same routine as with the ABCDE letters. By Magician's Choice, you arrive at a 7.

At this point, you say, "You have arrived at C, triangle, 7. Would you please open my prediction."

The trick is, obviously, better when you get C, triangle, 7 without having to go into Magician's Choice. More often than not, you'll only need Magician's Choice on one of the three items.

A peculiar thing, and one of the reasons why mental magicians believe in ESP, is that the oftener you do this trick, the higher your percentage of clean hits will be. I rarely have to resort to Magician's Choice any more—and when I started doing the trick, I had to call on it quite often.

Here's a completely impromptu mental trick that doesn't require any choices. I call it:

THE THREE-DIGIT TEST

Have the spectator write down a number containing three different digits, like 1,2,3, or 4,6,8. Then have him reverse his three-digit number and subtract the smaller from the larger. Have him concentrate on his result.

If you can get either the first or last digit of the total by watching the top of his pen or pencil as he writes it, you're in like Flynn. The total of the first and last digits will always be 9, and the middle digit of the final number will always be 9. Knowing that the first and last numbers always total 9, it's much less difficult to get one of them from watching the top of the pencil than you'd expect. If you think the third digit is 3, for example, watch for the first. It should be a 6, to confirm your original guess. The two outer digits will be combinations of 1 and 8, 2 and 7, 3 and 6, or 4 and 5, with an occasional 9 and 0. If you're not sure of one or the other, fish for it. Start by saying, "Concentrate on the middle digit. I get the impression that it's a 9. Is that correct? It is. "Now concentrate on the first digit. It's not quite clear, but I think it's a three. Is that right?"

If the spectator says "No," say: "Concentrate on the third digit. Is it a 7?" If he says "Yes," you know that the first digit is a 2.

Lightning Addition

A college math teacher showed this one to his students and impressed them with his ability to do lightning calculation.

He had a student write three numbers in a column, each number having an identical number of figures in it. "To make it more difficult," he suggested, "every figure in each number should be different from the others in that number."

As soon as the student had written his column of three numbers, the teacher put two additional numbers beneath them. He instantly announced the total as he handed the pad of paper to the student for addition, and he was always right.

All there was to it was that the teacher wrote figures in his first number that would total 9 in each line if added to the spectator's second number. For example, if the student's second number was 42718, the teacher wrote 57281 as the fourth number. For the teacher's second number, he followed the same procedure with the student's third number. If it were 81765, the teacher's second number became 18234.

Now, all he had to do to get the total was look at the student's first number, take away 2 from the end of it and put the 2 in front of the number. For example, if the student's first number were 96543, the teacher would immediately announce the total, 296541.

If the last digit of the first number is a 1, your subtraction of two affects the final two figures. For example, if the student's first number were 26541, the teacher's total would be 226539.

On rare occasions, I've had to come up with the middle digit, 9, and then say, "The second and third digits come through clearly, but the first is a complete blank. What is it?" When he tells you, you give the third digit without any chance of missing. You've only hit two out of three, but that's not bad for mental telepathy with an inexperienced subject.

The next trick is a particularly strong one for audiences of any size from 6 to 600 people. A version of it originally appeared in my book, *You, Too, Can Read Minds,* a book for advanced mental magicians. I call it:

MONEY TALKS

Five or six crisp, new $1 bills are folded identically, so that it's impossible to tell one from another. They're dropped into a cereal bowl or even a cup. A member of the audience is invited to remove one of the bills and have the serial number on it copied by another spectator, for future reference. He then refolds the bill so that it resembles the others, replaces it in the bowl and mixes the bills around. He admits that it would be impossible for him to pick the bill from among the others.

He now holds the left wrist of a third spectator, who is instructed to reach into the bowl and remove dollar bills, one at a time. He is to hand them to you until he decides to stop. If he doesn't stop until he picks up the last bill remaining in the bowl, that is the one of his choice.

Whenever he stops, regardless of how many bills remain in the bowl, he is told to give the bill of his choice to the spectator who copied the serial number on the bill chosen by the first spectator. The custodian

of the serial number confirms that he has selected the same bill as the one picked by the man who is holding his wrist.

He is told to concentrate on the serial number, and you haltingly divine it, digit by digit.

Pretty good, huh?

As in the Dollar Bill in Cigarette trick described elsewhere in this book, you erase the last digit of the serial number on new bills that run in sequence.

For this trick, you get nine new bills in sequence, and you erase the final digit on all of them, with a rubber eraser.

What you say explains why you use your own bills instead of borrowed ones.

"For this test," you say, "there must be no possibility that anyone could distinguish one bill from another. It wouldn't mean much if it were done with used bills that could be identified. And so I went to the bank and got brand new, crisp bills, fresh from the mint. They're folded identically, so that every one looks exactly like the others."

When the first spectator selects a bill from the bowl and has the serial number copied, he is cautioned to refold it on the original creases, exactly as it was. He is then instructed to mix the bills up in the bowl so that he can't tell one from another.

When the second spectator hands bills to you, one at a time, put each one, still folded, directly into your pocket. Should he stop on a bill before the last one, remove whatever bills are left in the bowl, counting them, and saying, "You had two (or whatever the number may be) more bills to choose from, but this is the one you took." Put the remaining bills into your pocket.

Whatever you do, don't say anything about the bills

"having different serial numbers." Take it for granted that *every* bill has a different serial number and that nobody could possibly have the ridiculous idea that the numbers might be identical.

Buildup is important in this trick. Make a big thing of having the first spectator hold the second one's left wrist, explaining that the muscular contact will cause the second spectator to unconsciously do what the first spectator desires. Don't hurry the trick. Everything should be done deliberately, so that the audience gets the full impact.

SIMPLE BOOK TEST

So-called "book tests" are always among the most impressive items in the mental magician's repertoire. Some of them require mechanical equipment and some require an elaborate setup.

This is a book test that can be done any time, anywhere, with no advance warning.

Basically, a book test involves having a spectator or committee pick a certain word on a certain page of a book. The mental magician then divines the chosen word.

In this version, you ask any spectator to pick any book at random from any bookshelf. You flip open the book and show that it is unprepared, that there are a certain number of pages in it, and that the words on each page are different. You hand the book to somebody to hold.

You hand someone a pad of paper and pencil and ask that a number of two different digits be thought of. The spectator is directed to write down his mentally selected number, reverse it, and subtract the smaller from the larger. He is then to add together the digits of the total thus arrived at. For example, if the total were 61, he would get 7. If it were 32, he would get 5. Whatever that final number is, he is to open the book to that page number and concentrate on the first word on the page.

You build up the revelation to suit your fancy, either getting the word a letter at a time or getting a mental picture of what the word means and finally, in one flash, the word.

How? When you showed that the book was unprepared, you deliberately turned to page 9 and got a quick glimpse of the first word on that page. You continued, of course, flipping pages rather quickly and casually.

Why did you remember the first word on **Page 9**?

ESP Knockout

Here's a trick that dealers would probably sell for $10. The letter from an old friend is self-explanatory.

"Dear George—Sure, you have permission to publish my ESP card trick. It's so simple that most magicians won't even bother to try it, and yet, it's a high spot in my club act.

"I use the Jumbo size ESP cards, although there's no reason the smaller size wouldn't work. I made two stands, each to hold a display of five cards. To make a stand, you trace around five ESP cards with a pencil on a piece of fairly thick plywood or composition board, lining up the cards in a row, an inch apart and flush with the top of the board or ¼-inch above it. Since the tops of the cards are flush, you mark around only three sides of them. Then you cut away (maybe I mean cut out) the outlines of the cards. You now screw or cement this cut-away board to a solid one the same size and spray-paint the whole thing dead black. You then cement or tack a ½-inch white molding around the four sides of the front. You now have a display rack with five slots, each of which will hold an ESP card inserted from the top opening. You then cut four pieces of cardboard to the size of an ESP card except for being ¼-inch short. These, too, are painted dead black. You make five sets of such black cards.

"Next, you lay out five sets of five ESP cards, all in the same order, and insert a black cardboard between every two cards. There are actually nine cards

in every set. You insert these five sets into one of the display racks, back out.

"You show this rack, along with the empty one. You hand a set of five ESP cards to a spectator along with the empty rack and tell him to insert the cards into the slots in any order he likes, faces out.

"Once he has done this, you display the racks, side by side. Since your five back-out cards in each slot are separated by short pieces of cardboard, it's a simple matter to pull out either one, two, three, four or all five cards from a slot and turn it or them around, so that the face will match that of the spectator's corresponding card. The black separator cardboard keeps any remaining cards in a slot from showing, and the sides of each slot keep the cards lined up as one while you lift them out and turn them around.

"You show the audience that the spectator arranged his five cards in the same order as those you previously placed face-down in one rack. For ease in handling, you may want to make the open slots a ¼-inch shorter than the cards, with the front molding hiding this. You turn the back-out cards to face the audience as quickly as possible, so that the thickness of the card(s) isn't noticed.

"The whole thing looks so innocent that nobody has ever asked to examine anything—not that I'd let them. Good luck with it.

Sincerely,
Mentalo"

Because you knew that 9 would be the Page Number ultimately arrived at. If the subtraction of the smaller from the larger two-digit number contains two digits, they will always add to 9. If it consists of only one digit, that digit will be a 9.

Don't worry about anyone seeing you getting the first word on Page 9 when you show the book. Unless you're pathetically obvious about it, such a thing will never happen. For one thing, the spectators don't know what the trick is going to be at the time you show the book. For another thing, it is astonishingly easy to get the first word on Page 9 quickly.

There are stronger book tests, but none simpler or easier.

The "9" page number is the weak part of the trick. Let's say you want a higher page number, like, for example, 36. Look at the first word on Page 36 and remember it. Then have someone write a single digit on your pad of paper. Have someone else write another digit directly beneath it. Keep adding as you go along. Whenever the total is within 9 of 36, stop. Say, "Now I want somebody else to add the numbers these people have written down." Boldly and quickly, write the digit that will bring the total to 36, right beneath the last number a spectator has written. Quickly and strongly, draw a line beneath the numbers and have another spectator, seated some distance from the last number picker, if possible, add. Have him announce his total.

If you're worried about getting caught while writing that last digit, you can say, "I'll draw a line beneath the numbers, and you add them." But take my word for it, the fact that you add a number to the line of digits is never noticed.

A total somewhere between 30 and 40 is about right. With single digits being written by each spectator, you'll get at least four numbers—and fewer would be bad, because the person who totals them might possibly remember that only three people wrote down digits.

A much stronger method requires preparation and a gimmick. Cut a slot in the lid of an old candy box. Tape a shallow sack inside the cover, around the slit so that any folded slip dropped through the slit would go into the sack, not into the box.

Write the same number on each of seven or eight slips, say 78, fold the slips, put them into the box and put the gimmicked lid on it. Now, have seven or eight people think of page numbers from one to 300, or whatever the last page of the book happens to be. Pick up the box, have them drop their slips through the slot, give the box a shake, remove the lid and have someone select one of the slips. Put the lid back on the box and put it back into your brief case or whatever you're carrying your equipment in. This simple force of a number, the invention of Otis Manning, has been used by many magicians in the performance of a wide variety of mental tricks. While it is not impromptu, it is far more convincing than having slips put into a "changing bag" or other contrivance that gives the impression of being tricky. It looks so innocent that nobody thinks a thing about it.

The whole trick hinges on forcing a page number. Getting the first word on the selected page is nothing. You now have three strong, simple, easy methods of forcing the number of your choice, two of them completely impromptu.

A book test is one of the strongest mental magic tests in existence. When reporters review a mental magician's performance, they almost invariably pick out the divination of a word from a book as one of the highlights of the performance.

Now, I'm going to give you an entirely different kind of book test that's an absolute knockout—a test in which you *predict* the word that will be chosen. And you use a metropolitan telephone directory for it. Sorry, most small-town directories won't do, for a reason which will eventually be evident.

You say, "I'm going to write a prediction. Once having written it, I won't touch it again. I'll put it into the hands of a spectator who will open it and show it at the proper time."

You have previously looked through a metropolitan phone book and found a last name which occupies a full page or more of listings. Don't pick the obvious Smith or Jones. In the Chicago directory, I have often used the name, "Miller." In any large city, you'll be surprised at the number of names that meet the necessary qualification. You print this name, preferably with a heavy marking pen, on a sheet of paper, large enough so that everyone will be able to see it at the proper time. I sometimes print it on a length of adding machine paper, in advance of performance, roll up the paper, put a rubber band around it and say, "I've written a prediction in advance."

What if you're doing the trick in a locality that has too small a phone book? You carry a metropolitan phone book with you and say, "For the purposes of this experiment, I won't use the local phone book, which would make what I'm about to do much easier, but will use one of the largest telephone directories in the world."

At this point, you employ a brazen tactic that is so audacious it's never questioned. You hand the phone book to a member of the audience and instruct him, "Riffle slowly through the pages. When a second spectator says stop, quit riffling and hold your finger at that spot."

You select another spectator to say "Stop" whenever the spirit moves him. He does.

You go immediately to the first spectator who is holding the phone book, a break at the point where he quit riffling pages. "All we care about," you announce, "is the Page Number, which happens to be—". You glance at the page number. Whatever it is, you call it as the page number on which the name "Miller" or whatever name you selected, happens to occupy the whole page. Let's say it's 374. You say, "All we care about is the page number, which happens to be 374." You close the book immediately and hand it to a third spectator.

"I want you to open the book to the page that was chosen by chance—Page No. 374," you instruct him. "Hold the book open on your lap." You take his right hand. "Point your forefinger. Don't look at the page." You move his hand in a small circle above the page and continue, "When I release your hand, let your finger drop to the page."

He does, and you ask, "What's the last name your finger happened to light on?"

He looks, and says, "Miller."

You close the phone book, thank him for his expert telepathic sensitivity, and instruct the spectator who is holding your prediction to open it. The name, "Miller," is printed on it in bold letters.

With a good buildup, this trick is one that will be talked about long after your performance. Be sure that everyone realizes the spectator let his forefinger drop to a name anywhere on the page. And close the phone book as soon as he's identified the name his finger touches.

If you don't like the bare-faced method of arriving at a page number, you may want to use the Otis Manning candy box, having a number of people write page numbers from 1 to 1,000 on slips of paper and putting them into the slot. Let me assure you, it isn't necessary. The fact that your prediction is written *before* a page is selected and that the spectator lets his finger fall wherever it may on the page eliminates any tendency to think that you may have miscalled the number.

INTERMEDIARY

This is a trick with numbers that has an unusual twist. A member of your audience divines the total of three numbers, a total that is apparently unknown to anyone other than the person who added the numbers together.

Hand a pad of paper and pencil to a spectator and ask him to write any three-digit number on it. Take the pencil and paper from him, go to a second spectator and ask him to "give me another three-digit number." He whispers the number to you and you apparently write it down as you move on to a third spectator, some distance removed from the second.

What you actually do is write beneath the first three digit number numerals that will bring the total of the two lines to 999. If a digit is 9, you write 0. If it's a six, you write three. Each two digits, reading up and down, total 9.

You ask a third person to write a three digit number beneath the two "that two other people have selected." handing him the pencil and pad of paper.

You get a quick glance at the third number, which is the only one that concerns you, as you hand the pad to a fourth person, instructing him to add the three numbers.

You, of course, already know the total. How? Whatever the third three-digit number is, subtract one from the end number and put it in front of the first numeral. For example, if the third number is 653, you know that the total of the three numbers is 1,652.

While the fourth spectator is adding the three numbers, you go to still a fifth spectator, near the one who is totaling the numbers, and say, "Neither you nor I knows the total of the numbers—but the gentleman who is now adding them will have that information. We're going to use him as a transmitter and you as a receiver, with me as a medium or intermediary." You grasp the closest wrist of the fifth spectator with your right hand. "Don't reveal your total," you say to the fourth spectator, "but let us know as soon as you have it."

When he says he has a total, you touch your left fingers lightly to his forehead and say to the fifth spectator, "We'll arrive at the correct figure one step at a time. We'll start with the first digit of the total. I'll call numerals from one through nine and zero, slowly, in random order. Whenever you feel you're getting a thought impulse from me, name that number."

You begin calling digits at random *not* starting with one. When you call "One" you give his wrist a little twitch with your right thumb, which is on the underside of his wrist. With some subjects, it is necessary to give almost a pinch on the first couple of digits, to let them get the idea.

If the subject doesn't catch what he is to do, thank him and try a different subject. Say to this second one, "You are to obey any impulse, mental, physical or auditory which you may receive. When you get the impulse, call out the number."

You call out digits, "twitching" his wrist at the proper time, until he's arrived at the number, 1,652, a digit at a time.

A friend of mine has an unusual way of signaling the spectator the proper digit. He has the bulb-end of one of those little "plate lifter" novelty devices pinned to his shirt pocket, beneath his coat. The other end, with the squeeze-bulb that activates the little soft-rubber bladder, is in his left-hand pants pocket. He instructs the spectator to hold his right hand firmly over the mentalist's heart. As he calls the digits, he squeezes the bulb in his pants pocket at the proper time. The spectator is always astonished, and there's certainly a pronounced clue to him as to the right digit.

When you get a really cooperative subject, there's an absolutely superlative way to signal the digits to

him, a method that is not only undetectable to the audience but leaves the subject in the dark. He will actually think he's received thought impulses from you.

Have him hold his open fingers lightly against either your right or left temple, and have the person who did the addition call out digits, slowly. When you want to signal the subject a digit, you merely press your teeth firmly together. "Clenching your jaw" might be one way to describe the movement.

Don't make a big thing of it. You don't *have* to clench the jaw pronouncedly. Just make a solid contact between the upper and lower teeth. Put your own fingers to your temple and try it. You'll feel a definite "bump" from the temple with very little jaw pressure.

The only explanation the subject can possibly give to account for getting the numbers right is that he "felt something in his fingers".

Mention of heartbeats reminds me of a weird trick that was taught me by an old-time performer named Fox. He had a hypnosis and mental show, and he got reputable physicians to swear that when Fox told a hypnotic subject his pulse would stop, it stopped.

STOPPING THE PULSE

To my way of thinking, it's not an audience trick, because nobody sees anything happen, but I used it years ago with hilarious results.

I was a college student, and had to undergo the customary physical examination, which was given by interns and medical students, as a rule. I knew that, as usual, somebody would take my pulse.

The intern who drew the assignment started to take my pulse, and then stopped, horrified. "You—your pulse has stopped," he declared.

I nodded, bored. "It does that all the time," I told him.

He called a second intern over. This fellow felt my wrist and said to the first one, "You're nuts. He has a good, strong pulse." His smirk changed to a look of horror. "He *did* have a good pulse. Now, it's gone."

A young nurse was brought into the picture, and she insisted that my pulse was as steady as anyone's.

"Then you make the count," the first intern said. She shrugged, nodded and took my wrist again.

"I had it," she mumbled, frowning. She looked at me sharply. "What's going on here?" she demanded.

"I guess you're taking my pulse," I replied. "Aren't you?"

The three got into a heated discussion as to whether they should report the problem to a superior. The nurse and the first intern were in favor of it, but the second intern was just as firmly opposed. "We'd just get involved in a big tsimmis," he said. "What the hell, these are supposed to be routine examinations."

"But this isn't a routine pulse," the other intern pointed out.

"You ever had any heart trouble, fellah?" the second intern asked me.

"Not that I know of," I answered.

"You must have had your pulse taken before."

"Oh, sure."

"Any problems?"

"Not that I was aware of."

He turned to the other two. "See? No problems."

"But Good Lord, Joe, a pulse that stops completely *is* a problem," the first intern objected.

The other one shook his head. "You're getting way behind. Look—a big line. Mark it normal and run the guy through or you're gonna jam up the whole routine."

Disrupting the routine was unthinkable. The first intern sighed, marked my pulse normal and passed me through.

Years later, I stopped my pulse for a doctor employed by an insurance company to give physical examinations to insurance applicants. He felt my wrist, probed briefly with his fingers, frowned and recorded a normal pulse beat, without comment.

How do you stop your pulse-beat? Nothing to it. Fox did it with a two-inch block of wood held under the armpit. Heavy pressure of the arm against the wooden block did the trick. Release of the pressure caused the beat to resume. I later learned that, for me, a golf ball worked just as well as the block of wood.

Blackstone did an impromptu version with a tightly knotted handkerchief pressed into his armpit.

MESSAGE READING

Secretly getting possession of something written down by a spectator is the backbone of mental magic. There are many, many ways of doing it, but, unfortunately, most of them are impractical for the inexperienced amateur.

The commonest impromptu method of obtaining written information is known in magic as the "torn center steal." A little rectangle of paper is folded into quarters, to make what the mental magician calls a "billet." It is unfolded, the mentalist draws an oval in the center of it, and asks the spectator to write, say, the name of any city in the world in the oval. He is instructed to refold the paper, which he does. The mentalist takes the folded slip, tears it into small pieces and burns them in an ash-tray.

Well, not quite. He burns all but one torn piece— the piece that was the center of the slip. He pulls this back with his left thumb as he drops the remaining pieces into an ash tray. And the tiny piece he holds back contains the oval.

A good mentalist does it casually and smoothly. I've never seen a rank amateur do it even passably well. He telegraphs everything that's happening, and he has egg all over his face. His attempt to read what's written on the little scrap of paper is so crude it's pitiful. He seldom fools anyone except himself.

What mental magicians call "the billet switch" is another fine way of getting written information, but again, not for the beginner. This involves having a duplicate billet hidden in the left hand. The right fingers take the folded billet, with writing on the inside, from the spectator. The fingers of both hands apparently crease the folds more firmly—and the blank slip has been substituted for the one with writing on it.

Not only the amateur fails to do this convincingly. I've seen successful professionals whose billet switch left much to be desired. The move requires skillful palming of the blank slip and a deft switch of it for the one with writing on it. Then the mentalist has the problem of getting the written slip unfolded and reading it without anyone being aware of what he's doing. This is sleight of hand that requires real skill. I know one professional who's been doing a billet switch for years who practices the various moves involved for a full hour every day.

Your best bet for a semi-impromptu method of getting written information involves an innocent-looking little gimmick I invented and released to the mental magic fraternity over twenty years ago. I call it:

MATCHBOOK MIND READING

It works on the same principle as the expensive and ingenious "file board" used by many professionals. In other words, it depends on getting a carbon impression of the spectator's writing. A file board would be completely out of place under most circumstances under which a modern mental magician works, but the matchbook gimmick is natural, normal and logical.

It's a do-it-yourself piece of equipment. I don't know of any place where you can buy it.

To start with, you have to peel the cover of a matchbook. By this, I mean that you separate the cardboard body of the cover from the printed paper outside surface.

You then have two covers, the inner one gray cardboard and the outer one a printed surface with some of the gray cardboard adhering to its inner surface.

If you rough one corner of the matchbook cover and start peeling the two surfaces apart from there, you shouldn't have too much trouble. If the problem of getting the two surfaces apart without tearing either one looks too difficult, soak the cover in water. While it is saturated, the two surfaces will peel apart with ease. Dry them out, preferably under a warm iron, so that they won't curl.

Next, you cut an opening in the gray cardboard part of the cover—an oblong hole almost as large as the space occupied by the twenty matches. The gray part of the cover that would normally fold down and clip under the front edge of the matchbook is left intact; just the back part has a hole in it.

You place a piece of good carbon paper between this opening and the printed part of the back, carbon impression side facing the opening. You cut the carbon paper to a width the tiniest fraction of an inch less than the width of the covers. You put rubber

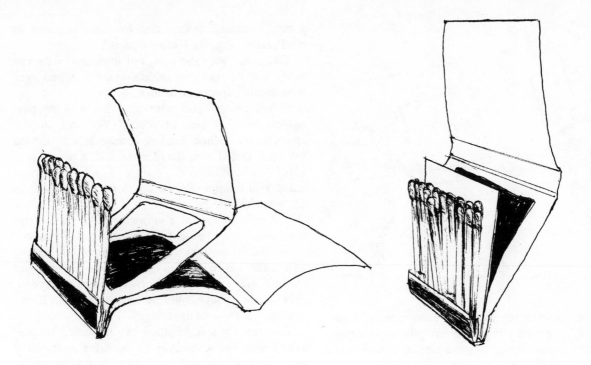

cement on the back side of the carbon paper and cement it to the thin exterior cover that has printing on the outside. Then you rubber cement the gray inner surface to the outer one.

You can handle this matchbook with reasonable freedom. From the outside, it looks like any other matchbook. With the book open, the carbon is hidden by the matches, unless you deliberately expose the inner back surface. Between the matches and the carbon, you insert a piece of business card or cardboard of similar thickness, cut to the proper size.

That's all there is to the matchbook gimmick. You'll find it's practical to make four or five of them at once, and it's a good idea to have a couple of them in your pockets.

When you're ready to perform, hand a spectator a little slip of paper about the size of the folded matchbook surface. You can tear a slip off a bridge score pad or even from the margin of a newspaper. The matchbook is still in your pocket.

Get the spectator to stand beside you, away from any table or writing surface. "Please stand apart from the others," you explain, "so that nobody can possibly see what you're doing. I want you to think of any city in the world. Think hard. In order to focus your mind on the city and nothing else, print its name on this little slip of paper. Here."

You hand the spectator the slip and a stubby, hard-lead pencil.

"As soon as you've fixed the name in your mind by printing it, you'll burn the slip." You pull out your special matchbook. "Don't ever let me touch the slip and fold it as soon as you've finished. Oh, you'll need something to write on, won't you? Here." You put the packet of paper matches under the slip in his hand.

"Now turn your back to me so that I can't see what you're writing, and print the city's name. Finished? Then fold the slip and drop it into an ash tray."

As he does this, you take the pack of matches from him, tear out a match, strike it and hand it to him. As you tear out the match with your right fingers, holding the packet in your left hand, it's easy to shove the little piece of cardboard into your left palm.

All eyes are on the spectator as he ignites the slip. Turn your back while it's burning, read the carbon impression, and put the matchbook and little piece of cardboard back into your pocket.

You have the information, and all that remains is to build up your divination.

You can use the carbon matchbook to get information on numbers, names of people, cities, even questions.

If there's a simpler, cleaner, more innocent method of getting written information, I've never found it.

A strong method that requires performing conditions where nobody can see the gimmick is:

THE WINDOW ENVELOPE

This is particularly effective under the right conditions. Whatever you do, don't let its simplicity get you so enthusiastic that you overdo its use.

Have a little packet of end-opening envelopes of the type commonly called "pay envelopes." With a razor blade, cut away most of the surface of the address side of one envelope. You start your cut about half an inch below the flap, so that the opening won't be visible from the flap side. The opening extends from this top to the bottom, leaving not much more than a quarter-inch paper ledge on three sides.

117

In addition to the packet of envelopes, with the prepared one on the bottom of the pile, flap-side up, you have some cards, cut to a size so that they fit fairly snugly into the envelopes.

You hand a spectator one of the cards and tell him that while your back is turned, he is to make a drawing on the card—"Something simple; I'm no artist." When he has the drawing completed, he is to turn it face down and write his initials on the back. When he's completed his drawing, you turn to face him, turn over the pile of envelopes so that the prepared one is on top, and ask him to slide the card, still face down, into the envelope. You immediately moisten the gummed surface and seal the envelope. You now prop the envelope up against a book or other solid object, flap side to the spectators. In removing the envelope from the packet to prop it up where it will be "visible to everyone," you get a fine view of the drawing.

You now take another of the cards and say, "I'm going to make a drawing, too. Please concentrate on

yours, because I want mine to come as close to duplicating yours as I can make it."

You make your drawing, put it in one of the envelopes, seal it, put your initials on the flap, and hand it to another spectator to hold.

"My drawing," you point out, "is out of my possession before I look at yours." You pick up the spectator's envelope, holding it address side toward the floor, and clip off the flap end with a pair of scissors. You reach into the open end and pull out the card. You crumple up the envelope and throw it in the wastebasket.

You hold the spectator's drawing up and nod. "You transmitted your thoughts to me very well," you say. You hand the scissors to the spectator who is holding your envelope, tell him to remove your drawing, and the two are now held up for everyone's inspection, side by side. They should be almost identical, if you can draw a copy of anything.

I invented a stage method of duplicating a spectator's drawing, which is in my book for professional mental magicians, *You, Too, Can Be a Mindreader.* It would be most impractical for close-up use and requires somewhat complicated special equipment— much more complicated than a window envelope.

A CLEAN REVELATION

Another good method of getting written information depends on—you'd never guess—a bar of white soap! That's right—soap.

You have a small note pad. You lift up the top sheet, turn it over, and rub the back of it briskly with the soap. When there's a thin waxy soap coating on the back of the paper, you fold the sheet back into its original position, so that the soaped side is now the under side.

Anything written on the top sheet when it is prepared like this will leave a wax impression on the

second sheet. Have the spectator do his writing, tear off the page, fold it and put it into his pocket.

He will not see anything wrong with the second page. You have to know what you're looking for to see it. When the second page is held at a certain angle so that the light hits it right, the wax impression will be visible.

As an excuse for continuing to use the pad, I always do some writing on the second sheet, something that pertains to the divination. As soon as I've seen the wax impression, I do a little more writing, find what I've written unsatisfactory, tear off the page, crumple it up and throw it away. The points I write down on the *next* sheet begin to make sense.

THE SEALED QUESTION ANSWERING ACT

The question-answering act, once so popular and profitable, is now old-hat. Too many unscrupulous charlatans used it for illegal fortune-telling purposes. Some of them bilked question-askers out of substantial sums of money.

Perhaps the best reason for not doing a question-answering act is that some members of your audience will believe you're infallible, that your answers are bound to be right. And, let's face it, most of us simply aren't qualified to answer questions about another person's personal affairs, particularly when we know none of the background leading up to the questions.

Certainly, only a doctor is legally qualified to give medical advice. A lawyer should be more competent to give legal advice than anyone else. The area of social and mental problems is equally sticky.

As for giving advice about financial matters, a so-called mentalist could do irreparable financial damage. Even a qualified financial counselor usually hedges his advice with numerous qualifications.

Back in the question-answering act's heyday, I heard mentalists answer questions with advice that should have gotten them jailed. Their sole interest was in coming up with sensational answers, and the effect of their words on their listeners meant nothing to them.

An intelligent, informed, conscientious performer can still have a question-answering segment in his performance, but he's careful not to diagnose, not to accuse anyone of anything, not to advise about money matters, not to give legal advice and not to recommend taking any specific course of action. In short, he shows his audience that he can "get" their questions —but he doesn't answer them. He not only talks in generalities, but much of what he says is double-talk.

There are many, many question-answering acts that can be purchased from magic supply houses. Some of them cost hundreds of dollars. Many of them require more than one person. Some of them, conceived by old-timers who worked big stage presentations, require not an assistant but a whole crew.

The best of the lot, in my opinion, is a method called Hewitt's "Modern Mindreading." The late Ted Annemann, most prolific of all mental magic inventors, first marketed it, and it is still being sold by magical supply houses. The price is low.

There is an expensive "wired wireless" method of answering questions which, at first glance, would seem to be just about perfect. It requires a team. One of the mindreaders goes through the audience and asks people to whisper their questions to him. The medium, on the platform, immediately answers. The member of the team who goes through the audience wears a tiny concealed microphone and the medium wears a concealed earphone.

It's not as good as it sounds. The medium has to keep talking, and hearing and retaining the questions under the circumstances is extremely difficult. If the medium doesn't grasp the question, he or she can hardly say, "Would you mind repeating that, please?" Smooth performance requires long and arduous practice.

Oral code methods of getting questions are highly impractical for most people. A team must first learn a complicated code—and the simplest of these aren't easy. Once both members of the team are thoroughly acquainted with the code, constant practice is required to keep the routine going smoothly. One mentalist who had been forced to take long layoffs while teaching a series of attractive young ladies his code, only to have them leave, reached the conclusion, "The only practical way to do a code act is to marry your assistant."

Another type of code act which still exists is the one in which the medium is blindfolded and the "sender" goes through the audience, touching various objects that are held out to him. The medium identifies and describes the objects.

The most amazing variation of this act I ever saw was one used by a mentalist who had grown tired of teaching his code to a series of assistants. He knew from experience what the preponderance of objects held out for his inspection would be. He typed a list of these on a little card, in a specific order, and his assistant held this list palmed in her left hand. Although blindfolded, she could see her hand perfectly by looking down the sides of her nose.

The mentalist roamed through the audience, touching the objects listed on the card, in order. If he coughed, it was a signal to his assistant to skip the next object on the list. Anything held up for his inspection that wasn't on the list was completely ignored.

He worked fast, and he tore all over the audience, apparently touching objects at random but looking wildly for the next one on the list. All of them were common objects, such as glasses, pens, wrist watches, rings, handkerchiefs, keys, purses, leather bags, hats, tie tacks and pocket combs. He kept up a running fire of chatter and didn't give his assistant time to describe any item—which she couldn't have done.

Surprisingly, the act pleased and mystified audiences, and was known as "the fastest mindreading act in the business."

"IN THE DARK" MINDREADING

On occasion, I've worked a message reading routine at parties that certainly is the ultimate in simplicity. You have to be prepared to do it, and the preparation consists of a specially prepared fountain-pen flashlight.

The glass over the bulb is covered with a layer of red tissue paper. This is held in place by black tape, applied so that only a tiny bit of red tissue is left exposed. A little experimentation is necessary to arrive at the pinpoint of red light that will make the writing on a card visible and won't be seen by your audience. When I'm going to do the trick, I have a heavy black silk handkerchief in my pocket and throw it over my hands before turning on the flashlight.

Questions or messages are written on the cards by members of the audience, and one of them gathers up the cards. He is instructed to stand beside me, the little pile of cards in hand, and not to hand them to me until the lights are turned off and the room is in complete darkness. He then fumbles his way back to his seat.

Once the room is dark, I pull out the handkerchief, throw it over my hands, and apply the flashlight beam to one of the cards. The handkerchief is spread in such a way that it masks any possible light from the audience but doesn't conceal the cards from my eyes.

I've had people tell me it's the most baffling demonstration of message reading they've ever seen. With the room in complete darkness, there seems to be no possible way for anybody to read anything.

A friend to whom I revealed the secret told me that he got caught with it the first time he tried it when one of the spectators tiptoed up behind him. After that experience, he said, he always did the trick while seated in a corner of the room, with solid walls on both sides and behind him.

A MESSAGE FROM ZOGRAPHOS

I particularly like this next trick because of the story I've worked out to go with it, but it would be a marvelous trick with no story at all.

You need one prop for it—a piece of heavy cardboard about four inches wide by six inches long. On one side of it, pencil in a card game score, with the game having been played by "Z" and "O", with "Z" the big winner. My cardboard has a gin rummy score on it, with "Z" winning three blitzes.

On the other side of the card, you write with a marking or show-card pen, "The last card removed from the deck will be the nine of Diamonds. Natch! What else? Turn it over and see. Nick Zographos."

Whenever you plan on doing this trick, you remove the nine of Diamonds from a deck of cards in advance and put it beneath the scorecard, which is message-side down.

When you're ready to perform, the scorecard is either on the table or in your kit, nine of Diamonds in place on the under side.

You hand a deck of cards to a spectator, minus the Nine, and have him shuffle and cut it. He keeps the deck in his hands.

"There's a theory," you say, "that a person's possessions carry a mysterious influence, even after the person has shuffled off this mortal coil. This theory is called psychometry."

You pick up the scorecard, thumb on top, fingers beneath, holding the nine of Diamonds in place on the bottom side.

"This scorecard was the property of Nick Zographos, the most famous member of the famous Greek gambling syndicate. It was used in the last Gin Rummy game he ever played. As you can see, Nick won roughly $8,000—which isn't bad for a half-hour's pleasant work.

"Nick Zographos' favorite gambling game was baccarat. At one time, he lost nearly $700,000 in a week of baccarat play at Cannes. Undaunted, he came into the game again with his last million francs —and bet the entire amount. His first two cards were face cards, which don't count in baccarat, but his third card was the nine of Diamonds, a certain winner. It signified the end of a run of bad luck, and he recouped his entire loss in a few evenings of play.

"From that time on, the nine of Diamonds was his

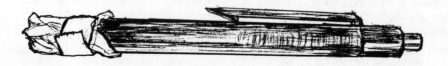

trademark. A tiny replica of it was on all his jewelry. A nine of Diamonds was embroidered on all his linen. His yacht flew a nine of Diamonds flag.

"Now, I want you to deal off cards, one at a time, onto this score card."

As each card is dealt onto the scorecard, which you're holding, you slide it off onto the table top into what forms a discard pile. After a few cards have been dealt off and handled in this way, you continue, "Now, whenever you get the impulse, stop dealing off cards."

You continue to slide off cards onto the discard pile until the spectator stops. At that point, say to him, "You felt an impulse to stop dealing. Now, do you want to use the top card on the discard pile, this one that's still on the scorecard or the one that's on top of the deck?"

If he says "The one that's on top of the deck," you tell him, as you slide off the previous card onto the discard pile, "Of course, it must come in contact with the Zographos scorecard in order for psychometry to work. Deal it off, please."

Whatever he says, you point to the top card of the discard pile and say, "This is now the card of your choice."

You drop the scorecard on top of the discard pile, so that the nine of Diamonds beneath it is added to the top of the pile. "Turn this scorecard over," you direct, "and see what it says on the other side."

He turns over the scorecard and reads the message. "Now," you continue, "follow Nick's instructions and turn up the last card you dealt."

He turns over the top card of the discard pile which is, of course, the nine of Diamonds.

NEWMANN'S NUMBERS

To the best of my knowledge, C.A. George Newmann was the person who made a sensation of the next trick. There have been many variations of it, and the origin has been attributed to four or five different performers, but I'd give the nod to Newmann. Whoever's responsible, it's a superlative trick. It can be performed as a prediction or a divination, whichever you prefer. Over a period of years, I've reached the conclusion that it's better as a divination, for the reason that making a prediction of the total of five five-digit numbers, written down by five different spectators, is too good to be true. A certain type of mentality reaches the conclusion that there must have been a switch of numbers—and that happens to be correct. Of course, the person who figures that out won't have the faintest idea of how the numbers were switched—but I still prefer the divination effect.

You need a small memo pad of plain white paper, about 4 x 6 in size. On the top sheet, you print four or five five-digit numbers, one beneath the other. While Newmann often used five, I prefer four, particularly when doing the trick for less than a couple of dozen people.

The memo pad has no cardboard backing. Whichever side faces up is the top side. On the top sheet, you have the four five-digit numbers—and you try to make them look like they'd been made by four different people.

You add the four numbers carefully, putting the total on another sheet of paper, not on the pad. After checking the total, you pencil it lightly, in small numerals, in the lower left-hand corner of a strip of cardboard. It should be small enough so that your

Pseudo-hypnosis

Here's an impressive demonstration of hypnotism that's easy to do. The magician asks a spectator to look straight ahead and then roll his eyeballs upward. He is instructed to keep them in that position.

He is then told to close his eyes but to keep his eyeballs looking upward.

"Keep your eyeballs looking toward the ceiling," the magician says. "Concentrate on it. Now, try to open your eyes. You can't do it. Keep looking above your head. Try as you will, you can't open your eyes."

And he can't. At least, nobody to date has been able to keep his eyeballs looking upward and open his eyelids while he's doing it.

Mock Sad Ali once tried this pseudo-hypnotic trick on a highly susceptible subject who, when he found he couldn't open his eyes, actually went into a hypnotic trance. The fellow later told everyone in the community that Mock Sad Ali was "a genuine hypnotist."

121

thumb will completely cover the number. It's there only for reference, so that you won't have to memorize the total.

You pick up the memo pad and a pencil and offer it to a spectator, asking him to put down any five-digit number. You take the pad from him and go immediately to a second spectator, then a third and finally a fourth, asking each to put another five-digit number directly below those already on the pad.

Now you move as far from the four number writers as is reasonably possible and tell a fifth spectator that you want him to total the four numbers. Your hand with the memo pad has dropped to your side as you walk to this fifth spectator, and as you hand him the pencil and pad, you have turned the pad over so that what was the bottom page is now the top page. You tell him to draw a line under the four numbers and add them carefully.

Don't worry about anyone turning over the pad. I can truthfully say that I've never had it happen, and Newmann, who performed the trick regularly, said it never happened to him.

I know some performers who use a pad with a spiral binding and a cover, and they flip the pad so that whichever side is on the bottom is concealed by the cover. There's nothing wrong with that, if it gives you added assurance. I've never found it necessary.

As the fifth spectator adds the numbers, you go back to the front and pick up the strip of cardboard and a marking pencil. You walk to a point about three yards in front of the person who's doing the addition. When he finishes, you tell him to double-check to be sure his addition is correct. And then you tell him to concentrate his mind on the first digit of the total. You make a big deal of concentrating, and you write the proper digit, large, on the strip. You don't show it at this point. You tell him to concentrate on the second digit and write a second numeral on the strip. When you've completed divining the total, you ask him to announce his total. He does, and you turn the card slowly toward the audience, showing that your total is identical with his.

You take the pad and pencil from him, stick them in your pocket and acknowledge the applause.

Don't throw away the four numbers written down by four different spectators, the numbers that are on the bottom of the pad. They'll be the four numbers you use the next time you do the trick. Each number is in different handwriting.

The directness and simplicity of this trick make it one of the best in the entire field of mental magic. The physical talent required is the ability to turn over a memo pad, and the ability to handle the pad without exposing the bottom of it at any time.

The *real* talent required is the ability to sell the trick as a demonstration of telepathy. Newmann had that ability to the nth degree. Oddly, he could do the test with a completely innocent memo pad if he chose to, relying on contact mindreading to get the correct total. He used this method because it was easier and required less effort on his part.

A Magic Art

Learning to "read" the top of a full-length pencil as someone is writing with it isn't easy—but it's a knack that can accomplish miracles.

It is much easier to read printed letters than words written in script, and capital letters are more legible from the top of the pencil than lower case ones.

The best way to learn is to print some words, yourself, studying the movement of the pencil top as each letter is put on paper. Once you think you've familiarized yourself with the formations, get a friend to print some words and see if you can grasp them.

The letters will be traced in the air by the pencil top in reverse. Some letters are much easier to get than others. It's not difficult to determine how many letters are contained in a word. Usually, if you can get a few letters clearly in a word, you can "fish" for the others and come up with the correct word.

Most pencil-top readers think reading numerals is easier than reading letters. Since there are only ten numerals and they are all distinctively shaped, this is probably true.

A magician doing mental telepathy who is adept at reading the pencil top can do trick after trick without resorting to anything else.

Give a spectator a typed cocktail menu listing Martini, Bronx, Old Fashioned, Daiquiri, Stinger, Alexander and Gin and Tonic. Tell him to mentally choose one and print it on a little piece of paper for future reference. It is comparatively easy to tell which of those choices he prints.

DOWSING RODS

Kenneth Roberts wrote a book about dowsers, or "water witches," as they're sometimes called. These men use a pair of L-shaped metal rods or a forked willow wand, most commonly to find water but sometimes to find mineral deposits.

In many rural areas, farmers swear by the dowser's ability to locate the best spot for a well. They'll give you stories of repeated unsuccessful attempts to dig a well, followed by bringing in a dowser who immediately found a spot where water would be available from a fairly shallow well.

I've never had any experience with the forked willow wand but have had a lot of fun with the L-shaped rods. They're easy to make. Cut off the top hooked part of a coat-hanger with a pair of wire-snips. Straighten out the remaining wire and then make a 90-degree bend in it about six inches from one end.

Prepare a second one in the same manner. The short ends of the L are the grips. You hold the rods in your fists, which are extended directly out from your body. The rods are spread completely apart so that they form a straight line, parallel with each other. If you'll walk around with a pair of these rods held in that position, sooner or later, they'll come together in front of you, apparently without any physical motivation. I imagine that the moving force is the same one that sets the Sex Indicator in motion.

They'll move together eventually, whether you're looking for anything or not, but it's amusing to conceal a glass of water somewhere in the room and have a spectator try to find it by use of the dowsing rods.

No matter how often you fool around with them, there's something uncanny about the way the rods pull together. I use them as part of a trick, the basic idea of which stemmed from the late Ted Annemann. I had a version of this trick in *You, Too, Can Read Minds,* but the variation I'm going to give you here is simpler and easier. Annemann called the original trick:

PSEUDO-PSYCHOMETRY

You pass out letter envelopes to five members of the audience. They are instructed to put some little personal possession in each of their respective envelopes, which they then seal. Your back is turned while they're doing this. A sixth spectator is told to gather up the five envelopes and mix them. He then hands them to you.

You hold one of the envelopes up to your forehead and "get an impression" of the kind of person whose object is concealed in it. This can be a kind of character analysis and can be both entertaining and accurate, since you know the owner of each object.

How do you know? You passed out envelopes that had been marked. You make a little thumb-nail indentation in the upper left-hand corner of the flap of an envelope. It becomes Envelope No. 1. A nail-nick is made in the flap of Envelope No. 2 half-way between the upper-left-hand corner and the tip of the flap. The same kind of mark is made in Envelope No. 3 at the tip of the flap. No. 4 has its thumb-nail indentation half-way between the flap tip and the right-hand corner, and No. 5 has the mark in the upper right-hand corner.

The envelopes are stacked in order, from one to

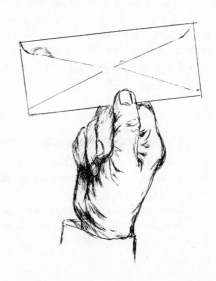

five, flap sides up. As you hand Envelope No. 1 to a spectator, you mentally paint a big, black Number One on his forehead. Handing No. 2 to a second spectator, you form a mental picture of a Number Two on his or her forehead, and use the same technique with the remaining three envelopes and three spectators. You can further simplify identification of the five people by passing out the five numbered envelopes in a pattern, the spectators running from your left to your right in numerical progression. You *must* be able to identify the five people, numbered from 1 to 5.

The rest of the trick is easy. You give each person a little character reading, without identifying him. Then you pick up the dowsing rods, the envelope pressed between your extended fists. You walk among the spectators and tilt the dowsing rods enough to make them come together in front of the proper person. It doesn't take a tilt that is noticeable to achieve the desired movement. Indeed, you have to watch closely to prevent the rods from swinging together before you want them to do it.

With the proper buildup, this trick takes time to do—but it always holds audience interest. I usually ask each person if the character analysis given before he was identified was reasonably accurate. Since I've been careful to make the analysis flattering and have

The Mercedes Act

Joe Mercedes and his wife had a "mental" act in vaudeville for many years that was a sensational headliner all over the world. The act, "Mercedes and Mlle. Stantone," couldn't have been done by many couples. Somehow, the right two people got together.

The act was simple but astounding. Joe passed through the audience and asked people to give him the names of songs, classical or pop, new or old, wellknown or obscure. And Mlle. Stantone, seated onstage at a piano, immediately played a few bars of the selection which had been whispered into Joe's ear. Her musical repertoire must have been prodigious. One magician who saw the act eight times, says, "People requested numbers I'd never even heard of, and she played 'em without the slightest hesitation. In the eight performances I saw, she was never stumped once."

After the demise of vaudeville, Joe came up with an act that tied right in with "talking" pictures. It was a "question-answering" act, in which a filmed Mlle. Stantone answered questions from the screen, in perfect lip sync. It added a new element of mystery to the mindreading act.

For many years following his retirement, Joe was manager of a Wisconsin travel and resort bureau office in Chicago.

included some obvious physical characteristics, I always get a "Yes."

While the trick is excellent, there's a lot of repetition in it, and so it needs a climax. Since you're doing the same thing five times, how do you get a climax?

My solution to the problem is to fail to get "any mental impressions" on Envelope No. 3. No character analysis. I put No. 3 aside, with obvious reluctance. After I've returned Envelopes No. 4 and 5, I return to No. 3. Still no mental impression. "I guess we'll have to depend entirely on the dowsing rods," I say, shaking my head. Using the rods, I return the envelope to the right person, who verifies that the object is his.

I ask him if he's only recently acquired it. If he says "Yes," I nod sagely. That explains my difficulty.

PAR-OPTIC VISION

This trick, basically, is a method of seeing while blindfolded. While the method differs from the one I used when I did the Blindfold Drive, the effect is identical. The trick was my bread-winner, and it brought in a lot of bread. The same effect made Kuda Bux famous. It has always been surefire, *if* it's convincing.

The method I used for the blindfold drive requires a cleverly-gimmicked black serge hangman's hood. Doing the trick indoors, the hood seems out of place. The method I used whenever I performed the trick without doing the blindfold drive is entirely different. In some ways, I reluctantly admit, it's better.

Most magicians who do a "Seeing with the Fingertips" routine employ the old dodge of seeing down the sides of their nose. This, to me, is the worst possible method. It's impossible to see anything at eye level, and you have to hold your head tilted back at an obviously uncomfortable angle to see anything at all.

Back when the late Bill Larsen was making his *Genii* magazine one of the greatest sources of good magic ideas of all time, he published a blindfold method that few readers ever tried. *Genii* was a labor of love and still is, perpetuated by his heirs. Most magicians had too little experience with blindfold tricks to recognize the excellence of the method, but they should have know that anything Bill approved for *Genii* had merit.

Where the method was revolutionary was that it depended on seeing from the *sides* of the nose instead of down its length. I don't remember the instructions. For that matter, I don't even recall the issue in which the trick appeared. I thought immediately that the principle was highly practical.

You need little *pads* of absorbent cotton. If you can't buy any that are the right size, cut your own.

I prefer pads that are roughly two inches by three. You have a supply of these in an absorbent cotton box or container.

You also need a roll of adhesive tape, preferably half-inch width, and a pair of scissors.

You put one of the cotton pads over your left eye, the two-inch width just above your eyebrow, the three-inch length extending down over the eye to the bony structure under it. You hold the pad in place while a member of the audience slaps an X of two strips of tape over it, the X ends clinging to the skin above and beneath the eye.

While you're holding the tape in place for the spectator to fasten it down with tape, it's ridiculously simple to handle the pad so that the side at the inner part of your eye, next to the nose, is fluffed slightly away from the eye. You don't need any glaring gap. If you've ever peered through a pin-hole in a paper bag, you already know that only a minute space is needed for vision.

Have the same kind of adhesive tape X applied to a pad over the right eye, handling the pad in the same way. Now, have a long strip of tape applied across your forehead so that it covers the top of both pads. Have another strip applied at the *bottom* of both pads, straight across, to the sideburns. Have it applied firmly, cautioning the spectator to make it tight, so you can't possibly see down the sides of your nose.

If the bottom strip is applied tightly, it cannot possibly grip the skin directly on either side of the nose, thanks to the nose's protrusion.

When this taping is completed, don't panic if you don't have ample vision from the inner corners of both eyes. Pat the pads in place, press firmly on the various tapes and call attention to the fact that you are now thoroughly blindfolded. During this casual patting and pressing, the thumb concealed by the fingers as they press on the top tapes, can get you the little opening between cotton and side of the nose that you want and must have.

When you demonstrate your ability to See with the Fingertips, you don't need to face the item you're describing. The item can be at either your right or left, with your head facing straight ahead. And you don't need to tilt your head back at an unnatural angle.

Don't worry that your audience will spot the tiny openings at the sides of your nose. The won't—unless you've made them glaringly large, which is completely unnecessary.

You use your left eye to see to your right and your right eye to see to your left. You have freedom of head movement that would be impossible if you used the "seeing down the sides of the nose" method.

Don't spend money buying expensive trick blindfolds, or complicated methods of using unprepared materials. One of two things are wrong with most of these. Either the materials will not stand rigid inspection or the blindfolding must be done by a confederate. Take my word for it that the method I've just explained is your best bet.

While it's simple and easy, it requires some practice. You have to get the feel of *any* blindfold routine. Have a personal friend, preferably a member of your own household, blindfold you a number of times, until you understand the trick's operation.

And knowing the trick isn't enough. You must have an interesting, entertaining routine with it. Describe a few objects held out near your fingertips by spectators — not too many. One demonstration that's effective is to have a pitcher of water and several empty tumblers of different sizes. You pick up the pitcher and pour each glass full to the brim without

Silly Quickie

You hand a common lead pencil for examination, pointing out that there is nothing peculiar about the black lead it contains.

When spectators admit that the pencil seems to be innocent of any preparation, you state that what looks like a black lead will actually write any color called for by any member of the audience.

"So that you know I'm not using a confederate," you continue, "I'll ask you people to decide which of your number asks for a color. And whatever color that person requests will be the one this apparently innocent pencil reproduces."

Let's say the requested color is lavender. "You picked an unusual color," you comment. "Watch closely."

You apply the pencil point to a piece of paper and write the word, "Lavender."

spilling any water. Another is to read something, apparently with the fingertips. Have a spectator reset his watch to any time. Hold your fingers lightly to the watch crystal and state the time the watch shows.

One of the most effective demonstrations is done with two sets of five ESP cards. Have a spectator line up one set, symbols facing the audience, in any order. You take the second set and put a matching card with each of the five. Since you can see both sets of cards, it's not much of a challenge to you.

Have a spectator circle any date on a monthly calendar sheet. Run your forefinger lightly above the sheet and let it come to rest on the circled number.

For some reason which I don't quite understand, reading the serial number on a borrowed dollar bill seems to have more impact than reading a number picked at random.

Don't overdo it. Make your routine just long enough to show that your par-optic vision is infallible. And when you complete the demonstration, don't remove the cotton and tape from your eyes, yourself. Have a spectator do it. This proves to the audience's satisfaction that everything is legitimate.

Whatever you do, don't pass up the blindfold demonstration because the method seems so simple. It's the simplicity that makes it so good.

This trick alone can establish you as an expert mental magician. I know, because it did the job for me. I know I'm prejudiced by the amount of money it once made for me, but my advice would be to learn to perform this trick well, whether you learn any other mental magic or not.

There's one restriction. If you need to wear glasses, you'll have to wear contact lenses while you're performing par-optic vision. Glasses simply won't work with the cotton pads and adhesive tape.

There's a legendary story in mental magic about the "clairvoyant" who performed without glasses until he got ready to answer questions that had been written on slips by members of the audience. At this point, he turned on a reading lamp just behind him and put on a pair of reading glasses!

Magicians thought it was hilarious. Strangely, the audiences before whom this man performed never seemed to find anything incongruous about it.

Eddie Clever once wrote a book, *Thought Wings Onward*, published by the Abbott Magic Co., which explained the performing attitude of the mental magician better than anyone else has done it.

A good mental magician never gives the impression that he's a magician. He probably has more nerve than any other public performer, but it doesn't show through. His audacity is concealed by a smooth air of innocence. He never flaunts his dexterity. Indeed, it's never apparent to the audience that he has any.

His greatest miracles are often the result of chance. He is on the alert throughout his performance, and he takes advantage of anything that happens.

He is careful of his claims. I've seen "strong" workers who brazenly announced their psychic powers, but the good mentalist today doesn't do such a thing. He discusses the *possibility* of psychic phenomena and says, "I make no claims. I'll present a few demonstrations or tests and let you be the judge as to whether they're the result of luck of happenstance, or whether they go beyond that. If you don't find these tests remarkable, I hope you'll at least find them entertaining."

The approach taken by Kreskin, a currently successful mentalist, is particularly good, in my opinion. He not only avoids extravagant claims but leans over backward to keep from being labeled a fake. Because he works so "clean," he is welcome as a guest entertainer on the top television shows. Years ago, the "mental" act appealed to an audience of low mentality —the ignorant and superstitious. Today, it attracts a sophisticated, intelligent audience. It's fun to do and it's fun to watch.

Revenge

Charles Maly once marketed a trick of his invention, and it was good enough so that all the magic supply houses stocked it, advertised it and, more important, sold it.

They sold it, that is, until Dunninger, the famous mentalist, hit the news stands with a dollar book that exposed hundreds of magical secrets, including the new Maly trick.

Maly was so enraged that he ran ads in the leading magical publications offering "The Complete Dunninger Mindreading Act" for 25¢.

Mindreading acts were selling at the time for prices ranging from $5 to $100.

Maly actually sent purchasers of the "twenty-five cent act" complete instructions on how to perform an act with all the tricks contained in the act for which Dunninger was receiving $1,000 a performance. He made no claim that the methods as outlined in his manuscript were identical to those used by Dunninger, but students of mental magic believed that they were at least extremely close.

The insult cost Maly some money, but he felt that his revenge was well worth it. Of course, his manuscript lacked the one ingredient that had made Dunninger's act so successful — the unique Dunninger showmanship.

Coin Tricks

Let me start this section of the book with a confession. I have never been an expert coin manipulator. Maybe it's just sour grapes, but most of the professional coin manipulators I've seen don't impress me as being great coin manipulators, either. Coins *must* be more difficult to manipulate than most of the magician's stock props, because the field of coin magic is loaded with special manipulative equipment, gimmicks and fake coins.

The taboo against trick decks of cards doesn't hold against trick coins, in my opinion. When the average person sees a good card trick, his first reaction is that it must be accomplished by trick cards. But that same person almost never raises the possibility of trick coins. Perhaps it's because such strict regulations existed for so many years against tampering with coins.

Most of the trick coins that are on the market today are beautifully constructed. The workmanship on them is superb. While the price for such coins is high, it's understandable. A fine piece of craftsmanship is almost never cheap.

In spite of my approval of good trick coins, I don't intend to cover tricks done with them. Without the prepared coins, you can't possibly do the tricks. And if you buy the trick coins, you can get detailed instructions for their use, right along with them.

One of the classic coin tricks of all time has been the "Coin in the Matchbox." Unfortunately, it was sold in great quantities a few years ago in dime stores and novelty shops across the country. It seemed to me that almost every other person I met had one of the trick matchboxes.

Most of them didn't know what to do with the trick once they bought it. The instructions that came with the equipment advised the purchaser to "borrow a penny, make it mysteriously vanish and then pull the match box from the pocket. When the spectator takes the rubber bands from around the box and removed the little velvet bag inside it, opens it and reaches inside, he will find his penny."

The purchaser's first major problem was that he had no idea how to "make the borrowed penny vanish mysteriously."

The simplest of all ways to vanish a borrowed coin is:

THE CLASSIC COIN FOLD

This coin fold enables you to vanish a coin of any size and still retain control of it.

All you need is a 4 x 6 inch sheet of paper. Fold the bottom up to within about three-fourths of an inch of the top. Put the borrowed coin into the creased fold. Now, fold over the right side and then the left side so that the packet is one-third the width of the original open paper. Then fold over the top away from yourself. Make all the creases sharp.

That top fold is the fooler. To the spectator, it looks like the paper is folded over so that the coin couldn't escape without unfolding. But that top fold leaves the side where the coin is completely open, thanks to the original fold up from the bottom having come three-quarters of an inch short of the top.

If you now turn the packet so that the folded-over top edge is at the bottom, the coin will drop into your hand.

There's no way for spectators to see this happen unless you deliberately show them. Don't hurry to put the hand that conceals the coin into your pocket.

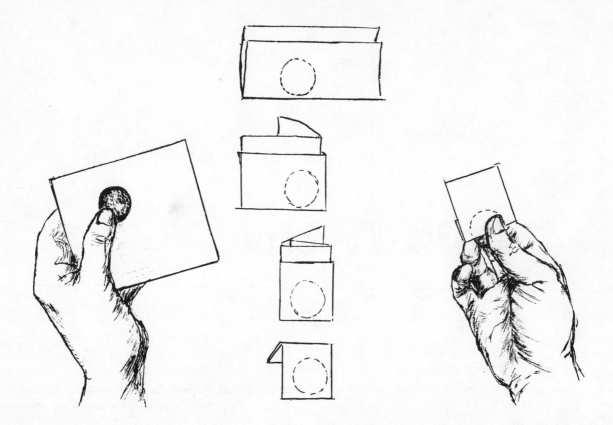

Don't reach into your pocket until there's a logical reason for such a move.

Now that you know the coin fold, let me say that the vanish of a borrowed coin becomes completely pointless unless there's proof that the coin you produce from another place is the same one. The reproduction of the penny from the rubber-band encased matchbox and bag was pointless unless the penny had been marked for identification. The magician knew it was the same penny, but the spectator didn't.

After the second time a spectator cut his finger while marking a coin with a pocket knife, I decided I had to have another means of coin marking. There's a type of sticky tape on the market that's used for labels and will take ink or pencil. I now clip a little snip of this tape, have the assisting spectator put it anywhere on the coin he chooses and then mark the tape with his initials. It's quicker, and it's not dangerous. You can also mark coins with a marking pen.

So the coin is marked. Now, after you let the spectators see that it's vanished, how are you going to reproduce it?

Not with the matchbox or the ancient ball of wool, I hope. The secrets of both are so widely known that you won't mystify many people with either of them.

Rubber cement gives you all kinds of possibilities for reproduction of the coin. Two rubber-cemented surfaces that have been allowed to dry but have been kept apart from each other will, when they make contact, adhere firmly and tightly. The surfaces must be kept apart until the proper time, and this may be done by having a piece of clean paper between them. The paper not only keeps the two surfaces from adhering prematurely but serves as a guide for the coin.

With a light coating of rubber cement over the mucilage surfaces of an envelope flap and envelope, it's easy to reproduce the coin from a sealed envelope. I prefer to rubber-cement the edges of two matching pieces of thin cardboard, bottom edge stuck together and other edges kept apart by a sheet of paper larger than the cardboard. On one side of the cardboard, I have written, "I.O.U. 25¢," and this card is in the open envelope. I put the coin between the two thicknesses of cardboard, withdraw the paper, and close the envelope flap. Don't worry about the two pieces of cardboard adhering to each other. Just closing the envelope usually makes them stick firmly. It it doesn't, handling the envelope to open it will do the trick.

As soon as the envelope is removed from the pocket and given to someone to hold, you pick up the coin-fold paper, which has been prominently displayed, and tear it to bits, letting the pieces drop into an ashtray. The coin has vanished. Direct the spectators to open the envelope and then the card. Don't touch the coin until its owner has identified it, or part of your audience will think you switched coins.

One of my favorite impromptu methods involves finding a male spectator who has patch pockets (without flaps) on his coat. I get him to stand up, as I stand at his right. With both hands, I take his elbows and move him so that he faces me, his left side toward the other spectators. As my left hand comes down from his right elbow, I drop the coin, which has been in my left palm, into his pocket. Then I give him the coin-fold paper and tell him to tear it to bits. The coin has vanished. From a distance, I direct him to see if it's in either of his coat pockets. It is!

A really fine method of reproducing the coin involves having a metal ash tray with a dab of beeswax on the bottom. You pick up the ash tray and rest it on your left palm, sticking the coin to the wax that's on the underside. The ash tray is immediately set atop a drinking glass. Now, you pick up the coin-fold paper as if it still contained the coin and put the paper in the ash tray. You set fire to the paper with a match and step back.

As the paper burns, the wax melts. There is an audible clink as the coin drops into the glass. You set the ash tray aside, pick up the glass and hand it to a spectator, who removes the coin and establishes its identity.

Another method involves a deck of cards. The coin-fold paper is resting against a tumbler and the coin is already in your left palm. You pick up a deck of cards with the right hand and put it on your left hand, at which point you immediately start fanning the cards from left to right, asking a spectator to touch one. He does, and peeks at it.

As you put the deck back together, you insert the coin just below the card that was looked at, under cover of the fanned deck. You square it up, pick up the coin-fold paper and tear it to bits.

"Now," you say to the spectator, "what was the card you looked at?"

He names it.

"Do you think you could cut the deck to that card?" you ask.

Whether he does or not, have him cut the cards. He can hardly keep from cutting at the selected card, since there is a break the thickness of the coin just beneath it. He picks up his cut and the coin is staring at him.

If he misses the cut, which almost never happens, you simply say, "I guess you have to know how to do it. Just cut to the missing coin." You cut to the coin as you say this, have him pick up the coin and take it to its owner.

An effective reproduction of the coin if you're performing at the lunch or dinner table is to pick up a saucer with your left hand, fingers on the bottom side, and show that there's nothing on the table beneath the dish. When you put the saucer down, you leave the coin beneath it. You now put the coin-fold paper on the saucer, giving it a snap with your right forefinger. You tear it up, showing it's empty. Have someone else lift the saucer and pick up the coin. The effect is that the coin penetrated the saucer.

The coin-fold is the easiest method of vanishing a coin and keeping control of it, but there are times when a bare-hand vanish of a coin is better. So here's my own pet method, which I call:

THE NO-SLEIGHT COIN VANISH

Clip the coin between the thumb and forefinger of the right hand, holding the coin by the edge so that most of it is exposed, if the palm side of your hand faces your audience. Lift the second, third and little fingers away from the thumb and forefinger, so that when the hand is palm-side down, the coin is completely visible.

With the fingers in this position, rest the coin against the open palm of the left hand and close the left fingers over it, retaining a tight grip on the coin with your right thumb and forefinger. Now, let the right second, third and little fingers relax to normal position. They will rest against the back of the left fingers, between the first and second joints.

Pull your left fist away as if it held the coin. Actually, the coin is still gripped by the right thumb and forefinger. Your eyes should follow the left fist. Reach into a pocket with your right hand immediately, drop the coin and remove a pen or pencil with which you tap the left wrist. Open the fist slowly and show it front and back.

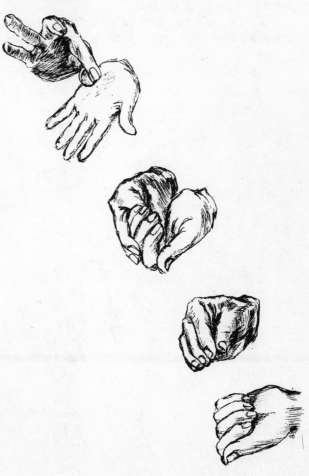

THE HAN PING CHIEN COIN TRICK

This and the "Miser's Dream" are the two classics of coin magic. While the Miser's Dream is ordinarily a trick that involves both mechanical apparatus and sleight of hand, and is a stage trick rather than a close-up one, the Han Ping Chien trick is done without apparatus and is perfect for close-up magic. As a matter of fact, it *must* be performed while seated at a table.

While the original trick was done with eight matching coins and a ring, I prefer to use six matching coins. Why? I think the trick is easier to do with three coins in each hand than with four—and the additional coin in each hand doesn't accomplish anything that I've ever been able to discover.

I hesitated to include this trick, because it involves sleight of hand. The description makes it *sound* difficult. However, I've run across four or five people who know nothing about magic and who only do one trick. It's the Han Ping Chien coin trick, and they've done it well enough to make it impressive.

I prefer to do the trick with six half-dollars, because the half-dollars seem easier for me to handle than smaller coins. However, I have done it with quarters and even with pennies. If the smaller coins are easier for you to handle, use them, by all means. The denomination of the coins has nothing to do with the effectiveness of the trick.

I usually use a ring with the six coins. I have, on occasion, used a poker chip. When I use six pennies,

I have sometimes used a quarter instead of a ring or poker chip.

Let's assume that you're doing the trick with six half-dollars and a ring. You're seated at a table. You line up the six half-dollars in two rows of three, extending out in front of you. The two rows are eight or nine inches apart. You put the ring at the inner end of the right-hand row, closest to you.

You pick up the coins. First, you take the ring into your right fist, gripping it against the palm with the third and little fingers. Then you pick up the three half-dollars with your thumb and first two fingers. As you close the fist, you actually grip the three half-dollars between the thumb and forefinger, the third finger holding the ring separately. The fist is closed so that neither the coins nor ring are now visible to your audience.

You now pick up the three coins in the left-hand row with your left hand, forming it into a fist. You put them into your face-down palm so that they rest against the palm, one on top of the other. When the fist is closed and held thumb up, the bottom edge of the coins is close to the table top.

Your right fist, thumb up, rests against the table-top as you turn the left fist palm down and slap the three coins to the table top, pulling the left hand away.

"Three coins in the left hand," you say. You line them up as before and pick them up exactly as you did the first time.

"And three coins and a ring in the right hand," you continue. You slap the coins down as you turn

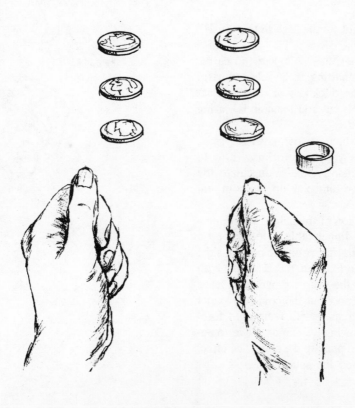

the right fist down and open it, pulling the hand away to reveal them.

You line these coins up as before and pick them up again.

Now, you rap the center of the table-top, sharply with your right knuckles. "The tabletop is solid," you say, "both on the upper side and—" you put the right fist under the table top and rap it sharply from the under side—"and on the bottom."

As you move your right fist back from beneath the center of the table-top, you leave the three half-dollars on your right knee, as quickly as possible. You bring the closed fist up into sight again. It rests toward the rear edge of the tabletop, thumb up.

"Three coins in the left hand," you repeat, turning over the left fist and slapping the coins to the table, pulling your hand away to reveal them. You pick them up as before.

Now comes the one sleight of hand move in the trick. The left fist rests against the tabletop, thumb up, the fist held so loosely that the bottom edge of the three half-dollars actually touches the table. The fist is three or four inches to the left of the right fist (which now contains only the ring).

"And three coins and a ring in the right hand," you say. Your turn the right fist down toward the left, bringing it almost directly over the left fist. At the instant when it is almost immediately above the left fist, you move the left fist six or seven inches to the left, out of the way—but leaving the three half-dollars behind. The right palm slaps down on top of them and lifts to reveal three half-dollars and the ring.

Done properly, the illusion is perfect. When you do it smoothly, you can't even detect, yourself, that the coins didn't come from the right fist. Once you've learned to do this move smoothly, you're ready to do the Han Ping Chien coin trick.

You gather up the three half-dollars and ring into your right fist and put it under the table. You immediately slap your left fist onto the table top and slowly spread the fingers. You lift the left palm and turn it up. It's empty. During this movement of the left hand, you have retrieved the three half-dollars from your right knee with your right hand, which you now bring to the tabletop and open, revealing all six half-dollars and the ring.

It's a beautiful trick and a baffling one. I once saw a radio announcer, a rank amateur as a magician, violate all the rules of magic by repeating the Han Ping Chien trick five times. His audience was more mystified the fifth time he did it than they'd been on his first run-through.

Get that one move, co-ordinating the left and right hands, down pat and you're all set. The move should *not* be lightning-fast. If you turn the right fist palm down with a wide flourish, preparatory to slapping the coins(?), actually just the ring, onto the tabletop,

it will completely cover the infinitesimal relaxing of the left fingers as they move easily to the left, leaving the three coins behind.

This trick has had over a dozen explanations in magic books written for professionals, and the methods vary widely. Magicians specializing in closeup magic have found that every method is workable if the timing is right. The entire illusion depends on slapping the right hand down onto the tabletop just as the left hand starts to move away. This is true of every method.

I mentioned another coin trick classic—without too much enthusiasm, you may have gathered. It's:

THE MISER'S DREAM

I'll give you two versions. Even with the easy one the effect of this trick is beautiful. Done by the average amateur, it's abysmal. The easy method I'm giving you first is *not* the method used by brilliant sleight-of-hand artists. It's a method you can do, although it will take more practice to do it well than the description might lead you to believe.

This is not a method for close-up performance under intimate conditions. It is for performing in *front* of an audience, with the people in the first row at least nine or ten feet away.

You will need some kind of receptacle in which to apparently toss the coins you produce, two half-dollars, a six or seven-inch length of fine catgut, and a length of black nylon filament or fine silk thread about two inches longer than twice the depth of the receptacle.

With tape or wax, you fasten one end of the black nylon filament to the bottom of the receptacle, on the outside, near the edge. You fasten the other end to a half-dollar. Both ends must be *firmly* affixed. Since neither of the fastenings will be seen by the audience, you can anchor both ends with good adhesive tape.

An empty coffee can makes a good receptacle. You drop the half-dollar into it. The filament or black thread should be just long enough so that the coin will rest flat on the bottom of the coffee can when your left thumb is under the thread, held flat against the can.

You fasten a catgut loop to the edge of the other half-dollar. Experiment with the length of this. With the loop over the right thumb, the coin should hang loosely on the palm of the hand. This coin is behind the coffee can, catgut loop up, when you get ready to perform.

Show both the right and left hands empty, front and back. As you reach for the coffee can with your left hand, your right thumb goes into the catgut loop. You immediately turn the right hand so that the back of the hand will face your audience. As you lift the

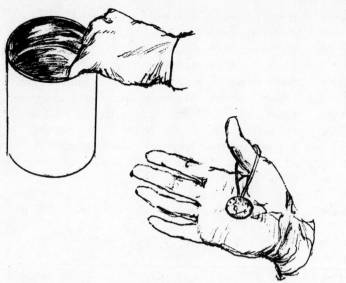

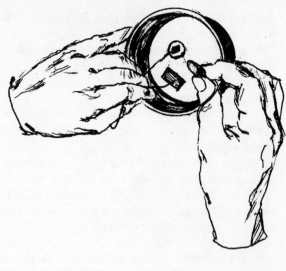

right hand, the coin will rest against the palm. The fingers may be spread wide apart. The spectator cannot believe that you could possibly be holding anything in your flat, wide open hand.

Your left hand picks up the coffee can, fingers inside the top edge, thumb on the outside. The thumb goes under the thread, on the outside, and is at the back of the can from the audience viewpoint. The grip looks natural.

You reach the right hand upward, to the left, swinging the coin with the catgut loop into audience view, grasping it between the thumb and first two fingers of the right hand. You must practice the swing of the hand so the half-dollar swings almost automatically into position.

Once the coin is gripped by the thumb and first two fingers, you can turn the hand palm downward and slightly facing the audience, so that everyone can see the only thing you're holding is that one coin.

You bring the right hand over toward the coffee can, a few inches above it, and make a motion of tossing it into the can. If you turn the back of your hand toward the audience as you release the coin from the thumb and fingers, it will drop back into its original palm position.

As you release this coin, your left thumb makes a sharp twitch against the nylon filament or black thread. This lifts the coin into the air and then lets it drop noisily against the metal bottom of the can.

The illusion is perfect. You've just produced a half-dollar from thin air, holding it at your finger-tips. You've tossed it into the can. Of course you have! It's no longer visible, your fingers are now open, and the sound of the coin dropping into the can has been heard by everyone.

You repeat the process about a dozen times. You need to produce about that many coins to get the impact. More than a dozen becomes too repetitious.

One finish of the trick involves having had 11 loose half-dollars in the can before you started. At the conclusion, you dump the coins from the can into a soup plate.

While it's a nice touch, I don't think it's at all necessary. Simply put the can onto the table, leaving the catgut loop coin on the right thumb behind it, and go into your next trick.

Done under proper, controlled conditions, it's a good trick. Magicians specializing in coin magic can do it under almost *any* conditions, but by a far more difficult method.

As I mentioned previously, equipment for the stage version of the trick is expensive. None of the elaborate coin pails look as innocent as the coffee can, in my opinion.

The bare-handed production of coins from the air, one after another, is brilliant sleight of hand. I've never been able to do it well enough to feel that I'd dare to attempt it in public. The coin with the catgut loop doesn't achieve the same effect, but it's easy.

I've bought tricks using such a loop, tricks that were advertised as close-up magic. Well—maybe they are, but a catgut loop over the thumb is *not* invisible when people are standing close to you and are looking for something. Such tricks can be close-up magic only when the performer has worked out a series of moves so that the hand is in constant motion or is held with the loop hidden while it's stationary.

Now for a sleight-of-hand version which requires no gimmicks. It is much better—and also more difficult.

You use an empty two-pound coffee can and six or seven half-dollars. That's all. The half-dollars are stacked right behind the coffee can, where they can't be seen.

When you get ready to do the trick, you reach for the upper rim of the coffee can with your right hand, to pick it up. At the same time, your left hand goes behind the can and grasps the stack of coins, the third and little fingers closing over them. For the moment, the back of this hand is kept facing the audience. You close all the fingers of this hand and rap the bottom of the can sharply with your knuckles. The open top of the can is turned by the right hand to face your audience.

At this point, you transfer the can from right hand to left. The left thumb grips the top edge of the can on the outside and the fingers are inside, the pile of coins beneath them and held against the side of the can.

You show the right hand unmistakably empty, front and back. This hand lunges out and up as if grabbing a coin from the air, comes immediately over to the top opening of the can in a throwing motion, and the left hand releases one of the coins, which clatters against the bottom of the container.

Your right hand reaches to the bottom of the can and picks up the coin, gripping it in the manner described in the "No Sleight Coin Vanish." You hold it up for everyone to see, the edge of the coin held between the thumb and forefinger. You now make the drop or throw motion again, turning the back of your hand toward the audience and letting the second, third and little fingers drop down into natural position, to conceal the coin. As you make the drop or throw motion, you release a coin from the left hand.

You now reach up into the air again with your right hand with a little lunge and lift the fingers to reveal the coin held by the thumb and forefinger. You bring the coin over to the top of the container and make the throwing motion, dropping a coin from the left

A Staple Stop

You can make a cute little gimmick trick with a piece of cardboard or construction paper 4½ inches wide and 10 inches long, and a stapler.

Fold over 1½ inches of the width of the sheet to the left. Then fold the left side over to the right, making a folded tube 10 inches long by 1½ inches wide. Unfold it. From the inside of the center fold, put through a staple, 5 inches down from the top of the paper. This staple goes through only one thickness of paper or cardboard, with the protruding ends of it on the back.

Then fold over the two sides as before, insert a ruler or something solid between them and the back of the tube, and put a staple through the front, 5 inches down from the top. Get it exactly in line with the first staple.

Now, dropping a coin into the tube from the front side of the top, you show that it can't possibly go through the tube because of the staple.

"But if you have a 'special disintegrating' coin," you explain, "it will go right through." This time you drop the coin into the back thickness of the tube. Since there's nothing to stop it, it goes right through.

hand and letting the fingers cover the coin in the right thumb and forefinger again.

You continue this until there are no more coins in the left hand. At this point, you tilt the can and shake it vigorously several times so that the audience hears the clank of coins. On the last shake, you shoot the coins up the side of the can under the left fingers, which grasp them again. If you don't grab all of them, it's perfectly all right. Continue producing coins until the second stack is gone. Then very deliberately, drop the coin in the right hand from well above the can.

This version gets away from having to front and back palm a half-dollar. The mistake most magicians make is in trying to hold too big a stack of coins in the left fingers. Six or seven is enough. With the ruse of shaking the coins in the container, you can continue as long as you like by simply shooting the coins in the can back up into the left fingers.

You must be able to release one coin at a time from the left fingers. You must be able to do the no-sleight coin vanish move, and you must time the "throw" of the coin and the dropping of a coin from the left fingers. Do these things smoothly and you have a beautiful close-up trick.

COINS ACROSS

Another sleight-of-hand trick with coins that I've greatly simplified for your use is Coins Across.

You'll need one of those little individual appetizer trays that are used at most cocktail parties—and you'll need to gimmick it. These trays have a very shallow edge, which is required for this trick.

Glue a fairly stiff cardboard flap to the bottom of such a tray. The piece of cardboard should be about three by three. Glue almost an inch of it to the underside of the tray, so that the loose outer edge of the flap is almost even with the tray's edge at either end. If you can find a fairly stiff piece of plastic the right size, it's even better than the cardboard.

Put two half-dollars into this flap. If the tray is

tilted downward at the end where the flap opening is, the two coins will slide out.

You need seven half-dollars in all. The audience is never aware that there are more than five. You also need an 8½ x 11 sheet of white paper for making the coin fold previously described.

You show the five half-dollars. "Since we can't divide five half-dollars evenly between two people, I'll be generous and give you three, while I retain two." You drop three of the coins onto the upper surface of the tray, at the end above the cardboard flap.

Move directly to a spectator as you continue, "Now, magicians are pretty sneaky. I'm going to dump these three coins into your right palm. I'll dump them from this little tray, without touching them. But close your fingers over them *instantly*, so that I don't have any chance of removing any of them. Hold them in your clenched fist, and don't ever relax your tight grip on them. Cup your palm so that your fingers can close over the coins the instant you have them."

You tilt the tray into the spectator's palm, and bring it squarely *over* his palm the instant the coins leave it. The tray conceals the fact that there are *five*, not three, coins in his hand. Don't move the tray away until his hand is formed into a fist.

Now you make the coin-fold, as previously described. You drop the two remaining coins into it singly, so that the second coin clicks against the first.

You complete the folds, ending up with the top fold that leaves a secret opening. Transfer the folded paper from the left hand to the right, turning it end for end in the process. Let the coins slip gently and quietly into your right palm.

Mysto Magic

The late A. C. Gilbert, who marketed the "Erector" toy building set and superb electric trains, started at least two generations of magic fans into the realm of conjuring with his Mysto Magic magic sets.

The sets ranged from an amazingly good little box of tricks that sold for a dollar to large, complex and excellent assortments of tricks that sold for as much as $25. Gilbert had, himself, been a semi-professional magician early in his career, and he picked the tricks for his Mysto Magic sets with a knowledge that could come only from experience.

Most youngsters started with the dollar box. If they had any "ham" quality in their makeup, they were soon demanding "step-up" sets to take them further along the magic trail.

Get a group of senior magicians together, mention Mysto Magic sets, and you'll start a series of fond reminiscences. While there have been numerous beginner's magic sets since the days of Mysto Magic, old-timers insist that nothing since the Gilbert sets has ever quite matched them.

"The object of this demonstration," you continue, "is to cause the two coins in this packet to fly across and join the three in your tightly clenched fist."

You reach into your left pocket with your obviously empty left hand, looking for a pencil. You don't find one. So you transfer the folded packet to your left hand and reach into another pocket with your right hand. A pencil is in that pocket, and you remove it, leaving the two coins behind.

"We'll make the coins fly across one at a time," you explain. You rap the packet sharply with the pencil, and then make a flipping motion with the pencil toward the spectator's fist. "Did you feel that?"

Whether he did or not, you rap the packet with the pencil again. You now deliberately and slowly tear the packet to bits. The two coins have vanished. You instruct the spectator to open his fist and count the coins one at a time onto the tray, which you hold out to receive them. Put the tray away while you're accepting your applause.

COIN CON

You can have a lot of fun with this little flimflam, which is more a con game than a magic trick. It's based on the fact utilized in Karrell Fox's Heads-and-Tails trick, that if the bottom coin held by the thumb and forefinger is released from the thumb only, it will indetectably turn over as it drops.

You have a dime between two half-dollars. The bottom half-dollar is tail-side up, the dime is head-side up, and the top half-dollar is head-side up. You arrange the coins in this order without showing them.

Then you quickly grasp them between the fingers at the front, thumb at the rear. The coins can only be seen from the front if you tilt the bottom one into sight.

You release the bottom half-dollar with the thumb only, letting it drop onto the open left palm, which is held seven or eight inches below the right hand. The coin drops head-side up, and you call attention to that. Unbeknownst to your audience, there is a dime beneath this coin on the palm, and it is now tail-side up. Don't worry about the dime. If you drop the half-dollar in the right way, the dime will automatically fall beneath it, out of sight.

You now drop the top half-dollar, releasing it from fingers and thumb. It drops head-side up on top of the other half-dollar already on the palm. You openly pull it a little to one side to show that both half-dollars are head-side up. Then, carefully, with the forefinger of the right hand, you move the top coin completely over the bottom half-dollar. There has been absolutely no possibility of turning over the bottom half-dollar. It is still head-side up.

"Now," you say, "would anyone care to bet that

the bottom coin is head-side up?" If you don't get any bet, offer to give $1 to a spectator if the bottom coin is head-side up.

Whatever happens, you slowly lift the two half-dollars, revealing that the bottom coin is tail-side up.

Whatever you do, don't talk about the lower half-dollar being tail-side up. Be sure to bet that the bottom *coin* is tail-side up.

I usually use this as a demonstration of a swindle. I have always made it a rule to refrain from any actual bets with spectators. While you may pick up a little money making such bets, you leave the spectator with a decidedly bad taste in his mouth when he realizes he's been swindled.

A big-time magician who at one time worked the best supper clubs in the country had what I felt was a particularly obnoxious way of getting tips when he worked the tables. At the conclusion of his table routine, he would ask the host to lend him a $5 bill for his next trick. He would then roll the bill into a tight little ball and place it in the host's fist, urging him to hold it tightly. Of course, he had switched a ball of tissue paper for the $5 bill in the process of rolling it up.

"Now," he would ask the host, "if I can remove the $5 bill without your knowledge, may I keep it?"

The host would invariably say "Yes," at which point the magician would say, "Thank you," and walk away from the table. The host would open his fist only to find that he held a wad of tissue. It may have been polite, subtle thievery, but it was still thievery.

When I'm performing a trick in which I want a spectator to make a bet with me, I usually say, "I won't ask you to bet your own money. I'll give you some of mine." I hand him a $1 bill, which he bets and, of course, loses. At that point, I say wryly, "I wish you'd try to be a little more careful of my money."

MINDREADING WITH COINS

This is a highly unusual trick, a mental trick with coins. Have a member of your audience gather a $1 bill, a penny, a nickel, a dime, a quarter and a half-dollar from various others in the group. He dumps everything into your hands, behind your back. You say, "I'll try to read the dates on everything from a penny to a dollar, without seeing the coins. Since the largest denomination is $1, I'll start with that. The date as I see it in my mind is 1969."

You bring the dollar bill from behind your back and hand it to the person who gathered the money for verification and for him to return it to its owner. He verifies that the date is 1969.

"Next," you continue, "I'll try to get the date on the half-dollar. It is 1967." You fish it out from the

coins behind your back, hand it to him for verification, and ask him to return it to its owner.

"Now we'll try the quarter," you continue. "As I see it, the date is 1954." It, too, is fished from the coins, handed to the volunteer assistant for verification, and is returned. You continue right on through to the penny, getting the date right on every coin.

It's the old "one-ahead" system.

At the outset, what you call as the "date" on the dollar bill is not really a date but the serial number. It is 1969 on all current dollar bills, although this changes from time to time. It's sufficient to know that the current serial numbers on all dollar bills in circulation are identical.

As you take the dollar bill from behind your back, you get the half-dollar into your palm. Look at the bill to verify the "date" yourself, and hand it to the assistant. Meanwhile, you have read the date on the half-dollar. If the coin is turned wrong-side up to read the date, a tilt of the palm will turn it over. Put the hand behind your back, fish out the quarter, put it into the palm and bring the half-dollar to your fingertips as you "get" the date on the half-dollar. Hand it to the volunteer, reach behind your back again, bring the quarter to the fingertips and hold the dime in your palm. You continue in this way until you've called the date on the penny.

You need good, sharp eyesight to do this trick well, particularly when you reach the nickel.

I taught this method to a friend whose vision wasn't all it should have been. He wanted to do the trick but didn't want to strain his eyes, and so he came up with a method of his own. He had coins from a penny through to fifty cents in his hip pocket, and had memorized the dates on all of them. He had a volunteer assistant gather the coins and bill and put them into his hands behind his back. He immediately put all the coins into his left hip pocket and removed those whose dates he had memorized from the right hip pocket. He now had the volunteer assistant take any coin or the bill from his hands, still behind his back and call out the denomination. He immediately gave the correct date without ever bringing his hands from behind his back. He had simplified the trick to the ultimate. He told me that his big problem was to keep the audience from seeing considerable movement behind his back as he switched coins. He practiced holding his elbows and upper arms rigid as he went through the necessary motions. But he still wasn't satisfied until he attached two little clips to the back of his belt, one containing the memorized coins and the other all set to take the ones that had been collected from the audience. He likes to do things the easy way, and I can't argue with him.

He does one trick with a borrowed dollar bill that reads like an impossibility but works beautifully in actual practice.

He puts a borrowed dollar bill into an envelope, using the Bluey-Bluey method described earlier in this book. His one variation is that the envelope is held in the right hand at the time the bill is removed through the slit on the address side. The owner of the bill has, of course, taken down the number on it.

While the envelope is burning in an ash tray, his right hand, containing the borrowed bill, is held behind his back. The left hand is exhibited very openly, front and back, fingers spread wide apart. It goes to his right inner coat pocket and pulls out a billfold. The billfold is opened, a dollar bill removed from it, and the bill is verified as being the one that was just borrowed and burned.

He uses a one-fold billfold, and it is hanging over the top edge of his inside coat pocket, opening down. As his left hand goes under the front right lapel for the coat pocket, his right hand, behind his back, goes up under the coat and holds out the dollar bill. The left fingers extend downward and grasp it, bringing it up and inside the mouth-down billfold as the billfold is removed, now closed.

From reading this, you wouldn't think it would fool anybody. Let me assure you that it's possible to transfer the bill from the right hand to the left under cover of the coat and fool *everybody*.

To the spectators, the distance between the two hands seems so great as to be unreachable. Actually, the move is easy and undetectable.

Try it in front of a mirror and convince yourself.

But I digress. We're supposed to be learning coin tricks. Since dollar bills somehow got into the picture, I'd like to give you one of my favorite coin tricks, one that I've been using in close-up work for many years. I call it:

BREAKING A BILL

You pick up four quarters from your pants pocket and hold them in the palm, under the third and fourth fingers, which are curled in, as you remove a dollar bill from the pocket. The dollar bill is shown openly as you crease it in half along its length and say, "Does anybody have a common lead pencil? If not, I have one right here. I'm about to show you an absolutely new and highly unusual trick, one I'm sure you've never seen. Grip the pencil firmly by the two ends and hold it out in front of you.

"You've never seen a trick like this before, I'm sure."

You bring the folded dollar bill down against the pencil several times, lightly. If you've built up what a new and unsual trick this is, somebody is bound to say, "Why, that isn't a new trick. It's the old one of breaking the pencil."

You shake your head. "No, I'd have to agree that breaking the pencil is an old, old trick. What *I* do is break the dollar bill."

You bring your hand down sharply, releasing the four quarters as you make the fast, sweeping move. And you don't stop the movement. You continue right through, dropping the bill in your side pocket as you turn that side from your audience. All eyes are on the quarters and it's not difficult to get rid of the bill.

Even if your audience sees the bill, the effect of the trick isn't nullified. There's a gag element that's always good, and the trick becomes secondary to the joke.

THE BENDING COIN

This trick is much like the last one in that it is as much a joke as a trick. Everyone has seen at least one amateur magician grip opposite edges of a coin between the thumbs and first two fingers of both hands. He bends his fingers vigorously, up and down, and the illusion is created that the coin is bending. It's similar in this respect to the Rubber Pencil trick.

The Bending Coin trick is fairly common knowledge. We add a variation that makes it much more amusing.

Now, I don't know what the legal regulations are on bending a coin. I do know that if you put a coin in a vise and apply pressure to the free half of it

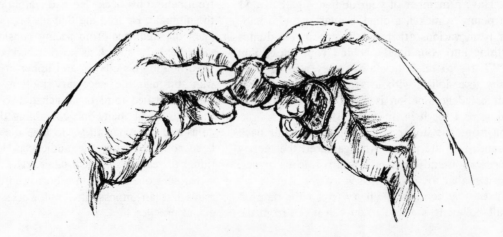

with a pair of pliers, the coin will bend. Also, I know that if you have a piece of cloth between the pliers and the coin, you avoid scratching it.

Maybe you should try to find a coin that's already been bent. I certainly wouldn't want you to do anything illegal.

However you acquire the bent coin, you have it in the palm of your right hand, the third and little fingers bent over it to hold it in place and covering it.

The simplest way to get it into position is to have it in your right-hand pants pocket, along with other coins. You'll have no trouble finding it by sense of touch, because of its odd shape. As you pull a matching and unbent coin from the pocket, you get the bent coin into the palm position.

When you start the bending movement of your fingers, nobody even considers that you might have another coin in your hand. Everyone has seen the little illusion before, and what you're doing seems to be standard routine.

After you've gone through the bending motions long enough to establish the illusion, you bring the thumbs and first two fingers together, sliding them along the surface of the coin until it is completely hidden by the fingers. Once it's hidden, you let it drop into the left hand, shoving it there with the right thumb and holding it in place with the left thumb. The left hand immediately drops to your left side as, right side toward your audience, you toss the bent coin out onto the table with your right hand, which is obviously otherwise empty. While the bent coin is being tossed to the table, the left hand has dropped the unbent coin into a left-side pocket.

You stare at the bent coin, shake your head sadly, and comment, "Sometimes I just don't know my own strength."

THE SYMPATHETIC COINS

T. Nelson Downs, in his era the most famous of all coin manipulators, called a certain trick The Sympathetic Coins. It's always been one of the most impressive of all coin tricks—if it's well done. And that has been the catch. It's been a difficult trick.

The effect is that four coins magically disappear, one at a time, and invisibly gather, one at a time, at another place. In most versions, four coins are laid out at the corners of a square, atop a table. The magician has two pieces of cardboard with which he covers two of the corners and coins at a time. A coin disappears from under one card, and two are revealed under the other. This continues until all four are under the one card. The effect has great audience impact.

When my daughter was in high school, she wanted to learn this trick. She had fine muscular coordination and was bright enough to later become a Phi Beta Kappa, but she was never able to do the trick well enough to fool anybody. The part of the routine that threw her completely was surreptitiously picking up a coin under one of the cards while holding a card in the hand, the card above and covering the coin. Picking up a coin with the back of one hand isn't easy, even if you aren't trying to hide the move. The problem is compounded by the fact that the card in the other hand must move over to the vacant spot just as the other card starts to leave it, so that the absence of the coin is not seen by the audience. As Max Adali used to say, "It ain't easy."

I fooled around with it for years before I arrived at a version I thought anybody could do. Even with this simplified version, nobody can do it well without practice. You must get the "feel" of it and do it often enough to make the moves smoothly and naturally.

I promise you, though, that if you take the trouble to learn it, this Simplex Sympathetic Coins will be one of your all-time favorite impromptu close-up tricks.

The requirements are a table-top on which to perform, one piece of cardboard, preferably about 4 X 6 inches, although the size isn't too important, a regulation-size newspaper and five quarters.

Notice that I say five quarters, not four. The audience is never aware of the existence of the fifth quarter. And notice that I say one card, not two. This, I think, is a decided improvement.

Only one sheet of the newspaper is used—four pages. The "fold" edge of the paper is facing you, the "open" edges at your left and right and the third open edge facing your audience.

Before you begin the trick, have the piece of cardboard in the right inner breast pocket of your suit coat. Have *three* quarters in your pants pocket. That's the extent of your preparation.

Lay the newspaper out on the table and reach into your pocket for the three quarters. Grip one of them back at the heel of the palm and bring out the other two held loosely between the thumb and forefinger, palm down. Drop the two quarters onto the center of the sheet of paper and say, "I seem to have only two quarters, and this demonstration requires four. Will one of you let me use two of your quarters? I promise that you'll get them back."

As you're saying this, your left hand, palm away from audience, reaches up to remove the piece of cardboard from your inner breast pocket. It drops its quarter into the right sleeve opening adjacent to the pocket. Since your right arm is naturally bent at the elbow, the coin will drop into your sleeve only as far as the elbow. As soon as you've dropped the quarter into the sleeve, your left hand removes the card from the pocket and tosses it onto the paper, along with the two quarters. "I also need this piece of cardboard," you continue, turning it over with your now empty left hand.

The point of finding only two quarters in your pocket is a subtle one that for some reason seems to establish the use of only four coins in the trick.

Take the two borrowed quarters into your left palm and lay them, along with the other two, out in a row in the center of the paper, about three inches apart from each other. Your obviously empty right hand assists in the arranging of the four quarters. Both hands are unmistakably empty. Now, your right hand drops casually to your side as your left hand picks up the card. You point out that the card, which seems to be innocent, actually has remarkable magical properties, and hand it to someone to inspect. You take it back with the left hand.

While this has been going on, the quarter that was lodged at your elbow in the right sleeve, completes its downward course, dropping out into the cupped right palm. You bring up the right hand, palm still cupped and away from audience, as your left hand puts the cardboard into it. The right fingers are on the bottom of it, thumb on top. The right fingers hold the concealed quarter firmly against the bottom of the card.

Holding your right fingers closely together, which is natural in holding the card, you turn the card over several times without releasing your grip, simply by turning your wrist to the left and then back to the right.

A Laugh with a Wand

You can always get a laugh and create a mysterious effect with a "special" magic wand. You can make it from a piece of dowel rod. Instead of painting it black, wrap it with black plastic tape of the type used by electricians.

At one end, have a heavy weight wrapped inside the tape. Heavy lead foil molded to the shape of the dowel rod and firmly compressed works well. If your length of dowel rod is 10 inches long, the lead end should be about another 5 inches. When the lead foil is wrapped inside the tape, cement white tips on both ends by wrapping them with 3-inch wide strips of white gloss enamel paper.

Better yet, use a 14-inch length of hollow aluminum tubing, and fill slightly less than half of it with lead or solder. Cover it with tape, as in the dowel rod version, with white gloss paper for tips.

Handle the wand just as you would any other one. However, when you put it down on the table, let the lead-weight end of the wand rest atop the table, with the major portion of the wand's length extending over the edge. If your weight is heavy enough, the wand will stay in position, balanced perfectly, although the bulk of the length is hanging in air. Don't call attention to it. By the time you've put the wand down several times after using it, your audience will be thoroughly impressed.

Your right hand next puts the card down onto the paper at the right corner, several inches in from both edges—not far enough to make the trick difficult of performance but far enough in from the edge so that the edge of the newspaper is clearly visible. As your right hand puts the card down, it leaves the quarter that was in the fingers behind, under the card.

Your right fingers immediately pick up one of the four quarters in the center of the paper. And now comes the most important move of the whole trick.

Your left hand lifts up the lower left side of the newspaper, fingers beneath the folded edge, thumb on top. You lift the edge of the paper not more than a couple of inches, just enough for the right fingers holding the quarter to go under the newsprint.

If you make the lifting move naturally with the left hand, you'll find that the left fingers beneath the edge of the paper do *not* point straight ahead. They extend under the paper diagonally to the right.

Your right hand goes under the paper where it's been lifted and apparently moves under the paper to the right to a point directly beneath the center of the card. Actually, the hand goes under the paper, drops the coin onto the left fingers and continues to the right in one unbroken motion. You leave the quarter on the left fingers, beneath the paper.

When your right hand reaches the area of the card that's on top of the paper, you make a little kneading motion with the fingers, pull out your empty hand and reach with it to pick up the card.

The left hand remains stationary. You pick up the card with your right hand to reveal the quarter beneath it. You put the card into the left hand, under the thumb, as you pick up the coin, turn it over and drop it a couple of times, to show that the coin is perfectly innocent.

The instant you put the card under the left thumb, your left hand comes away from the newspaper. The quarter that was dropped onto the left fingers is on the under-side of the card, which is transferred to the right hand and put down over the coin that was just shown. The second quarter is left behind under the card. Your right hand picks up one of the three quarters remaining in the center of the newspaper, and your left hand lifts the left folded edge again, just as it did previously. The right hand releases the quarter onto the fingers concealed by the newspaper and continues moving beneath the paper to the point where the card is. It comes out from under the edge of the paper, empty, picks up the card and reveals two quarters. It puts the card under the left thumb, just as before, and moves the two just-revealed coins around slightly as the left hand withdraws, quarter beneath the card.

The same procedure as before is followed until you get to the last coin on the center of the paper. This coin is deposited on the left fingers just as the others were, with the right hand then moving under the paper's edge to the right.

As the right hand moves to the right and makes its kneading motion, the left hand turns, back of the hand toward the audience, and comes out from under the paper to drop naturally to the side. It retains the coin on the palm.

You then invite a member of the audience to lift the card, revealing the four coins. You take the card from the spectator in the right hand and transfer it to the left hand, which immediately puts the card back into the inside right breast pocket, letting the left-over quarter drop into the pocket along with it.

A spectator has just had the card in his own hands, and now everything else may be examined without anyone discovering the slightest clue as to how the trick was accomplished.

Each time when you deposit the card at the lower right-hand corner of the newspaper, be sure that the coin you're leaving behind doesn't touch one of the coins that's already there. This is simple to do, since you see the coins at the corner and your right fingers know the location of the coin beneath the card. The two thicknesses of newsprint will deaden the sound of the quarter being deposited, but they wouldn't deaden the "click" if the coin were put down on top of one already there.

On your first trials, you'll have a tendency to make the depositing of the coin from the right hand into the left fingers noticeable as you start the movement of your right hand to the point beneath the card. This must be avoided by putting the right hand under the edge of the paper and moving it to the right without the slightest pause. You simply release the coin onto the left fingers as you move the right hand to the right.

Also, when you pick up the card to put it into the left hand, the left hand should start its movement out from under the paper as the right hand and card approach it.

A friend who learned this trick from me has an unusual way of taking the card into the left hand. He feels more comfortable with it than with the movement I use, and I'll have to admit that it doesn't reveal a thing.

His right hand brings the card over to the left corner of the paper, three or four inches above the paper and slightly to the rear. His left hand comes out from under the paper and grasps the card, with the card above the hand before the hand starts its movement. Experiment with both ways.

This method of doing a great trick is better, I think, than methods sold by some dealers for more than the price of this book.

CHIPS ARE MONEY

A superior version of this trick is sold by most dealers. It requires special equipment, including a beautifully made set of "gimmicked" quarters or half-dollars. If you like this trick well enough to want to

Truth in Advertising

Fly-by-night magic dealers have, from time to time, let their eagerness to make sales overcome their honesty in their direct-mail and trade journal advertising. Many a purchaser has been hard put to find any resemblance with the material he received and the material described in such glowing terms in the dealer's advertising.

One classic example was a Floating Glass of Milk trick. The dealer advertised, "No threads, cords or wires are attached to the glass at any time."

The purchaser of the trick read the instructions, "Instead of thread, cord or wire, this trick employs a fine silk line which is invisible from a short distance."

Another dealer, advertising a trick in which a billiard ball first appeared in an empty box and then, "removed from the box and held openly in the magician's hand, mysteriously vanishes without cover," sent customers a crude box with a black flap, a ball and instructions to "vanish the ball by your favorite method."

One dealer, advertising a card trick which could, to the best of his potential customers' knowledge, be done only with special cards, said "No trick cards employed." Instructions that came with the trick said, "You will notice that the cards we send you are the same size, weight and quality as those found in standard decks. They have, of course, been specially printed to meet the requirements of this magical effect."

A dealer advertised his Vanishing Alarm Clock trick with the words, "No trick boxes or canisters. You simply cover the clock with a silk handkerchief, and when you flip the silk into the air, the clock is gone!" Purchasers received instructions to "cut a hole in the top of your magic table large enough to take the alarm clock. Tack a loose piece of cloth to the under-side of the hole so that the clock won't fall through to the floor. The ring at the top of the clock is unattached. Put the handkerchief over the clock, grasp the ring through the silk, move the clock back to the hole in the table and flip the handkerchief into the air."

Reputable dealers describe their tricks in glowing terms, but accurately. If an established dealer says of a trick, "No sleight of hand required," you may be sure that you won't have to "vanish the water pitcher by your favorite method."

make it a feature, I suggest that you favor a dealer with your business. The trick is a classic, originally known as the Cap and Pence but commonly referred to by most magicians in this country as The Stack of Quarters.

Take four cardboard poker chips of the same color and cut away the inside of each chip enough so that a quarter will fit *loosely* inside the opening.

Put a quarter on a chip, exactly in the center, and draw a pencil line lightly around it. Then cut along the outer edge of the line. You'll need a sharp knife, but your workmanship doesn't need to be neat. All your audience will see of these four chips is their edges.

Next, cement these four hollowed-out chips together with clear plastic cement into a neat pile. Cement a whole chip of the same color to the top of the pile. Put a stack of five quarters into the hole and put a sixth loose chip of the same color on the bottom.

Have these six chips in a box of poker chips, with a chip of another color directly behind the loose chip. The stack is at the front of one of the compartments in the cardboard box in which chips are packaged.

Unlike the gimmicked coins which dealers sell, this pile is not movable, except for the bottom chip. The fact that the chips are neatly boxed in stacks and that the bottom chip is later removed somewhat offsets this deficiency.

The other thing you'll need is a tiny construction paper "dunce" cap or cone that will just barely rest on the surface of the table when placed over the pile of poker chips. Form your cone around the chips, so that the top fits firmly against the top chip. It fits in such a way that when it is resting over the chips, it will pick up the pile if your fingers exert a slight pressure against the sides of the cone.

When you get the size of the cone worked out precisely, cement it into permanent shape.

You're all set.

You tell a story about making some extremely wild bets while playing poker in a game that included an old-time professional gambler. He watched you, your story goes, with increasing distaste. Finally, when you drew two cards to a bob-tailed straight, he couldn't stand it any longer.

"Son," he said, "those chips you're throwin' around so reckless are money. Every one of 'em represents two bits. Here, I'll show you. Put five quarter chips in a stack on the back of your hand."

As you say this, you reach into the box and pull out *six* chips, the five-chip cemented stack with the loose chip on the bottom and five quarters inside. You pick them up neatly and put them carefully on the back of your hand. Maybe the bottom one is a little out of line and you carefully move the solid stack even with it.

You go on to say that he was a sharp-eyed old codger and that he spotted immediately that you'd picked up six chips instead of five. He counted the edges (from the top down) one, two, three, four, five, six. He pulled out the bottom chip (your finger has just counted the bottom chip as "six") and threw it back into the box.

"You've not only been acting like a dunce," he said, "but you've been making a dunce out of your money."

You pick up the tiny dunce cap and put it over the pile of five chips, holding it in place.

"Those five chips are the same as five quarters," he said, "and don't you ever forget it."

You lift the dunce cap, tilting the bottom opening back slightly toward yourself, and immediately rest your right hand with the cone against the edge of the table. It is a simple matter to let the solid stack of chips drop from the cone onto your lap. Everyone will be looking at the five quarters on the back of your hand. As soon as the cemented stack has dropped, you flip the dunce cap out onto the table.

You slide the coins from the back of your left hand onto the table and pick them up, one at a time, to put into your pants pocket. When you have them gathered, you *do* put them into your pocket, picking up the stack of chips on the way and leaving it with the coins.

A high school boy liked the trick so much that he drilled a hole in the four hollowed-out chips, just large enough for a kitchen matchstick, at one edge, in only about an eighth of an inch from the side. He fastened the top of the matchstick to the solid top chip with plastic cement, ran the body down through the hole in the other four chips that he'd drilled, cut off the matchstick flush with the bottom one, and cemented the bottom to the bottom chip with sealing wax. As a result, he has a stack of chips that he can spread or fan slightly and then even up. The four hollowed-out chips are not cemented together into a block but stay in place because of the matchstick.

Since I have a stack of the mechanical half-dollars, I've never bothered making such a stack of poker chips. I do the trick with half-dollars and quarters, instead of chips and quarters.

The critical part of the trick, whether you use chips or money, is getting rid of the mechanical stack when you lift the cone from the back of your hand. The audience's astonishment at what they see when you lift the cone usually permits you to get away with murder, but I hate to see any trick done sloppily.

The high school boy who made the movable stack got rid of it so clumsily from beneath the cone that I finally had him do this. He lifted the cone and started immediately to put it into his side coat pocket. As his hand approached the pocket, he let the open bottom of the cone go a fraction of an inch inside it, stopped abruptly and said, "Oh, maybe you'd like to look at the cone, too." He flipped it out onto the table, having dropped the stack when the cone's bottom was inside the pocket.

Maybe that procedure isn't great magic, but it was certainly a tremendous improvement over what he'd been doing.

Dai Vernon, one of the most brilliant magicians in the world, lifts off the cone and lets the stack drop immediately into his palm. With his thumb, he flips the cone out onto the table and drops his hand to his side. The flipping of the cone attracts everyone's eyes. Once he's dropped his hand, he either puts the stack into his pocket or gets rid of it in some other way.

With Vernon's ability as a manipulator, he could probably retain the stack in his hand and show the hand to you, front and back, without revealing the stack's presence.

HEADS OR TAILS

No coin trick could be simpler than this one, but don't knock it. It's good.

Toss five coins of any denomination onto the table. While your back is turned, a spectator is instructed to turn over two coins at a time—any two of the five, as many times as he likes. On each double turn, he may turn different coins. There is no restriction, just so he turns over two at a time. If he doesn't want you to know how many times he's done the double-turnover, it's perfectly all right for him to turn the coins silently.

When he gets through, he is to put his hand over any one of the coins. Only when he has a coin covered, do you, the magician, turn around. And you tell him immediately whether the coin he's covering is heads or tails!

Think it over. It's clean, without a single manipulative move. There is no make-ready. Neither is there any involved calculation. What coins the spectator will turn is completely unpredictable, and nobody can have any idea which coin he'll cover with his hand. And yet, you never miss calling the covered coin correctly, heads or tails.

The secret is ridiculously simple—which is why it's so good. When you toss the five coins onto the table, notice whether there's an odd or even number of heads-up coins. You don't have to count, and you don't have to pay any attention to the number of tails-up coins.

If the spectator turns over two coins at a time and you started with an even number of heads-up coins, you will have an even number of heads-up coins at the finish. If you start with an odd number of heads-up coins and he turns two at a time, you will have an odd number of heads-up coins at the finish. Simple?

All right. He covers one of the coins with the palm of his hand. Let's say you started with an even number of heads-up coins, and two of the uncovered coins are heads. You know that the coin he's covering is tails. Then let's say you start with an uneven number of heads-up coins. When you turn around and the spectator has his hand over one coin, you notice that there are two heads-up coins visible. You know that the covered coin is heads. For the purposes of this trick, one is odd and zero is even.

For example, if you started with two heads-up coins and when you turn around, four tails-up coins are showing, you know that the covered coin is tails. If the number of heads-up coins was either odd or even at the start, it must be the same at the finish.

Try this, by all means. It will often make more of an impression at the dinner table or in a casual gathering than a much more difficult trick. How good your audience thinks it is depends largely upon how hard you sell it.

Blackstone's Doughnuts

Harry Blackstone never passed up a chance at publicity, and he felt he should play the role of master magician to the hilt, both on-stage and off.

One morning while his big show was playing a week stand in Sioux City, Iowa, he stopped suddenly in front of a doughnut shop while on his way to breakfast. He went into the shop and ordered four doughnuts, a chocolate-covered one, a cinnamon-and-sugar coated concoction, a cocoanut-covered one and one covered with white frosting. He pinned one side of the sack to the inside of his suit coat and continued on to the restaurant where he was meeting two friends for breakfast.

He ordered a glass of orange juice, a cup of coffee and "one plain and one chocolate-covered doughnut."

The waitress had scarcely turned away from the table after delivering his order when he called her back. "Miss," he demanded, "what kind of doughnuts did I order?"

"One plain and one chocolate-covered," she replied —and then stared in bewilderment at his plate. It contained a plain doughnut and a white-frosted one.

"I guess they made a mistake," she stammered, and took the plate away, returning quickly with a plain and a chocolate-coated doughnut. She put it down on the table and left, but he called her back. She shook her head as she stared at two chocolate-covered doughnuts on the plate.

She changed his order five times before somebody told her that she was waiting on The Great Blackstone. Most of the restaurant employees were soon clustered around the table, and Harry did a few tricks for them.

The story appeared in both Sioux City newspapers.

The Challenge 100-Foot Rope Escape

Tricks that can be done outdoors, at picnics, rallies and similar gatherings are few and far between. The tricks have to be big enough for a crowd to see, and the magician can't control the placement of his audience. The tricks must be angle-proof.

Mark Wilson and the late Jack Gwynne both worked many lucrative open-air fair dates, but they depended largely on big illusions, and they worked from a stage, with a backdrop. Even so, I always marveled at their ability to capture and hold the interest of a large audience under such trying conditions.

You, however, are not a master illusionist. You probably don't even have a full-stage backdrop, let alone thousands of dollars' worth of stage illusions.

Back during the bottom of the depression, county fairs managed to survive, although their budgets were sharply curtailed. There were a substantial number of such fairs every Fall within a 50-mile radius of Wayne, Nebraska, where I was running a community newspaper.

These fairs, I found, were offering a fairly standard fee of $100 for grandstand acts, with one performance in the afternoon and another in the evening. Since all the dates were within commuting distance of Wayne, I wanted those $100 fees. Unfortunately, I didn't have an open-air act.

So I built an act from the 100-foot rope escape. It sold, and it satisfied.

Early in his career, Houdini did the 100-foot rope escape at every performance.

Five volunteers from the audience are handed a 100-foot hank of strong sashcord. Another spectator holds a stopwatch. At a signal from the timer, the five

men begin tying the performer, in any way they choose. When they finish tying him, it is up to him to escape in less time than it took the five men to tie him.

On the county fair circuit, the volunteers are usually

big, burly farmers. I weighed about 170 pounds at the time of my county fair routine, and they towered over me.

What with getting the five volunteers, having them examine the rope, some comedy "business" preparatory to being tied, instructions to the man with the stop watch and the actual escape, the act runs about 15 minutes.

I had tried the escape three or four times, just fooling around with it, when I got the contracts for the fair dates. I was young, brash and confident, or I'd have been scared speechless.

Why? Well, I knew the story about the time at the old New York Hippodrome when Houdini got five volunteers who were sailors from the same ship. They had practiced for days. They trussed Houdini up in roughly three minutes—and after nearly ten minutes of struggle, Houdini finally managed to free himself with embarrasment. The 100-foot rope escape ceased to be a highlight of his performance.

Knowing that, I had respect for the trick. But I also had confidence.

The confidence stemmed from several things.

First, and probably most important, it is an incontestable fact that if you start tying from one end of a rope and finish by tying the other end, there *must* be a slipknot at one of the two ends. It simply can't be avoided.

Houdini's sailors knew that, too, and they started from the middle of the rope. However, with a 100-foot length of rope, starting from the middle is almost out of the question, particularly if the rope is rolled into a hank at the outset. I have yet to see any five-man team start from the middle.

The closest I ever came was once when one of the volunteers *suggested* that it might be a good idea to start from the middle.

"That'd take all night," I protested. "It's my job to entertain this crowd, and they'd be bored stiff by the time you completed tying me." The man nodded understandingly, and the volunteers started, as usual, from one end of the rope.

On top of the slipknot factor, the 100-foot length is too long for efficient handling. The men could do a much more efficient job with a 50-foot length, but it wouldn't look so spectacular.

With 100 feet of rope, considerable slack is *almost* inevitable. Add to this the fact that you *steal* slack whenever you can during the tying process, and slack *is* inevitable.

The escape is made even easier because the tying process is disorganized. The five volunteers, even though their intentions are good, work at cross-purposes. They get in each other's way, they have different approaches to the tying, and they practically give you more slack than you need.

On top of all that, the volunteers are plagued by

a time element. They start tying the rope tightly, conscientiously, to the best of their ability. But 100 feet of rope is more than they thought it would be. It's such a lot of rope that the tying seems to take forever. Time drags, and by the end of the first 50 feet, the tying job begins to get sloppier. It gets worse as time goes on.

The volunteers usually pull themselves together when they reach the end of the rope, and they try to make it tight—but they're too late. Between the two ends, there's 99 feet of rope that's loaded with slack. And that end of the rope that was tied last may be tight, but it's almost never tied well.

By the time the tying is completed, you know where the slack is and you know which end is the slipknot. It has taken the volunteers close to five minutes, in most cases, to tie you up, and you could get out in 30 seconds.

You don't do it, though. You free yourself almost immediately, but you keep that mass of rope on your body for a few minutes, squirming and going through a variety of contortions which are strictly build-up. With less than a minute left, you begin to emerge from the rope. By the time you hold the mass of sashcord triumphantly over your head, there are probably not more than 30 seconds left.

I found early in the game that the trick needed a "kicker," and so I devised one. As I started to release myself, I stood directly in front of a stand microphone and began to recite a schmaltzy dramatic poem. I brought the poem to a climax and finale just as I held the mass of rope aloft.

The poem made the difference between good solid applause and a thundering ovation. It gave the audience something to hear as well as something to watch, and it built to a climax that aligned itself with the climax of the escape, giving double impact. Add to it the announcement of time every 30 seconds by the man who held the stopwatch, and you had a lively performance.

The simplest explanation of how you do the trick is that you just do it. You do exactly what the audience sees you do—you squirm free of the ropes.

Afraid to try it? Well, I've never shown it to anyone who couldn't do it—and most of those I've encouraged to do the trick haven't received anywhere near the background I've given you here.

It looks extremely difficult. If it didn't, the trick wouldn't amount to much. But I think you'll be amazed at how easy it is. The most difficult part of your performance, ordinarily, is to keep it from looking too easy.

There have been times when I've had to apply considerable force to ropes around my wrists, to get the slipknot to slide. But it doesn't need to slide far to permit you to pull your hands free.

Rope tightly tied around the ankles can be time-consuming, until you realize that kicking off your shoes makes escape from them easy.

Don't try the trick in public until you've had some private practice. One audacious youngster attempted the trick for the first time in front of an audience of about 400 people, and he panicked. The ropes were practically falling from his body, but he froze. Fortunately, he recovered in time to make his escape, but it was close.

For an outdoor gathering, it would be hard to find a better trick. It is equally good for a stage trick.

I once ran across a carnival magician who made his living with the 100-foot rope escape. He was a master showman, and he knew audience psychology.

He and his wife and one other man were the complete company. They had a tent that would accommodate about 300 people, with a platform in the center.

I saw him work in the little town of Bristow, Iowa, at a town celebration. On the ballyhoo platform in front of the tent he offered $10 a man, $50 in all, to any five volunteers who would tie him up so that he couldn't escape in less time than it took them to tie him.

He got five husky farmers onto the ballyhoo platform, and had them give their names. Then he announced that anyone who wanted to see what happened could do so by paying fifty cents and entering the tent.

He got about 100 customers, who trooped into the tent and shouted encouragement to the five farmers.

And he *failed to escape in the allotted time*. He was furious. He accused the volunteer timekeeper of misrepresenting the time. The argument was still raging as he stalked out to the ticket booth to get the money to pay the five men off, and the audience, whooping with glee, followed.

He thrust five $10 bills at the volunteers, being as ungracious as possible about it, and suggested that each of them should give part of their money to the timer.

By this time, he had an enormous crowd, and he suggested that if the town marshal would serve as timer for a second tying, they couldn't do it again.

The town marshal was found, and agreed to serve as timer.

And this time, he had the tent packed, with more than 300 people jammed together. He escaped in ten seconds less than the allotted time, and then made himself even more obnoxious. "You were just lucky the first time," he sneered. "You couldn't beat me again if you tried for ten years. As a matter of fact, I'll pay *$20* a man, $100 in all, if you tie me in less time than it takes me to get free again."

He had no trouble filling his tent for a third show, and a fourth. On the fifth show, he offered $100 a man, $500 in all, and the tent was jammed.

I visited with him over a cup of coffee later that night, and he told me, "Whenever the tip dwindles (the crowd gets too small), I let the towners beat me again, and the take goes right back up. The towners'll pay time after time in the hope of seeing the city slicker taken by their pals."

I remarked that I'd never seen the trick used in such a way, and he said, "This used to be a wrestling show—a dollar a minute for any local boy who could stay ten minutes with me. The money was pretty good, but some of the local talent is tough and mean. They didn't know enough about wrestling to take me, but they gave me a rough time, and I had bruises all over my body, day in and day out. The wrestling show works on the idea of letting the local boy stay and giving him his ten bucks. The crowd thinks the smartaleck carney hustler has been taken, and they come back to see him taken again. I decided to use the same psychology with the 100-foot rope escape, which I'd learned when I was doing magic in the ten-in-one show. The psychology works, and I'm making more with the rope escape than I did when I was letting the yokels batter me around."

The 100-foot rope escape is a great trick for sales conventions, maybe because it's physical and full of action. The five salesmen who volunteer to do the tying are usually extroverts, and they get a volley of suggestions from the rest of the audience. At a sales convention, I'd say that you get the ultimate in audience participation from this trick.

Don't knock it 'til you've tried it.

A Spectacular Illusion

As producer of a sales convention for a large corporation, I was once called upon to devise a spectacular, dramatic entrance for the company's sales manager. He was insistent that it had to be startling, and since he was the man who'd sign the contract for the following year's convention, I tried to oblige.

We made what amounted to a door frame, of cheap pine. It had braces at the front, to hold it upright. Then we fastened two hinges on each side of the frame, to which we affixed similar pine frames, about an inch shorter, so that they'd clear the floor when they swung. Cheap newsprint paper was thumbtacked to these frames to cover them, so that they became paper-paneled doors. Each of the two side-frames was hinged to swing a full 180 degrees. With both of the side-frames swung to a closed position from the rear, the audience saw what appeared to be a paper covered door.

This swinging set of doors was in place, well down toward the front of the stage, away from any drapes, when the curtains opened. Actually, the door that swung to the left was not completely closed. Between it and the door that would swing to the right, the sales manager had taken his position, hidden from audience view by the front paper covered frame, sandwiched between it and the other one.

Two pretty young models came on-stage and swung the left paper-covered frame out to the left so that it was parallel with the center-frame and the front one. They then moved to the other side. While they were doing that, the sales manager moved a few feet so that he was standing behind the opened paper-covered panel instead of behind the center frame. The girls

opened the right panel so that it, too, was parallel with the others, swinging it open from behind. The audience now saw the opposite side of the panels from those they'd seen when they were closed, with an empty, open frame between them.

As one of the models went around the front to the left side, the model on the right closed the right panel so that the paper covered the center frame. As soon as she did this, the sales manager took a couple of steps to a position behind the center and right frames. The model on the left then closed the left frame, this time slamming it tight-shut and thus breaking the newsprint that covered it. The instant it was closed, the sales manager burst through the center frame, leaving torn paper and no clues behind him.

This is one of the simplest illusions there is, and it's certainly inexpensive to build—at least, compared to most of the standard illusions.

The sales manager was absolutely delighted with it. He used the same frame for the magic production of a model holding one of his products in a number of trade shows. As a matter of fact, the illusion made him a magic fan and an amateur magician—a pretty bad one, I regret to say. He now has about $1,000 worth of mechanical tricks, a dozen decks of gimmicked cards, over $100 worth of mechanical coins and a captive audience, his sales force.

Mark Wilson has done considerable to sell the merits of magic for conventions and industrial shows. I have always favored it, not only because I love magic but because it can look big and flashy at less cost than other forms of entertainment. One good magician can do more to pep up a convention show

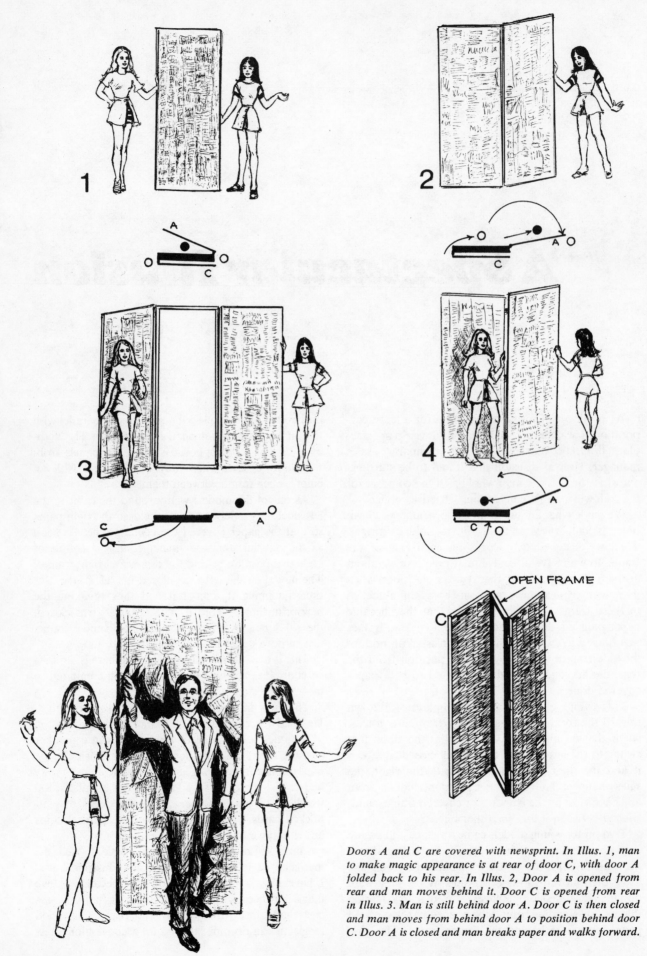

Doors A and C are covered with newsprint. In Illus. 1, man to make magic appearance is at rear of door C, with door A folded back to his rear. In Illus. 2, Door A is opened from rear and man moves behind it. Door C is opened from rear in Illus. 3. Man is still behind door A. Door C is then closed and man moves from behind door A to position behind door C. Door A is closed and man breaks paper and walks forward.

than a dozen talented performers from other areas of show business.

It is particularly good for the introduction of a new product. When the latest model of a product suddenly appears out of thin air, the impact is considerable. With small products, there are many ways of accomplishing the desired effect. With a large product, the problem can be sticky.

A friend of mine once drew the assignment of making a new model of a popular make of car appear instantly on-stage. The problem was complicated by my friend's having given the car manufacturer a "package price" for the convention show. This meant that any money spent in devising a way of producing the car would come out of his pocket.

I think he came up with the best possible solution. He called on the ancient "black art" magic principle.

He built a framework box large enough to hold the car and lined five sides of it with a cheap grade of black velvet or velveteen. The front of the frame was left open. The outside of the framework was covered with white wallboard, with a 6-inch panel of the wallboard running around the edges of the front frame. This was decorated with glitter, a sign-painter's accessory that flashes and glitters. He also affixed a fairly strong string of lights to the front edging of the open box, the lights all being on the *outside* of the paneling, with reflectors behind them, so that the light was thrown at the audience, not into the box.

When the time came for introduction of the new model car, the stagehands moved the box on-stage and the car was rolled into it from one end, which was hinged at the top. The end was then dropped into place and a piece of black velveteen was draped over the car to completely cover it from the front.

Two stagehands, who had been thoroughly coached, were shrouded in black velveteen from head to foot and wore black gloves. They entered the box and stood motionless at either end of the draped car, their hands gripping the black velveteen drape that covered the car from the front.

The lights around the front of the box were turned on and the curtain was raised. The sales manager, wearing a gray flannel suit, stood out in front of the box and began his sales pitch on the new model.

"You've all been waiting to see it," he said. "It's so completely different from current models that you'll hardly be able to believe it. You'll say that our engineers have accomplished miracles.

"The new model *is* a miracle, and so we want to present it to you in the most miraculous manner possible." He stepped over to the side of the open-front box and pointed his outstretched right forefinger. "Watch," he commanded. "I'm going to count to three, and at the count of three, you'll see a miracle."

He counted loudly and briskly. At the count of two, the stage hands whipped off the velveteen covering

and ducked down behind the car with it. At the count of three, a spotlight directed its glare on the automobile.

My friend tells me that the effect of having the new model appear out of thin air created pandemonium. It brought down the house. And the sales manager took full advantage of the trick's impact.

The automobile people were so pleased that they gave my friend a bonus which more than covered the cost of the black art illusion.

Long before his use of the black art principle, I had devised a black art box for a children's television show. The box was a three-foot cube, open at the front. We had semi-flexible black covers made of mesh wire covered with black velvet, in a variety of sizes, each with a black ring at the top. An object could be produced or vanished by removing one of the black covers or putting one on an object. The box was a running gag in the show and was used in every performance.

I once hired a black art guest act for the Magic Ranch television show on the ABC network. The show was filmed in color, and color film requires a great amount of light. In the studio, during the filming, with all the light that was thrown onto the black art stage, the guest act held no mystery for anybody. We had made careful tests before the filming of the show and knew that the act would revert to its original mystery when it appeared on the screen, but a sponsor representative who was present during the filming was almost hysterical. I tried to reassure him, but he told me that the cost of the entire show would be on me if the act failed to come off. I knew our tests proved that everything would be fine, but I couldn't help but develop into a nervous wreck during the production of that show.

The president of one company wanted to make a dramatic entrance into the firm's sales convention. He was just about my build, and that gave me a bright idea.

In the auditorium where the convention was being held, there was a set of wooden steps, about four feet high, open at the back but solid wood in front. I think they'd been used as steps for a performer to use in going down into the audience from the stage.

We put the steps at center stage. The president of the company, draped with a white sheet to look like a ghost, was hidden behind and beneath them.

I came out onto the stage, with a sheet under my arm, mounted the steps and proceeded to drape myself with the sheet, saying that I was going to present a little illusion known as "The Ghost Walks."

A stagehand brought out a drape affixed to a curtain rod. The rod was about 7 feet long and the drape was attached to hang the full width. The drape was rolled up. I unrolled it, from the top of the steps. As I recall, it was 8 or 9 feet long, so that when I held the rod at waist length, it hung down to the floor.

I stepped down the steps and remarked, "As you can see, this drape is long enough to completely cover me when I hold it up over my head." As I held the sheet up over my head, the president of the company emerged from the back of the steps and gripped the rod from the bottom as I released my hold on it. I raced for the back of the steps and crouched inside them.

The president of the company lowered the drape and stepped back, draping it completely over the steps and letting the curtain rod clank to the floor behind the steps. Shrouded in the sheet, he then walked down to the apron of the stage and made some passes toward the steps with his hands.

At that point, I had removed the sheet and stuffed it into a corner of the inside part of the steps. I emerged gingerly and the audience saw something begin to form and grow under the drape. I walked up the steps and let the drape drop, revealing myself without the ghost costume.

It got considerable applause. But then, when the president of the company took off his ghost costume and waved to the crowd, he stopped the show cold. That audience went wild. And don't think the president didn't enjoy it. He was grinning from ear to ear.

When the riot finally subsided, I said, waving a hand toward the president, "I told you this illusion was known as The Ghost Walks. And here, gentlemen, is the man who bears the final responsibility for *making* the ghost walk for all of you."

THE NEST OF BOXES

Stage illusionists sometimes do a "nest of boxes" illusion in which the three nesting boxes are highly lacquered and ornately painted. For a sales convention, I and my associates once made a set of three corrugated cardboard boxes identical in appearance to those in which merchandise is commonly shipped. Each box consisted of six pieces of corrugated cardboard, held together with the tough, heavy gummed tape that is used to seal such boxes. There is a type of gummed tape that has tough threads running through it, and it won't tear.

The inner box was a four-foot cube. A sashcord sling was fastened to it with the gummed tape so that there were rope handles to grasp in lifting the box from the middle box. The middle box was cut to a size just large enough for the inner box to fit into it. This box, too, had rope "handles" to simplify its handling. A third outer box was made enough larger than the middle box so that all three could be nested. A rope sling was also affixed to its outer surface.

Everything was as innocent as it appeared to be except that the inner box had one side that was a loose flap, fastened to the rest of the box only at the

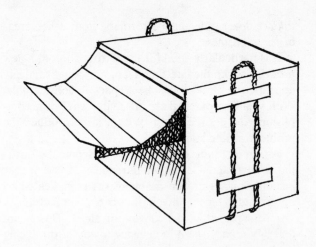

top. After some experimentation, we cut this flap side into four strips and taped them together, so that the flap was flexible, a curtain of four parallel strips.

We made a small but easy-to-see identifying mark with a pen on both the outer and second boxes to show which of the four sides of the inner box had the loose flap.

This nest of three boxes, completely empty, hung from the balcony, held in place by a rope on the balcony rail.

When we got ready to do the trick, an attractive model emerged from the right wing and took her position at a chalk-marked spot, about two feet in from the wing. A stagehand brought out a loosely rolled drape, 6 feet wide by 10 feet long, wrapped around a 6-foot curtain rod. When the drape is almost rolled up, a floor mop is inserted and the rolling completed. The stage hand held out one end of the roll to me and we started to unroll the drape, holding it about chest height. I was standing behind the drape so that I could hold the floor mop without it being seen. We were both in front of the model, with the drape between her and the audience. I beckoned her to move in closer to center-stage and moved over toward her as she moved toward me. At this point, I lifted the rod so that it was above her head. The stage-hand holding the other end of the rod was forced off-stage by my movement and the girl ran off-stage behind the drape. The minute she was behind the wing, I held the mop perpendicular to the floor, mop-end up, and started to drape the cloth over it, moving back toward center-stage.

At that point, I was close to the middle of the curtain rod, and with the drape over the mop end, the rod hanging down several feet behind it, I moved back toward the far end of the rod, retaining my grip. With the mop balanced on end, I moved quickly to one side, shouting, "Go!" The mop toppled to the floor, the drape along with it. I reached down, pulled the mop up into sight and tossed the drape off-stage.

We had rehearsed that part of the routine more than a dozen times, and everything went smoothly.

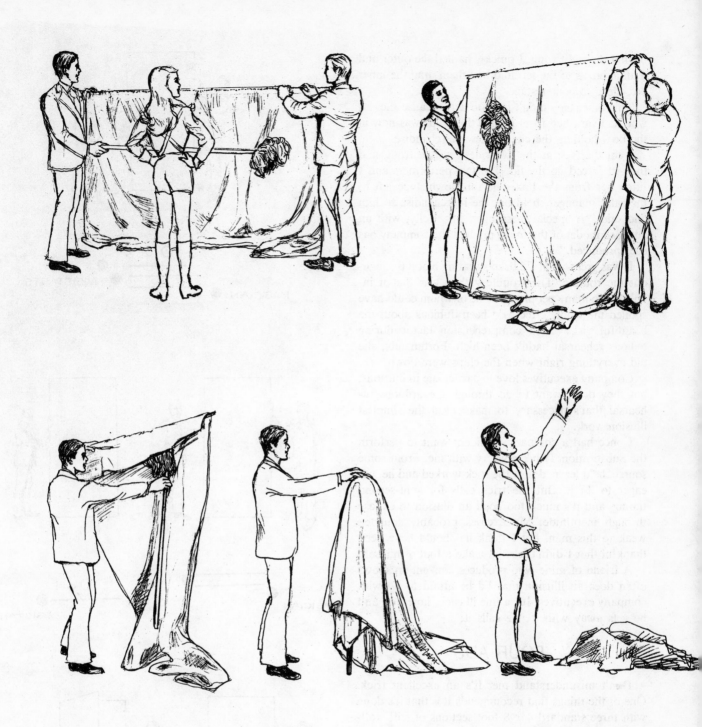

I stopped the applause—well, not *too* quickly—and directed attention to the corrugated box hanging from the balcony. Two convention show performers stood directly under it as a third, stationed on the balcony, untied the rope and lowered the box.

The two performers carried the nest of empty cardboard boxes up to the stage in the rope sling, handling it as if it weighed a ton. They really hammed it up. A chalk mark in line with the right front wing and 13 feet in toward center stage showed the two performers where to put the box. They continued to ham it up, one of them wiping the sweat from his brow with his handkerchief.

The top of each of the three boxes was hinged with gummed tape at the back. Three strips of paper gummed tape, not the kind with threads in it, held the sides and front sealed. I picked up a sharp knife from a taboret and cut the tape at the front and two sides, pulling back the lid. The two performers grabbed the rope grips at either side and lifted the middle box out, putting it down to the right of the first box. Again, they made the weight of what they were lifting seem terrific. I cut the tapes at the sides and front of the middle box, threw back the lid, and they hauled out the third box, putting it to the right of the middle one.

Seven or eight inches of the inner box were now

behind the right wing. I quickly hauled the outer and middle boxes to the left and had them drag the inner box close to center stage.

This time, they didn't have to act, because the girl who had vanished from behind the drape was now in the box, holding the client's new merchandise.

I cut the tape at the two sides and the front, and the girl forced up the lid. The two performers and I lifted her from the box. She ran down-stage left to the sales manager, held out the merchandise to him and said, "A special messenger, Mr. Kelly, with an advance model of the finest product the company has ever produced."

It was great—but I'd been sweating blood throughout the routine. The trouble with it was that it involved too many people, any one of whom could have spoiled the whole effect. I'd been dubious about the beautiful girl, whose comprehension factor during tedious rehearsal hadn't been high. Fortunately, she did everything right when the chips were down.

Company executives love to participate in illusions, but they don't want to go through the arduous rehearsal that's necessary to make even the simplest illusion work.

I once had a company president want to perform the Substitution Trunk mystery with me. From some source, he'd learned how the trick worked and he was eager to do it. But the trick calls for split-second timing, and it's much too good an illusion to expose through ineptitude. My excuses probably sounded weak to this man, but I think he should have been thankful that I didn't let him make a fool of himself.

A friend of mine who produces convention shows often does an illusion that I'd be afraid to do with company executives. It's a fine illusion, however, and he gets away with it. He calls it:

FOUR ADS

Don't misunderstand me. It's an excellent trick. One of the things that recommends it is that it's done with three standard 4 x 8 foot sections of stiff wallboard or plasterboard.

Three different ads for the company sponsoring the convention are painted on the three boards, which are stacked, held upright, upstage right, by the magician. An attractive girl model is standing directly behind the three stacked boards. The magician points to the front board and says, "Ad Number One." Assistant Number One steps in front of it, grasps the side edges with both hands and slides it along the floor to center-stage.

As he starts to slide it, the girl, who is behind Board Number Three, moves to the left with it, staying behind it all the way. The boards are heavy and awkward enough to handle so that the slow, careful movement of Assistant Number One doesn't seem incongruous.

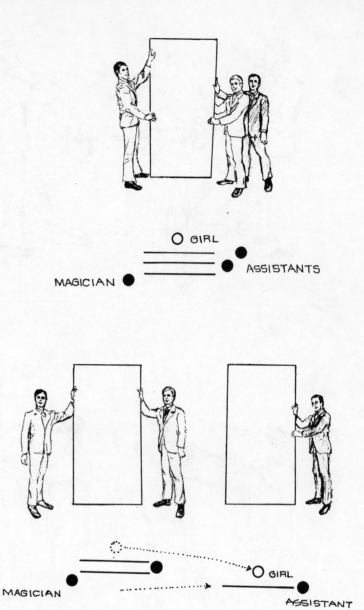

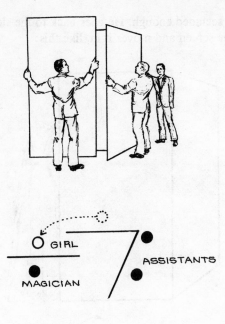

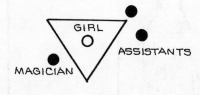

When he gets to center stage, he steps to one side and holds the board up so that it faces the audience.

The magician says, "Ad Number Two," pointing to the board that is now the front one of the stack. Assistant Number Two steps in front of it and slides it over to center stage, in front and to the left of Board Number One. He brings the right side of his board into contact with the left side of board Number One and moves the left side forward and then to the right so that it forms a V that will eventually be the apex of a triangle.

The magician says, "Ad Number Three." He steps in front of the third board and slides it to center stage so that it is in front of and parallel to Board Number One, its left side overlapping Board One by about a foot and a half. The girl steps to the right to a position behind Board Number Three, now in front of Board Number One. The magician moves Board Three farther to the left so that its right side and the right side of Board One touch, and then swings the left side out so that it completes the apex of the triangle.

"Where's Ad Number Four?" a shill shouts from off-stage. "You said there'd be four ads."

"Ad Number Four is an Ad-orable," the magician responds.

"What's an ad-orable?" the offstage voice shouts.

"I'll show you," the magician answers. He and Assistant Number Two swing the front ends of their boards outward, revealing the girl. The three men prop up their boards at the back of the stage while the girl walks off, and they remain there throughout the rest of the show.

The 11 drawings make the movement self-explanatory. The two critical times in the illusion are the times when the girl model moves from behind one board to behind another. Assistant Number One and the girl must work in perfect coordination, and the magician must watch his angles very carefully when he moves the third board into position to complete the triangle.

My friend tells me that he found a smart girl model and that he hires her whenever he's going to do the trick. Assistant Number One would worry me, even so, because if he inadvertently exposes the girl when he's moving his board to center-stage, there's no illusion left.

An illusion that I've done with an inexperienced assistant, always with misgivings, is called:

THE GIFT OF THE MAGI

You need a three-fold screen that's at least 7 feet high and two identical "Magi" costumes. These consist of a loose, flowing robe that reaches to the floor, even dragging on it, and a 'magi' latex face mask and hood. One of these costumes hangs on a hook on the

rear side of the center fold of the screen. The other is on a chair on-stage. The screen is propped against a wing, folded, the costume hanging on the inside of it.

The assistant is handed a rolled piece of adding machine tape about five feet long. The magician says, "Guard this with your life, because it contains the secret that has made this company great. Don't open it, under penalty of the direst consequences. Your job is to divine this great secret. You'll do it through solitary meditation. And you're about to go into solitary meditation right now."

The magician goes to the wing and picks up the three-fold screen, bringing it to center stage and opening it out like this:

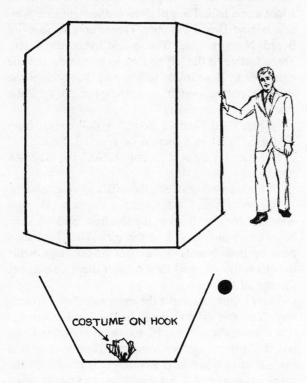

The costume hanging on the hook is on the side away from the audience.

"This is your meditation cell," the magician continues. "Enter it, and ponder the secret of this company's success."

The assistant goes behind the screen, where he quickly dons the robe, along with the latex mask and hood.

The magician, standing out in front of the screen says, "The great secret is the Gift of the Magi, and to impart it to our meditator, I must become a magi." He picks up the robe, puts it on, puts on the latex mask and hood, and says, "Now I'm a magi. Has the secret been revealed to you as yet?" The assistant calls out "Not yet."

"Perhaps," the magician says, "your meditation cell

isn't secluded enough. He goes back to the side panel of the screen and moves it in, like this:

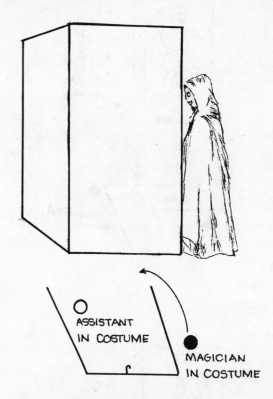

He now walks behind the screen and moves the other rear panel in, like this:

At least, that's *apparently* what happens. As he walks in behind the screen, his assistant, in identical magi costume, moves to the other rear panel, closes it in slightly and walks on around to the front. The magician has taken the roll of adding machine paper from him as they pass.

The assistant stands directly in front of the screen, facing it, his back to the audience. The magician, taking off his costume and hanging it on the hook, shouts, "If you haven't discovered the secret at the count of five, I'll have to tell it to you. One . . . two . . . three . . . four . . . five." He holds his hands high above the screen as they unroll the adding machine tape. "The secret, the priceless secret which keeps this company consistently in the forefront, is leadership." The tape has the word, "LEADERSHIP," printed on it in large letters.

He walks around from behind the screen, holding the strip of tape in front of him as the assistant turns to the audience and removes his costume. The magician folds the screen and the assistant carries it offstage during the applause.

Any substitution illusion always has enormous impact on an audience, and this one is no exception. While it's simple, everything depends on the timing when the magician moves in the ends of the screen from the rear, trading places with his assistant as he does so.

The illusions we've just discussed are all simple ones. Not one of them requires the intricate, elaborate props that are necessary in some illusions. Unlike

most of the tricks in this book, they are for stage use and *only* for stage use. And they *all* require practice and rehearsal. While illusions seldom require sleight of hand, they require skill. Their success hinges on perfect timing and smooth performance. What little work I've done with illusions has given me deep respect for the old masters in the field of big illusions. Doing a trick in which everything depends on you is much easier than doing one whose success depends on yourself and one or more other people, all working in perfect coordination.

If you want an illusion for a sales convention or big stage show of any kind, I'd strongly recommend the first one in this section, the one with the door frame and two paper-covered doors, as being the easiest.

I'd also recommend the Challenge 100-foot Rope Escape as an alternative. It depends on you, and when you've tried it a few times, you'll be confident that you can do it. It also has plenty of audience participation.

Of course, the ultimate in illusions as far as the average viewer is concerned is The Floating Lady, referred to by magicians as a "levitation." When I produced the Magic Ranch television show, I passed up routines with far more entertainment value in favor of a levitation for the first show of the series. The Floating Lady is Magic with a capital M to most people.

Unfortunately, I know of no levitation method that can be put together by an amateur. Every Floating Lady illusion that's worth anything requires special equipment beyond most people's construction ability.

If you're determined to have a Floating Lady illusion as the highlight of your club act, I would strongly recommend Abbott's "Super X" illusion. It will cost less than one hundred dollars, but it'll be worth it if you do many shows. To be properly done, it requires one assistant, although I suppose it could be done solo. It also requires a "floating lady." However, I've seen some good performers do it with a "volunteer levitee," a girl from the audience. Even after she'd been suspended in the air, the volunteer had no idea of how she'd been levitated.

For the most part, I'd recommend that you stay away from big illusions. The occasions when they might be useful to you will be few and far between. My own interest in them has been academic. I sometimes buy books, manuscripts and blueprints of illusions—but not with the idea of ever performing them. Perhaps wanting to be in the know is part of it, but I think the major reason why I've tried to keep informed about magic illusions is that I admire the thinking behind them so much. Most of them are ingenious. Some of them are so clever that their modus operandi almost overwhelms me. I know how they're done, but the odds against my ever doing them are exorbitant.

A Close-up Routine

In the United States, close-up magic has become the most important magic there is. The Magic Castle, that successful private club on the West Coast, packs 'em in night after night, week after week, with nothing but the finest close-up magic to be found anywhere in the country. In nearly every city of any size, there's a club or pub that features close-up magic, and it does healthy business.

Matt Schulein of Chicago probably started the craze for close-up magic in restaurants and bars. At least, he parlayed it into a tremendously successful business. He had one trick, throwing a pack of cards at the ceiling and having the previously chosen card stick, while the rest of the deck came down, that made him a legend. I've never been in an American city where somebody didn't ask me about Matt and tell me about that card trick.

Johnny Paul and Johnny Platt, both of Chicago, pioneered the "magic bartender" idea, which rapidly spread. Don Alan, one of this country's most successful magicians, got his start with close-up magic, with Matt Schulein, in his own restaurant and then with others. "Senator" Crandall achieved such national fame, working as a close-up magician in Chicago, that he was summoned to the Magic Castle.

The late Bert Allerton brought prestige to the field when he became what amounted to resident close-up magician at the famous Pump Room in Chicago's Ambassador East hotel.

The list of highly successful close-up magicians could go on and on. But they are actually a small part of close-up magic. The amateur and semi-pro magicians all over the United States who perform magic

for fun or profit or both but who insist upon enjoying it, themselves, have recognized close-up magic as the most practical form of the art and have embraced it.

Most people take up magic as a hobby because they think it would be fun to be able to do a few good tricks—not on the stage, but at convivial gatherings. Too many of them buy a few mechanical tricks that are really meant for stage performance. Others acquire a repertoire of tricks that require elaborate, lengthy "setting up."

Let's face it. The average close-up magician doesn't have either the time or the opportunity for extensive setting up of equipment. If he's going to perform at all, he must be ready at the drop of a hat.

By its nature, close-up magic is intimate. And because it's done right under the audience's respective noses, without a lot of phony equipment, it is the most impressive magic of all.

Most of the time at social gatherings, you'll do one or two tricks and let it go at that. But there are occasions when you want and can use a whole routine of close-up magic. With a group seated around a table, yourself at one end, you'd like to be able to perform for anywhere from 15 to 30 minutes. Ideally, this shouldn't be a hit-or-miss performance. The tricks should have sequence, and your routine should "build," with your real block-buster saved for last.

Magicians commonly refer to what they say during a routine as their "patter," and I've always disliked the term. I think immediately of "the patter of little feet," something childish. Sad to say, the words that pour out of some performers' mouths *are* childish. The major patter offense, though, is stilted, mechanical, memorized words that don't fit the magician's personality and give the impression of rote.

Close-up magic gives the performer an opportunity to be warm and friendly, to get on intimate terms with his audience. What he says should *never* be "recited."

It should, however, have purpose and direction. You should know the *essence* of what you're going to say and you should know how you're going to lead from one trick into another.

The first routine I'm going to give you is a brief one that employs nothing but a babushka, scarf or ascot—in other words, a 36-inch square of silk or nylon. You may want to carry one with you, although it's a rare group where one of the women won't be wearing one or the hostess can't go to her bedroom and get one for you.

The Silk Routine

As soon as you get the silk, spin it into a loose rope, holding the top left corner between your left thumb and forefinger and the bottom right corner between your right thumb and forefinger. If, during the routine, the "rope" unfurls too much, give it another spin.

As you're spinning it, your comment runs something like this. "In this permissive age, audiences seem to like their entertainment slightly on the naughty side—and this is a naughty silk. I hope you won't find it too offensive. I'll show you how naughty it is."

At this point, you tie the Dissolving Knot, as explained under that heading. You extend the silk with the dissolving knot in it toward one of the ladies. "If this is too naughty, just blow on it."

As she blows on it, you pull the two ends imperceptibly and the knot dissolves.

"You see, getting rid of one offensive knot is easy. More than one takes a bit of doing." At this point, you do the:

DOUBLE-KNOT VANISH

You hold the ends of the silk in your hands and apparently tie a single knot in them. Actually, you wrap the ends around each other, waving your hands slightly as you do it. Each end returns to the fingers that originally held it. Now, grasp the "twist" or apparent knot firmly between the right thumb and forefinger and ask one of the spectators to tie a second knot "on top of the first," tying it so that it's firm and tight. This knot, incidentally, *should* be tight. Still holding the silk at the cross-over, you examine the second knot critically. "When I said tight, I didn't mean for you to overdo it. This is going to take a really big blow. But since you're so strong, maybe you have a strong breath, too."

Your fingers take their hold about an inch from both sides of the knot, holding it carefully. The knot will "hold" in position.

"Blow on it, please—hard!"

As he blows, pull the two sides of the silk gently, imperceptibly. The knots will spin furiously apart.

"Congratulations! I'll bet that held you breathless, didn't it?" Give the ends of the silken rope a little spin and drape it over the side of the right hand in readiness for the Appearing Knot. "Getting rid of knots is easy—for a magician. Making knots appear is slightly more difficult."

Make a knot appear in the silken rope, using whichever of the two methods previously described is most comfortable for you.

"Now, here's the world's fastest knot."

WORLD'S FASTEST KNOT

Lay the left end of the silken rope across the left face-up palm, letting the end hang down through the crotch of the thumb about 6 inches. Grasp the other end in the right hand, palm down, the right end extending about 6 inches from the fist, the silk being gripped by the crotch of the thumb. Now, if you'll turn the hands so the two palms face each other and bring the palms together, you can nip each opposite hanging end between the first and second fingers. Pull the

hands apart, gripping the two ends, and there will be a knot in the center of the silken rope. Don't try to hurry this, but do it quickly and smoothly. Keep your eyes on the silken rope and your fingers as you do it. After a few trials, you'll be able to make the knot appear with amazing speed. Untie it and say, "And now, here's the world's fastest bow."

WORLD'S FASTEST BOW-TIE

The bow is tied exactly as is the plain knot, except that the hands are held about 6 inches apart, with long ends hanging. You nip opposite ends with a thumb-and-forefinger grip, just as before, except that you take the grip, not at the end but where the thumb and forefinger touch the silk. Pull the hands apart and you'll have a bow-knot. While this looks much more difficult than tying a simple knot, the action is identical.

Pull the ends of the bow-knot to untie it, and ask for the loan of two bracelets. Preferably, they should be noticeably different in appearance. Let's say you get a gold wire bracelet and a plastic one. Have the owner of the plastic bracelet hold it in her fingertips.

BRACELET FROM SILK

Hold the left end of the silken rope between the first and second fingers, 8 or 9 inches of it hanging over. Lower the free end of the rope through the bracelet, grasp it in the right hand and bring it up toward you, putting the end between the thumb and first finger of the left hand. The silken rope is in position to tie the Dissolving Knot, which you do, tying it firmly before you release your second finger of the left hand from the little bight that holds the knot in place.

Have the spectator hold the gold wire bracelet directly behind the plastic one. With your right hand, put the free, hanging end of the silken rope through

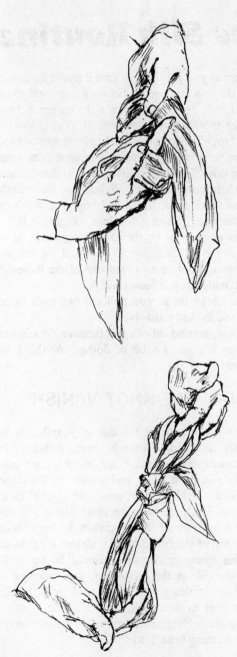

both bracelets, away from you. It goes through the plastic bracelet first and then the gold wire one. Once it's through the bracelets, bring it up and tie two more legitimate knots at the top, bringing them down on top of the dissolving knot. Ask the owner of the plastic bracelet to release her hold. You're holding both ends of the silken rope in your left fingers.

"Now," you ask, "which one of the bracelets do you want?"

If she says, "The plastic one," you simply pull it free and hand it to her. If she says, "The gold one," you pull the plastic one free and hand her the silk, which has the gold one tied to it, both knots being legitimate.

"This is a very delicate, sensitive kind of silk," you remark. "So for this next demonstration, I need a sensitive person."

SILK THROUGH THE ARM

You have a spectator grip both hands tightly together, holding them outstretched. You hold the silk in the left hand between first and second fingers and lower the free end through the circle made by the

Flash Production

"Dear George—I know you do a close-up routine in which 24 or 36-inch silk handkerchiefs play an important part. How would you like to produce a couple of such handkerchiefs from thin air, instantly and cleanly?

"Okay. Tie a catgut loop around one corner of each silk, loosely, about two inches in from the end of the silk as it hangs down from the corner. The loop should be large enough for easy insertion of the thumb.

"Fold each silk up from the bottom to the top, twice —three times if the smaller packet is easier for you to handle. Now, tuck these two packets under your belt, a few inches to the right and left of the belt buckle, with only the catgut loop extending above the belt.

"Show both hands, unmistakably empty, front and back, fingers spread wide apart. Rest your wide-open hands against your waist at the front, hooking the two thumbs into the two catgut loops. Count one, two, and then sharply, three, as you thrust your hands out and up away from you in what is almost a lunge of the hands. Large silks will be hanging from both hands. The instant appearance is beautiful magic.

"Now, in putting the silks onto the table, pull each one from the catgut loop (that's why the loop was tied loosely). The loops will drop off your thumbs unnoticed, behind the silks. Proceed with your silk tricks.

"I know you can have fun with this.

Very truly yours,
Marty"

spectator's joined hands. You bring the free end up toward yourself, put it under the left thumb in position to tie the dissolving knot, and tie it. You then bring the hanging end up through the spectator's arms, on the side away from you, and tie two legitimate knots.

"Watch closely," you caution, "because you're about to witness a miracle, a demonstration of solid through solid." Give the ends of the silk a gentle tug and the silk lifts free of the spectator's arms. You untie the knots that remain in it.

"In conclusion," you continue, "I'm going to violate the magician's code by showing you how to tie a knot in a silk without letting go of either end. And I don't mean that old business of folding your arms and then grasping the ends of the silk. Watch closely."

You go into the business of tying a knot without letting go of either end. You do it twice, and then have the ends tied around your thumbs, to prove conclusively that you do *not* release either end. Then you have spectators try it, with their failing to get any knot. You take the ends from them and have them "slip out their wrists" and they get a knot. A knot appears or doesn't appear at your whim. You explain that "it's all in the wrist movement." You can make this part of the routine as long or as brief as you choose. Believe me, it will last a long time if you don't deliberately stop it.

Here's the way the routine runs:

THE SILK ROUTINE

Dissolving Knot
Double-Knot Vanish
World's Fastest Knot
World's Fastest Bow Knot
Bracelet from Silk
Silk Through the Arm
Tying a Knot Without Letting Go of Either End

This is a *great* routine, and it's about as impromptu and casual as any magic routine could be. It's loaded with audience participation, and the length of time it takes can be controlled. Best of all, it uses only one prop, and that happens to be a prop that can be found in almost every home. I've often done it while wearing an ascot tie with a sports shirt, removing the tie from around my neck and going into action.

There are only two moves in the entire routine that require much practice—the dissolving knot and tying a knot without releasing the ends of the silk. Neither is hard to learn, and they're both worth knowing.

If you have difficulty with any of the other knots— which you shouldn't—don't worry. Just leave them out of the routine until you can do them well.

The next routine is longer and employs a greater variety of props. It, too, however, is about as impromptu as a routine could be.

Impromptu Close-up Routine

Here's what you'll need: a dollar bill, folded over from right to left into eighths and then doubled over, two paper clips, two rubber bands, a yard length of heavy string or twine, a pencil, a sheet of paper and a table knife. The only "make-ready" is to have the folded dollar bill palmed in your left hand, held at the base of the third and fourth fingers by those fingers. The bill is folded with the "gray" side out, as opposed to the "green" side. You can hold your hand naturally, not, of course, turning it with the palm toward spectators.

THE BILL SWITCH

"My first trick," you say, "is best performed with a borrowed $1,000 bill. I don't like to use my own, because the audience becomes suspicious that it's prepared in some way. Would someone please hand me a $1,000 bill? No? Well, the trick *can* be done with a $100 bill. A $100 bill, please?" You sigh. "Sometimes, I have to do it with a $5 or $10 bill, and that makes it really difficult. I can see that this is going to be one of those nights. How about it?"

Borrow a $5 or $10 bill, taking it in your outstretched and empty right hand. Drape it immediately over your left hand, so that it covers the folded dollar. Put it on the left hand so that the top of the folded dollar is roughly half-way down the length of the bill. The left thumb holds the $10 bill, pressing the dollar flat beneath it. You turn the left hand palm up the instant the $10 bill covers the dollar. This calls attention to the fact (?) that there is nothing else in either hand, without your mentioning it.

Now, as you bring both hands up in front of you preparatory to folding the $10 bill, the backs of the hands face the audience. Move the $10 bill slightly to the right and then back, with the right hand, putting the surface of the $10 bill *beneath* the $1 instead of on top of it. Fold over the top half of the tenspot toward yourself, over the already-folded $1, which overlaps half an inch to the left. Your left thumb conceals it.

Bringing up the bottom edges of the tenspot, you fold the bill into quarters and then into eighths, "gray" side exposed. At this point, you can handle it rather carelessly, without danger of anyone detecting the dollar bill's presence. Hold the folded tenspot very openly in the left hand, the thumb hiding the extending edge of the folded dollar.

Now comes the critical move. Fold the top part of the tenspot over onto the bottom part, folding it in

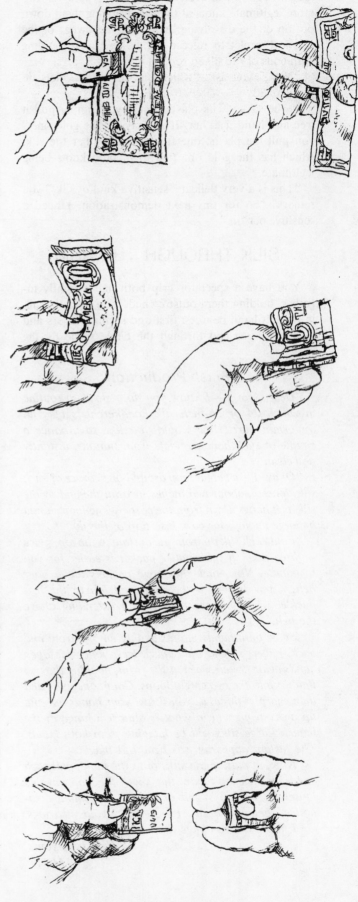

half so that it is identical in size with the dollar. Your right thumb folds it over, and at this point, for a second or two, both bills are hidden by the backs of your hands. Grip the folded tenspot firmly between the thumb and fingers of the right hand, pulling it back and down into "palm" position as the left thumb pushes the end of the dollar out into view. Don't make a big deal of this. It appears to the audience that you simply folded over the bill and put it back into view. Hold out your left thumb and forefinger, the folded dollar clipped between them, toward whoever furnished the tenspot and ask him to grip it tightly in his fist.

As you're doing this, your right hand goes into your right side pocket and comes out with a pencil and you say, "I don't know why it is, but I have to shove the pointed end of a pencil into your fist or this trick won't work."

You, of course, left the tenspot in your pocket when you removed the pencil. You insert the pencil gently, point down, into his fist.

"At this point," you continue, "you'd think it would be impossible for me to get that $10 bill or any part of it away from you without your knowledge, wouldn't you? And you'd be right. It would take a magician to do such a thing. But I claim to be a magician. Would you believe that your $10 bill is now gone? Peek into your fist and see."

After he's peeked into his fist, continue, "Satisfied? Would you bet that you still have it? Well, I won't bet because I'd have a sure thing. Open your fist and see for yourself."

He opens his fist, usually looking triumphant. If he doesn't start to unfold the bill, direct him to do so. As he starts to unfold it, take back the pencil from him with your right hand and put it back into your pocket, getting the folded tenspot back into palm position in the right hand. You can do this very casually, because everyone will be watching the visible bill as it's unfolded. If there's a coffee cup on the table, pick it up, casually, fingers of the right hand inside, and turn it mouth down, leaving the bill beneath it. If there isn't a coffee cup, pick up almost anything that's on the table and turn it over, leaving the bill under it.

When the bill is completely unfolded and the audience sees that it's a dollar instead of a tenspot, the impact is terrific.

"Don't worry. I wouldn't rob you," you assure him. "Just turn over this coffee cup."

On occasion, sitting at a table, I have bent over slightly and put the tenspot into my right shoe, at the instep. This is easy to do. At the finish of the trick, you put your right foot up onto the chair seat, remove your shoe and shake out the $10 bill, saying, "I wanted to be sure it didn't get lost, so I put it away for safe-keeping."

Give him back his $10 bill, thank him, and take the dollar. "This dollar bill reminds me," you continue, "of the time I got clipped for a buck."

You take one of the rubber bands and the two paper clips from your left-hand coat pocket and do Clipped for a Buck, as described earlier in the book. This trick is self-working.

At the conclusion of this trick, you remove the paper clips from the rubber band and put the band over the first and second fingers of your right hand. You remove the second band from your left coat pocket and interlace it over the four right hand fingertips. You then do the Jumping Rubber Band trick as described earlier.

At the finish, you put both rubber bands on the table and interlace one of them over the four fingertips of the left hand, stretching the fingers to show that they're held tightly together.

BRACELET OVER RUBBER BAND

You borrow a bracelet, preferably a plastic one, from a spectator. As you reach out to get it, your left palm up, your second finger pulls out of the rubber band as you take the bracelet in your right. You simply bend the first joint of the finger slightly and move it back. Then you put it back so that it presses firmly against the two thicknesses of rubber band that are now in front of it. You hold up the palm

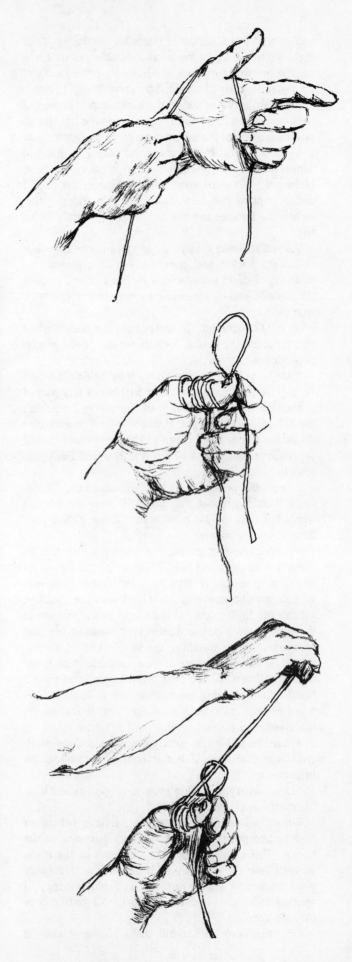

of the hand toward your audience immediately. From the front, all four fingers are still held in place by the band. Bring the bracelet down quickly over the second fingertip, and let it drop. Your right palm momentarily covers the left second finger as you do this. The instant the bracelet is on the finger, you press the fingertip forward against one thickness of the band and the twist goes back over the finger just as it originally was. Hold out the hand to the spectators and have them try to remove the bracelet without removing the band. It can't be done.

Take off the rubber band and put the bracelet on the table in front of you as you reach into your pocket and pull out the yard of heavy cord or string. You are now ready for:

THE BRACELET ON THE STRING

Stretch the string out in a straight line on the table. "It would seem to be impossible to get the bracelet onto the string without threading it over one end or the other, wouldn't it? Not so! There's a way to do it. I'll show you. Watch both ends of the string, please, and notice that the bracelet never goes over either of them. Instead, we put the bracelet down over the *center* of the string, like this."

You now pull up a little loop of string through the center of the bracelet and tie it around the right end of the string.

"The bracelet is now held to the string," you continue, "but, of course, it isn't really *on* the string. This is simply a slipknot." Pull the two ends of the string and the slipknot comes out, leaving the ring atop the string as it was. Tie the slipknot again, exactly as before, using both your right and left hands to do it. A small loop of the string is pulled up from under the bracelet and you insert your left thumb in it. At this point, take the right end of the string in the right fingers, and hand it to one of the spectators, preferably one in front of you rather than to the side. Do this rather quickly. As you hand the end of the string to the spectator, the loop over the thumb pulls the left end of the string through the bracelet. It is impossible to detect. As far as the viewers are concerned, neither end of the string has been out of sight and the ring hasn't been anywhere near either end.

Direct the spectator to hold both ends of the string and pull out the slipknot. He does, and finds that the bracelet is on the string.

Pick up the string and hang one end of it inside the crotch of your left thumb, letting 6 or 7 inches hang down. You are getting ready for:

THREADING THE NEEDLE

Wrap the long end of the string around your left thumb six or seven turns, wrapping under, away from yourself and over toward yourself. When you have six or seven turns of string, bring up a loop in the long end and give it a half-twist to the left, taking the loop between the left thumb and forefinger. The loop should be about 2 inches high, although you may prefer to make it smaller. The free end of the string, extending down from the loop, is behind and under the other end that is wrapped around the thumb.

"I always had trouble threading a needle," you remark, "until an old magician showed me how to do it. Consider this loop as the eye of the needle."

Pick up the short end of the string that hangs down from the thumb crotch, grip it tightly between the right thumb and forefinger, and make a sharp, quick, lunging motion forward with it, directly at the loop and out past it.

The end will be threaded through the loop. You can pull it out of the loop and repeat the action several times.

This simple little trick is as old as the proverbial hills—so old, in fact, that few of the present generation recall ever having seen it. And the illusion it creates is beautiful.

Unwrap the string and get ready for

ON AGAIN, OFF AGAIN

Thread the bracelet onto the center of the string and take one end of the string in each hand. Cross the ends and grip them between the thumb and forefinger of the left hand. Be sure to cross them so that the original right end, which now extends to the left, is under or behind the left end, which now extends to the right.

Pick up the bracelet with your right hand and put it over the end of the cord that extends to your right.

Call attention to exactly what you do and to the fact that the right end goes under the left end every time.

After you thread the bracelet over the end that extends to your right, you grip the two ends and re-

lease the crossed-over hold. The bracelet either stays on the cord or drops free of it, at your whim.

Nobody can detect the slightest difference in what you do. You can let members of your audience do it and tell them before they release the ends whether the ring will stay on the cord or be free of it.

If the continuation of the string that has its end pointing to the left is on the far side, away from you, when you put the ring over the end extending to the right, the ring will drop off, free. of the string. If the end is on the near side, toward you, the ring will stay on the string. You can control this with ease when you're doing it yourself. And all you have to do is look at the string to know what will happen when someone else does it.

And now it's time to do:

THE PADDLE TRICK

Technically, this trick is sleight of hand. Don't let that upset you, though, because nothing could be easier. The "paddle move" is one of the greatest manipulative moves in magic, and it is a beautiful illustration of the magic law that a broad move covers a small one.

If you're any good at whittling, you can make excellent paddles from the wooden tongue depressors that doctors so often use. Just whittle away the part illustrated in gray, except for a handle about a quarter of an inch wide.

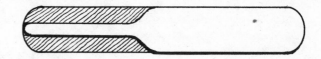

The paddle move has a purpose, which is to apparently show both sides of the paddle while actually showing only one side. Let's say you have an "X" marked on one side of the paddle and don't want your audience to know it until later. You show the clean side of the paddle, holding the handle between the thumb and forefinger so that pressure of the thumb forward or backward will cause the paddle end to roll over. The handle is resting on your forefinger, the end of it pointing toward your body. Your thumb grips it from the top. A slight thumb movement to the left turns the paddle over to the left, and a slight thumb movement to the right turns it over to the right.

You hold the clean side of the paddle facing your audience, the paddle end pointing slightly downward. Now you're going to show the other side. You twist your wrist toward your body, bringing the end of the paddle that is pointing downward up in a half circle. As you make this sweeping arc, your thumb moves either to the right or left, just enough to turn over the paddle. The move is absolutely indetectable to any human eye.

As a matter of fact, a friend of mine wanted to teach the paddle move with a film, and so he filmed it in slow motion to show viewers what happened. The film was no good, because even in slow motion, you couldn't see the move.

With the paddle pointed upward, you apparently show the other side. You now turn the wrist to bring the paddle to a downward position again, reversing the movement of the thumb on the handle.

If the hand were held completely still, the move would be glaringly apparent, but the sweep of the end of the paddle covers it completely as you turn your wrist.

For this particular paddle trick, you may either use a tongue depressor paddle or a table knife. If you use a tongue depressor paddle, you make three X's on each side of it with chalk, making them look as much alike as possible and putting them in the same position on both sides.

For this routine, I think the table knife is preferable. You tear six little strips of paper to a size anywhere from a quarter to half-inch square, and dip them into water. Newsprint paper is fine. The paper should be wet enough and light enough to adhere to the knife blade. You affix three paper strips to each side. Then you hold the knife handle between the right thumb and forefinger, in position for the paddle move.

are two strips on the bottom, you make the paddle move, flipping the knife blade up and back with the wrist as you turn it over with the thumb.

You move it back and forth, up and down, several times, making it clear to your viewers that there are now only two paper strips on each side. Now, with the knife blade pointed down, you remove a second paper strip, apparently from both sides but actually only from the top. You repeat the paddle move several times to show that now only one strip remains on each side.

"If we take away the last paper strip on each side," you continue, "the knife blade will be clean again." You make the same move as with the previous two strips, removing the top one and rolling it between the fingers prior to throwing it away.

You apparently show both sides of the blade bare, making the paddle move several times. "Now, you might wonder why I went to all the trouble of putting the strips on the knife blade if all I was going to do was take them off and throw them away. Not much of a trick, that. The trick comes in bringing the strips back again."

The bare side of the blade is showing, pointed downward, as you say this. You turn the wrist to bring the blade upward, but this time you don't make the paddle move. "It's as simple as the flick of a wrist," you observe, taking the blade in the left hand and holding it out for closer inspection. There's no question about it, the three strips have come back.

"Getting them back onto the other side is just

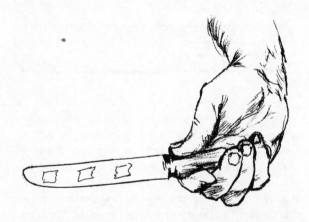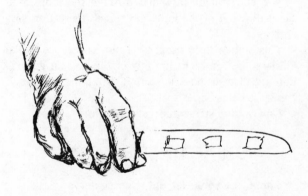

"We'll take away one paper strip from each side," you say, putting your thumb over the strip on top, at the farthest end of the knife. The fingers go underneath. You pull the left thumb and fingers to the left, taking away the paper strip from the top side, but not the one from the bottom side. You immediately roll the strip between your thumb and forefinger and drop it into an ashtray.

"Now," you observe, "we have only two strips on each side." There *are* only two strips on the top side, but three remain on the bottom. To show that there

as easy," you continue. "Watch." You put the knife handle back between the right thumb and forefinger, with the strips visible on the front of the blade. "One, two, three," you count, and swing the blade upward to show the other side, making the paddle move. You make it several times, up and down, back and forth. There are apparently six strips of paper back on the knife again, three on each side.

"The strips on both sides are sympathetic," you say. You reach down onto the blade with your left thumb and slide off the forward strip, being careful not to bring your fingers near the bottom side. "Take away one from this side, and one disappears from the other side, acting in sympathy." You make the paddle move again, showing two strips on each side. Then you take off the second paper strip from the top side of the blade and show, by means of the paddle move, that there is now only one strip on each side.

"The paper strips are very sensitive," you observe. "Sometimes, knowing what's about to happen, they'll disappear before they're supposed to." You lift the blade to the "up" position without making the paddle move and show that the one on the bottom has already disappeared. You drop the knife to the table and offer, "You may keep the last paper strip as a souvenir."

"Don't give me any credit for what happened to the strips," you continue. "Actually, I did nothing. The spirits did the trick. You don't believe in spirits? Then let me introduce you to Chief Running Bear, my spirit guide."

You reach into your pocket and pull out the pencil again, holding it to your ear. "How about convincing these people, Chief?"

You nod. "How many of you people understand the Apache language?" Talk to the blunt end of the pencil. "Palefaces no can rap with you, Chief. No diggum your language." Hold the blunt end of the pencil up to your ear. "He says he can still rap with you by means of the pencil—one rap for yes, two raps for no."

THE RAPPING PENCIL

Don't underestimate this trick. It's the one, remember, that I told you was so marvelously effective in the hands of Gene Bernstein.

The pencil you use should be the type that doesn't have an eraser on the end. A pencil with hexagonal sides works best, although I've done the trick with a round pencil. One of the Bic ballpoint pens, with the cap discarded, will also work.

You put your right forefinger on top of the blunt end of the pencil. Your second finger presses against the right side, and is touching your forefinger. Your thumb is on the other side, also just touching the edge of the forefinger. It looks like you're holding the pencil between the thumb and second finger, with the forefinger resting on top. Actually, you are holding it erect against the table top with your forefinger, which exerts considerable pressure. Your thumb should be thoroughly dry, and so should the pencil. If you press the ball of the thumb hard against the side of the pencil and move it toward the forefinger, it will make a tiny, jerky motion that creates a distinct sound, the sound of a rap. The thumb is hidden from the spectators by the forefinger and second finger,

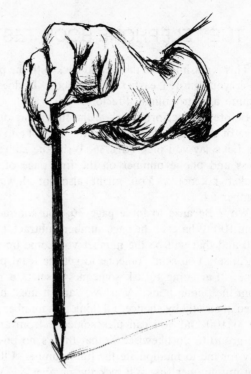

but I've done the trick with people all around me, and the movement of the thumb is so slight that it is never detectable. To show you how slight it is, I usually get about 12 distinct raps before I have to change the thumb's position.

The principle is somewhat the same as that of drawing a rosined bow across a violin cord. The sound is created by the bow, in this case your thumb, moving against the string, in this case the pencil. If you rest the tip of the pencil against the top of a wooden box, the sound will be greatly amplified. I have found that resting the tip of the pencil against the front cover of a heavy book will amplify the sound, strange as that seems. On occasion, I've rested it against the bottom of an inverted coffee cup, with good effect.

Another interesting thing is that you can rest the tip of the pencil against the palm of a spectator's hand, and that person will swear that he "feels" the raps, although the pencil apparently doesn't make the slightest movement.

Getting the raps is admittedly a knack, and you have to experiment around before you do the trick with maximum effect. Once you catch on, however, you have a little gem. Both the pencil and your thumb must be perfectly dry. On occasion, I've tried rubbing a little powdered rosin into the pencil. Maybe it's my imagination, but I think it helped. Once when I'd been doing some manual labor and my thumb was calloused, I got tremendous results.

You can get some good laughs with the "Yes" and "No" answers. It's always good for a laugh to give one rap in answer to a question that calls for an obvious "no." Shake your head, and let the second rap come, delayed.

The trick is an ideal lead into your final trick,

THE TELEPHONE BOOK TEST

This is dissimilar to the mental trick with the phone book you learned earlier in the book. It does *not* require a metropolitan directory.

Before you perform, look at the first name on any page of the local phone book from Page 11 to Page 49. Let's say you pick Page 36. Write the name, address and phone number on the first page of your pocket notebook. You might also jot down the number 64.

Why? Because to force page 36, you subtract 36 from 100. Whatever the page number, subtract it from 100 and that will be the number you come up with.

All set. You send someone to get the local phone book. "I'm going to ask someone to select a name from the phone book," you say, "and it must be arrived at strictly by chance. I'll think of a number from 50 to 100 and you can pick someone from among the group to do likewise. So that there's no possible way for me to manipulate the final number, I'll give you my number first. I'll pick the number 64. Write it down, please. Now, I don't even want to know your number. Just pick any number from 50 to 100 and jot it down directly under my number, 64. Add the two numbers together. Don't tell me the total, but if it's over 99, eliminate the one. Just use the last two digits."

Incidentally, with two numbers from 50 to 100, the total will *always* be over 100.

"Now," you continue, "so that my number will

Gus Rapp

Gus Rapp was the last of the Wizards of the Sticks. He played the smallest villages, hamlets and cross-roads settlements throughout his career, offering a full evening show that his audiences loved.

Sticking to the same territory, he built up a following over the years that insured a big enough turn-out at every performance to be profitable. Neither Blackstone nor Thurston, Big Time contemporaries of his, would have taken in enough money to pay their stage-hands, if booked into the Rapp villages.

Rapp didn't get to the magic conventions until late in his career, and his act was quite different from what was being done by other performers. When some of the leading magicians in the country finally saw his performance, they admitted that they'd never seen some of his tricks before nor even heard of them.

When offered bookings into larger communities at more money, Gus always shrugged, smiled and said, "I'm happy where I am." When he retired, however, it was to a large city, Milwaukee, Wisc. The story of his life, published by Magic, Inc., is a charming picture of a kind of show business most of today's generation never knew.

have no influence on the final choice, subtract those two digits from *your* number—not the total of our two numbers but from your number, alone. The resulting number will determine the Page Number of the phone book, and I think that you'll agree there's no possible way I could know what it is—not that it would help me if I did know. Anyway, turn to that page number and concentrate on the first name on the page."

Let's assume, for purposes of illustration, that the spectator took the number 51. Adding that number to yours, he got a total of 115. Discarding the first digit, he had 15. Subtracting 15 from 51, he got 36. No matter what number he chose, from 50 to 100, the final result will be 36.

Had you elected to use the name and phone number on Page 48, your original number would have been 52—and regardless of his number, when added to 52 and the final two digits of the total subtracted from his number, he would have arrived at 48.

The number in this case, however, is 36. I sometimes use a precautionary measure. People have been known to make mistakes in addition and subtraction. I say, "First, concentrate on the page number. I get the impression of a 3 and—a 6. Page 36! Is that correct?"

In the rare event that he says "No," have someone else check his arithmetic and have him turn to the correct page.

Take your pocket notebook and pencil from your pocket and tear off a strip from the bottom of the first page, printing the name on it. Don't be too fast about this, and stare at the volunteer spectator, asking him to concentrate one letter at a time. Don't announce the name. Just print it on the slip, fold the slip and put it on the table.

You should have the address and phone number firmly in mind by this time, having just looked at them for several minutes. Put the notebook away and say, "Now, concentrate on the address. I get the impression—" Give the address haltingly, and then ask him for the name. When he gives it, tell him to open the folded slip you just put on the table. It's the same name.

"Now comes the most difficult part," you continue. "Concentrate on the phone number." Give the phone number, one digit at a time, and get his acknowledgement that it's correct.

It would be unwise to try to follow this trick with another, because topping it would be almost impossible.

If you're going to do an encore trick, get into something with a lot of participation, like tying the knot in the silk without releasing either end.

This is a good, strong impromptu routine that grabs attention right away with the bill switch and holds it throughout.

Here's the routine:

Bill Switch.
Clipped for a Buck.
Jumping Rubber Band.
Bracelet over Rubber Band.
Bracelet on String.
Threading the Needle.
Off Again, On Again.
The Paddle Trick, With a Table Knife.
The Spirit Rapping Pencil.
Telephone Book Test.

The final trick, alone, is enough to establish you as a magician, as far as your audience is concerned.

A great many would-be magicians, particularly men, want a "Card Act." They'd like to be able to do a routine with nothing but playing cards—and borrowed cards, at that.

Routine with Borrowed Cards

The only preliminary preparation is to remove the nine of Diamonds from a deck of cards and put it under a piece of cardboard on which you've written the Zographos message, in preparation for a trick that's been explained in the section of the book on card tricks.

You have borrowed a pair of bridge decks, and the nine of Diamonds has been removed from one of them, as explained. You also have with you a cheap deck of cards that has been baked in the oven. This is not brought out until you get ready to do the last trick in your routine.

You open by saying, "I've been asked to do some card tricks. And let me confess that while I've always had an interest in magic, I'm no expert card manipulator. I like card tricks, however, and so I've tried to combine magic and mindreading. If a trick is beyond my capabilities as far as magic is concerned, I rely on mindreading. Here's an example of what I mean."

You toss out the deck that's short one card, and have it shuffled.

"Now I've heard about magicians who could take a shuffled deck of cards, fan it, and force a member of the audience to take one particular card out of the 52. I wonder. It always sounds a little farfetched to me. At any rate, I can't do it. I'll simply fan the deck into as even a fan as I possibly can. And I'm going to need some help on this trick. Frankly, I can't do it alone. Here's a fellow who looks like he has the makings of a fine magician."

You've fanned the cards from right to left, face down, as explained in the Hoax Think of a Card trick. You motion the person you've picked for an assistant to join you and stand directly behind you. Then you turn your back on the rest of the audience and hold the faces of the deck of cards up in front of him. "Now, as I've said, this trick is going to depend on you," you tell him. "I'm going to ask you to think of any card you see in this fan that particularly impresses you, that stands out for one reason or another. Concentrate on it. Don't forget its name. You have one? Good. You may sit down again."

MAGIC OR MINDREADING

The only card in the deck that the volunteer assistant could possibly identify is the bottom card, and you leave it right on the bottom of the deck. You announce, "Now, there are many different ways of shuffling a deck of cards—and some of them, confidentially, don't do a very good job. The best way to shuffle, in my opinion, is to mix the cards up every which way, even face up and face down."

You are holding the deck in your left hand, as if ready to deal. You reach over to the deck with your right hand, palm down. You thumb off a small block of cards to the right with your left hand and take these cards in your right hand, fingers on top, thumb beneath. You now turn your right hand palm up, thumb off another little block of cards with your left

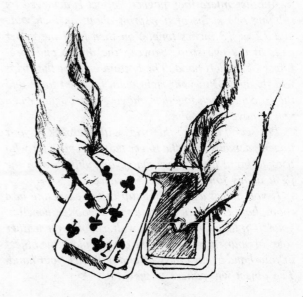

hand, and take these beneath those you're already holding. The two blocks of cards face in opposite directions. The top block is face up and the bottom block is face down. You turn your right hand palm down again, take off another block of cards with it, beneath the bottom cards in your hands, turn the hand over again and thumb off another block, putting it against those now on the bottom. You continue this way, up, down, up, down, until you get to the last card of the deck. You put it face down on *top* of the face-up cards in your right hand.

If you've done this briskly, you now apparently hold a deck that is hopelessly mixed up, with cards alternating face up and face down throughout the deck. Actually, the top half of the deck is all face up with the exception of the top card, and the bottom half of the deck is all face down. It is very easy to split the deck at the division point, so that all the cards in each hand face one way with the exception of the top card in the right hand. If you have any trouble

Personal Magnetism

Lay a nickel on the outstretched palm of either your right or left hand. Give a clothes brush to a spectator and tell him that he cannot brush the nickel off your palm—at least, not with the clothes brush.

He can't. The explanation is—well, you figure it out.

Another magnetic effect is achieved by putting two matches on the table top, a couple of inches apart. You rub your thumb and forefinger briskly together and move them above and between the two matches. The matches roll farther apart as you continue to rub your fingers. When you stop rubbing, the matches stop rolling.

Of course, while you're rubbing, you're blowing your breath gently onto the table top between the two matches.

Another interesting magnetic effect is achieved by rubbing two strips of newsprint about an inch wide and 12 or 13 inches long. You then hold the upper ends of the two strips between the thumb and forefinger of the left hand. The bottom ends of the strips will fly apart. Put your right palm between them and they'll come back together, moving apart again when you remove your palm.

The secret is to rub the strips with the back *of your fingers, actually with the finger nails. A spectator who tries to build up a static charge by rubbing with the flesh of his fingers will get nowhere.*

If you detect a static buildup in the carpeting in a room, hold a pack of cigarettes or a wooden pencil in your right hand, walk up to a wall, rubbing the leather soles of your shoes against the carpet, place the object in your hand against the wall and pull back your hand. The object will adhere to the wall.

splitting the deck at the right place, riffle the edges. You should seldom have to do this, however, because cards that have been used much are all slightly bent in the same direction and when the two halves of the deck are back to back, they form a natural break.

Turn the cards in the left hand face up and give the two halves of the deck a quick riffle shuffle, leaving the one face-down card on top. Cut this card to the center of the deck and turn the deck face down, neatly squared. Put it on the table.

"That mixes the cards even more," you observe. "And now," nodding to the volunteer assistant, "I remember that you looked at the fanned deck and merely thought of a card you saw there. You didn't remove it. You didn't even touch it. For the first time, what is the card you're thinking of?"

He tells you, and you spread the deck out across the table. Every card in the deck is face down except one card in the middle—and that is the card that was mentally selected!

Sure, the volunteer assistant knows that he had a mental choice of only one card—but he hasn't the faintest idea of how you got that card reversed or how you mixed all the cards in the deck face up and face down and got them all back facing the same way. He wouldn't even know where to start to do the trick, himself. As far as the rest of your audience is concerned, it has just seen one of the best card tricks that any member of the group has ever witnessed.

Next, you do the Card Spelling trick as explained in the card section, but you don't do the follow-up in which the spelled card is reversed. You've just done a reversed card trick.

After the card spelling, you fan through the deck and remove the four Aces, face up, tossing them to the table. While somebody is mixing them up, face down, you get a break with the little finger of your left hand under the top three cards of the deck, as explained in the card section, and do the four-Ace trick that utilizes the addition of those three cards to the pile of four Aces.

At the conclusion of this trick, you put the four Aces on top of the deck, face down, give the deck a false cut, pulling a pile from the bottom with your right hand and slapping the top half back down on top of them. You then do a riffle shuffle, not disturbing the four Aces on top of the deck, do another false cut, and have the deck cut into four piles, as the start of the Three Under and Three Across four-Ace trick previously explained.

After you've gone through the formula, three under and three across with each pile, you say, "This trick illustrates again how I call on mindreading rather than sleight of hand. I mentally willed you to cut those four piles exactly as you did, and you obliged." Have the spectator turn the top card of each pile face up and reveal an Ace atop of each pile.

Next, you do the 12-Card Count or Cards Across trick, employing either the simple method with two ordinary envelopes or using the sleight-of-hand method that adds three cards to the right-hand pile from the left-hand one.

If you like, you may interject the Poker Hand demonstration previously explained. It's hardly necessary, because you've already shown your control of the four Aces, but a lot of people like it. Suit yourself. Whether you do the poker deals or not, you next do the Zographos Prediction, and put the nine of Diamonds back into the deck.

For the first time, you use the second deck as you perform You Do As I Do, one of the easiest tricks in the whole routine and certainly a strong one.

Then, giving the spectators a choice of either deck, you perform the Golden Miracle trick. If you hold the penny between the right thumb and forefinger, thumb beneath it, forefinger on top, have the spectator grasp it in exactly the same way and have it directly above the center card of the five, the penny should drop onto that card, the chosen one, without the slightest difficulty. If, as seldom happens, he drops it onto another card, you know how to handle the situation.

"And now," you continue, "I'm going to use my own deck of cards for my final demonstration. Don't, please, think that it's a trick deck. You may examine the cards and shuffle them to your heart's content. The reason I use my own cards is because the deck gets destroyed in the process of doing the trick, and I'd like to be invited back here. Also, our host's cards are of superior quality, and this deck is as cheap as they come."

Smudge

While moving an ash tray to a spot in front of you, get a good-sized gob of ashes on the ball of your right third finger. When you set the ash tray down, curl this third finger in toward the palm, which is a natural position for it.

Now, ask a spectator to hold out his right hand, palm down. With your left thumb and first two fingers, pick up a few ashes from the tray and put them on the back of his hand.

As you say, "Now, close your hand into a fist," reach your right first and second fingers to the back of his extended fingers, third and little fingers of your own under them. You close his fingers. "Keep your hand tightly closed," you instruct him.

Now, you gently rub the ashes on the back of his hand. They will practically disappear. Tell him to turn over his hand and open his fist, and he will see that the ashes went through from the back to the palm of his hand.

Some magicians close the spectator's hand into a fist before they put the ashes on the back of his hand. It's a matter of personal preference.

You have the cards examined, shuffled, a card chosen and put back into the deck. You bring it to the top as explained in the trick, Tearing a Deck of Cards in Half. Then you tear the deck in half, pick up one torn half of the deck and thumb off card pieces until the person who chose the card says "Stop." You hand him what has remained the top card throughout, a torn half of his card. Another person says "Stop" as you deal off pieces of card from the other half in the same manner, holding back the top torn piece of card.

You've wound up your act, and believe me, it's a sock finish when the two torn pieces of card not only match but are the chosen card. With Zographos, The Golden Miracle and Tearing the Deck as your final three tricks, you should make your exit in a blaze of glory.

The routine is:

Magic or Mindreading?
Card Spelling
Four-Ace Trick
Three Under, Three Across
Poker Demonstration (Optional)
Zographos Prediction
The Golden Miracle
Tearing a Deck in Half, Plus.

If you feel uncomfortable with any of the tricks in the routine, substitute others for them. Miraskill is hard to beat.

Some people want a close-up routine that's a little easier than the strictly impromptu one I've already given you. For them, here's the Stebbins Stacked Deck Routine.

Card Routine with a Stacked Deck

Many amateur magicians, I've found, want a routine of card tricks with a stacked deck. There's nothing wrong with that if you know how to handle the cards so that nobody in your audience has the faintest idea you're using such a thing.

If you're going to use a stacked deck for a series of card tricks, you should certainly learn the false riffle shuffle described in the card section of this book. And I don't mean you should be able to do it after a fashion. You should be able to do it so well that it passes as a legitimate shuffle.

The routine I'm going to show you is done with a Si Stebbins stack. For years, this has been the simplest and most popular of stacked deck arrangements. In it, the suits run in a set order, Clubs, Hearts, Diamonds and Spades. The word CHaSeD is your key.

To stack your deck, sort out the four suits and arrange each suit with the cards in order from Ace to King. Lay out the four piles in order from left to right: Clubs, Hearts, Spades and Diamonds. The face-up Club pile has the Ace at the top, the King directly beneath it and the remainder of the suit in order running down to the deuce. Cut the Heart pile so that the Four is the top face-up card. Then cut the Spade pile so that the seven is the top card and cut the Diamond pile so that the ten-spot is on top.

Pick up the Ace of Clubs. On top of it, put the face-up four of Hearts. Next, put the face-up seven of Spades, then the ten of Diamonds. The King of Clubs goes on top of this, followed by the three of Hearts. Continue stacking the cards in this manner until the whole deck is stacked.

No matter how often you cut this deck, the order of cards remains the same. Each suit runs through the deck in order, A,K,Q,J,10,9,8,7,6,5,4,3,2 — with three cards of the three other suits between each two. If a Diamond is on the bottom of the deck, a Club three spots higher will be on the top. For example, with the six of Diamonds on the bottom, you know that the top card is the nine of Clubs. With the four of Spades on the bottom, you know that the top card is the seven of Diamonds. With the eight of Hearts on the bottom, you know that the top card is the Jack of Spades. The top card is always three higher than the bottom one, in the following suit in the CHaSeD progression.

A Switch

Cut the flap off of an envelope with a razor blade.

If you put this envelope on top of a pile of matching envelopes, flap side up, the flap of the second envelope will seem to be the flap of the gimmicked top one.

Fold down the top flap and have a spectator initial it. Then lift the flap and insert the card or any small flat object into the envelope. Let's say that it's a card and that it's the three of Spades.

Grab the top envelope by what is apparently the loose flap and pull it away from the pile with your right hand, the left thumb and fingers holding the remainder of the pile in line. The back of the left hand should be tilted slightly toward the audience as the flap is pulled away.

Hand the initialed envelope to a spectator to seal.

When the sealed envelope is torn open by another spectator, the three of Spades that was originally put into it is seen to have changed to another card. The other card was, of course, inserted into the second envelope, the top one with a flap, prior to the performance.

In addition to using this technique for switching a card, coin, or piece of paper, it may also be used to vanish whatever is put into the flapless envelope. In this case, the second envelope down from the top is empty at the start of the trick.

You fan the deck and have someone remove a card —a free choice. You cut the deck just above the selected card, bringing those cards to the bottom. Let's say that the card just above the chosen card is the three of Spades. You cut it to the bottom and know that the chosen card is the six of Diamonds. When you complete your trick, you replace the six of Diamonds on top of the deck and cut the cards. The order of the entire deck is still intact.

Cut your stacked deck so that the Ace of Clubs is on the bottom. Put the deck in your left hip pocket, facing your body.

You start the routine with a matching deck that is unstacked. You hand this unprepared deck to someone to shuffle. You take the shuffled deck and put it quickly behind your back, without looking at it.

"For my first trick," you say, "I'm going to try to find one card of each of the four suits, with the shuffled deck behind my back. While I might have been able to catch a quick glimpse of the bottom card, I think you'll agree that it would have been impossible for me to locate four cards of four different suits."

As you say this, you remove the stacked deck from the left hip pocket with your left hand and put the shuffled deck into your right hip pocket with your right hand.

You take the top card from the stacked deck that is still held behind your back. "First, I'll remove a Heart," you say. "How about the Four of Hearts?" You toss the four of Hearts face up onto the table. "The other major suit is Spades. How about the seven of Spades?" You toss the next card, the seven of Spades, face up on top of the four of Hearts. "Now, let's look for a Diamond. Let's say, the ten of Diamonds." You toss it face up onto the seven of Spades. "And that leaves Clubs. We don't have a picture card yet. How about the King of Clubs?" You toss it on top of the other three cards. You bring the deck around to the front, turn the face-up cards over and put them face down on the deck, following immediately with a cut that brings them somewhere near the center.

"I know what you're thinking. You think there's something on each card that I can feel. So let's try to identify a card without my even touching it." You fan the face down deck and offer it for selection of a card. The person who takes the card is told to look at it and stick it in his pocket while your back is turned. You turn around, having looked at the card directly above the chosen one and cut it to the bottom. Let's say it's the King of Hearts.

"I'm going to try to determine the identity of your card by Lip Reading," you announce. "I'll put one finger lightly on your upper lip and one on your lower lip. I'll keep my head turned aside. Now, just form the name of your card with your lips. Don't say it—

don't even whisper it. Just form the words silently with your lips."

As soon as you've felt movement of his lips, declare, "The card you selected is the three of Spades. Is that correct?"

As soon as he acknowledges it, put his card back onto the deck and cut the cards. This Lip Reading idea first came to my attention in a routine devised by Howard Albright, and I've found that audiences are fascinated by it. Let several other people take cards and "read their lips."

"Now," you announce, "I'm going to try something even more difficult." Put the deck face-down on the table. "Cut the cards, any way you choose, a deep cut, a shallow one or a medium one. Take the top three cards and hold them tightly against your chest." You pick up the deck, showing him how he's to hold the cards "against his chest." Once you've seen the bottom card, you put the deck down and turn your back.

Let's say the bottom card was the five of Clubs. You know that the cards he's holding are the eight of Hearts, the Jack of Spades and the Ace of Diamonds.

"Fan your three cards faces toward yourself," you instruct the volunteer assistant. "I get the impression that one of the cards is a picture card. Concentrate on it. It's a black card. It's a Spade. It's the Jack of Spades. Put it down on the table and concentrate on the other two. Pick one of them in your mind. No, no, you're thinking of *both* of them. Think of the less desirable of the two. Forget the other one for the time being. That's right. Put the eight of Hearts on the table with the Jack of Spades. You now have one card left. I get the feeling that it's a good card. It's a Diamond. Oh, now it comes through clearly. It's the Ace of Diamonds." You turn around, take the Ace from him and put the three cards back into the deck, face down, in their original order. You cut the cards.

"One of the easiest ways to determine a card that's been removed from the deck," you continue, "is to simply look at the deck and see what card is missing. While my back is turned, remove a card from anywhere in the deck and put it into your pocket without even looking at it. You may cut the cards or leave them as they are, whichever you choose. All set?"

You turn around, pick up the deck, and fan the cards facing yourself. At only one place in the fan will there be two adjacent cards of the same color. Looking at them tells you immediately what the missing card is. For example, if the matching color cards are the ten of Diamonds and four of Hearts, you know immediately that the missing card is the seven of Spades. Cut the deck at the matching cards so that one goes on the bottom and one on top. Tell the assistant to remove the card from his pocket and look at it for the first time. It is the seven of Spades. Put it on top of the deck.

You now have two choices of procedure. If you can do a convincing false riffle shuffle, do it and offer the deck for cutting.

If you can't do a good false shuffle, put the deck behind your back and say, "I'm now going to show you how I can rearrange the entire deck by sense of touch, in less than five seconds, holding the cards behind my back." You have put the stacked deck in your right-hand hip pocket and removed the straight deck.

"Oh, wait a minute," you say, bringing the straight deck around to the front. "I should have let you shuffle the cards first." You offer the deck for shuffling. You then take it, put it behind your back and exchange it again for the stacked deck as you count sharply, "One, two, three, four, five." You bring the deck around to the front and announce, "I'm going to deal four hands of Bridge. Please don't look at your cards until I tell you to. Perhaps somebody would like to cut again."

When the cards have been cut, see what suit is on the bottom. If it happens to be a Spade, deal four hands, dealing the last hand to yourself. If it isn't a Spade, deal the hands to four spectators. If a Diamond is on the bottom, you know that the four players will receive Clubs, Hearts, Spades and Diamonds in order. With a Club on the bottom, you know that the players will receive Hearts, Spades, Diamonds and Clubs in order. Keep track of the Spade hand.

When the cards are all dealt, ask one player to look at his hand and say whether he'd bid on it or not. Since he holds 13 cards of one suit, he most certainly would. Ask the other two if they'd bid on their hands, holding back the Spade hand 'til last. They'd bid, too.

"Each of you three thinks he has a sure thing," you say, "but you couldn't even get the bid, because this

Locater Cards II

The simplest of all "locater" cards is a double-thickness playing card. Why it's never detected by spectators is a mystery to me, but it never is.

Where do you get one of these double-thickness cards? You don't. You make it.

You decide what card you want to use as a locater, let's say the three of Clubs. You put a thin coat of rubber cement on the back of it. You coat the face of one of the Jokers similarly, line the two cards up carefully and press them together.

Whether you start with this card on the bottom of the deck or somewhere in the middle, it's ridiculously easy to find by sense of touch. Have a chosen card replaced beneath it, the deck squared and cut, and you could find the chosen card while thoroughly blindfolded. Dealing off cards face down, one at a time, you know when you feel the heavy card that the next one will be the spectator's.

man would bid seven Spades." All the hands are turned up, showing that you've dealt four perfect bridge hands.

You've completed your routine, and the cards may now be examined to everyone's satisfaction without revealing any secrets.

When Bert Allerton was amazing guests in the Pump Room at the Ambassador East Hotel in Chicago, he often used as many as four or five stacked decks in the course of a close-up performance. The cards were frequently shuffled by spectators and nobody had any idea that most of his eye-popping card tricks were done with stacked hands. They'd have been willing to swear that only one deck was used in the course of his routine.

Everything was right for the use of stacked decks. Since guests almost never carry decks of cards to dinner, nobody expected him to do tricks with a borrowed deck.

The Nikola system of stacking a deck, explained in detail in the revised *Encyclopedia of Card Tricks,* is probably the ultimate. The tricks that can be done with it are almost too good, but memorizing the stack and the mnemonics system that goes with it is no easy task. As much study as it requires, however, I'd learn it if I were going to depend on stacked decks.

Because the cards progress by three in the Si Stebbins system, some magicians favor the "Eight Kings" stack, in which the arrangement follows no mathematical pattern. You memorize the sentence, "Eight Kings threatened (3-10) to (2) save (7) ninety-five (9-5) ladies (Queens) for (4) one (1) sick (6) knave (Jack).

It may be a less detectable arrangement, but it is also slower—and if a stacked deck routine is done briskly, nobody will recognize the three progression.

Doc Mahendra worked out all kinds of mathematical formulae for the Si Stebbins stack, so that he could tell you the position of any given card in the pack. His Si Stebbins routine was superb, but a major factor was his ability to handle a stacked deck so that

The Great Unknown

Comparatively few magic fans have ever heard of Eddie Tulloch. Most amusement seekers wouldn't recognize his name.

And yet, Eddie Tulloch, working about nine months of the year and taking it easy for the other three, probably earned more money as a performer last year than anyone else doing magic.

And he did it with one prop, a deck of cards. A specialist in the Industrial Show field, he enjoys an income that few magicians even come close to attaining. He doesn't go after personal publicity or acclaim —just dollars.

And he gets them!

audiences never for an instant considered one might be in use. For the average amateur to know the position in the pack of any card called for is, I think, a glaring tipoff that a stacked deck is responsible.

There's no denying that some beautiful tricks can be done with stacked cards, particularly in the field of poker deals. However, if your experience is anything like mine, you'll abandon stacks as you become more familiar and at ease with cards. You simply won't want to be bothered getting cards ready.

At the conclusion of the Si Stebbins routine I've given you, the original stacked deck can be thoroughly shuffled and you can wind up with Miraskill, a superior card trick explained in the card section of this book. I have a feeling you'll find it the most satisfying trick in the routine.

The Stebbins routine offers little challenge to the performer, aside from a convincing riffle shuffle and a smooth switch of a straight deck for a stacked one. A professional magician who is going to do the deck switch behind the back probably won't use the hip pockets for it. He will have a couple of holders hanging from the belt at the back. These can be made of heavy cardboard, half an inch wider and about the same increase in thickness over the size of a standard card case. They are about two-thirds the length of a card case and are open at the top. They are often made in one unit, with a divider between them to keep the two decks from getting mixed up.

Probably the most effective and simple way to switch a stacked deck into use utilizes the right-hand inside breast pocket. The stacked deck of cards is there, beside a pen or pencil. You have a deck with matching backs shuffled and take it in your left hand. Now, you must contrive some seemingly logical reason why you need a pen or pencil. One of the simplest is to make your first trick with the stacked deck a "prediction" trick, but that's not always something you want to do. One of the most brazen—and best— is to say, "So that you know I don't switch cards on you, I want you to make some little identifying mark on the face of the top card of the deck."

You hold open the right side of your coat with your right hand. The left hand, holding the shuffled deck, reaches into the pocket for the pen or pencil and drops the shuffled deck as it grabs the stacked deck and writing instrument. If the pocket isn't large enough to make a smooth exchange of cards, put the shuffled deck in your armpit, gripping it firmly with your upper arm. After you've had the top card marked, take back the pen or pencil and replace it in your pocket, at the same time taking the deck from the armpit and dropping it into the pocket, too.

Once you have a few performances under your belt, you won't get much kick from doing a routine with a stacked deck of cards. Probably the most satisfying kind of close-up routine is one you do with a little kit of paraphernalia. You don't need the kit for mechanical apparatus, but to offer tricks with a wide variety of objects. This kind of a routine gives you opportunity to show versatility and is the type of performance that most professional "table workers" employ. It gives the impression of being much more professional than a routine with a deck of cards or a piece of rope, and it is wider in its appeal.

It purposely includes some almost self-working tricks which are good magic and which give you an occasional "breather." The three most difficult tricks of the routine come at the end, by which time you should have plenty of confidence. Simple as the routine is, when you can do it well, you're a magician.

"Kit" Impromptu Table Routine

In your equipment kit, you have: a hank of soft sash cord, a metal or plastic ring about 3 inches in diameter, one of the strips of paper coated with rubber cement and talcum powder as described in the "Ice Breaker" section, four sponge balls, a set of Afghan Bands (to be described), an end-opening envelope with a slit across the address side, a card to fit inside the envelope, a slate and chalk, a fairly stiff card, 3 inches square and the same on both sides, six half-dollars and a poker chip.

You start the routine by draping a length of rope over your left thumb and forefinger, which are spread, facing your audience. You pick up the ring and show that to get it onto the rope, you have to bring it up over either end. It won't go on by pressing it against the middle, the part between your left thumb and forefinger.

"I do my first trick with a piece of rope," you say. "I use rope because it has strange properties. I've heard that rope comes from the same source as hashish, a powerful narcotic—and I can believe it, because sometimes a piece of rope can make you think you're seeing strange things. Now, you *know* it's impossible to put this ring onto the rope by pressing it down against the middle of the rope." Your left hand turns so that the back of it now faces your audience, and the thumb comes out from under the rope as the right hand starts to slide the ring down it. The left thumb goes back under the rope but through the ring, as the right fingers lower the ring in a continuous motion. By the time the downward pressure has brought the two ends up to the left fingers, the ring is obviously and undisputably threaded onto the rope. "Now, you know darned well you didn't see such a thing happen, but you *think* you did, and as far as a magician's concerned, that's just as good."

You slide the ring off and stretch the rope between your hands. "Now, where's the center of this rope?" you ask. Somebody points to a spot, and you have him hold the rope at that point, while you let go of the two ends. The ends hang down from his fingers, and it's easy to see how close he came to guessing the exact midway point of the rope. You're now ready to do the:

SQUARE KNOT CUT AND RESTORED ROPE

There are many excellent cut and restored rope tricks, some using gimmicks and some depending on sleight of hand. This is one of the best, and certainly the simplest and easiest.

"With the strange hypnotic powers of rope in mind, we're going to mark the exact center of this length of rope," you announce, "so that there can't be any question about it." You bring up one end and tie it into a square knot at the point where he's marking the center. It *must* be a genuine square knot, not a granny. Half of the rope is now in a loop and the other half hangs free. You take the rope from the assistant, grasping it by the loop, a few inches above the square knot. With a knife or sharp pair of scissors, you now cut the rope, right at the extending end of the square knot. It's a good idea to cut through the rope and the

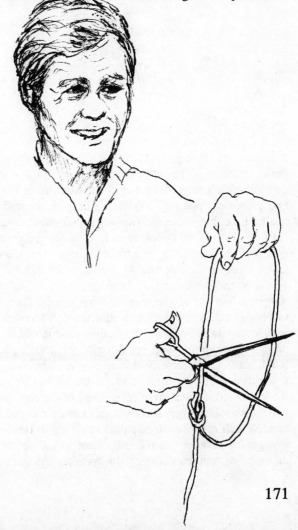

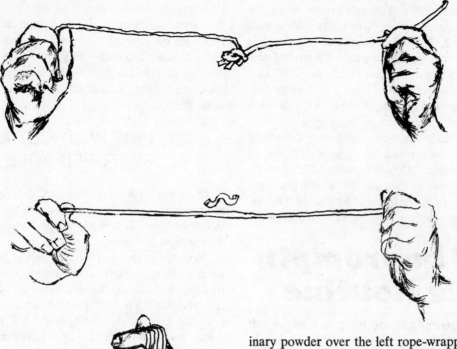

loose end of the square knot, nipping off a part of the knot's surplus. The rope immediately drops down, and the knot is now in the middle of what looks like two pieces of rope tied together. The trick is practically done, but there are two ways to finish it. The easy way is to grasp the other end of the rope in your right hand, the hands outstretched, rope between them, knot in the middle. At the count of "Three" you give the rope ends a sharp jerk and the knot jumps visibly off of the rope, leaving a solid length of rope intact. The other way, and the one I prefer, is to start wrapping the rope around your left hand, doing the wrapping with your right. As your right hand reaches the knot, which is inside, away from the audience, you continue to wrap, but you hold onto the knot, and it slides right off the end of the rope as you finish the wrapping. It is concealed in the right hand, which reaches into the pocket for some "invisible goofus powder," leaving the knot in the pocket and coming out immediately to sprinkle the imag-

inary powder over the left rope-wrapped hand. Have the assistant take hold of the free end and the two of you pull the rope out into a straight length. The knot has vanished and the rope is restored! If there's a cleaner, easier, no-gimmick method of cutting and restoring a rope, I've never seen it.

"Now, you know *that* didn't really happen, either," you continue. "I tell you this rope is tricky stuff. And *two* lengths of rope are twice as tricky as one."

You take a second length of rope, hang the two lengths over a pencil, tie them together and do the Ropes Through the Coat tricks as earlier outlined and explained.

"Maybe we better forget about rope. I don't trust the stuff." You put the 3-inch square card on the table. "I like to work with straight material, and nothing's straighter than an arrow. You remember Straight Arrow, don't you, from the movie of the same name? I really should have the services of a top-notch commercial artist for this next trick, because we have to draw a straight arrow on this card. I'll draw one on one side, to show you what I want. Like this." You draw an arrow through the center of the card, putting the arrow point at the top.

Now comes an important move. You grasp the lower right corner of the card between your right thumb and forefinger and lift that end from the table. The front end of the card is down, still touching the table. You lift the card 4 or 5 inches above the table and turn it over, without changing the position of your fingers, again bringing the outer side to the table-top first. "Now, you draw an arrow in the same position on this side." You illustrate by moving your finger or the pen or pencil up and down across the middle. "Arrow point at the top, just as on the other side." you remind him.

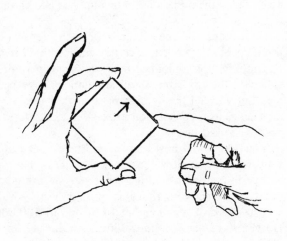

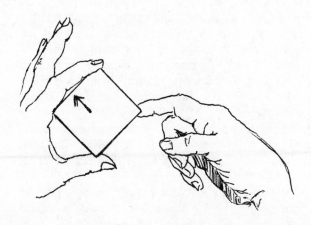

Now you pick up the card with the right hand and put diagonal corners of it between the thumb and first finger of the left hand, so that the point-end of the arrow points to the right.

You revolve the card slowly by pressing against the side with your right forefinger. "Let me call attention to the remarkable fact that the arrow tips point the same way."

You take the card by the lower right-hand corner again, between the right thumb and forefinger, and turn it back and forth with the same move as you used previously. "No question about it, the arrow tips point the same way. Two straight arrows, heading in the same direction."

You put the card back between the left thumb and forefinger, but this time, you put it so that the top arrow extends to the left, pointing to the left. With the diagonal corners held by the thumb and forefinger, you pivot the card again—but now, the arrow-heads are at opposite ends. One points up and one points down. You grasp the card between the left-hand thumb and forefinger at the left inner corner and do the turn-over move, and there's no question about it, the arrow heads point in opposite directions.

You shake your head and put the card on the table, arrow-head pointing away from you. "It's that dog-goned loose lead again (or running ink)." You very slowly pivot the card on the table back toward you, turning it over. And now, the arrow on the other side extends to the right and left instead of forward and backward. This move should be made very slowly, so that everyone can see that the two arrows don't even extend in the same direction.

"It's getting worse." You shake your head. "Let's forget the whole thing. Let's face it, Straight Arrow is crooked."

You bring out the rubber-cemented strip of paper. You have used a column of stock-market reports for it. "As a matter of fact, you don't know who you can trust any more. I went to my broker the other day with a list of what looked like good stocks I'd clipped from the market reports in the paper.

"Now, I don't want to consider any stock that's being manipulated," I told him. He took the list, looked it over, folded the paper in the middle, and picked up a pair of scissors. "In that case," he said, "we'll have to eliminate a few." You snip a small piece from the folded end of the paper and pick up the top end, showing that the strip is still intact.

"Another thing," I told him, "I don't want to consider any stock that isn't paying dividends." You fold the paper back up and snip off another piece from the folded center, saying, "He seemed to think that would eliminate a few more, and he clipped another hunk out of my column." You lift the top end of the paper again, to show the strip still intact, despite its having been cut across the middle a second time.

"What I really want," I told him, "is a sure thing—a stock that can't go wrong." This time, you cut away most of the paper, leaving little more than an inch on either side of the fold. "He really ruined my list from the paper at that point," you continue. You open up the short remaining piece. "He said, 'About all you've got left is U. S. Savings Bonds.' "

You can prolong the story, if you like, making more qualifications and clipping away more pieces.

"Everybody tries to take you," you continue. "The last one I had trouble with wasn't a crook; he was just a sponger. But I got even with him, I swiped his sponges."

You remove three sponge balls from the kit. The fourth hidden one is already in place. And now you do as long or as short a sponge ball routine as you like.

At its conclusion, you observe, "Not all people are spongers by any means, but everybody today seems to be a competitor. Everybody's competing with everyone else. So to stay in tune with the times, I've planned a little competition to see who's best at cutting red tape."

You have three circles of cheap red cambric or red paper, prepared for:

THE AFGHAN BANDS

This is an old, old trick. It requires no skill on your part, since two members of the audience actually do it, so it gives you a breather.

You need three 36-inch strips of red tissue or cheap cloth, each strip anywhere from an inch to an inch and a half wide. You sew or cement the ends of one strip together, making it a circle. You make a half-twist in one end of the second tape before you cement the ends together, and you make a full twist in the third tape, bringing the top of one end over to the bottom and right on over so that it's the top side again.

With the three circles of tape, you pick up the "straight" one and cut it down the middle so that it becomes two separate circles. You hand one of the other tapes to a spectator and the other tape to a second spectator, along with a pair of scissors for each.

"Now, you two are going to run a race at cutting red tape," you say. "The first one to cut his tape circle into two separate circles will be the winner. There's quite a trick to it. You want to sever the tape into halves as quickly as possible, in order to win—but if you try to cut it too fast, you may cut part of the tape completely apart so that it becomes a strip rather than a circle—which would put you out of the race. The race is well worth winning, too. The first one of you who cuts his tape into two separate and unconnected circles of the original size but half the original width will be awarded a new color television set. On your marks—get ready—go!"

They start cutting, as you encourage them. And when they finish, one spectator has two circles, one linked within the other—not separate and unconnected. The other has one circle twice the size of the original one.

This trick should be called "the Moebius strip" rather than "the Afghan Bands," since it was invented by Alfred Ferdinand Moebius, an astronomer, to illustrate a mathematical principle. Over the years, magicians have come up with many variations of it.

One of these starts with a 36-inch circle of cloth 4½ inches wide. One end of the strip of cloth is solid, while the other end is cut into three strips about 3 inches long, 1½ inches in from each side, making the end consist of three 1½-inch-wide tabs. One of these is given a half twist, the center one is left straight, and the other is given a full twist before cementing or sewing together. This cloth is quickly cut apart into three circles, continuing from the two cuts.

The center strip, if cut into two circles will result in two separate circles, while one of the outside strips will form a double-size circle and the other will form two circles linked together.

In a pinch, you can make three circles on the spot, cutting three strips 1½ inches wide from a newspaper and making them into circles by applying Scotch tape to the ends.

It's a matter of one minute's work to prepare the three strips, if you connect the ends with cement. Regretfully, you announce that you're not permitted to award the prize unless all stipulations have been met, but you tell the contestants that they may keep their tapes as a consolation prize—"in case you ever need some red tape."

You add, "And now that the red tape's out of the way, we can get down to serious business. Do you believe in mental telepathy? Well, you, sir, are going to try to project your thoughts into my head. I want you to think of any number from one to 100,000. Do you have one in mind? Fine. Concentrate on it. I don't seem to get any mental vibrations. Sometimes, it helps you to make a mental image of your number if you write it down. Write it in large numerals on the center of this card, but wait until my back is turned to do it." You turn your back as he writes down his number. "Got it written down." Your back is still turned. "Look at it. Now, turn it face down so that I can't see it."

As you turn around, you pick up an end-opening envelope, a little longer and a full inch wider than the card. Buy the envelopes and then cut the cards to proper size.

"So that there's no chance of my getting a glimpse of the number you've written down, we'll just seal it in this envelope and leave it in plain sight."

You hold the envelope flap side up and hold it right down to the level of the table top, where the face-down card is resting. You shove the face-down card into the envelope without any false moves, dip your forefinger into a glass of water and moisten the flap, and then seal the flap. It should be obvious to everyone that you haven't had the slightest chance of getting even a quick glimpse of the number.

You now prop the envelope up against a book or anything solid. If there's nothing available, just lay it flat on the table top, in front of your place.

Here's what has happened. The end-opening envelope has a slit in the address side, made with a sharp razor blade. The slit extends across, slightly more than the full width of the card—just enough more so that no forcing of the card is necessary. The slit is almost an inch under the exposed inside of the envelope on the flap side, so that when you shove the card into the envelope, you're able to shove the other end through the slit so that most of the card is on the back outside of the envelope. When you pick up the envelope to put it "on display, out of the way," you can look right at the number. A quick glimpse is all you need.

Now that you know the number, you tell the spectator to think of his number one digit at a time. You pick up the slate and a piece of chalk and, very hesitantly, write the number on the slate, which you then turn face down and put in front of the spectator.

Fu Manchu

David Bamberg, son of the illustrious Theo Bamberg, known throughout the world during his lifetime as Okito, is the eighth generation of magicians in the Bamberg family.

Touring his show mostly through Spanish-speaking countries, he has always worked professionally as Fu Manchu. His magical background came not only from his family but from early associations with Houdini, Rosini, Nate Leipzig and the Zanzigs, all magical starts of magnitude.

"Charm" is a word which most reviewers have used in describing the Fu Manchu performance. His personality projects warmly to his audiences, and his performing ability is such that he has had a separate career as a star of Spanish-language movies.

His comedic sense is strong, and even the most baffling illusions in his show have been designed to incorporate plenty of laughs. Few people in the world know every phase of magic as thoroughly as David Bamberg, and yet he wants to be known as a magical entertainer instead of as a great magician.

One of his magical masterpieces has always been the Floating Ball trick originated by his father. His injection of comedy into such illusions as his original Chinese Pagoda effect puts a unique Bamberg stamp on everything he does.

"I've tried to write your number on this slate," you say. "Let's see how close I've come."

You pick up the envelope, tear open the flap, very openly reach inside, to the end of the card and pull it from the envelope. There should be no question but what the card comes from inside the envelope. You hand the card to a second spectator, smiling, and say, "Would you please call out the number this other gentleman thought of."

You crumple up the empty, torn envelope and throw it into your kit, out of the way, as the second spectator reads the number. You now direct the first spectator to turn over the slate. You have written the same number on it!

"We've had such success with one number," you remark, "that I'm tempted to try something more difficult—a test with four numbers thought of by four different people."

You pick up a pencil and piece of paper and write a number on it. You then fold the paper and ask someone to hold it.

You then have one spectator write down the year of any important event in his life. A second spectator writes beneath that the year of his birth, and a third writes under the first two numbers whatever he considers the best year of his life to date. You say to the fourth person, "Oh, just write down any year that pops into your mind."

You take the slate, saying, "Now, I'll add up the four numbers. First, I better draw a line under them." As you draw the line, you *erase* the fourth number that was given, leaving a blank space just above the line.

"This row is written pretty lightly," you observe. "I'll make it a little heavier." As you say this, you write the predicted total *beneath* the line that's under the three numbers and the blank space.

"Now, I'll add them up," you remark. What you actually do is fill in a number on the fourth line that will bring the total you've written at the bottom. For example, let's say that the first three numbers are 1930, 1945, and 1960.

Let's say, for the purpose of illustration, that the number you predicted is 7,892. Your slate at this point reads:

$$1930$$
$$1945$$
$$1960$$
$$\overline{}$$
$$7,892$$

In the fourth blank space you fill in: working from right to left, a 7; next a 5, next a 0, and to the left of it a 2. The number you've filled in, reads normally from left to right 2057.

You hand the slate to someone who hasn't given a number—someone who isn't sitting too close to the fourth number writer—to check your addition. You then have each of the first three numbers verified by the people who wrote them down, erasing each number as it's verified. You start to hand the slate to the fourth number writer, but stop abruptly. "No," you say, "I don't want this man to see the slate because it has the total on it, and I'm going to ask him to open my original prediction before he sees the total on the slate."

As you say this, you erase the fourth number, leaving nothing on the slate but the total, 7,892. The writer of the fourth number opens your prediction paper and reads the number you predicted. You turn the slate around and it contains the same number!

I believe that U. F. Grant, a prolific inventor of fine magical effects, first came up with this great idea.

You used the slate just prior to doing this trick—for a good reason. You want a gray, dirty slate, not a clean black one.

"You people did a superb job of projecting your thoughts," you congratulate your aides. "And now that we've demonstrated the projection of thoughts, let's try to project solid objects—in this case, money."

You bring out the six half-dollars and the poker chip and line them up on the table in preparation for the Han Ping Chien coin trick, which was described in detail in the section of the book dealing with coin tricks.

You've given your audience a little of almost everything, except card tricks. If you want to wind up with a card trick, do The Golden Miracle.

This routine is a nice blend of manipulative magic and tricks that are almost self-working. It has considerable variety, yet everything fits together.

How do you get from the Han Ping Chien coin trick to a card trick, The Golden Miracle? Easy. "Well, the half-dollars were agreeable to showing their magic powers. Now that we've been successful with silver, let's see what we can do with gold." You pull a penny from your pocket and say, "This $20 gold piece came from an old pioneer Western gambler, who found it particularly lucky in card games—so we'll do a card trick with it."

The run-down of the routine is:

Ring and Rope
Square Knot Cut and Restored Rope
Ropes Through the Coat
Straight Arrow
Strip of Paper and Scissors
Sponge Ball Routine
The Afghan Bands
Number Divination
Four Numbers and a Slate
Han Ping Chien Coin Trick
The Power of Gold

A number of props are used in the routine, and I've seen close-up magicians work in two different ways. One will finish with a bare table in front of him; the other will have a table strewn with equipment and props. It takes him almost as long to "clean up" after he's through as it did for his performance.

Get into the habit of putting the props for a trick away when the trick is completed. When you finish the sponge ball routine, for example, put the sponge balls back in your kit. If you haven't already gotten rid of the hidden extra sponge ball, that's a good way to do it.

Material from previous tricks is distracting, and litter is unattractive.

Litter! If you cut up pieces of paper, don't let them fall on the floor. Things that are destroyed in the course of a trick should go into a waste basket or should at least be cleaned up. Don't leave a mess.

At one time, I let the pieces of torn cards flutter to the floor when I did the Tearing the Deck in Half trick. I thought it had dramatic impact. Then I discovered that if I unfolded a newspaper and put it on the table, letting the pieces fall onto it, the effect was just as good. All I had to do to clean up at the finish of the trick was fold up the newspaper and put it in a wastebasket.

One magician who does an elaborate full-evening show is the talk of the profession, not because of the high quality of his performance but because of his efficiency. He's arranged his show so that he literally packs each trick right on stage, at its completion. Protective slip-cases go over the already-packed material at the conclusion of the show, and he's off and running. He says he got tired of spending as much time packing as performing and decided to do something about it.

Close-up "table worker" magicians in restaurants and clubs pack as they go from economic necessity. The only way they can make money is by doing a routine, collecting their fee and getting on to another table. There's no reason why an amateur magician shouldn't be ready to leave the party when he concludes his performance.

The magicians I know who do close-up magic professionally have spent considerable time on their prop kits. When Don Alan was doing close-up magic almost exclusively, he carried an attaché case that contained materials with which he could do an hour and a half show, if necessary. And that case was neat as a pin. Gimmicks didn't roll around loose in it. Everything was held firmly in its place.

When you're going to perform, you don't need to *look* like an amateur, even if you are one. It's one of the first earmarks of professionalism to have your props in order, ready to go, with a minimum of set-up. And it brands a performer as an amateur when he leaves a mess behind him.

Make neatness and efficiency a part of *every* magic routine you do.

Here's another close-up routine — a routine of mental magic, which happens to be my favorite type of legerdemain. I've done some of the tricks in this routine before audiences of several thousand people. They're all strong tricks, simple as they are.

Close-up Mental Routine

Your whole bearing and attitude when you perform mental magic should be different from when you're doing standard magic. To your audience, you're not a magician. You're a telepathist.

You don't roll up your sleeves, you don't show your hands empty, front and back. You don't pass props out for examination. Instead of giving the audience the impression that you're going to try to mystify them, you take the approach that you're going to attempt some experiments in extrasensory perception.

And while "anything goes" in magic, as far as claims are concerned, you should be more circumspect when you're doing a mental act. The audience *expects* a magician to misdirect and even misrepresent. It knows he will try to fool its members. But the audience doesn't think of a mentalist as a magician. You might be surprised how many people sincerely believe everything a mentalist says. They *want* to believe, in many instances.

And their willingness to believe isn't groundless. Extrasensory perception exists. It manifests itself in unexplainable ways.

In doing performances of mental magic, I sometimes ask that anyone in the audience who has never had a psychic experience hold up his hand. You'd be amazed at the paucity of raised hands.

I've had such experiences, myself. So, probably, have you. In the performance of contact mindreading, I've had things happen that could be accounted for in no way other than telepathy.

But don't make yourself ridiculous by making claims you can't possibly substantiate. Don't say you're a clairvoyant unless you believe you are. And don't say that anything is "for real" unless it is. If you're doing a trick, don't assert that it is *not* a trick.

How can you handle such a problem?

I usually do it in my introductory remarks, in which I point out that we're living in an age of miracles. "When I first became interested in mindreading," I say, "I was told that there was just about as much chance of my ever being able to read minds as there was of man's walking on the surface of the moon."

I point out all the serious experimentation that's been done and is being done in the field of extrasensory perception, leaning heavily on the Dr. J. B. Rhine experiments at Duke University.

I continue by saying that I've seen many alleged mindreaders who were frauds, pure and simple, who accomplished all of their seeming miracles by trickery. "I've seen others," I continue, "who at times show what I must regard as positive proof of their psychic ability. At times. And at times, they, too, resort to trickery. Psychic power isn't something even a clairvoyant can control. He can't turn it on and off at will. If he's serious about it, he makes it his life work — and he must make a living, just like anyone else. If he's paid to come up with psychic miracles and can't do it, he'll do whatever he can to please the people who are paying for his performance. Whether or not he is getting intuitive flashes, he is usually a skilled psychologist. When he can't be sure, he guesses — and his guesses are based on exceptional ability to read character.

"For example, some of the greatest character analysts I've ever known have been fortune tellers, some of them uneducated almost to the point of illiteracy. They are keenly observant and sensitive. They can look at a person and see things that most of us are blind to. Sometimes, too, they see things that simply aren't there. They make what seem to be impossible predictions and those predictions come true. Is this guesswork? I don't think so. I think they work so constantly with extra-sensory perception that their sixth sense becomes highly developed.

"I've known so-called mindreaders who began as out-and-out charlatans and fakers, relying solely upon trickery. Thanks to working in the *field* of telepathic communication regularly, they have, much to their own astonishment, brought their ESP to life.

"I'm not going to make the slightest claim that what I'm about to do is clairvoyance. I'm so intensely interested in the subject that I hope some of it will be.

Magnetism

Here's a quickie that's hard for a spectator to explain. You tell him about your magnetic powers, and ask him to hold out either hand.

You grasp his wrist in your left fingers and close his hand with your right hand, forming it into a fist and then rubbing it vigorously. When you've done this for at least a full minute, you ask the spectator to open his hand. As he does so, you touch each of the fingers with your right forefinger and then touch the forefinger to his palm and lift it.

The spectator will admit that he feels an electric shock or a magnetic pull.

Why? All the time you're rubbing his fist, you're squeezing his wrist with your left fingers. When you lift your forefinger from his palm, you also release the pressure on his wrist. Blood circulation in the hand has been cut off, and the sudden rush of blood to the fingers is responsible for the magnetic or electric effect.

Whether it is or not, I'll leave up to you. If I can't come up with any conclusive demonstrations of ESP, I'll still try to entertain you. And I'll try to arouse your interest in the fascinating world of ESP, one of the few areas of scientific research that hasn't yet been explored to any great degree.

"I have a theory on telepathic communication that makes sense—at least, to me. I believe that every thought a human being has creates a physical action or reaction of some kind. I think, for example, that if a person tells a deliberate lie, he shows it physically in some way, although there's no oral or written communication. If you become angry, those around you sense it, whether you express your anger or not, because you have an involuntary physical reaction.

"I think much of what, for want of a better term, we call mindreading stems from a physical source. Much of what I'm going to do is a perfect illustration of this theory.

"Starting with my basic premise that thought creates action or reaction, let me illustrate with this simple little device that's been around for years. It's called, of all things, a Sex Detector."

You open the mental routine with the Sex Detector, which is fully explained in the Mental section of this book.

At the conclusion of your demonstration with the Sex Detector, you say, "Now, I don't believe for one minute that this little string and weight detects sex. I think it works by the power of suggestion. I suggest to you that the pendulum will swing back and forth if held over a male and in a circle if held over a female. That registers a thought on the brain, and the thought creates an involuntary and unwitting physical reaction."

There can be no argument about your statement, because it's true. You continue, "And now, I'm going to attempt an experiment that's entirely different and works, when it does work, as a result of physical contact—touch."

You are leading into an old but effective:

LIVING AND DEAD TEST

You pick up a sheet of good quality bond stationery and tear it into six or seven strips. You start tearing from the bottom and *do not,* I repeat, *not,* use the final top strip. Let's say you're using six strips. Five of the strips will have ragged edges at both top and bottom. The strip that was the original bottom of the sheet of paper will have one ragged edge but one sharp, smooth edge.

You pass out a couple of the strips, apparently indiscriminately, and say that you want the people who receive them to write the name of a living person on their slip and then fold it into quarters or eighths. You hand *one* person the strip with one sharp, smooth

edge and instruct him to write the name of a dead person. The remaining strips are passed out with instruction that names of living people should be written on them.

A member of the audience collects the slips in a bowl or hat and stirs them up "so that it would be impossible for anyone to know who wrote on any one slip."

With your head turned aside, you reach into the bowl an pull out a slip, saying, "Living." You pull out two or three more, and assert that they contain the names of live people. Then you pull one out and announce, "I get a quite different feeling from this one. It bears the name of someone who is now dead." You give it to the person who has been holding the bowl and instruct him to open it. You turn to the person who wrote the name of the dead man and ask, "And what name did you write on your slip?" He calls out the name, and the audience volunteer verifies that this is the name on the slip you handed him.

You've performed this seeming miracle by the means you gave your audience at the outset—the sense of touch. The only slip with a sharp, smooth edge *has* to be the one that contains the name of the dead man.

You now get ready to perform a trick called:

PSYCHIC DRAWING

"One of the most difficult tests ever attempted by any clairvoyant," you declare, "is the telepathic transmission of a drawing. Duplicating a drawing done by a member of my audience is particularly difficult for me because I'm not an artist. For that reason, I'd like to have a volunteer who isn't an artist, either."

You hand the volunteer a plain white card that will just fit snugly into a fairly large end-opening envelope. You turn your back while the drawing is being made and pick up a pile of such envelopes. They are all flap-side up. You turn the pile over in your hand and gesture with what was the bottom envelope as you instruct the volunteer artist behind you to turn the card face down when the drawing is completed.

At the signal from the artist, you turn around. The packet of envelopes in your hands is now flap side up. You take the top envelope, lower it to the face-down card and slide the card into the envelope. You touch your forefinger to your tongue, moisten the flap of the envelope with it, and seal the envelope. You ask the spectator his or her initials, which you print in large letters on the flap.

You put the envelope back on the pile and look for some place to display it prominently, picking it up as you look around. If there isn't a book or some logical place to prop it up, you shrug and put it back onto the pile, calling attention to the fact that it's identified by the initials on the flap.

You now pick up another card or a slate and chalk and stand near the volunteer artist as you start to draw. You complete your drawing, let someone hold it face down, and walk back and pick up the envelope, which you open. You remove the face down card and hand it to the artist, asking for verification that it's his or her original drawing. You've crumpled up the envelope and thrown it away.

Now, as dramatically as you can, you ask the artist and the person holding the face down slate to turn both of them so that the audience can see them.

"The two drawings," you remark, "are enough

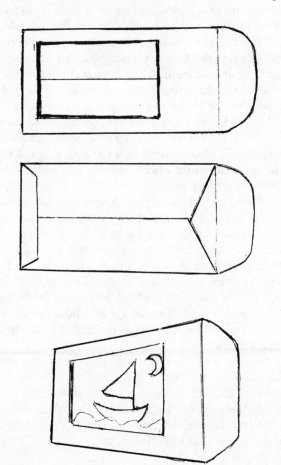

alike, I think you'll agree, to completely rule out chance or happenstance."

They should be. The envelope into which you slid the face-down drawing was what is known to mental magicians as a "window" envelope. The address side of it is completely cut away except for a narrow ledge on the bottom and sides. At the top, it's cut away so that the opening stops just below the tip of the flap, under the opening on the back through which the card is inserted.

When you hold up the envelope, looking for a place to display it, you see the spectator's drawing. It's facing you.

The window envelope has many uses in mental magic, but I think it's particularly strong for the duplication of a drawing.

In my book for professional magicians, *You, Too, Can Read Minds,* I describe in detail a method whereby you and the spectator face each other and make drawings simultaneously. The two drawings are held up for audience inspection the instant they're completed—and they're identical.

It is, in my opinion, the best method for duplicating a drawing ever devised—but it requires mechanical equipment and is, I think, too difficult for the average amateur.

The next experiment is one that I got from Ted Annemann many years ago. Annemann had the most inventive mind that ever hit mental magic. I'd say that well over half of the mental magic tricks that are being done today stemmed from his brain. He was a great believer in simplicity, and he sold me completely on the idea that the simplest way of doing any trick is the best way. This trick is so simple and direct that it's disarming—and it's remained one of my favorites over the years. I call it:

SPECTATOR AND SLATE

You hand a spectator a slate and piece of chalk, as you escort him to a far corner of the room where he can't hear what's happening. As you lead him to the corner, you say to him, "Give me a number from 40 to 50." Whatever number he gives you, say 46, you tell him, "Fine. Keep that number in mind, 46, and when I ask you to, write it on the slate."

You go back to your audience, pick up a note pad and pencil, and say, "I want somebody to put a single number at the top of this pad, any digit from zero through 9." You hand the pad and pencil to a spectator, who writes down a number. You approach a second spectator, close by, and say, "Put a second one-digit number directly beneath it." You get a third spectator to follow suit.

You add the numbers as you go, which is easy, since there's plenty of time as you hand the pad from person to person. You keep having numbers written, one under the other, until you get within 9 of the number the spectator with the slate originally gave you—in this case, 46. Once the numbers hit 37 or more, you stop.

"I'll draw a line across the bottom of the numbers," you announce, "and ask someone to add them up."

As you say this you very deliberately write another one-digit number beneath those already on the pad, and make a heavy line beneath them, making it with a flourish.

Let's say your total was 39. You add a 7 to the list while you're explaining that you'll add a line at the bottom and ask someone to total the numbers. You add whatever number is necessary to bring the total to 46.

The instant you hand the pad to the person who's going to do the addition, you call out to the spectator in the corner, "I want you to think of a number from 1 to 100. You have one in mind right now, haven't you? Write it on the slate. Write it in numerals big enough for everyone to see."

Simplicity

Production of seemingly innumerable lighted cigarettes from the bare hands enjoyed a magic vogue for some years that was almost an epidemic.

Annemann, the great inventor of tricks, was offered an attractive engagement "if he would do the lighted cigarette production trick."

Anneman wasn't known for his manipulative skill. He was not what he patronizingly referred to as a "finger flinger." He wanted the date and the money that went with it, however, and so he agreed to do the trick.

He bought a number of little metal receptacles that were designed to keep a cigarette lit, and soldered safety pins to the outside of them. He placed one under each coat lapel, one under each armpit, one just inside the back of his shirt collar, and one in each pants cuff, each loaded with a lighted cigarette. A few of the imitation lighted cigarettes sold in most novelty stores were in his coat pockets, in his handkerchief in his breast pocket, just inside his shirt front and under the waistband of his trousers.

He walked out onto the stage, slowly and deliberately showed his hands unquestionably empty, reached under his coat lapel, pulled out a lighted cigarette, took a few puffs on it and tossed it into a large ash tray. He produced a few more, just as deliberately, flicking sparks from them, and then removed the imitation lighted cigarettes from his pockets and the other places where they'd been hidden, winding up by reaching behind his neck and producing a cigarette which he puffed vigorously as he took his bow.

He drew heavy applause—just as enthusiastic as if he'd produced the cigarettes through manipulative skill.

As soon as he's written his number, in this case, 46, on the slate, you tell him to rejoin the group but to keep his number concealed.

As soon as the man with the pad has a total, ask him to announce it. He does, and it's 46. You ask the spectator with the slate to hold up his slate. It, too, bears the number 46.

I think you add immeasurably to the routine with what you say to introduce the next trick, which I call:

THE RAPPING CRICKET

"And now," you continue, "I'm going to show you something that's pure trickery, an out-and-out fraud. I saw it done by a spirit medium in Omaha, Nebraska, and it drove me out of my skull. I think I know most of the tricks of fraudulent spirit mediums, but this one had me baffled. I finally hit on a solution, and the medium reluctantly admitted I was right. I hope it will baffle you, too, even though you know it's a trick."

You put out on the table a tin cricket, one of those little noisemaking devices that have been sold to youngsters for years. A pressure on it makes a loud click. You click it a few times to demonstrate.

You now show an innocent little cardboard box, just large enough to hold the cricket. The box is just as innocent as it looks—as free from trickery, in fact, as the cricket. You pass both items around the table.

"This is a spirit medium," you announce, "let everyone examine the little toy cricket and an apparently unprepared cardboard box and cover. Both items are so simple in construction that it would be virtually impossible for either to contain any secret devices."

The cricket and box go around the table and come back to you. "I had seen spirit rapping hands in seances, but I had never seen a spirit rapping cricket. The medium put the cricket into the box and put the cover on very gingerly.

"There was absolutely nothing concealed in his hands, and he kept them both on the table, motionless. I looked under the table at his feet from time to time, and they didn't move either. But he called on the cricket to answer questions by rapping once for yes and twice for no—and it did! The sound of the raps was even slightly muffled, accounted for by the box. The man didn't make a single false move. Go ahead and ask some questions, and I'll illustrate what I mean."

The spectators ask questions and the cricket raps out answers. You don't make a move. During the course of the demonstration, you can invite any member of the audience to remove the box lid and take a look at the cricket, then replacing it. All there is in the box is that little tin cricket.

How is it done?

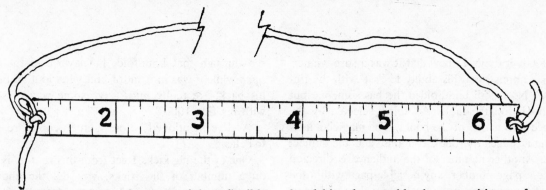

You cut off 5 or 6 inches from one of those flexible steel rules that wind up into a round container. You may need to experiment to get the length of steel tape that works best for you. Bend it against its curvature and you get a click that is identical with that of the tin cricket.

Drill a small hole at each end of the little piece of steel tape. Tie a piece of fairly heavy cord through one of the holes and bring the other end around through the hole at the other end of the tape. Put it around your waist, just above your belt but under your shirt. The tape is at the front, above your belt buckle. Pull the cord up just tight enough so that the tape is on the verge of bending. This tape belt should fit fairly snugly. Hold the second end in place by tying a bow or slipknot so that you can take the gadget off without a lot of fumbling.

Remember, it fits snugly enough not to hang loose, but not tightly enough so that the tape is bent back on its curvature.

With this belt on, all you have to do to make the cricket rap is tense your stomach muscles. When you do, the tape bends back against the grain and you get a distinct rap, slightly muffled by your shirt. That's all there is to it. Since you're sitting directly behind the cricket, the illusion that the rap comes from the little box is perfect.

Clever, huh?

Now, you get back to mental magic. The break has been good entertainment, and the fact that you so readily admit it's a trick has strengthened the rest of your performance. The next is a quickie, done with:

MATCHBOOK MINDREADING

Remember the little matchbook with the carbon paper inside the back, the one I described in the section on mental magic? You use it.

You say, "And now I want to do a little demonstration of visual teletransmission. The spectator visualizes something and I visualize the same thing. We must both see the same thing for it to be effective. I'm going to ask you to think of any city in the world. It's hard to visualize a whole city, so I'll ask you to print the name of the city on a little slip of paper and visualize the name, in type."

You have the spectator standing away from the table "so I can't see what you print on the slip." You

hand him the matchbook as a writing surface, after explaining that you'll have him burn the slip once he's formed a good mental picture of the printing on it.

You have him fold the slip and put it on an ashtray. You take back the matches, pull one from the packet, light it and hand it to him, telling him that you'll turn your back while the slip burns.

You get the name of the city while your back is turned, by looking at the card inside the matchbook cover. You stick it into your pants pocket, turn around and ham it up, getting the name of the city letter by letter.

You've saved the blockbuster for your finale. You wind up the routine with Par-Optic Vision, a demonstration of seeing while blindfolded as explained in the mental magic section.

A friend of mine has a windup for Par-Optic Vision that seemed silly to me when I first heard about it. But

The Pill Boxes

Three tiny pill boxes are in a row on the table. One of the boxes contains a single pill which is glued to the bottom of the cardboard container. A fourth box, never seen by spectators, contains an identical pill which is loose and which rattles loudly when the box is shaken. This little pill box is wedged under the magician's watch strap or held to his left wrist by a rubber band, well concealed by the coat sleeve.

The magician removes the lids from the three boxes on the table, showing that one of them contains a pill and the other two are empty. He puts the lids back in place, picks up the box containing the cemented pill with his left hand, and shakes it. "This one rattles," he points out, "while the other two don't." He picks up the other two boxes one at a time with his right hand and shakes them without causing any sound.

"Watch the one that rattles," he says. "I'm going to show you that the hand is quicker than the eye." He changes the position of the three boxes and challenges a spectator to pick the one that rattles. The spectator picks one up and shakes it without drawing any sound. "No," the magician says, reaching for one of the other two with his left hand, "it was this one." He shakes it. "See? Let's try again."

No matter how many times the spectators try, they can never pick the box that rattles. Since the only box that does emit a sound is up the magician's sleeve, the spectator's failure is guaranteed.

when I saw it done, I knew that it was a sure winner.

He's demonstrated his ability to "see with the fingertips." Now, still blindfolded, he has someone put three books on the table. A subject selected by the audience selects one of the books. The magician asks how many pages the book contains, and the subject replies. Another member of the audience is directed to write a page number, any possible page within the limits of the number in the book, on a slate and hand the slate to the subject. The subject is instructed to open the book to the proper page number and look at the first word on the page. He is then told to write that word on the slate.

He is told to put the book back on the table with the other two and mix them up. Then he returns to his seat.

My friend "feels" his way to the table, picks up the correct book and puts it behind his back, without opening it. He riffles the pages loudly and brings the riffle to a stop. "I seem to have stopped on Page 214," he announces. At least, it *feels* like 214. And the first word on the page is 'Nevertheless'."

He brings the book back from behind his back and tosses it onto the table. With the book *behind his back,* he has gotten the right page and the right word.

Of course, he has! Both the page number and the word were written on the slate, which was plainly visible to him. The business behind the back is all showmanship.

He tells me than once he gets a quick glimpse of the word and page number, he moves *away* from the slate and trys to avoid facing it while he does the rest of the trick.

It's so simple, it's ridiculous. He's already proved that he can see in spite of being thoroughly blindfolded. And yet, he makes that "book test" the sensation of his act.

I heard one spectator say, after the performance I witnessed, "Even if there was some way he could

Beyond His Powers

Nicola for years, when he got ready to produce a live rabbit from a borrowed hat, asked a volunteer child assistant, "And now, what would you like more than anything else in the world for me to pull out of this hat?" The answer was always, "A bunny" or "A rabbit."

On this particular evening, the little girl who was asked the question pondered for almost a full minute before she answered.

And then she said, "A baby brother."

Nicola said later, "I have thousands of dollars' worth of illusions in my show, but that little girl topped 'em all. She drew the biggest laugh that any magic show ever produced. She stopped the show cold for a good five minutes."

see through that blindfold, he never had the book *open* while it was in front of him. He did it all behind his back. He really *must* have some way of seeing with his fingertips."

As I've mentioned before, some people are eager to believe.

One of the big kicks I get from this routine is that, on a number of the tricks, you tell the audience exactly how you're going to get the desired information. As you get acquainted with the routine, you'll enjoy it, too.

There's another kind of routine that is neither stage act nor close-up performance. It's a law unto itself. It's the magic you're asked to perform at a children's party, usually a birthday party. There's no way in the world to become proficient at it other than to plunge in and do it. And if you don't ever perform magic at a children's party, you've missed something. Harry Blackstone once observed that a magician who can please a kid audience can please anybody. Harry was a master at entertaining children, and his handling of a juvenile audience was a delight for any adult to watch.

A Routine for a Children's Show

You'll never get a more enthusiastic audience for magic than a group of children—and you'll never get a more challenging one. I have actually seen a magician at a children's birthday party literally mobbed by youngsters who wanted to examine a piece of his equipment more closely.

The first time I ever produced a live rabbit in a children's show, it was like being hit by the Green Bay Packer line. The kids had been sitting fairly quietly on the floor, but with the appearance of that rabbit, everything was up for grabs. And every youngster at the party wanted the rabbit. One little girl told me I was a chintzy cheap-skate because I wouldn't let her have it. "I saw how easy it was for you to get it," she said. "You could get one for me just as easy."

Right at the outset, let me say that you should *never* give a rabbit to the guest of honor at a children's show without first checking with that youngster's parents. You'd be surprised how many adults resent having a live rabbit join the family. And try telling a child who's been given a rabbit by a magician that he can't keep it. You try it. I want no part of it.

Card tricks are seldom winners in a children's show for the simple reason that the small fry aren't well-enough acquainted with cards. Tricks that involve fire are definitely out. So are tricks that involve any element of danger.

Don't worry about getting audience participation. You may get more of it than you want.

You have to establish that you're a magician, right from the start. A so-called sucker trick, that they bite on and then find themselves fooled, is almost mandatory early in the program. Children love such tricks, and they always rise to the bait.

Your tricks shouldn't be long unless they're lively, with plenty of action. They should be visual. Mental magic has no place in a children's program. Neither do tricks that require audience concentration.

It's almost inevitable that some small child will shout, "Oh, I know how you do that!" after every trick. Don't let it throw you. If you act amused by such claims, you'll do much better than if you let them annoy you. Act as if you thing their explanation of tricks are hilariously funny.

You must start in command and stay in command. If a kid becomes a problem, I usually announce that, now, he's going to do the same trick. I've never found one yet who could do it, and his attempt is greeted by catcalls and cries of "Siddown!"

Don't get the idea that doing a children's show isn't fun. It's a ball! Once you get into the swing of it, you'll enjoy a children's show more than any other. Make your humor broad and schmaltzy. And let your audience see that you're enjoying yourself.

I did a children's show for Grandson Number One's sixth birthday a few weeks ago, and it was a delight. But guess who gave me the most trouble. You guessed it—my grandson, who is a good little magician in his own right. I quickly deleted a few tricks that I'd taught him to do.

Don't make your children's show too long. The juvenile attention span is short and a restless audience of youngsters becomes an obstreperous one.

You open with a trick where they think they've caught you red-handed. It's the:

TORN AND RESTORED PAPER NAPKIN

You need not one but three paper napkins. One is left folded. The other two are wadded up into balls. One of these is put into your outer coat pocket with a handkerchief, in position so that it will fall out of the pocket onto the floor when you remove the handkerchief from the pocket. You bend apart a bobby pin slightly so that it will grip the other paper ball. This bobby pin is fastened with a small safety pin to the

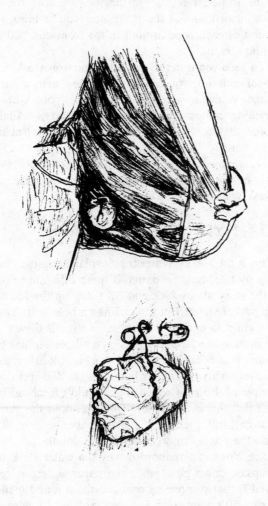

inside of your suit coat, on the left side, so that it hangs just above the bottom edge of the coat. If you bend your left fingers up under the edge of the coat, you can grasp the paper ball and pull it away. All this is advance preparation.

You start by telling the children that many magicians can make solid objects vanish and then bring them back but that only a few can destroy something and then restore it. You pick up the folded paper napkin and tear it into five or six strips which you then wad together and roll into a compact paper ball.

"Watch closely," you say. "I'm going to throw my handkerchief over the ball of paper shreds and when I take it away, the napkin will be restored."

You pull the handkerchief from your pocket and let the paper ball in it fall to the floor. You look crestfallen. The kids shout with glee.

"That wasn't supposed to slip out of the handkerchief," you admit. "Well, as long as you've seen it, I guess I might as well show you how the trick works."

You are holding the torn paper in your left finger tips. You turn your right side to your audience and bend over to pick the intact paper ball up from the floor. As you bend over, your left fingers, on the side away from the audience, put the torn paper into the trouser pocket and remove the intact one from the bobby pin. You pick up the ball from the floor and face front, a wadded napkin ball in each hand.

"You see," you explain, "this ball in my right hand was supposed to be hidden under the handkerchief. And when I throw my handkerchief over my hand, like this, I take the solid napkin ball in my left fingers and pull away the torn one, under the handkerchief."

You hand the handkerchief and ball in your right hand to one of the youngsters. "Nobody's supposed to know about this one," you explain. "It's the torn one. I open the one in my left hand, the only one the audience knows about, and show that it's whole again. If you don't know that the torn one is in the handker-

Silly Quickie

Solemnly announce that you're about to give a lesson in magician's arithmetic. The first lesson is that, in magic, two subtracted from four equals six.

Pick up a square piece of paper and ask a spectator to count the corners. There are four, of course.

"Four corners," you say, "and we'll subtract two of them."

You cut off two of the corners, cutting off triangles. "Having removed two corners," you sagely observe, "we now have six corners left." "And how many corners did we remove?" you ask. "Two? I'm afraid you weren't being observant. Here are the pieces I cut off and, as you can see, each one has three *corners, a total of six."*

chief, it's a good trick, isn't it? But unfortunately, you caught me. You know that the napkin I tore to pieces is still torn. When a thing like that happens, a magician has to do some real magic. I have to point my finger at the torn napkin and say Ostagazoozlum. Remember that word, Ostagazoozlum. No other word will work. And now, when I open the torn pieces, they've become an untorn napkin again."

You open out the second ball to show that it, too, is intact.

I've always loved the Ropes Around the Neck as a children's trick, thanks to the use of the mystic words that go with it. You're open to criticism, however, if you tie anything around your neck in a children's performance.

ALLAH PALOOZA

This is virtually the same trick as the Ropes Around the Neck. However, you drape the two equal lengths of rope over a wand or pencil and tie them together as explained in the Close-up magic section. You stretch the ropes behind the back of a little girl or little boy and proceed as if you were doing the Coat Off the Ropes trick, except that you tie both ropes into a lot of knots at the front after you've brought one end of each rope around to the front and tied a knot into them.

You get a youngster to say the magic words, adding to them each time you tie a knot, winding up by telling him that you've now come to the critical point where everything hinges on his saying properly, "Allah Palooza Paloo, Palip, Pazazza, Pazamzam, Racka Tacka Pontiac."

You remove the pencil or wand, tap the child lightly on the head with it, and pull the ropes free.

Next, you do the:

HYDROSTATIC GLASS

This is the Heavy Water trick explained in the On-Stage routine, but the patter is quite different. You tell the story about Jack and Jill going up the hill to get a pail of water. But the pail had a hole in it. You ask a child to examine the glass and see if there's a hole in it. When he says "No," you admonish him to examine it more critically. There's a big hole in it, right at the top, where you pour in the water. You sprinkle a couple of drops of water onto a child's forehead to prove that this is *wet* water. Then you pour the glass about half-full, pick up the heavy paper square, dip it into the pitcher and get the plastic double-disc behind it. Your explanation of why the water stays in the upside-down glass when the paper square is removed is that you blew a cold breath on it and made it freeze. It's now solid ice, you explain. To release it, you must blow a *hot* breath at it, which melts the ice.

Next, you do:

BANANAS

This trick is also explained in the On-Stage routine. With the sucker treatment, it's a terrific trick for children. You follow it with a children's version of a card trick that Harlan Tarbell taught me years ago. It's:

THE EDUCATED SNAKE

At a novelty counter, get one of those peanut brittle or jam cans that releases a spring snake when the lid is removed. The "snake," which is a long metal spring covered with cloth, compresses into the can and recoils to full length when released.

Remove the snake from the can and thread a length of heavy black linen thread up through the length of the body. The needle goes in at the base and comes out at the top. Put a small black button onto the thread at the point where it extends from the top of the snake, sew it firmly, and cut off the remaining thread. The end of the thread at the bottom of the snake should be firmly anchored with several big knots or by sewing it firmly to the bottom before threading the line up through the body.

The linen thread is only slightly longer than the snake, about half an inch. Now, punch a couple of holes into the bottom of the can and anchor the bottom of the snake to the bottom of the can with a couple of pieces of linen thread. The snake will spring out to full length but won't jump away from the can. This may not be necessary, but is done to avoid the danger of some child getting hit by the flying snake.

Compress the snake down into the can—but don't compress the linen thread. Pull it out to full length,

which will be at least a yard, depending on the size of the snake. Put the lid on the can to hold the snake in place, and you'll have a yard or more of black linen thread dangling from the top of the can. Put a good, thick coating of magician's wax or other strong adhesive onto the little black button at the end of the thread. The snake can is on your table, the linen thread emerging from the back and running along the table top to a point a couple of feet away from it.

That may seem like considerable preparation, but once the snake is set up for the trick, it can be used over and over again. The only preparation for each performance is to compress the snake back into the can, with the linen thread extending from the top.

The only other thing you need for the trick is a packet of 20 or so little white file cards, cut to roughly playing card size.

When you get ready to do the trick, you point to the snake can. "This isn't *really* a can of peanut brittle. It's the home of a snake—an educated snake. The snake that lives here can read and writhe. He's particularly good on reading. I'll show you. Who's a good writer? Can you write or print your name? Fine. Just write or print your name on one of these cards." You hand the child a card and a crayon. "The rest of the cards don't have any writing on them—not even a simple word like platitudinarianism." Once the youngster has put his name on the card, you put the card face down onto the pile, and do a false cut, leaving it at the top.

Now, turn the pile of cards face up and slap it down hard on the adhesive-coated black button. The card that presses against the adhesive is the one with the name on it. Press the packet down firmly and forget about it.

"Would you believe it," you continue, "the educated snake in this can can run through this little pile of cards and find the one with your name on it so fast you can't even see him. Watch." Nothing happens. "You see, he sneaked out, got the card with your

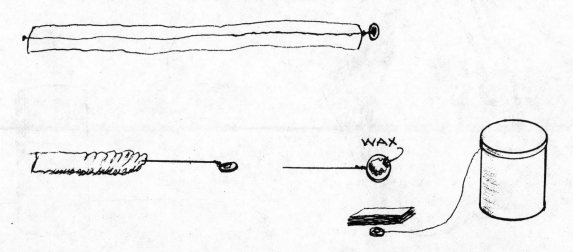

185

name on it and went back home so fast you didn't get even a tiny glimpse of him. You don't believe it? I'll show you."

Pick up the can and remove the lid. That's all you have to do. The snake leaps out to its full length and it's holding the right card at what must be its mouth. When the snake is released, the spring action pulls the card away from the bottom of the pile so quickly that nobody could possibly see it. The effect is both startling and indetectable. You remove the card from the waxed button and give it to the youngster.

THE RABBIT TUBES

If you're determined to produce a live rabbit, I'll give you what I think is the simplest method—but I'll do it with misgivings.

In the first place, just any old rabbit won't do. Some rabbits are extremely wild and some are huge. It should be a small, domesticated rabbit.

You'll need two tubes that fit one inside of the other. An electric can opener finishes off the edges of a can at both the top and bottom to make an acceptable magic tube, if you can get the right size cans. They'll need to be at least 12 inches tall. It's extremely difficult to make them from heavy cardboard, and such tubes don't stand up. If you can't find two tin cans that fit, your best bet is probably to have a tinsmith make them for you.

You will also need a "hook." It's a piece of stiff

wire shaped as in the illustration. The top hooked end will fit over the lip of both tubes or either one.

Next, sew four rings into the four corners of a square of dark, durable cloth. Put the live rabbit on the cloth and draw up the four corners at the top. Put the four rings over the bottom hook. The size of the cloth will depend on the size of the rabbit and the depth of the tubes and will be subject to experimentation. The rabbit and its cloth bag are on the hook, which is in turn hooked over both top lips of the tubes. They are sitting, nested, on your table. You pick them up as one, gripping them from the top, and let the lower tube emerge from the bottom. Put down the larger tube and show that the inner tube is empty. Slide it up over your arm and then off again. Now, show that it will go through the larger tube. Start it from the bottom, shove it up, grasp the top edge and pull it up through at the top, taking the hook and rabbit bag right along with it. Put it down on the table and run your arm through the larger tube, showing it empty, head-on. Put it down over the top of the smaller tube.

Now pick up both tubes and rest them on your left hand. Disengage the rings with your right fingers and lift both tubes, revealing a live rabbit on your left hand.

It's not easy to handle the tubes convincingly, but it's easier than what magicians call a "table load."

It's up to you. Nothing carries such a wallop with a child audience and the reaction is worth the effort— but don't try it until you're sure you can handle it. Most of all, don't try it with a "strange" rabbit.

My favorite closing trick is:

POPPING CORN IN A BORROWED HAT

You need special equipment for this, too, but it's easy to make. Glue in a false bottom about an inch and a half from the top of a cardboard box that could pass as a large container for shelled, unpopped popcorn.

Now, remove the bottom from the box with a razor blade. Move it up into the box for the distance of its width, attaching it with an adhesive hinge at the front. The inner flap should hang down almost to the bottom of the box. Run a stout thread through the center of the side opposite the flap hinge. Make a small puncture in the box at the back just below the false shelf and run the stout thread out through this little hole. With the bottom flap hanging down, put a small button onto the other end of the thread, on the outside of the box. It is there only to keep the thread from pulling free of the hole.

Turn the box upside down, with the flap open. Fill the space between the flap hinge and the shelf at the other end with popped, unsalted, unbuttered popcorn. Pull the button and thread tight to close the flap. The major part of the box interior will be filled with popped corn.

Pull the button and thread fairly taut. The button will be hanging down from the hole through which the thread runs. Cut a piece of cardboard about 1 inch wide by ¼-inch long and glue the ends of it to the

A Wild Hare

Few people know it, but a special dwarf breed of rabbit, docile and light in weight, is used almost exclusively by magicians who must magically produce a rabbit during the coure of a performance.

Jay Marshall of Magic, Inc., tells about a magician who was on the program at the annual Abbott Get-Together in Colon, Mich. Friends (?) substituted a wild jackrabbit for the tame, cuddly little rabbit that was hidden in a secret compartment of the magician's magic production box.

"When he reached into that production box to pull out his rabbit," Jay says, "you'd have thought a cyclone had hit that stage. It wasn't as funny as it had seemed when we planned it. That big rabbit knocked down most of the props on the stage before it took a flying leap from the stage into the middle aisle and tore for the exit. The man's act was a shambles."

Jay winds up the story with a sound piece of advice. "Before you produce any rabbits in a public performance," he says, "know your rabbit."

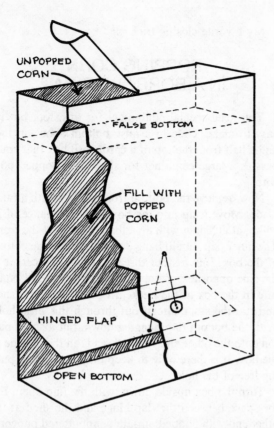

UNPOPPED CORN

FALSE BOTTOM

FILL WITH POPPED CORN

HINGED FLAP

OPEN BOTTOM

back of the box in the position where the button can be tucked into it from the bottom.

You'll find that if you pull the button free from the little cardboard tab, the bottom flap of the box will instantly drop open and release the popped corn.

With the popped corn loaded into the box and the button fixed in place, the box can be handled casually. You could even show the back of the box if you kept the cardboard strip and button covered with your thumb, but showing all sides of the box is rather pointless.

Put shelled, unpopped corn into the little top compartment and you're all set. Once the box is prepared, it may be used over and over.

You ask the youngsters what makes corn pop, and they'll tell you that heat does the trick.

"But heat is dangerous," you tell them, "if it involves fire. So the best way to pop popcorn is the magic way, with invisible magic heat."

You borrow a hat or use your own, showing it unmistakably empty. You open the top of the popcorn box and lift out a handful of shelled corn, letting it dribble back into the box. "We use regular hulled popcorn," you tell them. "There's nothing magic about it."

You now hand (?) a youngster an invisible magic candle. Get him to grip the imaginary candle in his

left fist. Then go through the motions of striking a match and hand him the imaginary match, warning him not to burn his fingers as he lights the candle wick. You approve of the imaginary flame, but reprimand him good-naturedly for dropping the match onto the floor.

Now, you hold the popcorn box above the hat, and take out a very small handful of hulled corn. You drop it into the hat a few grains at a time, lowering the bottom of the box so that it's inside the hat. You have released the button and the load of popped popcorn goes into the hat. Lift the box well above the hat as you dribble in a few more grains of hulled corn from your right hand. "It doesn't take much unpopped corn to make a lot of popped corn," you observe.

You now hold the hat above the imaginary lighted candle, high enough so the top of the hat is well above the children's eye level. You begin shaking the hat, gently at first and then more vigorously. You soon give it a few little up-and-down shakes that cause a few kernels of popped corn to jump over the rim of the hat. If you continue this jerking motion, it will seem that the corn in the hat is popping.

You then pour the popped corn out of the hat into a bowl and give it to the children to eat, warning them that there may be a few "old maids" in the bottom.

Children absolutely love this trick, and it always has them bug-eyed. The illusionary effect that the corn is actually popping in the hat is fascinating, and the "loading" of the popped corn into the hat is so smooth and easy that it's never detected. All you have to do is make sure that the bottom of the box is inside the hat, below the rim level, when you release the button on the back of the box.

This is a brief act, but it's the right length for a children's party. The only trouble spot is that rabbit production. Aw, why don't you just forget it?

One magician friend of mine gets around the rabbit problem by using the double-thickness paper cornucopia. Between the two thicknesses of newsprint that are cemented together along three edges, he puts a cloth cut-out of a rabbit. Eyes and nose are sewn onto the cloth in contrasting colors, and the haunches are marked in with a marking pen.

He shows the sheet of paper front and back and forms a cone with it. "To produce a rabbit," he explains, "you must have a sheet of newspaper. You roll it into a cone, reach in, and there's your rabbit!" He pulls out the rabbit cutout, shakes his head and says, "I guess it got flattened out going through the newspaper presses."

I don't like it, but the kids seem to think it's funny.

You're On-Stage

Everyone who does a few magic tricks passably well is called upon, sooner or later, to perform before a group—to do an act. Some who *don't* do even one trick passably well aren't called upon but solicit engagements with vigor and persistence.

I remember a tavern owner who wanted to appear on a television show I once produced. We used guest stars of the first magnitude every week, but Mr. Nadir thought his magic was superior to anything any of them had to offer. Why, he had over $7,000 worth of equipment.

I'm calling him Mr. Nadir because his magic was certainly the nadir in the field of mystification. He was a leading exponent of that school of magic buffs in which the value of your appartus is the status determinant. On his terms, he was a top-flight magician. Unquestionably, he had some of the finest tricks in the world. Unfortunately, he didn't know how to do them. Real magicians either laughed at him or growled about his being allowed to expose great tricks by performing them so ineptly. He wasn't famous, but he was notorious in the area where he operated.

We gave him the polite explanation that guest stars had already been contracted for the duration of the show, but he didn't give up.

Finally, the sponsor began to receive anonymous letters. The sponsor was being taken, these letters said, by a production staff whose members either didn't know what it was all about or were motivated by jealousy. "Within 50 miles of the TV studio," one of these letters said, "there's one of the world's greatest magicians—The Great Nadir. I understand he offered to appear on your show for nothing, if necessary, and

was turned down because the click (sic) in charge didn't want anybody to see how much better Nadir is than the star of your show."

Some of the letters described the marvelous tricks that Nadir featured in his act, and the descriptions would have intrigued almost anybody. The handwriting in all of the letters bore a marked similarity.

The sponsor finally asked about Mr. Nadir. Was it true that he had the marvelous tricks the letters described? Had he offered to work for nothing? If he was as bad as we seemed to think, how come he had the equipment for such wonderful tricks?

I suggested that the sponsor audition him. "After you've seen him perform," I said, "if you recommend that we use him, we'll be glad to do it."

Much to my surprise, the sponsor followed my suggestion. And he gave me a phone call after the audition. "I wouldn't have believed it," he said. "How can a grown man kid himself like that? Why, I've got a six-year old grandson who's more of a magician than that guy."

I recall a successful business man who, years ago, bought a big, full-evening magic show when the magician who owned it decided to retire. He actually went on tour with the show, featuring himself as its star. It was unquestionably one of the most pitiful exhibitions in the history of magic, but the man persisted in keeping the show on the road long after its financial losses had become severe. He was happy to operate at a loss. He was the star of a big magic show. Finally, it reached the point where nobody would book the show at any price.

And guess what he did then. He set up the show as

a charity operation, contributing it to any local charity, anywhere, that was looking for a way to make some money.

Now, this fellow wasn't an idiot. He was a successful, intelligent business man who was a leader in his field. He'd been bitten by the magic bug and the effects of the bite were incurable.

When you can do close-up magic that knocks 'em off their seats, don't get the idea that you can do the same thing on the stage. It's a different world, and the technique is, or should be, entirely different.

In some ways, it's easier than close-up magic. The distance from your audience makes it possible to get away with moves and gimmicks that you can't use when you're working right under people's noses. You can control the angles of viewing. You don't have to worry about anyone seeing something that he isn't supposed to see. You can use mechanical equipment that wouldn't survive the close scrutiny of a small group.

But that distance from the audience has disadvantages that offset its advantages. The most important disadvantage, in my opinion, is in the projection of your personality. It's easy to make personal impact on a close-up audience, and it's difficult to do the same

Dante

The most polished, sophisticated performer of any magician in this century was Dante, who presented the last of the "really big" full-stage illusion shows. He had a profusion of colorful, elaborate stage settings, lots of beautiful girl assistants, efficient male assistants, and a multitude of tremendous stage illusions, as well as considerable smaller magic. Most current theaters wouldn't be able to handle his show today; the last time he played the Oriental theater in Chicago, he had to leave out a number of his better illusions because of stage inadequacies.

In addition to having a beautiful, lavish, spectacular show, Dante wove humor all the way through his performance. Everything in the show was entertaining and Dante, himself, was a consummate entertainer. His opening entrance was made after four beautiful sets of curtains had parted, one after another. At one time, his spectacular opening routine was listed as "ten surprises in ten seconds."

Everything about his show was top-drawer, but nothing overshadowed his talent as a performer. His acknowledged skill as a magician was always secondary to his superb acting ability.

When the economics of show business compelled him to streamline his lavish magical revue for movie house stage presentations, he soon abandoned the show. Even were another performer of such talent to come along, it is extremely doubtful that such a gigantic presentation could ever be presented again.

thing from a stage. The intimacy isn't there. The gulf between the performer and the people in the rear of the house is a wide one.

Every trick you do must be visible to every member of the audience. Card and coin tricks that are superb in close-up magic will sometimes flop miserably from the stage, for this reason.

The stage act must, of necessity, be more firmly set than a close-up routine. Without the constant give-and-take with viewers, it must be "staged," planned to run a specific length of time. While you don't have to use memorized patter, everything you say must be carefully worked out to contribute to the performance and lead the audience in a straight line from your opening to your close.

You must have a definite "style." I've seen some fine, competent professional magicians who never achieved the success their talent merited because they had no style. Their otherwise flawless performances were nondescript. You might remember their tricks but you didn't remember *them,* because they didn't project any memorable characteristics.

Unless you're fortunate enough to have been born with an inherent style—and some people are—you have to be, in addition to a technician, an actor playing the role of an outstanding magician. The born comedian doesn't have to worry about style. Neither does the natural human dynamo whose personality overwhelms you, either on stage or off.

Most people are neither born comedians nor natural human dynamos. But as stage magicians, they must be *something.* If you perform like a colorless nonentity, that's what you'll be. Most people have to develop a stage character and then stick with it.

I know one man who has an unusual twang in his speech. It could conceivably be a handicap to him. But when he began doing a club magic act, it was the greatest thing he had. It made him different. It gave him personality, and it projected without any effort on his part. I know several performers with pronounced foreign dialects, and those dialects are decided assets to them. I've noticed that the dialect gets thicker and heavier the minute they step on-stage.

The finest magician I've ever known, from the standpoint of magical knowledge and flawless execution of difficult tricks, is the envy of every magician in the country for his craftsmanship. He's made it, big, with other magicians but he's never made it at all with the public because he lacks a dominant, memorable personality. Offstage, he's a likeable guy who makes friends easily, but the warmth doesn't register from the platform.

The magician who uses the canned patter that comes with a trick is doomed to failure. The material was probably prepared by the trick's inventor, and the chances are that it fits him perfectly. With patter for six tricks, from six different sources, at least five presentations are almost bound to be wrong. The *theme* of the presentation may be all right—may, indeed, be brilliant, but that theme must be adapted to the individual performer.

For this reason, the script of a magic act, written to fit anybody, usually fits nobody. When I don't have a specific performer in mind, I naturally write something that would be good for me. If it should happen to be good for you, too, that would be more luck than anything else.

One of the reasons why I encourage a semi-ad lib delivery for magicians is that it forces them to adapt material to their own personalities, at least to a degree.

There's another reason. A skilled professional actor can memorize lines and make them sound spontaneous. Few non-professionals can achieve that effect.

The first magic act I ever performed before a sizable audience was never written. It wasn't even planned. It was Chautauqua Week in Hawarden, Iowa, always one of the big weeks of the year, and the act that was to be the feature of the Friday afternoon performance had failed to make train connections. The unit manager wasn't about to refund somewhere between 600 and 700 paid admissions, and he was looking desperately for something, anything, to occupy the stage of the big tent for an hour and a half. He didn't care whether it was any good or not. Several townspeople told him about me.

I'd been an avid magic fan since I was five years old, and every penny I got my hands on went for magic equipment. I spent most of my spare time in front of a mirror, practicing tricks. When I wasn't practicing, I was reading magic books.

The Chautauqua unit manager asked me to do the afternoon show, an hour and a half. The longest I'd ever performed was slightly under an hour. But I had nearly two hours to get ready.

I was a brash kid, and I jumped at the chance. Most kids who are good at magic are gutsy, I've noticed.

I didn't think about what I'd say when I got out onto the stage. There wasn't time for anything as unimportant as that. I had to get out enough equipment and props to carry me through an hour and a half.

Let There Be Light

Marvin Roy, seeking something different, developed a magic act that is done entirely with light bulbs, ranging from flashlight size to big ones. Every trick is different, and the act is climaxed by the magical production out of thin air of a huge and attractive electric candelabra.

By adapting standard magic effects to light bulbs, he makes old tricks new. The originality of his routine has taken him into the smartest night spots around the world, where he never fails to command attention.

"Critics have to admit," he says, "that it's the brightest magic act they've ever seen."

By the time I went onstage, a new dimension had been added to my brashness. I was not only brash but frightened. Both came through, loud and clear. Those two qualities, brashness and fright, gave me a personality, some character. Not good or desirable character, maybe, but character.

A magician usually works against his audience. This time, the audience was with me, squarely behind the local boy. Seeing immediately that I was scared stiff did it.

I was much too frightened to try to act like a suave, assured adult, the first mistake that most kid magicians make. I'd chosen an opening trick that required no skill—the P & L Vanishing Wand. It's still a good trick and it's still being sold by the magic dealers.

My first four tricks were what a gin rummy player would describe as "no-brainers." They took longer to do than I'd anticipated, and I felt that I'd be able to pad the show out to an hour and a half without too much obvious stalling.

I did something that was contrary to all the rules. I said to the audience, "This next trick is just about the most difficult one I've ever tried, and I haven't had it long enough to practice it as much as I should have, so if I don't do it right, I hope you won't be too hard on me."

Miracle of miracles, I got through it, and pulled out my handkerchief to wipe the sweat off my face, elated and relieved. The applause was the sweetest music I'd ever heard.

And it built! That loyal hometown audience was determined to pull me through the performance. The show was an unrouted conglomeration of unrelated tricks, but the tricks worked.

It was undoubtedly one of the dullest, most disorganized magic shows ever presented from any stage, but the audience was determined to show the Chautauqua management that, by golly, we had pretty doggoned good talent right here in Hawarden without bringing in any ringers from the outside.

At the show's conclusion, I could have done a legitimate encore—if I'd had another trick. And I was hooked! A ham was born, right then and there.

I was full of confidence when I did my next public performance—too full of it, to the point of being glibly overbearing. And it wasn't Hawarden against the outside world. The audience was critical, I had no style, my patter was much too sophisticated for my appearance, I did some tricks that were beyond my capabilities and, in every way, I bombed.

But I'd heard applause, and I wasn't going to give up. I inflicted my performances on any captive audience I could find, all through high school. I didn't know what was wrong, but I tried to find out—and I learned a few things—not many, but a few.

I learned enough so that I was able to pay my way through college with magic. My biggest source of revenue came from driving automobiles blindfolded as a newspaper exploitation stunt.

And when I sold my first blindfold drive stunt, I also sold the local theater a stage act, making the sale on the basis of all the newspaper publicity that was an integral part of the blindfold automobile drive.

I sold the theater act, and then tried to throw it together. And it was then that I began to learn something about doing a magic act on a stage.

The theater was packed, thanks to the Blindfold Drive publicity. And the Blindfold Drive, itself, was terrific. The stage act was pretty bad, considering that I was getting money for it and should, therefore, have met professional standards, but it was saved by a blindfold demonstration for the finale—and that was what the cash customers had come to see.

After the performance, the theater manager took me into his office and paid me off. "Kid," he said, "I got no complaints. You packed the house. But for the luvva Mike, if you're gonna get paid for doing a magic act, you better get a magic act."

I didn't know what he meant.

"It ain't the tricks," he explained. "They're pretty good. That blindfold trick's a lulu. But you don't even know how to make an entrance. Your timing's bad. You don't know how to get applause when you've finished a trick. You don't even know how to take a bow."

"Where do I learn?" I asked him.

And he gave me what, at the time, in that area and under the circumstances, was the best possible advice.

"There's a tent rep show playin' in Osage," he said. "They do a repertoire of seven plays, a different one every night for a week's stand. They're good. They've got a stock director from Milwaukee. You go to him and offer to pay him to coach you. Get him to routine your act. Tell him to start from scratch and teach you what to do."

I went to Osage. The director was wise in all the tricks of stock. He charged me $25 and he worked with me for two whole days and it was the best money I had ever spent.

If you're going to do a stage act, try to get some professional guidance. It's almost impossible for a performer to direct himself, and competent direction can mean the difference between a poor act and a good one. Even an amateur dramatics coach can help you.

Nobody who walks out onto a stage, amateur or professional, wants to give a poor performance. If nothing else, your personal pride is on the line. You want to do the best you can, and you can't do it without help from an outside source. It's humanly impossible for most performers—and particularly novices, to be objective about their own work.

Where do you turn for competent help? One top professional magician once confided in me that he'd

been getting nowhere until a local minister coached him on delivery and stage deportment. One of the best amateurs I've ever seen put his stage act together with the help of a seasoned television actor who had ambitions to be a director and did the job for kicks. A likely youngster who gives promise of becoming a fine performer works for an hour every week with a high school speech teacher who doesn't know a thing about magic but knows considerable about public performances in general. One of the most entertaining magic acts in the country was routined for its star by a retired burlesque comedian. One of the most unique angles of approach I've ever encountered was taken by a dentist who sold a good Little Theater group on routining his magic act as a project. There are retired ex-vaudevillians all over the country, and anybody who was successful in vaudeville can be of great help to almost any beginning magician. One high school youngster's stage act has been improved at least 100 per cent by a circus clown who worked with him during the off-season.

With all this in mind, I'm going to try to give you the *basis* of a routine for the stage. What I'm talking about is an act that, for want of a better name, we'll call a Club Act. It's an act to perform when you're called on to appear in front of a group. It will *not*

Sorcar

The late Sorcar, who died while this book was in preparation, established himself as the greatest publicist of any magician since Houdini, perhaps the greatest of all time. Publicity on Sorcar and his Mysteries of India show went to every corner of the globe, even to places Sorcar had no intention of playing. He kept his name in all publications for magic fans, everywhere, and his show was billed like a circus. His son left college at Sorcar's death to finish the Mysteries of India tour as his father's replacement.

American opinions of his show differed sharply, but Jay Marshall, who saw it in India, insists that it was a fine, professional performance. While much of his magic was similar to that performed by other magicians, his famous "Cutting Off a Man's Tongue" trick is decidedly different—and gruesome. Sorcar boasted that thousands of people had fainted during the course of this presentation.

Jay's comment on the trick is, "Sure, it would be repulsive to our audiences. But his audience thinks it's terrific. It gives 'em a jolt that few magicians could duplicate. They remember it and talk about it—which is one reason why Sorcar draws such crowds."

In the finale, Sorcar presented a sensational black art illusion that was both colorful and mystifying. That he had a following was indisputable, because he played to packed houses throughout the Orient and Europe, year after year.

be a stage illusion show that requires seven assistants and three girls.

What goes into your Club Act routine *should* be influenced by the makeup of the groups before whom you'll appear. Generally speaking, men like card tricks more than women do. Women, on the other hand, have a much greater appreciation of tricks with silks than men have. Children and young teen-agers seldom dig mental magic. Some audiences will respond enthusiastically to sophisticated humor, while others will be bewildered by it. Cornball humor will bring guffaws from one audience and groans from another.

Since I don't know your audiences, what I'm going to give you will be a routine that is magically sound, entertaining and mystifying. It can be scripted to appeal to almost any audience, and the slant it takes will be up to you.

Club Act Routine

You should notice a decided difference in the *modus operandi* of most of the tricks in the club act from the methods employed in close-up magic.

The first thing you'll need is a table. It's important. I've seen performances ruined by the collapse or tipping over of a flimsy table balanced on three legs. I've also seen magicians working with tables that were much too small for the equipment they were employing. Your table should be big enough and sturdy enough to fill your needs. A kitchen table covered with a short but attractive cloth or drape is much better than a shaky folding card table, for example. An attractive tea cart may work out well.

Don Alan probably has the most unique table in the world in his stage act. He wheels on a table that is covered with an attractive drape. Almost immediately, he whips off the drape to reveal a garbage can on wheels. "This will give you some idea of the quality of my act," he says.

The inside of the garbage can is neatly and efficiently sectioned and equipped with firm shelves, hangers and whatever is necessary to keep all his props right where he wants them. The can has the added advantage of keeping equipment that is not in use out of sight, cutting distraction to a minimum.

Don't use it. It's Don's trademark, and it fits him perfectly. He's had enough exposure with it so that anyone else who uses such a table would be immediately branded as a copyist.

Everything you use in your act should have a definite place on the table, and that place should remain constant. If you have to fumble around to find what you want when you're performing, you ruin the pace of your act and annoy your audience.

Another thing, have a small tablecloth or even an old sheet to throw over the top of your table once you have it set, with every item in place. People are inquisitive, and they're particularly curious about a magician's props. Their intentions may be perfectly harmless, but they may pick up something and replace it in such a way that they give you a lot of trouble. Keep a cloth over the contents of your table until just before it's moved out into the audience's sight.

Your first trick is going to be a trick with a piece of rope—soft sash cord, actually. I'm going to give you two methods of doing it, both good, and you should use whichever one you prefer.

You walk onstage holding a piece of sash cord about 18 inches long in your right hand. You hold it up, shaking your head.

Right here, at the outset, a difference in style determines your approach. One magician may look like he's going to cry and say, "I asked for a piece of rope, but this is too short." Another may say indignantly, "Chee! I tell 'em I need a piece of rope and look what they give me! You'd think rope was $5 a yard. I've seen knots that had more rope in 'em than this."

Another may observe, "There's an old saying, give a magician enough rope and he'll do a rope trick. But this isn't enough rope for any rope trick I've ever seen. Magicians are often accused of stretching the truth. But I don't do that. I stretch ropes."

Without the rope ever leaving the sight of the audience, you proceed to stretch it to a length of about 12 feet. What you say as you do it will be determined by your style.

ROPE-STRETCHING

The first method I'm going to give you is my own. You pull out about an inch of the soft core of the 18-inch length of rope at one end and snip it off. Then you insert a tiny Alnico magnet. Wrap the end with a few turns of white thread to hold the magnet firmly in place. You can daub some white paint on the exposed end if you like, although I've never found it necessary. Repeat the process with one end of the 12-foot length of rope, using a second Alnico magnet, so that when the two ends with magnets in them are brought together, they will make a tight grip.

Next, you must prepare what magicians call a "tip-over" box. This may be of cardboard or wood and should be of cubic shape, the same dimensions on all six sides. Exact dimensions are unimportant, just so there's enough room to loop the 12 feet of rope in the bottom without danger of its being exposed when the lid is off.

The bottom of the box should be a separate piece.

If you're building a box, put together the four sides and then cut the bottom slightly smaller so that it will fit loosely inside the sides. Actually, you need two bottom pieces, identical in size. These are fastened together at right angles to form a unit shaped like this: ⌐

It should be firmly braced at the join, on the inside. This can be done with two small blocks of wood glued to both surfaces at right angles, and a couple of other blocks glued the same way along the width of the join. These are never exposed to the audience.

This unit is loosely hinged to the empty bottom of

grip on the rope so that the magnetic join hangs loose and the strain of the pull is on the long piece.

I loop the rope as I haul it from the box, and put the large coil of rope onto the table. The box is moved to the back of the table.

A friend of mine told me I was crazy to bother with the tip-over box. He simply coiled the long rope into a wastebasket which was sitting next to his table. He gingerly lowered the short length of rope part-way into the wastebasket after remarking that such a short rope might as well be thrown away. With one end in the wastebasket, he reconsidered and began pulling

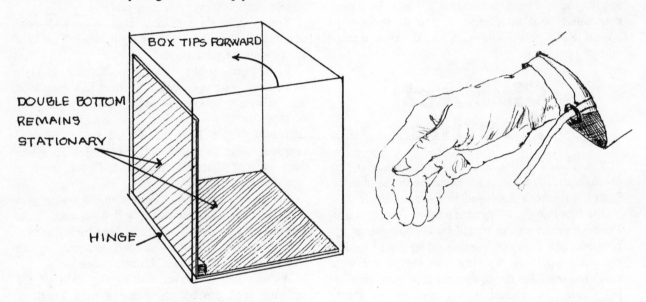

the box, at the front, at the join, so that when the bottom is in place, there are actually two thicknesses at the front side. The box should pivot easily on the hinge. Cloth gummed tape works satisfactorily with a cardboard box.

With the coil of rope in the box, if the open top is tilted over so that it faces the audience, the inner front side will become the bottom and the original bottom will be *behind* the open box.

I usually start with the back of the box facing the audience. I turn the box around, thus showing all sides without calling attention to that fact. I then tilt the box forward so that it rests on its front side, the top opening facing the audience. I run my hands casually around the empty inside of the box and flip it quickly back into upright position, which puts the ropes back into the box from their position behind it.

Then I gently lower the end of the 18-inch piece of rope that contains the Alnico magnet into the box, making sure to keep the other end in plain sight. I pull the 18-inch length up from the box, and the end of the long rope is now affixed to it. I keep pulling. As soon as I come to the magnetic join, I change my

out the rope to the full 12-foot length. Nobody in the audience seemed to be bothered by the fact that they hadn't seen the inside of the wastebasket.

The original Milbourne Christopher "Stretching a Rope" trick had the long length of rope looped in the inside breast pocket, one end running down the right sleeve to a point just above the cuff. One end of the short rope was shoved up into the right fist and apparently pulled out at the top. Actually, the rope end concealed under the cuff was pulled out. The performer continued to stretch the rope until he came to the far end of the long rope, which he gripped in his right fist against the hidden end of the short rope, so that the two long and short pieces looked like one continuous length of rope. There were no magnets, and there was no preparation other than the arrangement of the long rope in the pocket and down the sleeve.

I used the Alnico magnets, one in the short length and the other in the "far" end of the long rope. This enabled me to let the end of the rope swing free when it was finally fully stretched. I also wore a summer wristwatch band of nylon just above the wristbone of my right hand. I had affixed a small, smooth metal ring to this on the palm side, with the end of the rope running through the ring. This made for considerably easier handling and lessened the danger of the rope coming from the sleeve being exposed.

Whichever method you use, the long rope is loosely coiled and put on the table. You immediately pick up a pair of scissors and cut off a four or five foot length, observing that this is more like it. You now prepare to do the Square-Knot Cut and Restored Rope, as described in the close-up routines.

At the conclusion of the cut-and-restored rope trick, you measure off another length of rope against the first one, making them equal in length. You are getting ready for:

ROPES AROUND THE NECK

You drape the two ropes over the upper edge of the right hand, palm facing yourself, pulling the ends until all four ends are even. The four ends hang down, close together. As you reach to take a grip on the ropes with your left hand, you make a small loop in the right hand rope and shove this loop under the left length. You do this with both hands, covering it with a much broader movement as you apparently stretch the two ropes apart, parallel to each other. The right-hand rope is looped under and over the left rope as in the illustration. You bring this join to the back of your neck, up over your head, the two ends of each rope hanging down in front of your shoulders. You press the ropes firmly against the back of your neck and that little loop between your neck and the ropes holds them solidly in place as you tug on the ends with both hands. Actually you have the two ends of the free left-hand rope in your left fist and the two ends of the looped right-hand rope in your right fist. To all appearances, you simply have two ropes stretched around your neck.

You now bring the ends up and tie a firm knot in them, at the front. You tie a second, a third and a fourth knot on top of the first one. You can give the ropes a solid tug and the anchor loop at the back will hold. You apparently have two ropes tied tightly around your neck.

You reach up behind your neck with both hands and release the loop, quickly putting your thumbs in the two large loops as you bend your head forward and bring the two loops over your head to the front, stretching them out and holding them against each other. "The knots are still intact, both loops are intact, and they won't go over my head," you say as you

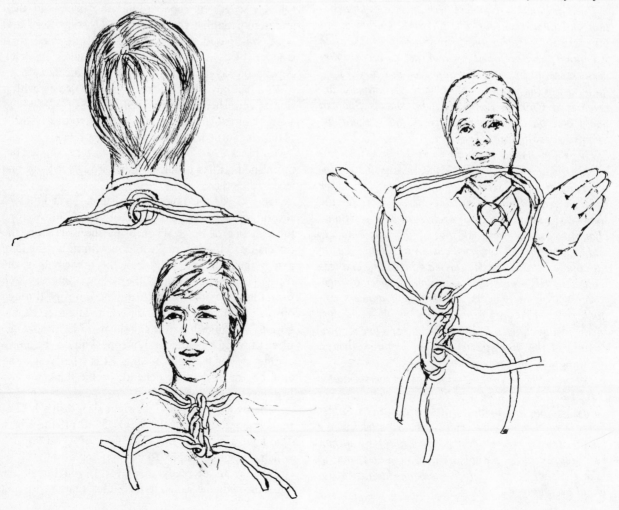

illustrate. They may be tossed out for examination, if you like.

While you're putting the ropes around your neck, you may want to say something like this: "They say that if you give the average person enough rope he'll hang himself. But magicians aren't average people. They have a vocabulary of magic words." As you tie the first word, you say the mystic word, "Allah." With the second knot, you say, "Allah Palooza." "Allah Palooza Paloo" accompanies the third knot, and "Allah Palooza Paloo Palip," the fourth. I use two additional magic words, "Pazazza" and "Pazamzam." Then as I remove the ropes from my neck, I shout, "Allah Palooza Palip Pazazza Pazamzam, Racka Tacka Pontiac!"

These were the magic words I first heard used with the trick when I was ten years old. A carnival barker used them, and I watched him enough times to memorize the incantation.

The sixth time I saw him do the trick, I discovered that he had a short length of white thread holding his two ropes together at their centers. When he put the ropes behind his neck, he switched ends so that he

Chang

Born in Panama, Chang entered magic as an assistant and interpreter for The Great Raymond about 60 years ago. After a tour of the world with Maurice Raymond, he developed his own act as an Arabian performer, but in 1913 first appeared in Chinese costume, using the name Li Ho Chang. His stage character is a Chinese comedian who speaks Spanish badly and makes numerous errors that delight his Spanish-speaking audiences.

His show had sometimes carried more than 30 people, including fine ballet dancers, and his equipment, lighting and scenery at the peak of his career weighed over 14 tons. A special musical score for the show was played by a full orchestra. The assistants changed costume for each unit of the performance, and Chang, himself, changed costume 25 times during the course of the show. He carried 45 costume changes with him. His show always contained specialty performers such as jugglers, acrobats and dancers. He made several large fortunes from magic—and lost them in unfortunate business ventures, such as production of the first Spanish talking picture. Always, his show was able to recoup.

Perhaps the keynote of the Chang performance was speed. Everything was done with lightning rapidity, without the slightest wait between tricks. Sometimes in the Chang performance, he did a trick while his assistants were setting the apparatus for another. He "stepped on" the applause as if he didn't want to take the time for it—which made the audience applaud even longer.

held both ends of one rope in each hand. And he broke the thread when he got ready to remove the double-noose.

Take my word for it, the loop in the rope is much better.

You now prepare to do the Block and Cord trick:

BLOCK AND CORD

Years ago, I saw Les Levant, the great Australian magician, do a trick with a block and a long length of red silk ribbon. The ribbon was threaded through a hole in the block and two spectators held the two ends. Levant grasped the block and slid it back and forth along the ribbon several times. Suddenly, he stepped back from the outstretched ribbon and held out the block, completely free of that ribbon. It was one of the highlights in a performance that was loaded with superlative tricks.

It was a beautiful mechanical trick to which Levant added his showmanship and polish. The trick was put on the magic market soon after Levant's visit to the United States, but his imitators never got the results from it that the Australian wonder worker did.

The ancient principle on which the old trick of tying a length of rope around the knee and then apparently pulling the rope through solid flesh and bone was based can be applied just as well to a wooden block as to the knee. This makes the trick depend on sleight of hand rather than mechanics.

You can buy the trick from a magic dealer, with a small, varnished or lacquered block of wood and a length of cord. You can also make it yourself, with a plain, unadorned, unfinished wooden block.

My block is a 4-inch length of 4x4 pine, sanded but unfinished. It has a hole drilled through it from one side to the other.

The size of the hole is important. Drill holes of several sizes in any old piece of wood. Put a rope through one of them. Then bring the rope from the underside to the top, make a loop with it, lay the loop across the hole and try to put the other end of the rope, the top end, through the hole, pulling the loop *firmly* into the hole as you bring the top rope through on the bottom and pull the end taut. The loop should go into the hole, but you should be able to hold the piece of wood by either end of rope without the loop's coming out of the hole. A snug fit is what you want, and the size of the hole depends on the thickness and firmness of your rope.

When you get the hole the right size, drill a hole of the same size through the block. Sand off the edges. You have a perfectly innocent block of wood through which a length of rope can be threaded.

When you get ready to perform, you thread the rope through the hole. It facilitates matters to coat

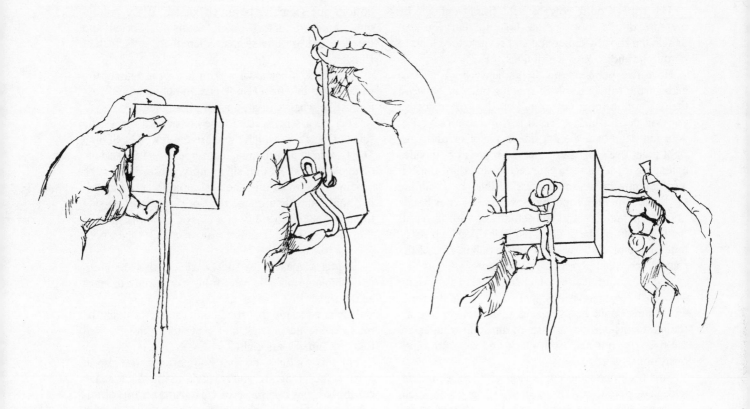

about 3 inches of each end of the rope with cement or glue to harden it and keep the end from fraying.

You hold the block, now threaded, in the left hand, forefinger on top, other fingers at the bottom and thumb at the rear. "Thumb at the rear" is the important thing.

Now, you bring the front end up behind the block with your right hand, from beneath, as if you were getting ready to thread that end through the block again. As much of it as touches the block is taut against the wood. You bring it slightly above the hole and hold it in place with your left thumb. There are now two ends of rope hanging down from the rear.

In the same motion with which you bring the front end up behind the block, your right thumb "hooks" the end of the rope that extends out of the rear opening of the hole. The right hand releases the front end

the instant the left thumb presses that extension against the block. The right hand then continues on up above the block with the rear end of the rope, finally grasping it near the end.

From the audience viewpoint, you have pulled the front end of the rope around to the rear and grasped it at the end preparatory to threading it through from the back.

Your left thumb moves the front rope over the hole. There will be a natural loop of rope under and extending from the left thumb. You put the rear end of the rope into the hole, *over* the loop, bring it out at the front, and pull it tight, pulling the loop *into* the hole. It appears that you have threaded a rope through the hole and then threaded one end through again so that the block is now held in a loop of rope. Actually, both ends are now coming out of the front end of the

hole but are held in place at opposite ends by loops inside the hole.

The rope should now be held firmly enough by pressure of the loops in the hole so that you can dangle the rope by either end and revolve the block to permit the audience to see all sides of it.

Have two people from the audience hold the two ends of the rope, the block hanging midway between them. Caution them not to pull on the ropes because you will need a little slack to perform a miracle. Put your left palm over the left side of the block and your right palm over the right side, the ropes at both sides extending from between your second and third fingers. You can now create the impression that you're sliding the block along the rope, by movement of your hands to the right and left, and you actually do slide it to pull the loops out of the ends of the hole. You step back, holding the block between your two palms, free of the rope which is held by the two spectators.

It is a beautiful effect, and the illusion is perfect. The block seems to visibly "melt" away from the rope. Everything could be examined at the conclusion, although I consider that a waste of time that would slow the pace of your act. Both block and rope are obviously unprepared.

This trick gives the impression of being a miracle, and you should sell it to your audience as such. Having done that, it's time for a little comedy relief. For that reason, you proceed to a trick which I call:

BANANAS

This is really nothing more than the old Boomerang optical illusion, dressed up. In this ancient optical illusion, two pieces of wood or cardboard are employed. They are identical in size and are shaped like this:

WHEN ALIGNED AT ONE END, LOWER BANANA APPEARS LARGER.

Held together, one against the other, they are the same length. But if one is held *above* the other, the bottom one seems to be much longer. If the bottom one is moved to the top, it seems to shorten and the new bottom one seems to lengthen. It is Instant Illusion.

As a trick, it has always been almost too good, too perfect. An intelligent audience quickly assumes that it must be what it is, an optical phenomenon.

There is a much-prized type of trick known as the "sucker" trick, of which there are too few. The Sliding Die Box in which the magician opens one front door of the box to show that side empty, closes it, tilts the box in that direction to the accompaniment of a sliding noise, and then opens the door on the other side to show that side empty is a classic example. Old as the trick is, it never fails to draw cries, "Open both doors at once."

The basic idea of the sucker trick is that the audience thinks it has discovered the secret, only to learn at the finish that it was mistaken.

It seemed to me that the boomerang trick might be made into a sucker trick, and experimentation showed that my hunch was right.

For this routine, cut your boomerangs to a size at least a foot long. If you're making them of heavy cardboard, put one piece of cardboard on top of another and cut through the two thicknesses so that they're perfectly matched for size. If you're making them of plywood, be sure that they're identical.

Your two boomerangs are going to represent two bananas. Paint one of them a pale green. Use a yellow, banana-colored base paint but make it green enough so there's no question but that it's a green banana.

Paint the other one yellow, and then put big splotches of dark brown on it, along with numerous

An Extra Trick

It's one of Don Alan's favorite magic stories.

A magician who was down on his luck and who also happened to be an expert ventriloquist conceived the idea of holding private spirit seances for a $1 fee. Those who came to him heard the voices of their departed friends and relatives, apparently coming out of the air. The voices were, of course, the result of ventriloquism.

A wealthy dowager heard about the fellow and approached him. "My good man," she said, pulling a $50 bill from her purse and holding it out in front of him, "do you suppose you could possible get me in touch with my late husband?"

The indigent magician stared at the $50 bill. "Lady," he said, "for that kind of money I'll not only get him to talk to you but I'll drink a glass of water while he's doing it."

brown speckles, so that it represents an overripe banana, one that's on the point of being *too* ripe.

Paint each boomerang the same on both sides. If you're not artistically inclined, find someone who is to do the job for you. Paint the background of the brown banana white and the background of the green banana gray.

With the two boomerangs painted, you're all set.

You hold one of the bananas in each hand, handling them rather gingerly and being obviously careful to keep one side of each facing the audience, as you relate the story of Benny Bananas.

Benny was a fruit vendor, and he was called Benny Bananas, not because his last name was Bananas but because bananas were the bane of his existence. For some reason, he was never able to correctly estimate the banana market. If he bought a lot of bananas, few people seemed to be interested in buying them. If he was short on bananas, the banana invariably became the most popular fruit on the market.

He got stuck with overripe bananas so often that

From a Borrowed Hat

Productions of objects from a borrowed hat are always impressive and can be hilariously funny if the objects tickle the funny bone. It's easy to "load" a borrowed hat in a stage performance, but not so easy when you're doing close-up magic.

One of the simplest and most daring "loads" is done by first putting the objects you intend to produce from the hat onto a silk handkerchief. Bring the four corners of the handkerchief together and tie them in place with a single twist of black silk thread, tied together so that you have a bundle in more or less the shape of a ball. Thread a few inches of surgical gut through the thread and tie it into a loop through which you can easily stick your thumb. The silk-covered "load" is in your kit or attaché case, along with a 12-inch square of plywood.

Holding the borrowed hat in your left hand, reach into your kit for the plywood board. Hook your right thumb into the catgut loop of the load and pick up the board with your fingers on the front of it, thumb at the back. Bring out the board facing your audience. Transfer the hat to your right fingers, the crown of it facing the audience. Pull the board away with your left hand to "show both sides of it." This will almost automatically load the silk into the hat, the brim of which should be tipped up in front so that nobody can see what's inside.

Put the board on four glass tumblers and rest the hat on it. Then break the thread that holds the ends of the silk together and start pulling items into view.

While you can't perform this trick with people behind you, the angles aren't bad. People may be fairly far to the sides, as long as they're in front of you.

he always bought green ones. In the slow periods, those green bananas ripened, and then became so brown and mushy that he'd finally throw them away.

As a result of his cautious buying, he always had two kinds of bananas in stock—green ones and overripe ones. Let's face it, some of his bananas weren't overripe; they were plain rotten.

Naturally, whenever one of the unexplainable banana booms started, he tried to sell the overripe bananas first. Here's how he did it. He would show the customer a green banana in his right hand and an overripe banana in his left hand.

"The price on the ripe bananas and on the green bananas is the same," he said, "but the ripe bananas are much longer, so they're a better buy."

As you quote Benny, you move the brown banana directly beneath the green one, the left ends in line with each other. The right end of the brown banana will extend considerably farther to the right than the end of the green one.

Then, you continue, when he'd gotten rid of all but one overripe banana, he kept it for purposes of comparison. If a customer complained that the bananas were too green, he said, "They'll ripen. And the green ones are so much longer than the ripe ones that they're a terrific buy."

As you quote Benny on this, you move the bottom boomerang to the top—but you do it in the most awkward manner possible. Holding one boomerang in each hand, you wave them around, turning each one over in what appears to be a sneaky attempt to fool the audience.

You do this several times, showing how Benny Bananas made either the green or brown ones longer, depending on his current supply. Make the exchange of boomerangs from top to bottom and back look awkward but surreptitious.

If you do this well—and don't be subtle about it—the audience will quickly get the idea that one boomerang *is* longer than the other, and that each boomerang has a green banana on one side and a brown one on the other. They'll ask to see the back of each banana.

You then appear uncomfortable and embarrassed. "But a banana doesn't have a back and a front," you protest. "Who ever heard of anyone peeling the back side of a banana?"

When you've "milked" it for all the effect you can get, you very slowly, with hands wide apart, turn over the banana boomerang in each hand.

"Oh, I see what you were thinking," you nod. "You thought this banana was overripe on one side and green on the other. But that simply couldn't be. Bananas don't ripen that way."

You then place the boomerangs in position for comparison. "You see," you explain, "the green one is actually much longer than the ripe one."

You slowly and deliberately move the ripe one to the bottom position, as you continue, "But since you've had the ripe ones longer than the green ones, they *look* longer."

If there's an easier trick to do, I don't know where you'd find it. And since you've made it as amusing as possible, you present the next trick in a more serious vein. It's called:

HEAVY WATER

You use a plain, clear glass water tumbler for this trick. Don't use a decorated or oddly shaped tumbler. It should appear to be exactly what it is, a plain water glass. A wide-mouthed water pitcher, about one-third full of water, is also on the table, along with a 4-inch square of heavy paper. A piece torn from the cover of a magazine is ideal.

The trick employs a gimmick. Draw a circle around the lip of the tumbler, on a piece of paper. Cut the paper to the form of the circle and then use it for a guide in cutting an identical circle of clear, colorless lightweight plastic. The thinner the plastic, the better. Now cut a circle of plastic about an eighth of an inch smaller than the first one. It should fit loosely *inside* the lip of the tumbler. Cement the two plastic circles together with clear, waterproof plastic cement. Let them dry.

This double thickness plastic circle is in the bottom of the water pitcher, the side with the inner circle attached facing downward.

You tell your audience that while everyone knows about the heavy water used in nuclear experiments, few people are aware of "light water." This is the water discovered in outer space by the astronauts. It's extremely difficult to bring back because of its tendency to float up out of a bucket into the air. You finally hit on the idea of mixing heavy water with it to create the weight you wanted.

You pour the tumbler about half-full of water. Then you pick up the square of paper, showing it on both sides, and dip it into the pitcher to moisten it. When you bring it out, you hold the plastic double disc behind it with your thumb. You then put the paper over the mouth of the glass, starting from the front, and get the double disc in place over the mouth. Slide the paper around, if necessary, to get the disc where you want it.

Now, put the glass on your right palm and bring your left palm down over the paper at the mouth of it. Turn the glass gently upside down and remove your left hand. It's a good idea to have the glass above the water pitcher while you're doing this.

The water remains suspended in the glass when you pull your hand away, you explain, due to the hydrostatic principle. However, with your mixture of heavy water and light water, you can go far beyond the hydrostatic principle.

With the left fingers, you carefully peel the paper away from the mouth of the glass—of course, leaving the double plastic disc in place. The water remains suspended, and the disc is invisible. The disc holds up the water by the same hydrostatic principle as did the heavy paper.

If you peel the moistened paper away with great delicacy, as if everything hinged on the way you do

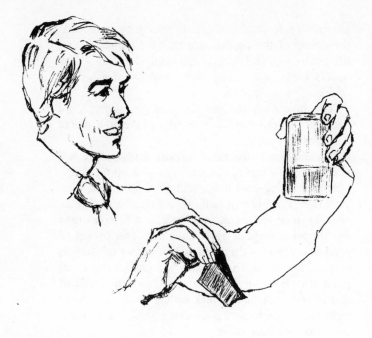

it, you will generate spontaneous applause when the audience sees the water still in the tumbler.

"There is only one way to release the water," you explain. You start to count, pointing your forefinger at the mouth of the upside glass with each count. "Nine, eight, seven, six, five, four, three, two, one—BLAST OFF!"

At the words, "Blast Off," you strike the plastic disc with your forefinger. Be sure that the glass is directly over the water pitcher. When the disc is struck, the water and the disc will fall immediately into the pitcher. The disc is not visible as it falls.

Your next trick is Pseudo-Psychometry, explained in the Mental Magic section. By all means, use the coat hanger dowsing rods to find the last person of those who put objects into envelopes.

This is a fine trick that will develop your showmanship. The oftener you perform it in public, the better it becomes.

You need a strong trick to follow it, and you'll have exactly that. You have built to your climax, to your blockbuster trick. It's:

THE NEEDLE TRICK

At this point, you become serious. "I'm about to perform a feat of magic which I do only on special occasions. I've had two special requests to do it in this performance.

"One reason I don't perform it more often is that it's one of the most dangerous feats of magic in the world. Only the Ching Ling Soo trick of catching a bullet in the teeth is considered more dangerous.

"It's a trick that was made famous by the immortal Harry Houdini. Don't labor under the delusion that it's simple—and after you've see it performed, *don't try to do it!* Professional magicians who venture to learn it have a physician on hand while they're attempting it. I had a doctor friend present the first 50 times I performed the feat. Houdini, who performed more death-defying feats than any magician in history, approached this piece of legerdemain with the utmost caution."

Don't use my words. Fit the thought to your own speech and to your audience. Incidentally, never do this trick for a children's show.

The first requirement for the Needle Trick is two paper packets of needles. I prefer the packet of assorted sizes, for no special reason.

Remove the needles from one packet and, gripping them as a unit, file down the points to blunt condition.

Thread these needles onto about a 6-foot length of heavy white cotton thread. The thread should be heavy enough to be clearly visible to the audience but not heavy enough to make the needle packet bulky. I measure off the thread from my shoulder blade to the tips of my fingers, taking off two such lengths before I break the thread.

Thread one of the needles onto an end of the white thread, moving it in about six inches. Tie a knot in the thread on both sides of the needle, to keep it from sliding. Thread the rest of the needles onto the thread with a somewhat irregular spacing between them, a knot on each side of each needle holding it in place. Thread and anchor the last needle six inches from the end opposite the one you started with. Now, hold the first two needles tightly together by the pointed end and wrap the thread between them

Two Great Tricks

Blackstone once told rather sheepishly about the well-dressed matron who came back-stage after his performance and buried him in an avalanche of praise.

Harry expanded under her glowing eulogy. Here, he felt, was one of the most perceptive women he had ever met.

"Which of my tricks," he finally asked, "did you like the best?"

"It's hard to say," she replied, "because they were all so marvelous. I think it would be a toss-up between two tricks."

"And which ones were they?" Harry asked, beaming.

Her reply deflated him. "The one where you tied a handkerchief to a black silk thread and then made it dance around on the stage, and the one where you made the bird cage go up your sleeve."

Harry never found out that the woman was the wife of a local magician who had coached her on what to say.

around the eye end, tightly. Bring the third needle up to the first two and wrap the thread between it and the second needle in the same position. Repeat the process with the fourth needle. When the needles are all wrapped, tie several knots in the loose end, right at the tip, and wedge it in between two of the outer needles at the eye end. Try to keep all the thread as close to the eye end of the needles as possible.

Another vital prop is a *large* spool of white cotton thread. The small spool used on sewing machines won't work. The wooden spool must be longer than your threaded packet of needles.

Remove the paper circle from the top of the spool, being careful not to tear it. Throw away the paper circle from the bottom of the spool.

With a brace and bit or a small file, ream out the core of the wooden spool. This hole must be large enough to hold the packet of threaded needles loosely, without any danger of their sticking. The packet should slide out when you tilt the spool opening downward. If it doesn't, you need a larger hole in the spool. The packet of needles, threaded and wrapped, is inserted in the hole points first. When you tilt the spool, the thread-wrapped end should drop out into your hand. Once the spool is properly reamed, glue the paper circle back on the top opening. The packet of threaded needles is inserted into the open bottom of the spool, points first. You will use the same spool and threaded needles over and over.

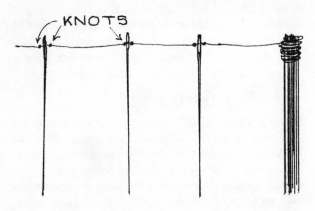

KNOTS

Another prop is a saucer or small individual pie tin. The pie tin is much preferable, because you can rattle loose needles against it and the audience can hear them. The little pie tin is on the table, with the other packet of needles in it. The only additional prop is a clean, folded white linen handkerchief in your left-hand suitcoat side pocket.

At the proper time in your performance, you hand the pie tin and packet of needles to someone in the front row. Ask him or her to remove the needles and place them in the pie tin, points all facing the same direction.

Have him pass several of the needles to those

around him for examination, to satisfy everyone that the points of the needles are sharp. Emphasize that the points must all face in the same direction. "One needle facing the wrong way could cause a serious accident," you explain.

You take back the pie tin, now containing loose needles. You put it at the front edge of the table where it is clearly visible.

"In addition to the needles," you explain, "we will need five or six feet of thread." You pick up the spool, open end facing your palm, with your left hand. With your right fingers, you pull off two lengths of thread, roughly three feet each, and break it off. You drape the thread over your right shoulder. The packet of needles previously threaded is now across the fingers of your left hand, thread-wrapped end to the right, pointed ends to the left. You put down the spool of thread and immediately pick up the pie tin with your right hand, bouncing the needles up and down a few times so that they rattle.

You tilt the pie tin to empty the needles from it into your left cupped palm. The needles go into your palm, and you show the tin empty without calling any particular attention to that fact.

You reach into the cupped left palm with your right thumb and fingers and pick up the threaded and wrapped packet of needles by the threaded end, the other end, the pointed end, sticking out in plain sight. You expose as much of the packet's length as you can without letting the thread be seen.

Holding this packet between your right thumb and fingers, you bring it up to your lips and shove the threaded end in and back so that the pointed ends extend outward. You pull the packet forward so that the points are visible between your lightly closed lips. You point to them with your right forefinger, and then with your tongue, pull them back into your mouth out of sight. You roll them immediately to the space between the inside of your left cheek and your left gums.

You now reach into your left-hand coat pocket with your left hand and bring out the handkerchief, leaving the loose needles behind. You open the handkerchief and drape it over your left wrist.

Next, you put the length of white thread hanging from your shoulder into your mouth, chewing it together into a tiny ball. You can palm the ball out as you stuff in the end of the thread. I prefer to put it between the cheek and the gum on the right side of the jaw.

You now pour a small drink of water and drink it. Then you hand the handkerchief to someone in the front row, open your mouth wide, and tell him to examine the inside of your mouth to assure himself that it is completely empty. The wider you open your mouth, the more thoroughly the needles and thread are concealed. I have on occasion even given spectators a pair of rubber gloves to don for the examination

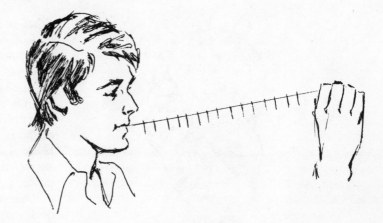

of my mouth, but it's time-consuming, unnecessary, and, frankly, it makes me nervous.

Bring the spectator who examined your mouth onto the stage. Spread the handkerchief on the floor and get down on one knee. Protection of your trousers from the floor is another reason for the handkerchief. Work the packet of needles up into your mouth and get the knotted end by feeling it with your tongue. Work it out between your lips. Instruct the spectator to take a hold of it and draw it out of your mouth slowly and cautiously. If you hold your left palm up toward him, it's a signal that he's pulling too fast.

He pulls out the length of thread, backing away from you until the full six feet of thread is extending between your lips and his hand, the threaded needles glistening along its length. Take the end of the thread from him, thank him and send him back to his seat as you hold the threaded needles aloft in a bid for applause.

With proper buildup, this is one of those tricks that nothing can successfully follow.

It is *not* a difficult trick to do. Every move is carefully worked out. Don't worry about anyone seeing the threaded packet of needles in your mouth. Spectators are hesitant to actually reach into your mouth, even with your handkerchief, and you can hold your jaws so wide open that nobody would believe anything could possibly be hidden.

Here's how the complete routine runs:

    Rope Stretching
    Square Knot Cut and Restored Rope
    Ropes Around the Neck
    Block and Cord
    Bananas
    Heavy Water
    Pseudo-Psychometry
    The Needle Trick.

You opened with a novelty, did some clean, uncluttered rope tricks, injected some humor, had a strong trick midway in your performance in the Block and Cord, followed it with a sucker trick and then began building to a smash finish with three strong tricks, Heavy Water, Pseudo-Psychometry and the Needle Trick.

There are many, many more good club act tricks that you can do without fear of failure. If you don't feel that the Needle Trick is for you, close with Par-Optic Vision, if you like.

"Break in" your club act on small groups. Get it "set."

If you want to include a card trick, the Tearing the Deck in Half trick is ideal. I'll give you another one, however, maybe for sentimental reasons. I first performed this trick in public in that long ago Chautauqua performance in Hawarden, Iowa, and I've done it many hundreds of times since. It's:

THE CARD IN THE ORANGE

Since you destroy two playing cards, one from each of two decks, every time you do this trick, keep two decks in reserve. When they get down to about 40 cards, use them for Tearing a Deck in Half.

You force a person to take a certain card in this trick. Some use the thumb riffle force, but maybe you should use the simple Cut Force, as described in the card section.

Let's say you're going to force the selection of the Jack of Hearts. It is put on top of the deck that will be used in the performance. Check just prior to doing your act to see that it's still there.

From the other deck, you take the Jack of Hearts and tear off one of the corners, one of the two identifying corners. This corner is on the deck, loose, on top of the face-down (or about to be chosen) card.

The Jack with the corner torn from it is rolled tightly around a lead pencil or slim pen. Take it off and you'll find that you can now roll it even tighter. It is rolled with the back of the card facing out, face in.

Carefully remove the top pip from a good-sized orange. Now, shove the tightly rolled card down into the orange, its full length. Put a tiny dab of cement on the pip, another on the surface of the orange where the pip came from, and replace the pip. The rolled

card is now inside the orange and the most careful examination of the fruit will not reveal that it has been tampered with.

Put this orange on a plate with two others and a paring knife. The "loaded" orange is pip-end down and the other two are pip-end up, for purpose of easy identification.

There are so many, many ways to force the selection of a specific card that I hardly know which one to recommend. I always use the Classic Force for this trick—the fan spread of the deck with the spectator taking a card from the fan. You'd probably be nervous about using it. When you pick the deck up from the table, you let the little torn piece slide off into your left hand and place the deck on top of it. A ridiculously simple force is one in which you ask the spectator to call out any number from one to 15.

The Hindu Rope Trick

The legendary Hindu Rope Trick is exactly that —legendary.

It's the trick in which the Hindu fakir throws a 50-foot length of rope into the air and it hangs suspended, without support. A small boy then climbs the rope, disappears, and the rope falls to the ground. According to legend, the trick is done outdoors, with the fakir surrounded by spectators.

Several magicians, traveling in India, have offered huge sums of money for anyone who would perform the trick, and there have been no takers. Stories about it, tracked down, have always come to a dead end. The person who is supposed to have seen it always turns out to have heard about somebody else who saw it.

The trick has been done as a stage illusion by at least half a dozen professional magicians—but with special scenery and lighting effects. In such a setting, it is not a particularly impressive trick.

Jack Kodell, originator of the magic act employing live parakeets, created a miniature version in which a parakeet climbs a two-foot length of rope and disappears.

When he's named a number, you illustrate what he's to do. "You're to count off that number of cards into a face-down pile, like this," you say. You count the cards off. Let's say the number is nine. You hold up the ninth card so it can be seen. "The ninth card is the one you're to keep," you tell him. You put it back onto the pile, put the pile back on top of the remainder of the deck and give the deck a false cut, pulling a block of cards from the bottom and slapping the balance of the deck on top of it. The card is now in the proper position.

When the spectator takes the force card from the deck, you take the balance of the deck from him and start to turn away, heading back for the stage. As you start to turn, you say, "I want you to tear the card right across the center, in half." You make a slight pause and add, "Mentally, of course. I certainly wouldn't want you to destroy the card." Time this so that the "Mentally, of course" comes the instant you hear the card being torn. You turn back toward the spectator, who is holding two halves of a card. This always gets a good laugh, particularly if the spectator looks sheepish.

You give a resigned shrug. "Oh, well, don't worry about it. As long as you've destroyed the card, might as well tear it into quarters. Go ahead."

"Now, tear it into eighths." He does. "Want to try for sixteenths?"

I've never quite understood why "Want to try for sixteenths?" gets a laugh, but it usually does. Few people can tear a card into sixteenths, but if he tries, stop him. Have him put the pieces onto your cupped right palm, reach over with your palm-down left hand and hand him the piece of card that was originally torn from the other Jack of Hearts. "You keep one piece as a claim check. Don't lose it."

Now, you must vanish the remaining seven pieces of card. I originally did it with a paper cone, which, for stage use, is as good a method as any. You cut two 12-inch squares of newsprint and rubber cement three of the edges together, leaving the top open. Trim all edges so they're even. You roll this piece of paper into a cornucopia, opening the top with your forefinger as you do it. You drop the pieces of card into the open end and then fold over the top, giving the cornucopia to someone to hold. The trick is practically done.

You pick up the plate with three oranges on it, keeping your eye on the loaded orange, and extend the plate to another spectator. "I want you to remove two of the oranges from the plate, please," you say.

If he leaves the loaded orange on the plate, you continue, "Keep one for yourself and give the other to someone else. When you get home, cut open those oranges and guess what you'll find inside. Vitamin C."

If one of the oranges he takes is the "loaded" one, keep your eye on it and continue, "Decisions, decisions! Now you have to decide which of the two we'll use for the experiment. Put either one of them into my hand."

If he returns the loaded orange, you hold it up. "You've made your decision and this is the one you've selected." If he keeps the loaded one, you say, "So that's the one you've selected."

For years, I had the spectator cut the loaded orange across the middle, revealing the rolled-up card. And then I had a nervous volunteer assistant cut his finger. Ever since that time, I've done the cutting.

At that point, you have the spectator pull the rolled-up card from the orange and open it out. You take it

to the spectator who is holding a piece of card, have him acknowledge that the card in the orange is the Jack of Hearts, the card he originally selected. Have him fit the piece he is holding to the torn corner. It fits perfectly.

As an afterthought, you open the folded-over top of the cornucopia, open it out and show both sides, empty!

For years, I opened the cornucopia and showed it

empty *before* the orange was sliced open. One night I forgot to do it and somebody in the audience called out, "What about the pieces in the paper?" I opened them and found that the vanish of the pieces drew a second round of applause. I've done it that way ever since.

Making the double sheets of paper for the cone is a nuisance. Some years ago, I acquired a Merv Taylor card box, a thin stainless steel box that can be examined minutely. You put the pieces of card into the box, close it and give it to someone to hold. When the person who is holding the box opens it, the pieces have vanished. If you do your club act with any frequency, you'll probably want a card box similar to the Taylor-made one. I doubt that you'll be able to find a Merv Taylor one any more, but there are other good makes.

If you want to "pad" your club act, make it run for a longer time, an ideal pad trick for stage use is the 100-foot Challenge Rope Escape.

Never change more than one trick at a time in your club act, once you get it set. Experimenting with new tricks is fun, but depend on tested and proven tricks for the bulk of your act.

Don't try to take bows at the conclusion of your act. Taking a bow gracefully is an art, and most amateurs do it badly and awkwardly. Instead of taking a bow, do a "Star." This is an old vaudeville technique in which you throw out both arms at right angles to your

The Ultimate Trick

The late, great Harry Blackstone once said in all seriousness that the ultimate in magic was bringing the dead back to life.

He had a trick that at least created such an effect. Unfortunately, it was a trick that couldn't be seen by a theater audience. Blackstone tried to work out some way of magnifying it so that a large audience could see it, but gave up.

The trick involved catching a live house fly. The live fly was then submerged in water, held under by a thimble or piece of screen, for eight hours or more. When the fly was removed from the water, it was a sodden, pulpy, inanimate thing. It was then exposed to the sun and its exterior surface dried.

The fly, Blackstone explained, wasn't really dead but was in a state of suspended animation. When he got ready to demonstrate "bringing the dead back to life," he simply laid one of his dormant flies out on a piece of paper and covered it with table salt.

The salt apparently absorbed the water inside the fly, because in a few minutes, what had passed as a dead fly emerged from the salt and walked groggily away. Harry thought it was one of the greatest tricks of all time and was frustrated by his inability to present it to audiences.

body as if you were about to embrace someone. Hold the pose until the applause starts. Then let your arms drop naturally to your sides, smile and walk off.

GREAT PERFORMERS

The late Dante was the all-time master. He had developed a surefire technique for getting applause. At the conclusion of every trick, he stepped up onto a three-foot square riser or platform, elevated only seven or eight inches above the floor. He faced the audience, held his hands together over his head, brought them down to a Star and said, "Sim Sala Bim." The words "Sim Sala Bim" became his trademark.

I would have to rate him the finest actor of any magician I've ever seen. He had a roguish face that could transmit any emotion to an audience, and his delivery of lines was flawless.

Blackstone was the greatest showman of all the magicians I've ever seen. He looked like a magician, and acted like "the world's greatest," both on and off-stage. He did everything with a flourish and had a bravura style that was unequaled. Magic was his life, and that came across to spectators.

I first saw Thurston toward the end of his career, and while he had a magnificent show, his voice and stage deportment were the things that most impressed me about him.

I saw Houdini do a full-length show in vaudeville. He packed the house and turned people away at every performance, the all-time master of exploitation and publicity. He was doing an escape act, and I thought it dragged noticeably here and there throughout the long performance. It's a great tribute to his ability that he could hold an audience through a full-length escape act. Most magicians who have tried it have failed miserably. The very nature of an escape act prohibits speed. Houdini had found that an escape act would draw bigger crowds than anything else he could do. I think he knew that escapes were "slow," but he's the one performer who was ever able to make such an act pay off consistently, year after year.

The two greatest technicians I've ever seen are Dai Vernon and Neil Foster. They're the ultimate in sheer magic, and their technique has made them favorites with other magicians, who drool at their performances. Cardini and LePaul added suave charm and showmanship to technique to make their performances tremendously enjoyable, among the all-time best.

For sheer personal pleasure, I find it hard to top the performances of Don Alan, Jay Marshall and Senator Crandall. They're expert technicians, but more importantly, they fracture me. They're *entertaining,* whether they're doing magic or just talking. Jay proved his ability as a comedian when he worked the top spots of the country with nothing but a floor mop, doing a comedy monologue, and when he worked Radio City Music Hall with nothing but a glove hand puppet, "Lefty." Crandall is, in my opinion, one of the great off-beat humorists of our time. Don Alan combines good magic and a breezy comedy style into a perfect blend.

The most enjoyable husband-and-wife team I've ever seen are The Johnstones, George and Betty, who came out of the old Blackstone show to work top spots everywhere. They're Beautiful People to start with, and they have a style all their own. Their magic has never flabbergasted me, but they've always entertained me.

The late Jack Gwynne had what must have been the greatest family magic act of all time. He knew magic from A to Z and could give you any kind of a performance you wanted, up to and including a big illusion show. The irrepressible Anne, Mrs. Gwynne, added striking beauty to the act, even after she was a grandmother, and the youngsters were among the best magician's assistants in the world. On top of that, their appearance was most attractive. The Gwynnes performed all over the world, and Jack, well past Social Security age, performed right up to the day of his death.

John Mulholland and J. Elder Blackledge had the best magic "lectures" I ever heard. Their styles were quite different, but both held their audiences in the palms of their hands. The late Harlan Tarbell, author of the famous Tarbell Magic Course, did a show that was a cross between a straight magic show and a lecture, a unique performance. On several occasions he worked the 6,000-plus seat Chicago Civic Opera House with a one-man show, without the "flash" of gigantic illusions—and anybody who can perform that miracle, has to be a real magician.

One of the greatest magicians I ever knew was Max Adali, who worked tent rep shows throughout the midwest under the name of Mock Sad Ali. He taught me some fine magic, and he knew a lot more than what he taught me during a too-brief summer on a tent rep show.

The funniest magic act I ever saw was Frank Van Hoeven's, a vaudeville act with stooges that broke audiences down into hysterical laughter. There were big time comedy acts that refused to work a bill with Van Hoeven, because they knew they couldn't top him.

High among the most artistic magic performances I've ever seen, I'd have to put Okito, the late Theo Bamberg, member of a continental Magic Royal Family. For some reason, the Oriental magic acts with their emphasis on mystification rather than comedy, plus their beautiful stage settings and costumes, were in a class by themselves.

For "inside" hilarity, the trio of Jay Marshall, Karrell Fox and Duke Stern can't be topped. They've become a three-man stock company at the magic conventions, and they lay their audiences in the aisles.

To anyone who knows magic and magicians, they're the funniest combination that ever walked a stage.

In the area of mental magic, I hesitate to mention the greatest performers I've ever seen, because some of them worked so "strong" that they should have been jailed. Dunninger would have to rate well up toward the top because of his superior showmanship. He has always commanded top fees and is certainly the best-known of all the mentalists.

Kreskin and David Hoy, of a younger generation, are both excellent. Hoy has the natural flamboyance that a mentalist needs, and his performance is always loaded with blockbusters. Kreskin has a new, mild and disarming approach that I find most refreshing. He's getting a wealth of network TV exposure because he deserves it.

Of the old school, I'd have to rate Rajah Raboid and Melroy among the most sensational. Their performances never failed to leave their audiences gasping, on the ropes.

For fantastic, unbelievable, sheer wizardry with a deck of cards, I pick a non-professional magician, Edward Marlo. Tell Eddie the effect you want him to achieve with a deck of cards and he'll do it. Among the "comers" in this field, I'd pick Allan Ackerman, a young semi-professional.

Magical Ego

The Great Julius was a struggling, unskilled magician working in a carnival sideshow. He became a key witness in a damage suit, and the attorney for the defense tried to discredit his testimony.

"What is your profession?" he asked.

"I am a magician," Julius answered proudly.

"How long have you been a magician?" the attorney asked.

"For nearly a year," Julius replied.

"And what is your salary?"

Julius hesitated to answer. Finally, reluctantly, he mumbled, "Twenty-five dollars a week."

"Are you a good magician?" the attorney asked.

"I, sir," Julius responded, "am a superb magician."

"Who," the lawyer continued, "would you say is the greatest magician in the entire world?"

Julius hesitated momentarily and then answered firmly, "I am."

The courtroom broke into uproarious laughter and the judge had to threaten removal of the spectators to stop the noise.

The defense attorney was furious. "You blithering idiot," he screamed at Julius, "didn't you realize that people would laugh you right out of court if you said you were the greatest magician in the world?"

"I was fully aware of what might happen," Julius replied with dignity. "But what could I do? I was under oath."

The top magical inventive geniuses, the creators of magical effects are, not necessarily in order of their ability, U.F. "Gen" Grant, Ted Annemann, Horace Goldin and—this might surprise you—Richard Himber. Himber, the retired orchestra leader, was a passionate magic devotee who took new approaches to magic. Some of the tricks he invented may not have been world-beaters but they were always different. His brash, abrasive personality and his penchant for outrageous practical jokes alienated him from a considerable number of magicians, but that had nothing to do with his inventive turn of mind. And, if you were his friend, there was nothing he wouldn't do for you. Annemann would have to be my favorite of all the magic inventors because his originalities were in the field that intrigued me most. He believed in the simplest way of doing any trick, and he streamlined some old, impractical ideas to the point where they were not only workable but good. He started and edited the weekly *Jinx* magazine for a number of years, and the old *Jinx* consistently published good magic, particularly in the mental and close-up fields. Ted's pen was often dipped in caustic, but everything he wrote was, in his opinion, for the good of magic. "Gen" Grant has created so many magical effects that some of them are to be found in almost every field of magic. Where the bulk of Goldin's creations would fall into the stage illusion category, Grant's forte is the club act kind of magic. I say, his forte, but he's invented close-up tricks, sleight of hand tricks, stage illusions—everything that's magical has had contributions from him.

Willard, the Wizard

Willard, the Wizard, was the last of the big tent show magicians.

His show played the Texas territory for years, and in the area where his show appeared, people said Willard was the greatest magician in the world. He was the son of a magician, and at one time Willard, his father and a brother were out with three almost identical tent shows, all billed as "Willard, the Wizard," and all thriving.

He survived the advent of talking pictures and he came through the depression years of the early 30's. It took tax problems to bring him down.

By the time he was honored as a feature performer at one of the national magic conventions, he was a tired, harrassed old man. His performance in no way resembled the Willard show at its peak, but he retained enough to let his critical audience see a trace of the greatness that had made him so popular for so many years. Magicians who knew him said that his inherent sense of what constituted good magic was remarkable and that his ability to sell a trick to an audience was superb.

Most new magic tricks are adaptations of old principles. Something that's really new in every respect is a rarity, and the people who come up with these innovations aren't prolific; at least, they don't invent many tricks.

The Number One magic family of the United States would, I think, have to be the Larsen family on the West Coast. When not only a husband and wife but the children have a passionate devotion to the art of conjuring, you have an exceptional family. The Larsens have been and are leaders in and promoters of everything magical.

There are some wonderful novelty magic acts. Perhaps I admire them most for their originality, the fact that they don't follow a set, traditional pattern. Marvin Roy's magic with electric lights is beautiful, mystifying and different. Jack Kodell's act with parakeets was one of the most original and delightful acts I've ever seen. Johnny Platt's fakir act is good magic, presented with a novel twist. The dove acts were great until there became an over-abundance of them. Norman Jensen's floating violin is without a peer. Ade and True Duval's Fantasy in Silks was exactly that. Think-a-Drink Hoffman had the one great magic bar act. Harry Lorrayne is a brilliant card manipulator, but it's his Giant Memory demonstration that makes him stand out. Doc Baker was billed as a protean headliner, but to me, his quick-change act was pure magic of the highest order. Karrell Fox, like Crandall, has a style of comedy that's all his own. Other performers have tried using the same patter Karrell employs, but the result is never even close. De Haviland's paper magic made him different. There may be other card manipulators who know their technique as well as Cardini, but the Cardini act simply can't be copied. Al Flosso's pitchman or carnival barker act always fractures me. Dominique has a pickpocket act that is absolutely superb, far superior in my opinion to similar acts done by others. John Shirley's balloon act is without an equal.

Probably the most dazzling act being performed today is that of Siegfried and Roy, who are headliners in Las Vegas at the time this is being written. The excitement mounts throughout their performance, with a climax at the finish where one of them is found to have been replaced by a live ocelot, a mean-looking, snarling beast.

A new Dante, not related to the original one, is said to have a superior escape act, although I haven't seen it. The act must be good to get the laudatory reviews it has received.

Mark Wilson's "Magic Circus" television specials are wonderful magic in the classic tradition. Mark's appearance, stage deportment, knowledge of magic and his ability combine to make him a major star.

Al Goshman is the perfect example of a man who learns to do a trick superbly well. Not a magician, he bought a trick from Okito—a coin trick—and followed Okito's advice to learn it well before he bought another trick. He took the advice so seriously that he was soon baffling magicians who knew and did the trick. Starting with that one simple trick, he grew into a stellar performer.

Rico is a fine magician who will fool any lay audience and most professionals. Julius Sundman and Marshall Brodien have to be rated as great magicians by any impartial judge. Al Koran has a special appeal for me because he does the kind of magic I enjoy most. I also find the Keeners particularly appealing because of their attractive freshness, good pacing and smooth performance.

Don Alan, whose name has been mentioned several times previously in this book, will always be one of my favorite performers, perhaps because I've worked with him so much under such a variety of circumstances. While he's a comedy performer, he takes his magic seriously. Everything he does, he does well. There's a reason. He works hard and will put in almost any amount of overtime to improve even a small segment of his performance. He doesn't "play" at being a magician. He makes his living from magic and gives it maximum respect and attention. I've seen him under almost impossible conditions, and I've seen him in situations where he had every right to a display of artistic temperament, but he never lost his "cool."

Few of the performers I've mentioned are great inventors of tricks. Many of them haven't originated anything they do in their acts. They have, however, developed specialties, refining and polishing the tricks they do until what they have becomes their own by virtue of the way they do them. And they don't follow the "store-boughten" instructions to the letter. They not only dare to be different but stoutly refuse to follow the set pattern.

Some of them do the same tricks, but with an entirely different approach. Each has an individual style that sets him apart from his confreres.

When you do your club act, don't pattern your style after any one of the greats. Make it distinctive—your own. And if you learn a trick that's done with a handkerchief and a piece of rope, don't be afraid to do it with a Turkish towel and length of chain if you think you can make it better or more entertaining.

If you're performing often for the same group, you'll have to learn some new tricks from time to time. But put them into your act one or two at a time and keep your best "old" tricks, which are audience-tested, as solid insurance for a good performance.

Blackstone came up with many new illusions over the years, but he always did his dancing handkerchief trick, as well as many other stand-bys. Any audience that had ever seen Neil Foster perform would feel short-changed if Neil didn't do the Zombie floating ball trick. If Jay Marshall doesn't bring out "Lefty," his tough little rabbit puppet, his audiences ask for it. I doubt that anyone ever saw Gene Bernstein perform without asking him to do his Spirit Rapping Pencil. When you do a trick well, and I mean really well, audiences want you to do it every time they watch your performance.

If any magic act is any good to start with, it should, like fine wine, improve with age. It should improve because your technique should improve. If you watch audience reactions to your tricks, you can't help but learn from them. And the more times you do a difficult trick, the better it becomes.

There are hundreds of amateurs whose magic is every bit as good as that of all except the top professionals. Many of them could be pros, were they so inclined. Their impact on their audiences is even greater than that of top professionals largely because their viewers know that magic is a hobby with them, not a business. Their talent is recognized and appreciated.

As with any other art, you can't buy success. Spending money on tricks won't make you a brilliant magician. You could probably assemble every trick in this book for an investment of $10 or $15, and if you learned to do even half of them with great skill you could outshine any "high-priced equipment" magician that ever lived.

Where Do We Go From Here?

You've decided you like magic and enjoy doing it. You've read the tricks in this book and you've learned to do some of them. You want to move on, full speed ahead.

Not so fast, chum!

Learn to do a few tricks well before you go on to more difficult ones. And when I say well, I don't mean passably well. One trick that you can do superbly well is worth a dozen that you can muddle through. That's the most difficult lesson of all for most amateurs to learn.

Be selective. Make your tricks fit you and your abilities. If a trick isn't to your liking, forget it. Find one that is, and then concentrate on it.

What about equipment? Isn't it the mark of a good magician to have fine apparatus?

Not so. If you have mechanical equipment, it should be the best, but I know plenty of self-styled magicians who are blessed with much more equipment than talent. I've stayed away from mechanical equipment in this book because you don't learn the basics of magic by pressing buttons or pulling levers. This doesn't mean that I'm against equipment.

If you go ahead with magic as a hobby, there's some basic equipment you'll want. I don't know a magician, amateur or professional, who hasn't at some time or another bought at least one thumb tip, a false metal thumb that fits over your own. I bought my first one for the Vanishing Lighted Cigarette in Handkerchief. It worked fine. After I learned some cigarette manipulation, I discarded it. Later, I used it to advantage in some mental magic tricks, until I learned how to do a decent billet switch. There are a good many tricks that can be done with it, but I don't use mine any more.

You should probably have a P & L reel or one of another make. This is a little gimmick that contains a spring-propelled reel of black thread. Dozens of tricks can be done with it, but you must learn how to handle it before you do *any* tricks with it. The first thing you need to know is how to keep your audience ignorant of its existence. And that's a pretty good trick in itself.

You may want a magic wand, although I never use one for close-up magic. I use a pencil or pen in situations that would call for a wand. But a wand says "Magician," and if it gives you any personal assurance, go ahead and get one.

If you're going to do a club act, you should probably have a production box of some kind. You show it empty and then produce solid objects, or what appear to be solid objects, from it. A "squared circle" production tube is good, and there are numerous other clever production units. None of them are any good, in my opinion, for close-up or table magic.

A good card box is a handy thing to have, but only if it looks innocent and is well made.

There are a few fine tricks that are best bought rather than made. At the top of the list, I'd put the classic Cups and Balls. You can practice with the cups and balls for years without ever learning all there is to know about them. They're great magic. A set of cups and balls seems expensive, when you consider what you get, three metal cups and four or five sponge balls. But the cups are specially made to fit the exact needs of the trick.

Years of thought have gone into their present construction, and a good set is a must if you're going to do the trick. Since the demand for these specially made cups is never going to be great, the chances of their ever being sold at a mass production price are minimal.

If the cups and balls require too much manipulation to suit you, get the great Al Wheatley "Chop" cup. You'll love it, and you'll be able to do tricks with one cup and one ball that look like the most advanced manipulation, but aren't. Even with the Chop cup, adding some sleight of hand makes a great deal of difference, however. While the trick is technically self-working, don't expect to duplicate a Don Alan performance with it until you've had a lot of practice.

The Linking Rings are another magic classic. I'd learn how to perform with them more for my own amusement than for use in public performance. They're fine magic, but few amateurs handle them well. That's too bad, because they're really not difficult to manipulate—with some practice and some guidance.

If you're going to do coin tricks, I'd not only give my blessing to your purchase of some "gimmicked" coins but would highly recommend it. The coins are beautifully constructed. Since they're individually made, and gimmicked by skilled craftsmen, they must of necessity command a high price. Bargain coin tricks are seldom bargains.

You'll probably want to learn how to use a "pull." This is a length of elastic with one of several kinds of holding devices at the free end. The other end, with a safety pin attached to it, fastens under your coat. The commonest pull is one for vanishing silk handkerchiefs, with an elongated cup into which the silk is stuffed. One pull holds a lighted cigarette. One, for vanishing small flat objects, has an adhesive on it. There are clip pulls and pulls with a catgut loop on the end. Once you get a pull, you must learn how to use it properly. It should be held and handled so that no spectator ever gets even a flash of the holding device or the elastic.

For some reason, nearly every amateur magician has a Milk Pitcher. It's a clever piece of equipment that appears to pour milk from its spout. The level of milk in the pitcher goes steadily downward as you pour, and nothing comes out. It's fine if you're doing a trick in which milk is to vanish from something. It's also overused.

One of the few trick decks of cards that can logically be included in a close-up magician's equipment is the Brain Wave deck. It's a terrific trick, worth more than its small cost.

If you're doing mental magic, you'll want to experiment with a thumbnail writer. This is a tiny gadget that enables you to write secretly with your thumb. I prefer the one that clips onto the thumbnail, but you should choose whichever of three types works best for you. A tiny concave mirror that you "palm" in your hand is another useful gadget. Perhaps you'll want a file board that takes carbon impressions of anything that is written on paper with it as a backstop. A pair of flap slates can be useful. Some mentalists think a crystal ball is a good prop.

There are lots of good mechanical tricks in every category of magic, but don't be misled into thinking that because they're mechanical, anyone can do them without practice. Some mechanical tricks require great skill. Others can be performed only under stage conditions.

Don't buy a trick just to add another to your repertory. Buy only tricks for which you have a "spot," a specific purpose.

Where do you buy your equipment?

My advice may make some purveyors of equipment angry. I'd buy from the mail-order supply houses that cater to professional, semi-professional and advanced amateur magicians. They don't depend on transient or one-shot business. The bulk of their sales are made to long-time steady customers and the fact that they've stayed in business for many years is proof that they're reputable.

The established magical supply houses don't *want* to sell you anything you won't be able to use to advantage. They don't want to discourage you, and they'd like you to become a steady customer.

If you'll level with them, letting them know your lack of experience, telling them what you *think* you want and asking their opinion on whether you'll be

The Bandana Vanish

Spread out an opaque bandana handkerchief and place a second one squarely on top of it. Sew the two handkerchiefs together along three edges.

When you get ready to vanish a small article, show the bandana on both sides and gather up the four corners to form a bag. Drop the item you wish to vanish into the open side.

When you want to show that the article has disappeared, grasp the open ends by the thumb and forefinger of both hands, letting the rest of the handkerchief drop. Show it front and back, and put it into your pocket.

Most magic supply houses sell a superior version, listed as the "Devil's Handkerchief." While the handkerchief is a useful utility, don't use it publicly until you've practiced with it enough to know how to handle it convincingly. Too heavy or too bulky an article will sometimes make a noticeable bulge that makes the Devil's Handkerchief unsatisfactory for close-up magic.

able to handle it or not, they'll give you conscientious advice.

Few magic tricks can be manufactured in quantity. Most of them must be built with precision or they're worthless. The bulk of the tricks on the market are not only handcrafted but had to be made by skilled workmen with a flair for magic.

The amount of profit the magic dealer makes on the sale of a single trick must be based on his gross volume and his overhead, just as in any other business. If the nature of a trick gives it a limited market, that trick must sell for a higher price than a trick that a lot of magic fans will want.

At the outset of the pursuit of the magic hobby, I'd recommend that you spend more money on books than on tricks. The books will give you the "feel" of magic and will show you which tricks are most practical for you. They'll give you a knowledge of what magic is all about.

You'll have to learn how to read magic books because most of them are written for people who already know something about the craft. You'll come across terminology that is meaningless to you until you figure it out or get the answer from another magic hobbyist.

Some of the books are slender volumes, many of them little more than pamphlets. Some of them are huge, *Greater Magic* by John Northern Hilliard, originally published by Carl Jones of Minneapolis, being a notable example. Some are expensive limited editions, the English *Locked Books* among others. Some cover a wide range of magical effects and some specialize in one narrow field. There are books devoted exclusively to card tricks, coin tricks, cigarette tricks, rope tricks, mental magic, and even a variety of applications of one piece of equipment. The *Tarbell Magic Course* books, published by Louis Tannen of

"The World's Greatest Magician"

Hundreds of magicians bill themselves as "The Great," and any number have tried to preempt the title of "The World's Greatest Magician."

MAGIC DIGEST's *nomination for the title of World's Greatest Magician is Fred Kaps.*

Who?

That's right—Fred Kaps, the most versatile top-flight magician currently performing. A native of Holland whose appearances in the United States have been few, Kaps is a superlative close-up magician, has a wonderful stage show, does a beautiful pantomime act, is an expert illusionist and does a stand-up talk act' that's hilariously funny and gets boff laughs even when performed in Dutch before a non-Dutch speaking audience.

A few magicians perform one kind of magic as well as Kaps, but his versatility and his superiority in every area set him apart from the Greats and entitle him to the "Greatest" title.

New York, on the other hand, run the gamut.

Magic, Inc., Jay and Frances Ireland Marshall's Chicago supply house, publishes in addition to its regular catalogue a second catalogue of nothing but magic books—and the book catalogue contains more than 140 pages!

A substantial number of magic enthusiasts have standing-orders for every new magic book that comes onto the market, regardless of the phase of magic it covers.

Unfortunately, many magic book buyers don't really read the books they purchase. They skim through them. They're collectors more than readers, and they want the satisfaction of owning every new book more than they want to know what it contains.

I once saw Jay Marshall do a terrific card trick for a customer, who flipped over it. "That's the greatest card trick I've seen in months," the customer exclaimed. "I've gotta have it. How much?"

Jay smiled at him. "You already have it," he said. "It's in the Harry Lorrayne card book you bought here over a month ago."

Such experiences are common to all dealers.

Books can give you a broad knowledge of magic that it would take you many years to acquire from any other source.

In general magic books, I would strong recommend the Tarbell Course books, C. Lang Neil's *The Modern Conjuror,* and any of Walter Gibson's books for beginning magicians.

In mental magic, one book is a "must," standing out above all others. It's Annemann's *Practical Mental Effects,* with hundreds of tricks of his own plus the best of others, given the added Annemann touch.

In card magic, I'd recommend *The Royal Road to Card Magic* as a good starting point. The card section of *Greater Magic,* now published as a separate book, is excellent. Once you get those digested, Hugard and Braue's *Expert Card Technique* will show you how much you have yet to learn. And if you *really* get hooked by card magic, you'll revel in the books of Dai Vernon, Ed Marlo, LePaul, Harry Lorrayne, Cliff Green and dozens of other card experts who don't write for beginners but turn out great material. You'll also want the standard card reference, *Expert at the Card Table,* by Erdnase.

In close-up magic, you'll want to advance to Ganson's *Art of Close-up Magic,* books by J. G. Thompson, Peter Warlock and Bruce Elliott.

In coin magic, you'll want to read J. B. Bobo's definitive *Modern Coin Magic.* You'll enjoy the Harold Rice *Encyclopedia of Silk Tricks,* and the Keith Clark *Encyclopedia of Cigarette Tricks.*

When you've read all these, you'll have barely scratched the surface.

And every month, you'll find new magic in the magazines. You can even buy a magic weekly, published in England, as well as a dozen small magazines devoted to specialized branches of magic. The supply of magical literature is endless, and it keeps coming.

In addition to books of tricks, there are great books on the history of magic, along with some fascinating biographies of both famous and infamous magicians. It's my belief that no other hobby in the world has been so thoroughly documented.

A new magic book is in the making at the time this book goes to press. It isn't to be a book of tricks or a book of sleight-of-hand moves. Frances Marshall, the author, refers to it as a "Success" book, and I'd recommend it without having seen a page of it for the good reason that Frances is writing it. She not only writes entertainingly, but she writes conscientiously, with the greatest respect for accuracy. And if anybody in magic is qualified to write about success in the field, she's the gal. She probably knows more magicians, amateur and professional, than anyone else in the country, and her insatiable curiosity has led her to learn what makes every one of them tick. She took over a small magic supply house that operated from an upstairs office in Chicago's Loop and built it into one of the finest firms in the business. When her first husband, Laurie Ireland, died, it was almost inevitable that she'd marry another magician—and she did. She and Jay Marshall are two of the most knowledgeable people in the business—and certainly among the nicest. The book contains 50 chapters, and one of them, "101 Ways to Make Money from Magic," runs 93 pages. She's called upon successful people in every phase of magic to augment her advice, and a good many lifetimes of experience will be put within reach of the reader.

Some of the finest books in magic aren't for the beginner. To list any group of books as the ten or 20 best for magic novices would be almost impossible. By the time a magic fan is able to judge the quality of such books, he's no longer a beginner and so his judgement is colored.

You can't go wrong with the Tarbell books, of course, and most of the books published by "regular" publishers for the general book trade are at least understandable. Some of them, unfortunately, "talk down" to the beginner and have been kept so simple that they're almost childish. Give a magic dealer some idea of your limited experience and let him recommend a book. The chances are that you'll do much better by taking his advice than by buying at random.

One thing you'll want to do is subscribe to *Genii* and *Tops* magazines. Both are excellent, with enough variety to keep your interest in magic aroused. To get *The Linking Ring,* another excellent magazine, you must join the International Brotherhood of Magicians.

The two major sizeable magic societies are the Society of American Magicians and the IBM. Many magicians belong to both. If you're fortunate enough to live in a community that has an active, organized group of either society, you'll get much more than your money's worth from your membership.

In addition to these two groups, there are many others—for junior magicians, for ministers, for collectors, for magicians with interests in one special kind of magic, and for advanced professionals. I won't list any of them because I'd surely overlook a few, causing great indignation on the part of their members.

Just being a magic fan makes you a member of the magic fraternity, and most of the brethren won't care which clubs, if any, you belong to, as long as your interest is strong and your knowledge at least passable.

And while you'll get a tremendous kick out of entertaining audiences with your brand of magic, you may find, as many have, that you get the most fun from getting acquainted with other magicians, swapping tricks with them, competing with them, corresponding with them and, whenever possible, visiting with them.

There are so many facets to the magic hobby that some one of them will appeal to everyone.

A friend of mine, a professional magician, points out that I haven't included any chemical tricks in this book. He's quite right. I don't think chemical tricks impress an audience as magic. It's my opinion that they belong in a chemistry book, not a magic book.

He also points out that I haven't included any thimble tricks, and again, he's right. Thimbles are easy to manipulate, and I know magicians who do a beautiful job with them. I happen to think they look ridiculous while most males are doing them. There's something about seeing any male solemnly performing with thimbles, doing beautiful flourishes and sleights with them, that makes me want to guffaw. If that insults some great thimble manipulator, I'm sorry, but that's how I feel.

I haven't included any mathematical card tricks, either—and there are many of them—far too many to suit me. They bore me stiff, and I think they have that effect on most audiences.

Why haven't I included more magic with cigarettes? The production of lighted cigarettes from the bare hands has long been a standard trick that gets strong applause. With the strength that the current anti-

Quantity or Quality?

An amateur magician once tried to impress David Devant, the great English conjuror, with a lengthy recital on the merits of his performance.

Devant interrupted the man's self-praise by asking, "How many tricks can you do?"

"Sixty-three," the amateur replied, his pride evident in his manner.

Devant shrugged his shoulders and quietly commented, "I do eight tricks."

cigarette movement has gained, I doubt that a straight cigarette act is a good idea. When you can't even advertise an item on television, I don't think it's smart to do an act based on it.

Many, many fine tricks have been considered for this book and eliminated because they require special apparatus that the amateur can't make for himself. They are "dealer" tricks and should be bought from a dealer if you want to do them.

Other tricks have been considered and tossed out, despite their obvious excellence, because they are too

Cardology

The "palm" sleight is the concealment of a card in the palm of the hand. The "front and back palm" is a difficult maneuver in which the back of the hand is shown and, while the hand is being turned over to show the palm, the card is transferred to the back of the hand.

Usually, a card is palmed from the top of the deck while the cards are in the left hand, being squared by the right hand. Under cover of the palm-down right hand, fingers at the front end, thumb at the back, the left thumb moves the top card to the right so that the right front and rear edges touch the left side of the right palm. As the right hand moves away from the deck, the right little finger and the base of the palm grip the card.

Jean Hugard is generally credited with a beautiful move, the One-Hand top palm. The right hand holds the deck from above, fingers at the front end, thumb at the rear, with the palm arched. As the right hand gives the deck to a spectator for shuffling, the right little finger rests firmly on the right front corner of the deck. The tip of this finger moves slightly outward and then to the left, which pivots the top card and levers it up into the palm, where it is held in place by the heel of the hand and the little finger. If the little finger levers off two cards instead of one, there is nothing to worry about. When the hand takes the deck back, it simply deposits both cards, which accomplishes the desired purpose of leaving the original top card in its proper place.

difficult of smooth accomplishment for a beginner. I've seen some beautiful tricks shamefully exposed to the public by eager amateurs who tried to perform them and couldn't, and I think that's a pity. A writer who gives such tricks to beginners not only does a disservice to the entire magic fraternity but makes his reader look like a bumbling fool.

In the area of card tricks with a borrowed deck, for example, there are well over a thousand good, entertaining, exciting tricks. Most of them require manipulative skill. I've only included card tricks that I think are exceptionally good and which I also think you can do well. I've simplified some card tricks that have always required considerable skill, so that you *can* do them.

There are dozens of good cut and restored rope tricks. I've included only one—one I'm sure you can do smoothly and expertly.

Mental magic is my favorite kind of magic. I like it because it has such impact, because it doesn't require a lot of paraphernalia and because I find it easy to do. I haven't included some of my favorite mental magic because it requires a billet switch or the use of a nail writer. I hope you'll eventually become adept enough to do a good billet switch and use a nail writer without detection—but I think it would be wrong to encourage you to try either when you're getting started. You should learn to creep before you learn to walk.

I want you to become a rabid amateur magician, a real enthusiast. I love magic as a hobby and want to bring you into it. It's the amateurs who keep magic alive, and the more there are of them, the healthier magic will be. Every good magician started as an amateur. There's no other way to begin. Without the steady birth of amateur magicians, there would eventually be no experts.

Start by learning to do one simple trick well. Learn to do it so well that it becomes a gem in your hands. Then learn to do another, equally as well. Remember, you're a magician when you do one trick that mystifies your audience. You're only a *would-be* magician when you do 50 tricks that don't fool anybody.

214

Let's Buy a Trick

It's fun to do tricks, particularly if you can do them well, but it's also tremendous fun to *buy* new tricks.

To any case-hardened magic fan, the arrival of a new magic catalogue is a red-letter event. Reading a new catalogue is, in some ways, even more fun than reading the secret of a trick.

The dealer who publishes the catalogue describes the *effect* of each trick in detail. If the trick involves a new method, he confounds his reader by stating that the trick is *not* done by the means that would be expected.

The description of each trick gives the effect created when the trick is competently done. If the trick is extremely difficult, most dealers will at least give a hint that it isn't for the rank beginner, but no dealer ever belittles the tricks he's advertising. He talks about his stock in trade the same way an automobile dealer talks about his cars—in superlatives. You shouldn't be any more incensed about that than you are about product claims made in every newspaper and magazine you read. Any merchant tries to *sell,* and naturally presents what he's selling in the best possible light.

I've been reading magic catalogues, off and on, since I was nine years old, and they've given me thousands of hours of pleasure. Sometimes, when a trick has intrigued me so much that I've ordered it, I've been disappointed—but far more often, the purchase has given me additional hours of fun, particularly if it happened to be a trick that required a little work on my part to make it presentable.

Let me say that whether a trick is good or not is a matter of personal opinion. I once bought a trick that

I thought was an absolute dog, unworthy of even trying. I commented on what a sorry trick it was when I talked to a brother magic fan a few weeks later, and he was amazed.

"Why, that's one of the best tricks I've run across in years," he exclaimed. "I put it into my act a week after I got it, and it's knocking 'em in the aisles. If you want to talk about gyps, I'd put BLANK's Card in the Pocketbook trick at the top of the list. What a dud! What a waste of money."

I didn't dispute him, because we were both right. The Card in the Pocketbook trick he mentioned as his nomination for an all-time clinker happened to be one of my favorite tricks. I enjoyed doing it, and viewers seemed to be completely baffled by it.

It was a bad trick for him, and the one I'd mentioned was a bad trick for me—but both tricks were fine for people who could do them well.

The magic magazines have, on occasion, run a "My Ten Favorite Tricks" series, in which any magician who cared to participate could send in the list of the 10 tricks he liked best. Few of the lists ever bore any resemblance.

You may pay $10 or $15 for the classic Cups and Balls trick. With a good set of cups and balls, it's possible to perform absolute miracles. I've seen magicians completely confound an audience for 15 or 20 minutes with nothing but a set of cups and balls, with one surprise topping another.

But you must learn how to *use* your set of cups and balls after you get it. The instructions that come with the set, included in the purchase price, are usually brief and casual. The *real* miracles come from manuscripts devoted wholly to the trick in which marvelous routines have been worked out.

Now, a beginner who buys a set of cups and balls without getting either a good routine or personal instructions won't have much. He may be disgusted with his purchase, because he doesn't know what to do with it after he has it. But for him to say that the trick is no good is nonsense. It's a superlative trick when it's properly mastered.

Every dealer has "pet" tricks that he pushes. Since the tricks are his favorites, it's only natural that he encourages their sale. But a dealer's favorite tricks may not be at all to your liking.

There was an Okito Coin Box in the first Gilbert Mysto Magic Set I got when I was a youngster. I fooled around with it for a few hours and dismissed it as a nothing. Then, many years later, I met Theo Bamberg, Okito, and he showed me how simple it was to perform really startling tricks with this versatile little piece of equipment. It became one of my favorite pocket tricks and in one of the Ireland Year Books, I even described how to use it in performing mental magic.

Okito's son, Dave Bamberg, known professionally as Fu Manchu, has just marketed a new version of the Okito Coin Box that is a really great addition—but probably some of the people who buy it will decide it's no great shakes and dismiss it.

The dealer sells you the equipment and the instructions, but he can't do your performance for you. If the equipment has any merit at all, how good the trick is depends upon you.

Floyd Thayer

The giant among magic dealers during the first half of this century was Thayer Manufacturing Company, a Los Angeles organization operated by Floyd Thayer. Superb Thayer quality was particularly evident in wooden equipment, sturdily built and painstakingly constructed for perfect fit and concealment of secret gimmicks.

Thayer advertisements on new tricks were masterpieces that never failed to intrigue magic fans. The Thayer ads never misrepresented, but their wording was always such as to make the reader feel the described trick could only be accomplished by mystical powers.

The handsome, profusely illustrated Thayer catalogue was required reading for every magician, amateur and professional.

When Floyd Thayer decided it was time to retire, it became apparent that the success of his business had depended on him. There was nobody around with enough time to devote to the business.

Today, some of the Thayer craftsmanship that is still in existence sells at a premium.

When I was about 12 years old, I used to read about a new trick in the old Thayer catalogue. Money didn't come easily, and so, if I thought I wanted a trick, I first wrote Thayer a letter in which I described what I wanted to do with the trick and mentioned my limitations in certain areas of sleight of hand. "If I buy this trick," I concluded each letter, "will I be able to do what I want to do with it?"

Mr. Thayer must have been an extremely patient man. He always answered my letters, and sometimes he told me to forget the trick about which I'd made inquiry. I particularly remember one time when he wrote, "This trick is intended for platform use. I gather that you have mostly close-up audiences. I don't think I'd be able to fool anyone with this at a distance of less than 10 feet away, so you probably wouldn't, either. Forget it."

Remembering how cautiously I spent my magic money in those days, I'm amazed at the nonchalance with which today's youngsters buy expensive apparatus. At an Abbott get-together in Colon, Michigan, a couple of years ago, I saw a 12-year old saunter up to the Abbott counter and buy a Germaine mechanical production tube for roughly $50. And he went on from there, buying a couple of hundred dollars worth of equipment as casually as I'd have bought a 10¢ candy bar.

When I produced the Magic Ranch television series, we had a junior magician doing a two or three minute segment in every show—and some of those youngsters came onto the film set with two or three tricks that had cost them several hundred dollars. They talked casually about what a "good buy" a new trick was at $25.

Regrettably, the ones with the most expensive equipment were usually the poorest magicians. They depended on equipment rather than ability. One boy who came onto the show with nothing but a piece of rope and a pair of scissors made them look like rank amateurs. He had taken a standard rope trick and developed it into a classic by adding some unusual twists and some novel presentation.

When the dealers describe their tricks in glowing terms, they are optimistically describing the effect of a trick on an audience—and the effect on the audience is what you want.

I know a teen-ager who reads a description of a good trick in a catalogue and then tries to work out his own method of achieving the described effect. Sometimes, he succeeds. If he doesn't and really wants the effect that the catalogue describes, he buys it.

The longer you enjoy magic as a hobby, the more you'll enjoy reading the dealer catalogues. As you progress, many of the catalogue items will become familiar to you—but there will always be enough you can't fathom to make challenging reading.

In Nebraska and Iowa, where I lived as a child, farmers and their wives referred to the Sears, Roebuck catalogue as the "wush" book. A few of them called it the "wish" book. The arrival of the Sears catalogue was a big event, and the whole family sat around evening after evening, reading the descriptions of all the wonderful merchandise, looking at the pictures, and "wushing."

Dealer catalogues are the magic fan's "wush" books. If you can leaf through a catalogue and not "wush" for something, you're not a real magic bug.

The catalogues play such an important part in the magic enthusiast's life that we've secured permission from two of the best magic supply houses, Magic, Inc., and Lou Tannen's, to reproduce part of their new catalogues in this book. The entire catalogue of either firm may be secured by ordering directly from the company.

Neither Magic, Inc., nor Tannen's has paid any fee for inclusion of their catalogue pages. The material is presented as a service to the reader, in an effort to give a well-rounded picture of magic as a hobby. We have made an arbitrary selection of pages from both catalogues, without either firm having anything to say about our choice.

The Tannen catalogue is unique in that it comes in hard-bound covers, just like a novel or non-fiction book. The Magic, Inc., catalogue has the reputation of being one of the best-written catalogues in the field, and we found the "Magic Is Alive and Well" cover particularly attractive.

While both Tannen and Magic, Inc., have been among the leading dealers for many years and both enjoy fine reputations within the magic fraternity, they are by no means the only good, dependable dealers. Abbott's, for example, is generally considered the largest supply house in the United States, and many smaller dealers give excellent service to their customers.

Please do not consider our re-publication of these catalogue pages an endorsement by us of the material appearing on the pages. Frankly, we don't even know how some of the tricks catalogued by both firms are done. We have never even seen some of them performed. Knowing the excellent reputations of both houses, we can't imagine that anything in either catalogue is other than as represented, but, as has been mentioned, the excellence or lack of it in any trick is a matter of personal opinion.

Do not buy tricks from *any* dealer with the expectation of returning them in the event that you don't like what you get. It isn't like buying a shirt or a new pair of slacks. If the tricks don't fit you, you've still bought them.

Why does this policy prevail in magic? When you buy a trick, the most important thing you're buying is the secret of how that trick is done. Once you get the merchandise, you've acquired the secret. In some tricks, all you receive from the dealer is detailed,

profusely illustrated instructions for their accomplishment. Once you're read those instructions, there's really nothing that's returnable.

The best thing you can do to avoid disappointment is to consider what you would do with a specific trick after you bought it. Where would you use it? How would you use it? Would it fit into what you're now doing? Do you think you could make it entertaining?

A big $100 stage trick is bound to look intriguing in the catalogue. When you read the description of it, your first impulse may be to buy it. But what would you do with it after it arrived? How many stage performances a year do you do? *Could* it be performed under the conditions that usually confront you, with a close-up audience on all sides? Would it be too cumbersome for you to carry?

Unless you learn to be practical about your purchases, you can invest a lot of money in seldom-used material.

Of course, if you're wealthy, maybe you'd like to be a magic collector. Such people exist, and the dealers love 'em. It is not uncommon for a front-rank collector to have a standing order with every dealer, both in the United States and in Europe, for every new trick that comes onto the market. Some classic equipment, no longer manufactured, sells to collectors for fabulous prices.

I know one collector who doesn't even know, himself, what tricks he has. He simply buys everything that comes along. He's never even *tried* to do many of the tricks in his collection. Whether he already has it or not is far more important to him than whether it's a good trick or a poor one.

I have a fairly large assortment of magic books and manuscripts, but it's nothing compared to the libraries of the avid magic book collectors. However, I've read every word of every magic book I own, and there's a type of book collector who never reads his books. He simply wants to own them. He baffles me.

Dealers tell me that many book purchasers who aren't confirmed collectors never learn to do most of

The Thumb Tie

Properly done, the Thumb Tie is one of the all-time great tricks.

The classic method of performing it, first shown in this country by an Oriental magician, requires a special kind of cord or binding for the thumbs that is available only through magic dealers.

Dealers sell a number of excellent methods. One of the easiest to do is the "Jaspernese" Thumb Tie, invented by Jay Marshall. In this version, the thumbs are wired together with pipe cleaners, and then the performer catches a solid steel ring on his arm, with the thumbs still wired together.

Most versions of the trick as explained in magic books have been unsatisfactory for the amateur.

the tricks that are explained in the books they buy. They simply skim through the books and get a vague idea of how each trick is done, without trying to do it. I don't understand them, either.

One magician friend who skims through his books defends himself by saying, "I don't want to do all that reading. I take a quick look, and if I see a trick that interests me, I learn it. If I get one good trick out of a book, it's paid for itself."

The average beginner, visiting his first magic shop or reading his first catalogue, is startled by the prices. He sees a simple little coin trick that sells for $5 and he can't understand why it should cost that much.

The truth is that the coin trick could be made to sell for much less. But it depends on a "gimmicked" coin, and unless the coin is gimmicked by hand, with real craftsmanship, the trick wouldn't fool anybody.

It's possible to buy a Magic Milk Pitcher in a fairly wide price range. Anyone who wants to fool an audience and who examines the various pitchers will usually end up buying the most expensive one. He sees that it's well worth the money. A poorly made piece of equipment that doesn't fool an audience isn't worth anything.

I once argued with a magic dealer about the price of a superbly made Rising Card trick. "Sure, the price is high," he agreed. "That deck is beautifully made, by hand."

"The price is still too high," I argued.

He smiled at me and asked, "George, did you ever know a really wealthy magic dealer?"

Most of them do all right, but, come to think of it, I've never known a dealer who was what some of my friends refer to as "stinking rich."

If you're going to buy magic equipment, pay for the good stuff. And if the price seems high, recognize the economics of the business. Griping won't solve the problem, and neither will buying what magicians refer to as "slum equipment."

Dealers contribute a great deal to magic. A good dealer draws many new recruits into the fold because it's good business for him, but in so doing, he helps everyone connected with the art.

There are dealers in many cities outside of the major metropolises who keep magic alive in their communities almost single-handedly. They organize magic clubs, they offer personal instruction, they work with youngsters, they encourage the use of their shops as magic hang-outs, and they keep abreast of everything that's happening in the magic field. Some of them undoubtedly deserve more reward from magic than they get, but it's a labor of love.

The public magic counter or shop that depends on big-city traffic may be perfectly satisfactory and, in most cases, is. There are, however, a few "counter demonstrators" in a few such shops who are out to take every transient for all they can get—and they're good at getting it.

I once saw such an operator sell a prosperous manufacturer and his young nephew $1,600 worth of magic in less than an hour. Neither the manufacturer nor his nephew would have been able to do the tricks they bought without a year of diligent study and practice, but they left that counter firm in the belief that they were now ready to baffle the world.

These counter demonstrators are particularly adept at what they call "counter" tricks. They present these tricks to the customer as good close-up magic, and the customer is always impressed. The counter behind which these men work contributes much to the effect. The customer can't see behind it, and it is so set up that the demonstrator can switch articles, get rid of cumbersome gimmicks, drop duplicate items, etc., without being detected. The trick buyer soon discovers that he doesn't have such a counter to work behind, but needs one. The counter, it turns out, is the most important part of the equipment.

I once criticized the proprietor of such a magic counter for loading a transient with equipment beyond his capabilities, and he was so outraged that he snarled at me in answering.

"Listen," he said, "I start out trying to sell simple little tricks they can do. If they buy, that's all I sell 'em. But a lot of 'em will let you demonstrate tricks for a couple of hours without buying a dime's worth. They're seeing a free show, and they'll take all the free entertainment they can get. I make my living running this counter, and it wouldn't be much of a living if I didn't put some pressure on the 'lookers.' When you go into a store, you expect the salesman to try to sell you something. I don't know why you shouldn't expect a magic demonstrator to try to sell. Really,

Laurant

Eugene Laurant was one of the last of the Lyceum Course magicians, and a good one. He played, mostly under auspices and nearly always with a guarantee of a certain amount of money, with a full evening show of standard magic. He was one of the first of the full-evening performers to abandon large illusions, and he proved conclusively that he didn't need them. While his show was neither large nor flashy, it gave solid satisfaction.

Toward the end of his career, he grew weary of the routine. A magician who went backstage to meet him after a performance at Aurora, Ill., was greeted politely but cooly with, "Look, I'm not a magic nut. I don't live, breathe and eat magic as I've heard some performers do. I have other interests, and when a performance is over, I forget about magic until my next appearance on-stage. Doing the show gives me all the magic I want. Thanks for saying you enjoyed my performance. Good evening."

what you're criticizing me for is that I'm good at selling my stock."

He had a point. I've seen both youngsters and adults stand around a magic shop all afternoon, watching demonstrations and asking questions, without buying anything. I'll have to admit that if I'd been behind the counter, I'd have been annoyed.

I remember one moderately well-to-do magic nut who was the bane of every magic dealer's existence. He'd become interested in, let's say, a $5 trick, so he'd visit a dealer's shop to investigate it. He'd have the man behind the counter do the trick for him. Then he'd start asking questions about it. He'd get the dealer to repeat the trick two or three times.

He'd say, for example, "Vanishing the silk handkerchief is an important part of the trick. If you make it disappear by using a pull, (a length of elastic cord attached to the performer's belt under his coat, with a device on the end of it that will hold the handkerchief compressed and will snap it out of sight faster than the eye can see) I already have a good pull. If it uses a pull, how much would the trick cost without it?"

At the end of an hour and a half or two hours, he'd have at least a vague idea of the trick's modus operandi. He'd go home and try to work it out. If he couldn't do it, he'd visit the shop again, with more questions. Occasionally, he'd end up buying the trick

A Minor Detail

Karrell Fox likes the story about the magician who featured a trick with a baby chick. The chick was placed in a little wire cage that rested on a pedestal. Several yards away, an apparently identical cage was displayed, empty, on another pedestal. The magician fired a shot at the baby chick which instantly disappeared and as quickly appeared in the other cage.

It was the magician's assistant's job to buy two yellow baby chicks in every town. He concealed one of the chicks in the spring false bottom of one cage, ready to appear at the pull of a thread. He was extremely careless about his work.

At this particular performance, the magician put a cute, fluffy, little yellow chick in the cage and fired a blank shot at it. The chick disappeared according to schedule, but the chick that appeared instantly in the other cage was mottled black and yellow.

An elderly farmer, seated in the third row, shouted out, "Jumpin' Jehosephat! Lookit the powder burns!"

after several lengthy visits to the shop, but only if he was convinced there was no other way to get it.

I was in a shop one afternoon when he came in and said to the proprietor, "I'm interested in that new Adhero trick you're advertising for a dollar and a half. Now, tell me—"

The dealer reached behind him onto a shelf and pulled down the trick, wrapped for mailing. "Here, take it," he said, shoving it into the man's hands.

"But I haven't decided—"

"I'm not asking you to buy," the dealer interrupted. "It's a gift—from me to you. No charge."

The man looked bewildered.

"I can't afford to sell you a dollar and a half trick, John," the dealer said. "I'll be ahead of the game if you'll just take it right now with my compliments."

The man thanked him and left the shop with the trick in his pocket. I don't think he knew he'd been insulted.

Maybe what I'm trying to say is that there are more undesirable customers than undesirable dealers in the magic business.

If you're buying magic equipment, find a dealer you like and stick with him. He'll soon become your friend as well as your supplier, even though all your business with him is conducted by mail.

I remember walking into the late Max Holden's magic shop in New York City for the first time, after having done business with him by mail for a couple of years. He had quoted me in his catalogue on the merits of some Ted Annemann tricks. I introduced myself and was treated like a long-lost buddy. Max introduced me to a number of magicians who had been nothing but names to me up to then. He made arrangements for me to watch some of them work. He knocked himself out to be nice to me, and his attitude was so warm and friendly that it had to be sincere.

Most dealers are right guys. If you're interested in magic, they consider you a friend, whether you buy from them or not. Most of them, too, are excellent magicians and their suggestions on how to get the most from a trick are valuable.

Now, here are some sample pages from the Magic, Inc., and Tannen catalogues. If you find them as interesting as I do, you'll want to get the whole catalogue from each firm, as well as catalogues from other magic supply houses.

CLOSE-UP MAGIC

DI-MINISH

Another great pocket trick..... A fancy rhinestone die is shown and placed on back of your hand, a plastic cover is now exhibited and placed over the die. Performer patters about making the die pass through his hand by simply tapping the plastic cover, as he says these words he taps the plastic cover and the dice is seen to pass through his hand, but wait a minute, this dice diminished in size, as a matter of fact it's half size. Price $1.50

Color Clairvoyance

A clever "SECOND SIGHT" trick that can be done any time. Four plastic chips colored red, blue, green and yellow are placed in an attractive plastic box and closed. All this done while performer's back is turned. He looks at box and immediately names the position the colors are in. CLEVER...$5.00

LUCKY LIGHT

A small plastic box with THREE NUMBERED BUTTONS. You explain that one of the buttons, if pressed, will Light the Light. First spectator now presses the button . . . result NO light! Second spectator presses another button. Result—NO light. You press the button. . . . Result JACKPOT . . . IT LIGHTS! Ll You now explain how it is done . . . and repeat the trick in different ways . . . BUT they FAIL each time. . . . You always hit the JACKPOT. . . . IT'S an

ELECTRONIC 3 SHELL GAME. . . . Try to find the button that lights the LUCKY LIGHT. YES . . . LUCKY LIGHT is an all-action-laugh-packed five minute routine. . . . Entirely self-contained. Can be performed immediately. . . . Our new small size (3" x 2½" x 1") makes this a dandy pocket trick. .... $ 8.50

ELECTRONIC LUCKY LIGHT $110.00

222

DOLLAR BILL TO MATCHES   No. 10

Effect: A dollar bill (stage money) is shown; hands otherwise empty. Bill is slowly folded in half, then into thirds. The bill apparently vanishes into thin air, but everyone knows by this time that it is in the right hand.

Then that hand is opened to show a pack of matches which is slowly shown on all sides and then opened to show the matches (no bill!) on the inside. A match is pulled out and lit.

Self contained, easy to do, fools magicians. We send you a packet ready to work, and another to use with a real dollar. Invented by pro Lu Brent, patter by Sid Lorraine. $1.50

EARL MORGAN'S SNAPO   No. 16

Effect: Spectator threads a small rubber band on a cord and slips band over performer's thumb, as in the sketch; he holds ends of cord. Performer now jerks his hand, stretching the rubber band. The band snaps back against the thumb and the cord falls free, having apparently passed thru the band, which still encircles the thumb. Cord and band are now passed for inspection. Everything for $1.00

BILL TUBE   No.15

One of the finest close up effects of all time. Sketch shows the appearance of the Bill Tube, made with a cap, and a small padlock locks tube and cap securely together.

There is no way anything could enter the tube, apparently yet a borrowed dollar is marked and caused to vanish from a handkerchief, to appear in the locked tube, held by a spectator. Simple to use, but very baffling even to the smart ones. Comes in an all metal, imported version, at $5.50
All plastic version, good considering it only costs $1.50

HANDY MAGIC WALLET

Be a magician all the time and keep people talking about you. That's how you get a reputation. For instance, lay your dollar bills flat in this plastic wallet. Close it and open it at once, and the bills are magically locked under the strips of plastic. Close it and open it again and they are magically locked under different strips on the other side of the wallet. Attract attention to your magic ability every time you give out or take in a dollar bill! No. 530 $1.00

Our big (144 page) Book Catalogue free with any order for $5.00 or over. The entire world of magic books is represented in this catalogue.

No. 125—THE MAGIC STAMP ALBUM

Here is a clever trick that will appeal to everyone. A stamp album is shown with all pages blank. Then a piece of newspaper is rolled up into the shape of a cone. Performer introduces a bag full of stamps and places these loose stamps into the paper cone. A few magic passes are made over the cone, which is then opened and shown to be empty. The stamps have mysteriously vanished. The album is picked up and opened to show that the stamps are now nicely in place.

Very easy to do. . . . Complete with instructions. $3.50

BLONDINO

THE TIGHT-ROPE BALL

No. 126—

This is a lovely novelty presentation and introduces an original effect that will suit either drawing room or stage.

The performer has a little stand on which he places the ball. This is done to a romantic patter story, which tells that the little box containing these treasures is the gift from Satan!

Displaying a length of silken rope, he taps everything with his wand, and then reading from the instructions, touches the ball with the outstretched rope.

THE BALL AT ONCE SITS ON THE ROPE!

The Rope is now lifted well clear of the stand, and on command the Ball rolls gently to and fro along the Rope!

It's all good fun and good entertainment, and it's all done by magic. The routine and amusing patter has been specially contributed by Wilfred Tyler, who makes a big feature of it in his current show. It is a 'hit feature' in his lecture on Children's Tricks.

VERY EASY, DONE AT ANY TIME. DONE ANYWHERE. NO SET UP.

Price only $2.50

No. 127—JUMBO BILLS

When we say these imitations of a dollar bill are JUMBO, we mean they are large, and that's putting it mildly—they are BIG! If you use some of these you will also get the BIGGEST laugh of the century. Put a couple in your wallet and ask someone if he has change of a large bill, then watch the expression on his face when you take one of the JUMBO bills out of your pocket. Tell your audience you're in the big money now and pull out a wad of our jumbo bills. Use it to pay your assistants. Can be used in a dozen different ways. . . . . 12 for 25¢
50 for $1.00

POCKET TRICKS

THE CHANGING SPOT CARD   No.92

The best of all tricks to carry in your pocket or
wallet for action, any time, anywhere.

Learn to do it in two minutes, but make their
eyes pop out. You use a bridge size plastic card
with six dots on it, like a domino. Show them
six dots on this side, three dots on this side.
(turning it over) and FOUR dots on this side
(turning it over again), and ONE spot on this
side (turning it over again). By now, you've
got them crazy.

As you try to put it away, they want to see it, of course. Toss it to them to
figure out. They can't - you gave them the fair card of the set. One of our
most popular fun makers. Very durable. The set, with instructions $1.25

NICKEL TO PENNY TO DIME   No. 94

A mechanical coin trick that is a dandy to use under any
conditions. Work it as soon as you get it. An attractive
red plastic box is used. Right before their eyes, you
lay a nickel in the box and it changes, first to a penny,
then to a dime. They take the box and the dime and
try to make it vanish but nobody can do it but you. Very good. $1.25

MAGICAL COIN VANISHING BLOCK   No. 96

Baffling to the spectators, but a very easy trick to do.
The spectator has a penny lying on his outstretched hand.
Instantly it changes to a dime. Or, for a different effect,
the penny vanishes entirely. When the coin is covered with
the magical block, it changes or vanishes, and they can try
it for themselves. Everything you need to do the trick $1.00

TELECOLOR CARDS   No. 93

One of our top pocket tricks. So easy to do, but impossible to figure out.

Five oblongs of cardboard, each a different brilliant
color, are laid down. Performer turns his back while
spectator turns over one or more of the cards. Per -
former immediately tells him which cards he touched,
and it may be any of them, all of them, or none. There is no trick like this
in magic. They can examine it freely. Do it at once and use nothing but
the cards sent. Excellent. $1.00

No. 173—Color Changing Knife

A double close-up effect that's tops in impromptu bewilderment!

An attractive white pearl handled pocket knife is shown on both sides. The performer closes his hand over it and it emerges from his fist with a different colored handle, instead of the pearl. Again he shows it on both sides, places it in his fist and it emerges with the pearl handle!

The knife is given for examination and the spectator requested to open the blade. However, he finds it impossible to do so. The performer takes the knife and opens it immediately.

No matter how much the spectator examines the knife, he cannot discover the secrets. Very mystifying and easy to do.

DeLuxe Model...$4.00 — — - Price $2.50
De Luxe Staghorn Model, 3 knives $8.95

RATTLE BALL

Here's a real brain-teasing, nifty, pocket perplexer! The little ball rattles when shaken—but—when you give it the command it STOPS! Yes, you shake it, but now it no longer rattles, but stays completely silent. Ball is handed to a spectator but he is unable to stop the ball from rattling. No hidden rattle gimmicks. The ball definitely does rattle or stop as you wish. By using 2 or 3 Rattle Balls spectator can be asked to try to locate the one that rattles as the balls are moved around. You definitely prove only ONE rattles but spectators are unable to find it. It's a new idea and the season's HIT POCKET TRICK. . . . . Price $1.50

No. 175
THE SCOTCH PURSE

A nicely made, colored cloth purse is shown. The performer places a coin in it and defies anyone to get it out. Apparently there are no openings in the purse, and although the coin can be plainly felt inside its removal is virtually impossible by anyone but the performer for whom it is an easy matter and takes but a moment.

The sublety of the secret makes possible the most rigid examination of the purse.

Price $1.25

SIBERIAN CHAIN ESCAPE
No.85

Performer has spectators chain his wrists securely and convincingly, then padlock the chain. Presto! Performer is free! Chain is passed out, still padlocked, for examination. Good quality heavy chain, lock and keys. $2.00

THE FOLDING COIN
No.89

A large coin which can be folded into thirds, so that you can make it appear in an empty bottle, or pass it thru a ring, etc. Easy to do, entirely mechanical. $1.00

THE IMP BOTTLE
No. 30

Nobody but you can put the little bottle down on its side, altho everyone tries. For you it lays down; for the other guy, it pops right up. A great little trick you can do at once.   75¢

RED SNAPPER
No. 90

As shown in the sketch, a red cylinder with a hook, the idea being to catch the hook on a rubber band inside the cylinder You do it to perfection, but nobody else can. A fine little gag which you will be pulling on your friends right away. $.75

UTTERLY IMPOSSIBLE COIN VANISH
No.91

Made possible by Don Alan!

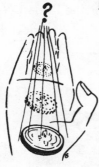

Effect: A borrowed half dollar is spun on the table, and then covered with one hand by the magician, as spectator is asked to call heads or tails. When the spectator calls the coin, the magician slowly turns his hand, palm up, showing both sides, fingers wide apart -- the coin has vanished!

Sure it's a gimmick, but a very, very clever one. Machine shop made, very durable and capable of vanishing other things similar to coins. Easy to use.

In Don's hands, this trick is a beauty. Nice clear instructions by him, so that every possibility is explained. $2.00

FUNNY RATTLE BARS
No. 9

Three red wooden bars are shown, one of which contains a rattle which sounds when bar is shaken. Try as they will, spectators can never pick out the one with the rattle. They are all examined - everyone knows that one of the bars contains a rattle, but which one? It drives everyone crazy and the performer always wins. Easy to do, right size to carry in the pocket. $1.50

CARD tricks

No. 233
DIPPY MAGNET (Harbin)

Anybody shuffles anybody's pack, removes any card which is shuffled back into the pack. Cards are spread out, backs up on table or floor. Now, the "Card Detectivo" or Dippy Magnet is introduced, this consisting of a small horseshoe magnet suspended from a cord. A magnet won't pick up cardboard, hence the name, The performer swings the magnet over the cards and one single card finally attaches itself to the magnet as the latter is lifted. THE SPECTATOR REMOVES THE CARD—it's his card!! He may tear the card to pieces—it's unprepared. The magnet will not now pick up that or any other card, and everything may be examined. No substitutions, no extra or added cards, you use only the borrowed pack. Will pick out the "Dead Name Slip," etc. Complete ready to work, and a pocket trick. . . . . Price $1.50

James Swoger's
"A CASE OF ESP"

Here is one of the simplest, yet most clever methods of gaining secret knowledge of a chosen ESP symbol yet devised. The spectator is given a set of 5 ESP symbols. He is told to secretly select one and to discard it. The performer then lays out, FACE DOWN, another set of symbols. The spectator is asked to select one of these. He has an absolute free choice! This card is placed to one side. The spectator then lays his remaining four cards face up on the table. Naturally one of the symbols is missing. The selected card from the performers group is turned over - it is the missing symbol- and is identical to the symbol that the spectator discarded. Coincidence or chance? ....Price $2.00

228

Louis Tannen, Inc.

A GREAT BUY IN CARD TRIX!

ANY FOUR FOR $2.00 - ALL TWELVE FOR $5.00

ALL TRICK CARDS - MECHANICAL - EASY TO DO

RIDICULOUS SUBTRACTION

Five cards are placed in a handkerchief, two are removed. The other three disappear.

THE MIND READER

Three cards are placed face up on table. You can predict which one will be chosen.

MYSTERIOUS HEARTS

The 8,9 and 10 of hearts placed in a glass, change places with the 6, and 7, held by a spectator.

LUCKY SEVEN

Four cards, all 4 of Diamonds, are placed on table. Two of them change to the 7 of Clubs.

RIGHT BEFORE YOUR EYES

Four cards are put in a hat. One is removed. The rest turn out to be blank cards.

INVISIBLE PASS

The two fives change places with the two blank cards.

GUESS AGAIN

Two cards are shown. One is placed behind your back. No one can name the card in your hand.

COLOR SWITCH

The three of clubs, and three of spades, change to diamonds and hearts.

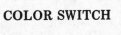

FLIP DEUCE

The deuce of any suit can be named by your audience. It is always found upside down.

NO. 220 - order by name of trick.

CONTINUED ON NEXT PAGE

NO SKILL REQUIRED

No. 282—THE HAUNTED PACK (Louis Tannen)

This is a pack that you must have and it is guaranteed to be one of the cleverest effects in modern magic. To see it is to buy—so take our word for it. Be one of the first to get it. You can work it, there's no skill required. A spooky and uncanny effect.

Performer produces a pack of cards and has two or three cards selected. Cards are replaced in the center of the pack each one separately. Cards are now riffled from one hand to the other to show the absence of any mechanical device. Pack is now placed on the palm of the performer's hand and in a spooky fashion the pack commences to move. At least a part of the deck moves sideways, then moves back leaving a card protruding. Again the pack moves forward and then back leaving another card protruding. Then for the third and final time it moves leaving a card protruding, as in the illustration. The protruding cards are now removed and found to be the selected cards. Haunting indeed! .... Price $1.50

No. 283—THE SVENGALI DECK

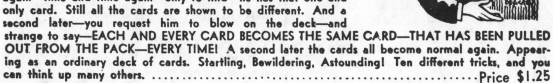

The wonder deck of the universe. Every card shown to be different—still you can compel the other fellow to take the same card every time. The most astounding trick pack of cards ever invented. You request a spectator to take a card. But—be sure to take the so and so "card" you request him. He grabs any card—only to find that he has the card you named. He tries again—time and time again—only to find—he has that one and only card. Still all the cards are shown to be different. And a second later—you request him to blow on the deck—and strange to say—EACH AND EVERY CARD BECOMES THE SAME CARD—THAT HAS BEEN PULLED OUT FROM THE PACK—EVERY TIME! A second later the cards all become normal again. Appearing as an ordinary deck of cards. Startling, Bewildering, Astounding! Ten different tricks, and you can think up many others. .... Price $1.25

No. 284—SIX CARD REPEAT

This card trick has become a classic. A purely mechanical version that's as easy as it is mystifying. Six cards are counted from hand to hand and then three counted on the table. You should have but three left in your hand. But, no, strangely enough, you still have—six! This is repeated five times and each repetition brings mounting amazement! Well made of standard cards and a complete routine is supplied. Absolutely no skill or sleights. We guarantee you'll love it. .... Price $1.00

A ULTIMATE ACES   A   No. 153
♣ A new and unusual card trick! ♦

Effect: The plot follows that of the modern Four Ace assembly, but with a new and formidable condition included - - the aces have blue backs and the rest of the cards used have red backs!

How's that for intrigue? If you like the progressive, the new, the novel, the offbeat, you'll enjoy this one. In printed booklet form by Lynn Searles, including needed cards. $1.00

MARVEL CARD   No. 215

A gimmicked playing card devised by John Morrissy. Here are a few of the tricks you can do with it:

After showing both hands empty, produce a playing card. Change a playing card to a bouquet of spring flowers. Vanish a card at your fingertips. Change a card to a silk, a dollar bill, a key, a coin. All these and more are possible with Marvel Card. Easy to do. $1.00

INSTANT CARD LOCATION   No. 133
....A WONDERFUL GAG....

After having a barrel of fun with it, the Amazing Dr. Clutterhouse (Elmer Gylleck) is marketing his pet trick: Instant Card Locator. It is always good for a laugh - sometimes they want to swat you, but no one can deny you DO locate the card!

Do it at once. Your deck of cards is put in the jacket pocket and you explain that you will have your hand on the deck, ready to find their card. All they have to do is to think of any card and name it.

The moment they name their card, you toss it on the table. They turn it over...and then comes the big laugh! Sure enough, just like you said, you located their card! We send you a supply for $1.00

GYPSY WITCH FORTUNE TELLING CARDS   No. 198

This specially printed deck permits you to tell fortunes with no effort or practice. Satisfies everyone. You are often asked to tell fortunes in connection with fairs, bazaars and other family type affairs. It brings in extra revenue and now you can do it easily. This deck, combined with a pleasant manner of speaking, and you're in business. High grade cards with full color or printing. $2.00

• SILK EFFECTS •

For "MUTILATED SUNSHADE"

HAT CHANGER

"FOR GLOVES TO DOVE"

'FOR SWITCHING A LIVE DOVE FOR A RUBBER ONE'

Now with the hat changer you can turn any Opera or Top Hat into a Changing Device, merely by pushing the special feke inside it. It rests on the bottom of the hat and divides it into two. A spring flap moves from side to side exposing one side or the other as required. Thanks to the feke being covered with black material the hat can be casually shown empty. Has many uses as illustrated. Yes you can use this idea in many ways to enhance your magic.   Price $8.00.

The Acrobatic Silks

Hanging from a 14" pole are three 18" silks . . . two yellow & a blue. Performer claims the blue is an "Acrobat" and when placed behind the performer's back it jumps to opposite end of pole, then back again, etc.

Up to this point "SO WHAT?" . . . but "WAIT" . . . The best is yet to come. THE BLUE SILK & ONE OF THE YELLOW SILKS *VISIBLY CHANGE PLACES.* THEN ALL HANDED FOR EXAMINATION.

No gimmicks . . . No threads . . . No wires . . . No springs, nylon & No moving parts.

YES . . . Can be done . . . Close up . . . Surrounded . . . Shows up on stage . . . Flashy . . . Well made . . . NOTHING ADDED OR TAKEN AWAY.

TRY to figure it out before you read the instructions . . . Can't be done. GIVE UP & READ INSTRUCTIONS AND SEE HOW NICE IT WORKS. Complete with three 18" silks. $6.00

"ALWAYS SOMETHING NEW AT LOU TANNEN'S"

WHERE MAGICIANS SHOP BY MAIL

BEER CAN MAGIC

No. FP62

One of the best known articles in the United States is the common ordinary beer can. Rich and poor, young and old, drinkers and non-drinkers......... everybody recognizes it instantly.

This makes it an almost perfect item with which to do magic - and we have some great routines with it.

The first routine with the Beer Can is done with balls -- they vanish from the can, appear in the pocket, vanish from the pocket, back in the can, until the audience is utterly bewildered. Just about then, with their own hand on the can, a big ball appears which fills the can. The ball is rolled away - again they hold the can - and there's a scream as another big ball appears under it!

This is great close up magic. The balls are very, very special, being our new felt-covered balls -- absolutely superior in every way to any other kind of ball. Each ball has two bright colors on it. Big balls match the small ones.

Other routines included are by **Mike Rogers**, and performed with rings, ribbons, etc. - a completely different type of routine, but still BEER CAN MAGIC!!!

Would you believe....everything, the Beer Can, all the felt covered balls, rings, ribbon, and all routines, only: $8.00

FELT COVERED BALLS

A new idea - great for various manipulative uses. Felt covered, one inch balls. Two bright colors to each ball, felt put on in "baseball" manner. Superior to the crocheted balls and much more masculine.

Sets for cups and balls, four felt covered balls to the set:No.111$2.75
Replacement sets for the Chop Cup, two to the set No. 112 $2.00
Large, 2½" balls to match, for loads, each ball No. 112A $l.50

No. 625   DELUXE FLAG BLENDO (Rice)

Rice's new silk flags make this effect ideal. Heretofore the heavier commercial flags were too bulky.

Performer exhibits 3—18" Spectrum solid color red, white and blue silks. The silks are tied together, and they change instantly into a huge American Flag measuring 24" x 36". Flag can be shown on both sides as the effect is self contained. Our Flag Blendo requires no skill when our simple instructions are followed. Due to the soft compacting qualities of our new exclusive line of flags, the entire effect packs into less than half the space occupied by other flag blendos on the market. We know our deluxe outfit will make a hit with you! Complete $27.50

No. 626—JUNIOR FLAG BLENDO (Rice)

As above, but 3—12" Spectrum solid color silks change into a 16" x 24" flag. This can be worked at close range and is even easier to handle than the larger size.

Junior Flag Blendo, complete with routine. . . . . **Price $20.00**

No. 627—   DECEPTIVE CHANGING BAG

The new   bag, we can safely say, is the most deceptive bag that has been placed upon the market, as we have entirely eliminated the puckering bunch at the bottom of the bag, which has always been an object of suspicion. This bag can be used for close work when necessary.

For disappearing, appearing and exchanging such articles as rings, watches, cards, or handkerchiefs it cannot be equaled. It can be shown inside and out—yet instantly it is filled with handkerchiefs, flags, etc.—or articles placed in the bag may be vanished just as magically.

Beautifully made, easy to work, as it only requires one hand on the handle. It also is of special value in connection with spirit question work.

Total length 16¾ inches—top or opening ring 4½ inches in diameter.

Price **$15.00**

No. 628—SUPER GIANT CHANGING BAG

$28.50

Okito's THRU THE NEEDLE'S EYE   No. 338

Exciting and bewildering! You can do it, because the right equipment makes it possible.
A large, polished lucite "needle" makes for
perfect working of the trick.

Effect: A spectator threads the bright red
needle with a long ribbon while a second
spectator examines a silk. Performer takes
the props and before their unbelieving eyes,
he miraculously penetrates the silk with the needle! After the penetration,
he draws the long ribbon thru as well.

Silk is shaken out to show unharmed - everything examined. Wonderful !

This Okito close up miracle, with all props, is only $2.00

TOPIT!   No. 319

One second the man has a glass in his
hand. The next second, it's GONE!

That's TOPIT! The most amazing
vanisher ever conceived. In full view,
you can vanish a deck of cards, balls,
a glass; any object you can hold in
your hand easily, you can vanish.

You can exchange objects, too.
There are hundreds of uses for Topit.
The foremost exponent of Topit, the
late George Davenport, once vanished
a live kitten! Our demonstrator, Ross
Johnson, was using Topit for every
sort of vanish, just a day or two
after he first saw it.

This absolutely wonderful gimmick
comes with the Topit Handbook,
which carefully describes the many
uses and tricks possible. Written by
Patrick Page, whose work with Topit
has to be seen to be believed.

You can use Topit anywhere. Actually, the closer the spectator, the more
he is fooled! How about that? Topit and Handbook: $3.00

No. 700—INSTANTO ROPE (Moore)

At last the perfect cut and restored rope. No fuss, no mess, no bother. A piece of rope tied in a circle is shown. It is then cut in half. Make no mistake, the rope is really cut and held at the finger tips, hand conceals nothing. Instantly the rope is visibly restored and you again have the complete circle. Once more the rope is cut. This time it's restored visibly into one long piece of rope, and your hands are absolutely empty. Best of all it may be done over and over. Nothing additional to buy. Once you have INSTANTO you don't have to buy any more rope. It works like a charm.

Price $2.50

A piece of rope is shown and performer causes it to stand straight up. Performer blows on the rope and it falls over. If you think the rope is prepared then you can examine it! Here it is, and Presto the Rope changes to a Handkerchief. The white rope wasn't rope any longer but a brightly colored silk handkerchief........................Price $3.00

No. 702—WONDEROPE

If you want real mystery here it is. . . . Performer uncoils a piece of rope. With a few mystic passes the rope is rigid . . . then it starts to rise above the performers' head . . . it's real spooky . . . performer grabs the rope and it slowly rises up-up-up—out of his hand . . . you don't have to be on a stage to do this effect . . . we do it right in the store . . . only a few feet away from spectators . . . it's an audience pleaser . . . they all talk about it. . . . . A low $3.00

Louis Tannen, Inc.

LINKING RINGS

One of the true classics of magic. Used by
many professionals. Can be worked into a
great comedy routine, as per Jay Marshall, or
done in all seriousness as a magical experiment.
The popular designs with the rings appear in many
routines, including the Tarbell. Linking Rings can be
done as a one man routine with no examination of the
rings, or can be worked with two or more assistants from the
audience. The small sets can be used in the midst of a group, as a
pocket trick.

In the general effect, a set of eight solid metal rings are shown, and
these rings proceed to link and unlink themselves, form into patterns,
separate and link seemingly in the hands of the spectators, etc. In the
end, they are only eight single and separate rings as when you began.

Like all the classics, they are just as suitable for showing to children
as to adults; they suit themselves to any kind of show, patter or theme.

We are very proud of our quality stage size set:
Chrome plated, 8" diameter, ¼" stock, (No. 698), per set of 8 rings, $25.00

Contact us for heavier weight rings, extras, etc. We are sometimes able to
furnish these special items.

Small Show size, 4½" diameter, heavy gauge, No. 355, set   3.00
Pocket size, 3" diameter, light gauge stock, No. 356, set   1.50

All sets include full routine. For additional effects and routine, get
Ireland's "LINKING RING ROUTINE", fully illustrated, $2.00

EARL MORGAN'S NESTO CANDLES   No. 226

A new mechanical idea of great simplicity, for the appearance
and vanish of one to eight flaming candles at the fingertips.
You have seen it used by Jimmy Reneaux, Fantasio and others
on TV.

Candles can be made to jump from one hand to the other and can be vanished one at a time. Hands need never come together in this routine.
Action can take place in both hands at the same time. One candle lights
another as they multiply.

The most perfect production of candles on sale today. Beautifully precision made, all metal. Easiest trick of its kind ever devised. Takes very
little practice to get down. For left or right hand. Set of four candles,
with full directions, illustrated. $12.50

No. 752—NICKLES TO DIMES

Another easy trick you will enjoy doing for your friends. Four nickels are shown, then covered with a brass cap. When it is lifted, the nickels are gone and it is seen that they have changed to four dimes. Cap and coins can be rigidly examined. No skill required. Everything is sent for you to do the trick right away.

$1.00

No. 752—A The Sliding Wine Box

Great Sucker Effect A La Die Box

A new version of the double compartment, four-door "sucker" die box, incorporating new ideas that make it even more puzzling. A small Cabinet represents a "Wine Cellar," and you remove an empty glass from it, and fill it with wine from a bottle nearby. The box is opened, all four doors, and finally the glass of wine is placed in one side of the box and doors closed.

The glass of wine vanishes, first one side then the other side of the box being shown empty—but the audience is suspicious of the tilting of the box and the accompanying "sliding noise," demanding that you open all four doors at the same time. This you do, after the usual by-play, and there is no trace of the glass of wine!

What became of the glass of wine? Back in the Wine Cellar, of course—and you open the Cabinet and remove the glass as final proof of your magical powers.

A handsome outfit, finished in Chinese red, with gold lacquer and brass hardware. This great comedy effect includes the Box, Cabinet, Bottle, Glass, directions and patter, and is quite EASY TO DO **$28.50**

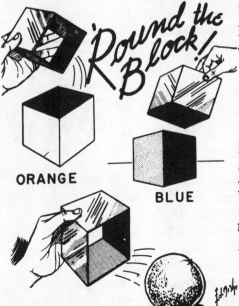

'Round the Block!

ORANGE

BLUE

You start by showing a large blue block, this is covered with a small tube and changed into an orange block. However the audience is not fooled, for all the magician has done is turned the block around. He continues to do this several times until the audience begins to shout, "You turned it round." To their astonishment, he lifts the tube and reveals a ROUND ball. Performer says: "You're correct." I did turn it ROUND!

Price $6.00

WATCHES BY MAGIC

So easy to do, almost automatic, but it looks like beautiful manipulation. Big enough for a stage, clever enough for a living room.

Effect: Performer takes a gold watch from his pocket, passes it to the left hand where it disappears, only to be found back in his pocket again. The watch is taken in the left hand and dropped in the left coat pocket.

Suddenly another watch appears in the right finger tips. This watch is also taken by the left hand, freely shown and then dropped into the left coat pocket. Again another watch appears in the right finger tips. While showing this watch back and front, both hands are seen to be absolutely empty.

This watch is also placed in the coat pocket, whereupon another watch appears in the right finger tips. This watch is placed in the mouth and swallowed. Then it is reproduced from under the vest. With the palm of his hand toward audience, performer tosses the watch into the air, it vanishes, is reproduced at right elbow. Then it is dropped into the pocket.

AS MANY WATCHES AS YOU WANT CAN BE PRODUCED AND DROPPED INTO THE POCKET. DO IT THE DAY YOU GET THE TRICK!

A special gimmicked watch makes it all possible. You get all necessary watches, gold colored, light weight, plus illustrated manuscript of a routine so clever you will fool yourself in a mirror.   No. 221   Everything for only $ 2.50

 # *BALLS A PLENTY* No. 227

$1.25

Gives the impression of really clever sleight of hand....only you know it isn't!

In this continuous ball production, performer takes a ball from his right hand and places it in his pocket. Suddenly another ball appears in his left hand. This is repeated several times, but for a surprise, now a colored ball shows up. Performer "swallows" ball, but it reappears on his left hand. Instructions include further possibilities and variations. Comes with the necessary balls. $1.25

No. 858—"3-D" PRODUCTION BOX

A very wonderful idea. Magician asks the audience if they'd like to see a rabbit. Answer is YES, of course! So he picks up a slate and proceeds to draw a rabbit with chalk on the slate. This is not what the audience expects or WANTS! So he says, "Oh, you want to see a real rabbit?" Suiting the action to the word he places the slate in a box and opens the box so the audience can see the drawing inside, NOTHING ELSE! He closes the box, and Hocus Pocus out pops a real live bunny. Beautifully made, new principle and holds an incredible load. Will produce anything as well as bunnies! And not only that, the box can be examined afterward. A real find. Box is approx. 10" x 12" x 9". $22.50

NEW FRENCH GUILLOTINE

This solid, realistic looking guillotine stands almost six feet high. The large heavy blade ZOOMS down thru the neck stock and OUT THE BOTTOM CLEAR TO THE FLOOR! As suggested and used by Jack Gwynne.

The effect with this new model is really startling. You can feature it in any show. Use a comedy presentation, a dramatic, sensational climax. Wonderful publicity possibilities.

This new model guillotine is very sturdily built and looks its part. Still, it folds down small for easy carrying.

The size when folded is 34 by 20 by 6 inches. It can be set up in two minutes!

Quality construction. A big illusion at an illusionette price. Shipped express charges collect.   Price $74.50

**VISIT OUR STORE ANYTIME,
PROFESSIONAL DEMONSTRATIONS WILL
MAKE YOUR VISIT A PLEASURABLE EXPERIENCE**

H-BOMB PREDICTION   No. 137

One of our dandiest card tricks, entirely mechanical, so you can do it at once. It is fast, fooling, foolproof and fascinating. Takes no skill.

Effect: Performer writes a prediction on a bit of paper and tucks it in the spectator's pocket. Then he gives him the pencil and cards and suggests he put them out of sight behind him, mix them up and mark one of them with the pencil.

When the spectator takes out the prediction and reads it, then looks at the card he marked, he is bowled over. THEY ARE THE SAME! Sounds impossible, but that's what happens. We send you all necessary props, plus all detailed instructions. $1.00

PHANTOM POKER   No. 136

An Ace of a pocket trick- highly recommended.

Trick is done with an interesting prop - a specially printed playing card with two poker hands appearing on each side of the card.

Effect: Performer challenges spectator to merely THINK of a card, any card in the deck. When the spectator says he has done so, the performer hands him a card with four poker hands displayed, two on each side. He is asked to examine the top hand and to state whether or not it contains a card of the same VALUE as the one he is thinking of. This repeated with each of the other three hands that appear on the card. On the last two hands, the performer also asks if the suit of the spectator's card appears in either hand. Immediately the performer names the card spectator is thinking of.. $1.00

RADAR MAGIC

A top notch pocket trick, a very clever gimmick. Reveals cards hidden in a deck not touched by performer. Spectator shuffles any deck. Cuts into several piles, selects card from any pile, returns it anywhere, and assembles deck. Performer, without touching deck, locates the card!

Everything for only $ 2.00   No.513

DR.RHINE OUTDONE

No. 563

This is Dr. Faust's fine mental trick - so easy
to do, suitable for anywhere.

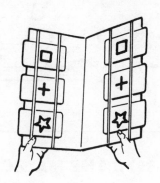

Effect: Board is shown with six cards inserted behind elastic strips. Performer removes three cards,
spectator removes three cards. Performer returns
his cards to the board, face down.   Then spectator is shown that the outside of the board has numbers, 1, 2, 3. He is asked to mix up his three cards,
and without looking, hand them to you, one at a
time, each time saying which number he wants them inserted at.

When all cards are thus returned, the board is opened - the result is as in the
sketch. The two sets of cards match exactly! The possibility of such matching is about 386 to 1 ... so it's a little miracle!

Made for bridge size E.S.P. cards. Excellent for living room and club use.
Price $4.00

No. 564

SPELLBOUND

The amazing part about these effects is that ANYONE can do them.
You apparently cause anyone to become SPELLBOUND so they
are unable to stand, raise a gun,read, etc.

Five effects: 1. A person is commanded to become Spellbound,
so they cannot rise from their chair.
2. A person given a gun is unable to raise their arm to aim it.
3. Person faces you, and you tell them they will feel a breeze
from your fingertips, so much so that they will fall backward.
They do!

4. You apparently cause a person to lose their sight, so they cannot
read.
5. A man becomes Spellbound so that he cannot walk over to a pretty
girl and kiss her.

Five more effects, all trickery of the cleverest type. You will say,
"Why didn't I think of that myself?"

These ten mysteries are direct from Bizarre India.   All for $ 2.00

No. 997A-THE MAGIC LOLLIPOPS
(Len Belcher)

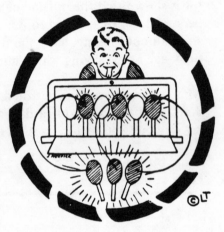

A whole store window full of luscious lollipops. That's the setting for one of the most appealing stories you could possibly do for the youngsters. Magician displays a stand with a door. Behind the door are revealed a line of six brilliantly colored lollipops. (Not real of course, but brightly painted on wood.) Relating a very cute story the magician removes three of the lollipops, the cherry, lemon and the "Dentist's delight." These are placed in a paper bag and the store door is closed. Ripping open the bag the lollipops have vanished! Where can they be? Opening the door of the candy store the lollipops are seen to be back where they were before. A very clever routine that is easy to do, utilizing a colorful piece of apparatus that works like a dream. But the low price is no dream, it's a real buy! . . . . Price $10.00

No. 998—CANDY FACTORY

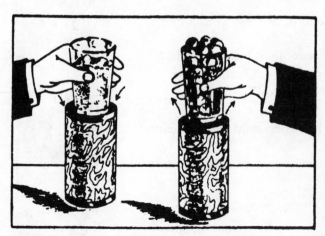

A glass overflowing with sugar is shown. You can pour out some of the sugar and let them taste it. You then show a fancy metal tube and poke your wand through it to prove it is empty. The tube is placed over the glass. You then remove the tube and it is seen that the sugar has VAN-ISHED and the glass is filled with delicious candy which may be passed out to the audience. With this device, you can also change a glass of tobacco into a glass of cigarettes and vanish a glass of milk. No skill required. Complete apparatus and instructions. . . . . Price $3.75

Louis Tannen, Inc.

WHITE FUR PRODUCTION RABBIT   No. FP13

Soft, real white fur rabbit. Spring in body permits it to fold
down nicely for production from a hat, box or screen, or for
vanish in a Flip Over Box. Can be made to look alive. $8.00

RUBBER CANARIES, small and soft for bird cage use $1.50
                                                    No. 364
RUBBER PARAKEETS, natural size, various colors. No. 362
                                                Each $2.50

DOVES & CHICKENS

RUBBER LIFELIKE DOVE. Many uses in dove magic, produc-
tions, vanishes, exchanges. FP13A $5.00
RUBBER PLUCKED CHICKEN. Very real, folds down small.
Opens up to full size chicken. Large No. FP13B $7.50
Smaller size rubber plucked chicken, No. FP13C   5.00

SPRING DUCK. Full size duck, feathered wings, cloth body,
springs in body for folding down. Great comedy production
item. Fire a shot and bird falls from a height, for a big laff. No FP13D $8.00

CARD IN BALLOON No. PL4

Beautifully made of brilliant lucite. A fast
moving and exciting trick - makes a very good
finish for a group of card tricks. A fine program trick for the stage show.

Apparatus is shown in the sketch. Balloons
are passed out to several spectators and the
one blown up first is put in the wire rings, as
shown.

A spectator selects a card, which is torn to
pieces. He retains one corner and lays the
rest of the pieces in a box offered by performer. The box is closed and the pieces
vanished. Performer calls attention to the
balloon, and as he does so, it bursts with a loud bang! There, in the wire rings,
is the selected card, all restored except for the missing piece. Spectator finds
that his corner matches exactly!

A one man trick, entirely mechanical, easy to do. $12.00

GIRL IN PLASTIC BAG
(SVEN KINDBOM)

A REPUTATION BUILDER. . . Here is an escape illusion that is nothing short of sensational, with the simplest of props. This effect consists of a large plastic bag and a roll of colored scotch tape. A girl assistant or magician himself gets into bag and bag is taped and initialed on top making an escape impossible. Performer with the help of a spectator holds up a large sheet in front of bag. In seconds girl makes her escape. Can be done any place. Everything stands examination before and after escape as a novelty assistant can change her costume while in the bag. Easy to carry—Easy to do. Complete with 2 bags. Price $5.00

"GWENDOLYN"
(SENATOR CRANDALL)

Senator Crandall and his Gwendolyn were a laugh riot at Lou Tannen's Magicians' Jubilee. We are fortunate to be able to put out the apparatus and the Senator's hilarious routine. Gwendolyn, in case you didn't know, is a duck. An educated duck that finds selected cards. She may be made of wood but her personality is winning. You'll love her and so will your audiences. Gwendolyn comes to you all dressed for action wearing a straw hat, feathers and is gaily painted. She can pick cards right from your hand or from an easily attached feed box. A beautifully dressed Gwendolyn and Senator Crandall's laugh-filled routine: $20.00

We also have the standard painted all white Duck with feed box permanently attached for
$18.50

Doves on Perch

An eye-appealing production that can be done close up and surrounded. After much experimentation, here is an ideal Dove production where, upon command, two Doves appear on the wand-like perch. Perch can then be removed to use Doves for any other effect. This is beautifully painted in blue, red, black and gold. Clear plastic front and back. An instant flash production . . . A real bargain.

$29.50

Marconick's CONTINUOUS PRODUCTION of SILKS

Beautiful!

Such pretty magic! So easy to do! So amazing to the audience!

Effect: The magician is holding a silk handkerchief. He gives it a shake, and from it falls a second silk. Laying the first one on his table or chair, he shakes the second silk, and from it produces a third. This action of taking away a silk and producing another can be repeated a number of times.

This pretty, graceful flow of silks makes a very favorable impression on an audience, and looks just great on stage or platform.

You will be surprised how simple the trick is and how quickly you will be performing it, after you get it.

We send you a set up for production of five eighteen inch silks, each a different color. You can add to this, if you wish, or can work with two of the set ups.

Price, which includes all special silks, detailed illustrated instructions: **$7.50**   No.475

Marconick's Glass of Water Production

Another clever item we arranged to handle during Mr. Marconick's visit.

Effect: Magician shows a heavy silk on both sides, slightly crumples it in his hands, reaches under the silk and produces a glass full of water. Can be done anywhere.

No. 476

A new approach. All plastic. Comes with suitable silk, special gimmicked glass, detailed illustrated instructions. All for **$3.00**

247

WESTGATE BOWL OF WATER PRODUCTION

If you have been wanting to produce a bowl with live GOLD FISH in your show that is NEW and DIFFERENT, then this is what you want. Can be done surrounded. No false moves. No bulky body or table loads. All moves are natural and mystifying. Performer picks up a tray about ½" thick, on top of which is a four sided box. A foulard is folded over the box. He takes each corner of the foulard and drops them to a hanging position. Lifting up the decorated box he shows audience that nothing is on the tray or in the box. Pulling the foulard off through the box and laying it aside, he starts producing from the box yards of streamers, a Coca Cola bottle, a string of HOT DOGS, HANDKERCHIEFS, etc. FOR THE CLIMAX . . . you lift the box and, right before their eyes stands a bowl of water with live gold fish swimming around in it! We highly recommend this effect and you will agree that this new principle will do wonders for your show. REMEMBER . . . you can do it surrounded. Comes to you ready to work—BOWL—TRAY—FOULARD and instructions. . . . . PRICE $28.50

JR. SILVER FLASH VANISHING BIRD CAGE

(SIMMS)

A masterpiece of fine workmanship, this new cage size 5" x 3½" x 3½" stands rigid when held in one hand, and can be vanished holding it this way. Constructed competely of metal and smooth on all sides. Due to its small size it flies out of sight in a FLASH. . . . Use it CLOSE-UP . . . USE it to OPEN your show with . . . Use it to CLOSE your show with. . . . No juggling or awkward get-ready. With this new size cage you can do the trick expertly with very little effort. No bird supplied. . . . . PRICE $22.50
Rubber Canary . . $1.50 Rubber Parakeet . . $2.50

Louis Tannen, Inc.

SILKS FROM NEWSPAPER

One of our most popular tricks. Easy to do and such good magic! A sheet of newspaper, or a magazine page is shown on both sides. It is unprepared. Hands are shown empty.

Performer thrusts his forefinger thru a picture on the page and pulls out a silk handkerchief. He pulls it half way thru the paper, then turns the back of the sheet, so they can see the other half hanging out the back. In this same manner, he produces three other silks. The newspaper and silks hanging from it are handed to the audience.

Good trick to emphasize details in advertising, etc. for commercial or trade show use.

No. 292, complete with four 12" silks, $3.50

SILK KING EXCLUSIVES

The finest magic silks in our profession - magnificent colors, superlative quality, tiny, flat hems.

No. 546, 12", all colors, $1.50 each
No. 547, 18", all colors, $2.50 each
No. 548, 24", all colors, $6.00 each
No. 549 Twentieth Century Silk Trick
       18" size, $15.00
No. 550 36" full color picture silks,
     like Dragon shown here, Butterfly
     Clown,Devil,Cards, $15.00 each

No.551 12x18" American Flag,$3.00 each
No.551A 24x36" Am.Flag, $9.00 each
No.552 12" Design Silks, $2.50 each
No. 553 18" Design Silks, $4.50 each
No.554 Vari-color Streamer, 6"x10 feet,
    pure silk, $7.50
No.555 Same,25 foot length, $18.75
No.556 Message Silks, Thank You, Good
    Night,etc. 27"   Each $10.00

Write us of your needs in this pure silk line. We either stock or can order any Silk King items.

CHECKER PRODUCTION TUBE

Magician shows stack of red and yellow checkers topped by one blue checker. Empty tube is shown and placed over checkers. When tube is lifted blue checker has traveled to magician's pocket. Magician now removes top red and yellow checkers from top of stack, places tube over remaining stack, drops yellow checker into top of tube, then red, lastly the blue. When tube is lifted, blue checker has traveled to position under red and yellow checkers. Once again, Magician covers stack of checkers with tube. However, this time when tube is lifted <u>All</u> the checkers have vanished and in their place now stands a dove or fish bowl with live fish. Self-contained, ready to perform. Includes tube, checker, and fish bowl. Overall size 4]/4" diameter x 12". Our low price.......$11.00

THE CASE OF THE MISSING HAT!

You will have fun with this one . . . You tell a story about ten of the greatest magicians gathered for their annual meeting. Each one checked his hat, during the meeting one hat was stolen. Still when the magicians claim their hats from the hat check room each one had a hat. You —will find this an easy and puzzling trick to show your friends. Comes complete with picture cards showing ten hats and ten magicians and then the fun begins. **$2.50**

WORLD'S GREATEST

No.F10

Get a good laugh anywhere in the show. Use in the following ways:

1. Pick your wand up off the table and wave it. It unrolls into the banner seen at the left.

2. Have your wand on the front edge of your table. At the desired moment, give it a flick, and it unrolls into the banner, and remains hanging there the rest of the show. When you do an especially good trick, take out a little feather duster and dust off the sign. (ala Ballantine.)

Very well made, strong and durable. Sharp, black lettering silk screened on yellow sign cloth. Weighted ends. Wand is black and white, forms part of the banner. Size, 12x25 inches.

Even if you are an armchair magician, this makes a fun decoration for your magic room. $3.50

MUTILATED PARASOL

No. F-11

One of the prettiest and most popular effects in magic. Very nice to perform with a girl assistant, but magician can do the trick alone if desired.

Effect: Parasol is shown and wrapped in paper, ends still showing. Silks are shown and put in a handbag. When the handbag is opened, the silks are gone, and instead there is the cover of the parasol. When the parasol is withdrawn from paper, it has no cover, but a silk hangs from every rib. Parasol is returned to the paper, cover to the handbag. Presto! The cover is shown back on the parasol and the silks are now in the handbag.

A mechanical trick which takes no skill. Only at Ireland's can you get the brilliant silk "beach type" umbrella, with every section a different bright color. This trick looks best done on a stage for big or small shows. Price, everything you require to perform, for $35.00

JUNIOR SIZE. Here we furnish a short umbrella, so it can be carried in a week-end size suitcase. Otherwise, identical with above. $32.50

"Ciget"

(Electric, Self-Lighting, Cigarette Dropper, DeLuxe)

Just received from England this improved cigarette dropper. It holds ten cigarettes and gives you the freedom and certainty of performance that make for peace of mind. It is worn under the coat and by pressure of the fingers, a single cigarette is instantly lighted and droppped into your hand, all done secretly and positively. It lights and delivers one at a time at ANY TIME during the act. Price $15.00

NEW METHOD RICE BOWLS

(AL BAKER)

Now in stock. The perfect Rice-Bowls. Now you can do this CLASSIC without worry or danger. Rice placed in bowls multiples. Both bowls are now emptied and again placed mouth to mouth. A few magic passes are made and this time, when separated the bowls are seen filled with water. 5" crockery bowls and a perfect hand-made gimmick, Al Baker's own illustrated instructions plus Sir Felix Koran's own routine and patter. . . . It's a real professional presentation. You can put it in your program immediately. . . . You will be delighted with it. WE THINK IT'S GREAT. . . Price $9.50

FOTO-THOUGHT

Two blank cards 5 x 8 inches in size are freely shown and given to a spectator to hold. He is asked to concentrate on anything he wishes. The boards, says the performer, are highly sensitized and will picture his thoughts. When shown they are still blank! Again he tries thinking of something else, with the same results. The pay-off comes when he chooses a card from the pack and when the boards are separated THERE IS A GIANT PICTURE OF THE CHOSEN CARD. There is nothing to add or take away. With additional routines. $2.00

MAGIC, INC. 5082 N. Lincoln Ave., Chicago, Ill. 60625

THE JASPERNESE THUMB-TIE

No. 358

Originated by Jay Marshall

Now YOU will be able to do this famous trick.

This method eliminates the drawbacks of the older methods. Clean, simple, sure fire. All you need are two standard pipe cleaners and you are ready to do the trick.

Effect: Take the two wire pipe cleaners and twist one around the other at the center. Then wire a spectator's thumbs together, to show him what it is like. He won't be able to move his thumbs apart in the slightest degree. Now let him wire your thumbs together in the same way, twisting the wires until the blood circulation stops, if he wants to get touch about it.

However, you can instantly put your hands around his arm, showing your thumbs still securely wired together at any time. Or he can toss a ring at your hands and you catch it in midair on your arm - - thumbs still securely wired together. All the tests of the thumb tie tricks are possible with this method.

Thumbs are really joined together; no gimmicks; use borrowed pi pe cleaners if you like. Do it anywhere, instantly. Guaranteed to permit you to fool everybody, even your smart fellow magicians.

Explained in printed booklet form, with a supply of pipe cleaners included. Highly recommended. For stage or close-up, anywhere. $1.00

METAMORPHO SPOTS

No. FP21

A big hit for any show. Lends itself well to the story angle. Entirely mechanical.

A black container with white spots is shown, and black and white silks put into it. You do some whimsical patter about the black silk turning white and the white silk turning black, and show the silks again. They don't believe it? Then you have to use magic.

You wave your hand or wand over the container, and the spots vanish from the walls. They are now all black. You pull out the silks, and they are covered with the spots ! ! !

This trick is further useful in that the routine can be reversed or changed to suit your own patter or purpose. New! Great! Easy! Mailed: $8.00

No. 1526

THE DOLL'S HOUSE ILLUSION

The performance of this illusion is always a pleasurable experience. A magical effect that the audience invariably appreciates. A perfect opening for a magician and his assistant.

The magician exhibits a small doll house raised from the floor on four legs, turns it around, showing all sides. He opens the front showing it filled and completely furnished with miniature furniture, otherwise empty. He removes all the furniture and closes the doors, again he spins it around showing all sides. Lo and behold, at his command, the roof bursts open, the front swings aside to reveal a beautifully costumed girl whose size and height are twice the capacity of the house itself. The house is a joy to behold, a little gem of a doll house. Finely decorated, inside and out. Folds flat for packing. A guaranteed hit for your show. A perfect effect for clubs.

Workshop Plans $2.50

Superior Professional Model, made to order. .... Price

No. 1527

MECHANICAL CUT OFF BUZZ SAW ILLUSION

The modern up to date method of sawing a woman in half. Eliminates all thoughts of two girls being used or a trick box. An illusion for superior shows.

The magician's assistant is placed on a flat board and secured by shackles, under a motor driven buzz saw suspended from a trestle. She remains in full view at all times. The motor is turned on, revolving with a wicked whine. Slowly the saw is swung over until it suddenly rips its way through the girl's body severing the upper and lower parts. A weird and spine tingling effect that leaves the audience gasping with horror and finally with relief when the girl is restored to life without bodily harm.

A sensational effect to say the least and an entirely safe and improved method that eliminates all hazard. A feature illusion with many of our leading magicians. Ask anyone who has seen Riciardil

Workshop Plans $5.00

Superior Professional Model, made to order. .... Price

A fine stage effect that can be used in a living room, or surrounded.

Magician exhibits a Colonial china cabinet, just big enough for one plate. Plate is seen thru the large openings in the front doors. The thin back of the cabinet is hinged, to be opened to show the interior from the rear.

Plate is taken from cabinet, handed to a spectator. With a hammer, he breaks the plate into small pieces, retaining one piece. The others are wrapped in tissue paper and put in the Fire Box. Paper is lit, there is a flash of fire and smoke, and the box is turned over to show nothing remains but a few ashes!

Now a pistol is given to the spectator, while magician holds the china cabinet. The spectator fires at the cabinet, and instantly and visibly the plate appears inside! It is taken out and shown to be completely restored with the exception of the missing piece. Spectator has been holding the piece, and he now fits it exactly into the plate!

Everything done right out in the open, no secret moves, exchanges, etc. Takes no skill. No time for setting up, may be taken to show ready to work. One of the most perfect stage effects we know. Everything included. No. 654 $27.50

EGYPTIAN WATER BOX

Box is shown empty, silks are produced from it. Water is then poured into the box and the water vanished. A glass of wine is then poured from the box. The wine is poured back into the box and it vanishes.

Many other routines are possible with this box, which is so incredibly clever that it handles dry loads and wet loads with a nonchalance that can only be magic! No covers of any kind are used to keep liquids from spilling.

A New Idea. We recommend it highly. Easy to do and mechanical. Size 7x 5½x4½". Well made, very attractive. No. 681. $12.50

No.584

EXTREMELY FINE MONOFILAMENT, FINE BLACK SILK THREAD, HEAVY BLACK SILK THREAD. Order by name. Each, generous spool,$1

TRIPLE ESCAPE MYSTERY

No. 1557

A well built and attractive cabinet that will bear the closest inspection. Interior is provided with a series of double cleats at the sides between which are three shelves. These shelves divide at the center and contain openings just large enough to secure the occupant "stock" fashion at neck, waist, wrists, and ankles. Forward parts of shelves are removed and performer takes his place in cabinet, after which each shelf is chained and padlocked by committee from audience. Door of box is then closed and locked on outside so that escape seems impossible. Yet performer makes his escape single-handed and in less time than it takes to secure him within cabinet. A feature of novelty and mystery that is far out of the ordinary.

Price upor application.

Price, Master blue print plans. . .$2.00

THE TRIANGLE ILLUSION

No. 1558

The performer opens his act with the mysterious production of a young lady assistant from a three panel screen mounted on a triangular frame and platform.

At the opening of the act the screen stands closed on the stage. The performer opens all three panels showing the cabinet to be empty. The panels are then closed, and the cabinet is wheeled around to show all sides. At command the two front panels of the cabinet fly open and out steps a smiling young lady costumed to suit the act as desired.

"The Bathing Beauty" would provide a desirable feature. This illusion is very easy to present, packs close and convient for travel. Its decorative features are highly attractive.

Price upon application.

Price, Master blue print plans. . .$2.00

No. 1559—SAWING A LADY IN TWO

The performer's lady assistant is placed in the box with her feet and ankles projecting from one end and her head from the other. Her feet and head are then secured with stocks which slide down in metal grooves at each end of the box. By means of an ordinary crosscut saw, the box is then cut exactly in half, after which the two sections of the box are separated and moved some distance apart.

With our version of this baffling effect, only one lady is used and the box is easily reconstructed for performing the effect over and over.

Master blue print plans. $2.00

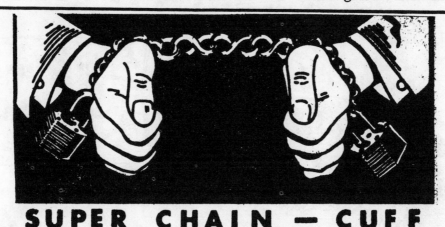

No. 1583—The Cannon and Crystal Box

Standing on one side of stage is a large cannon, and on the other side is a platform with a number of sheets of plate glass.

Performer builds up a box of glass on the platform, (as per Crystal Box No. 1334). A large hoop covered with paper and having cross feet so that it stands in an upright position, is placed in front of glass box. Next, he introduces a lady assistant and loads her into cannon—taking aim at glass chest, he fires cannon—a flash, a puff of smoke, a large hole is torn in·paper hoop, and assistant is seen reclining in Crystal Box.

Price, upon application.

Price, master blue print plans **$5.00**

No. 1584—From Bombay to London

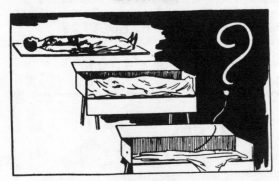

An ordinary and very thin looking table stands on the stage. Near this table, and supported on trestles rests a coffin-like box, the top of which is folded back, and the front is folded down so the audience can view the inside freely.

A girl is placed on the table and covered with a sheet, after which she is carried, still covered to the box and gently placed therein. Then box is closed. Presto! the box is opened and nothing remains except the sheet, which is removed. The girl may reappear elsewhere if desired. Very baffling.

Price upon application.

Price, master blue print
plans **$2.50**

No. 1585—The Vanishing Lady and Trunk

A trunk-like box rests on a very shallow platform in about center stage. A lady gets inside and the lid is closed over her.

A large cloth is next placed over the trunk and lines are let down from the flies which fasten to metal rings at each of the four top corners of the box, which pass through small holes in the cloth cover.

When secured the box and lady are hoisted well into the air. At a pistol shot, the cloth drops to floor, the trunk and lady having vanished completely. A mysterious and startling effect.

Price upon application

Price, master blue print
plans **$2.50**

Louis Tannen, Inc.

259

The Collector

Magicians are avid collectors. Some collect books, some collect ancient magic equipment, some collect posters and memorabilia, and others collect everything they can find.

A convention of magic book collectors was held in Chicago late in March, 1972, with Bert Pratt, English authority on magic books, as the guest of honor. Pratt's advice to his fellow collectors was, "Always aim for quality rather than quantity."

"Must" books for the collector are: *Bibliography of Books on Conjuring in English,* 1580/1850; Heyl's *A Contribution to Conjuring Bibliography,* English Language, and Hades' *Master Index to Magic in Print.* A definitive article on collecting is "How's Your Magic Library?" by James Findlay, in the Ireland Yearbook for 1969-70.

The posters of magicians are collectors' items that possess great color and romance. Many a magic fan who can't be labeled a full-blown collector has his den decorated with posters that date back to magic's golden age.

Since most magicians of the present era neither need nor have posters, the poster collector deals largely with the past—and the prices of old posters go up as the years roll by. Many poster collectors augment their collections with the glossy photographs performers past and present have used in their publicity. To be of top value, these photographs must be autographed by the pictured performer.

Some old posters are in such demand that reproductions of them have been made and are sold by specialists in the collecting field, but the true collector vastly prefers originals.

Collecting old magic equipment is probably the most difficult of all phases of collecting. Ancient equipment is hard to find, hard to document, and exists in such small quantities that a substantial collection is extremely hard to build.

The immortal Houdini was, himself, a collector. When a collector of any note dies and his collection is not willed to a specific person or group, magic collectors try to buy the entire collection to add to their own. Some privately owned collections are actually accumulations of half a dozen or more collections, each of which was built up over a lifetime.

The posters included in MAGIC DIGEST, some of them extremely rare, represent only a small fraction of the posters to be found in any good collection. They are the posters used by magicians who are representative of various phases of magic and who have made noteworthy contributions to the magic art.

"The Black Art Exposed," originally a slender magic book, is reproduced from a now-out-of-print magic book published in 1900.

EUROPE'S ECLIPSING SENSATION
HOUDINI
THE WORLD'S HANDCUFF KING & PRISON BREAKER
"NOTHING ON EARTH
CAN HOLD
HOUDINI
A PRISONER"

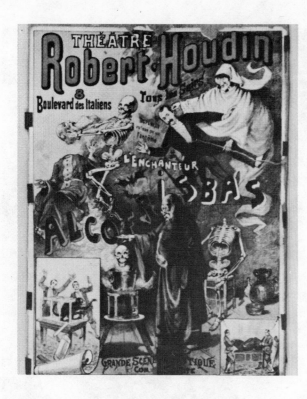

ROBERT-HOUDIN

John Eugene Robert was born in Blois, France, on Dec. 6, 1805. He learned the watchmaking trade and in 1829 married Josephe Houdin, daughter of a prominent watchmaker, at which time he added her name to his to become Robert-Houdin.

Always interested in magic, he opened a magic show in Paris in 1845 and met with immediate success. He toured England and Germany, and then opened his own theater in Paris. Even after his retirement, the theater continued to be successful. It was there that George Melies, the motion picture producer, made some of his pioneer films.

The French government sent Robert-Houdin to Algiers in 1856 to quell an Arab uprising—which he did. In recognition of his services, he was decorated by the government.

His interesting autobiography caught the imagination of a young man named Erich Weiss, who changed his own name to Houdini.

Robert-Houdin was also the author of an excellent magic text book, Secrets of Conjuring and Magic.

He died at St. Gervais, a suburb of Blois, on June 16, 1871. On the 100th anniversary of his death, the French issued a postage stamp in honor of the country's greatest magician.

HARRY HOUDINI

Controversy exists as to the birthplace of Erich Weiss, who became renowned as Harry Houdini.

While he wanted it believed that he was born in Appleton, Wisconsin, on April 6, 1874, evidence indicates that he was actually born in Budapest, Hungary, on March 25, 1874, and was brought to the United States as a baby.

His parents moved from Appleton to Milwaukee and then to New York City, where he learned to cut neckties. He read the biography of Robert-Houdin, and the book aroused a great interest in magic. He made little tricks for sale and then performed with with his brother, Theo, under the name of Houdini Brothers. When he married Beatrice "Bessie" Rahner, they traveled as The Houdinis, working in Chicago at the time of the 1893 World's Fair and touring with circuses, as well as playing dime museums and theaters.

Around 1900, he decided to specialize in escapes, and soon became a headliner in England. After his advertising was challenged by police in Germany and he had won a court case as well as an apology from the German government, his rise became meteoric.

He escaped from ropes, handcuffs, boxes, coffins, jails and straight jackets. Nothing could hold him. He continued to perform some magic in his show and became interested in exposing fraudulent spirit mediums.

An early aviation pioneer, he is credited with being the first man to fly an airplane in Australia. He became a motion picture star, but none of his film appearances made any great amount of money.

Houdini died in Grace Hospital in Detroit, Mich., on Oct. 31, 1926, of a ruptured appendix and peritonitis. He is the only magician to have his name become a verb in the dictionary.

264

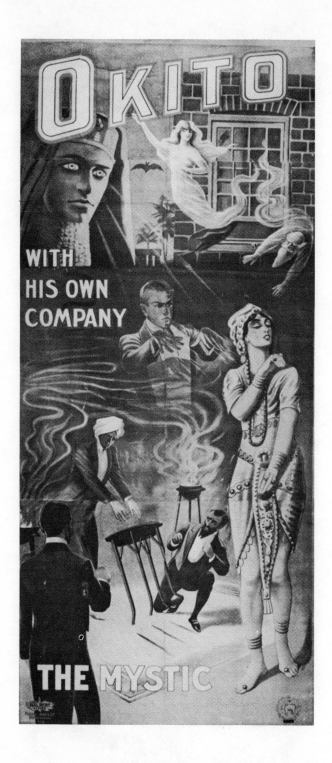

OKITO

Theo Bamberg, whose father was court magician to King William III of Holland, was the sixth consecutive generation of outstanding magicians in the Bamberg family. His son, David, known professionally as Fu Manchu, is the seventh.

As "Okito," in beautiful Oriental robes and make-up, Theo's magic took him twice around the world between World Wars I and II. At one time, his "shadowgraph" act was a feature of the Thurston show. After a South American and European tour in 1932, he decided to return to Holland and settle down. His son, David, who had established himself in South America, persuaded him to come to visit, and Okito arrived in South America just as the Nazis invaded Belgium and Holland. All of his possessions were either destroyed or confiscated.

He spent the last years of his life in Chicago, where he quickly won the friendship and admiration of everyone interested in magic.

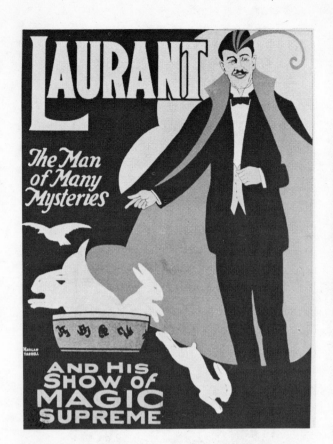

266

ALEXANDER HERRMANN

Herrmann was born in France on February 11, 1843. His father, a physician, was also a skillful conjuror and had performed for Napoleon I.

His oldest brother was a fine magician and performed in Europe under the name of Carl Herrmann. Young Alexander became an assistant to his brother and came to the United States, where he achieved tremendous fame as Herrmann the Great. He established the vogue among magicians of wearing a moustache and goatee, a magical trademark for many years after his death.

Herrmann died of a heart attack on board his private railway car while traveling from Rochester, N. Y. to Erie, Penn., on December 17, 1896.

He had operated his own magic theater in New York City and had much valuable property on Long Island at the time of his death. His chief assistant, William Robinson, later achieved fame as Chung Ling Soo, the marvelous Chinese conjurer.

Herrmann owned a yacht and had a cabin boy who later became as well known as Herrmann, himself. His cabin boy became Oscar of the Waldorf.

HARRY KELLAR

Kellar was born Heinrich Keller on July 11, 1849, in Erie, Penn. He left home at an early age because, he later said, "of a cruel stepmother," and became assistant to I. H. Hughes, a magician billed as "The Fakir of Ava." Following that, he worked at promotion of the Davenport Brothers and their Spirit Seance show, and then opened his own show.

He promoted his own theater in Philadelphia, calling it Egyptian Hall after the famed magic theater in London. His greatest trick was the "Levitation," in which a girl floated up from a couch five feet into the air, at which Kellar passed a hoop around her to show that she was floating. He had the Otis Elevator company build a version of the trick that could be moved from theater to theater.

Kellar's most successful years were from 1896, after Alexander Herrmann's death, to 1908, when he sold his show to Howard Thurston. He retired to Los Angeles with a substantial fortune and lived there with his niece until his death on March 10, 1922.

Kellar set six qualifications for being a great magician: 1. The Desire. 2. Manual dexterity. 3. Physical strength. 4. Ability to perform automatically. 5. A good memory. 6. Knowledge of a number of languages, the more the better.

MASKELYNE'S MYSTERIES

Egyptian Hall in London was the first home of the Maskelyne and Cooke magic shows, which played matinee and evening performances there from 1873 to 1905, when Egyptian Hall was destroyed. The show then moved to St. George's Hall at Langham Place, London, presented by Nevil Maskelyne in partnership with David Devant. They continued under the direction of the magical Maskelyne family until the British Broadcasting company acquired St. George's Hall for a broadcasting studio.

The original Egyptian Hall was constructed for magic, and had an air of mystery about it that enhanced the performance. The hall seated about 200 people, had an admission price that, for the times, was high, and was nearly always filled to capacity.

HARRY BLACKSTONE

Henri Bouton was born in Chicago, Ill., on Sept. 27, 1885. He teamed with his brother, Pete, to present an act, "Pete and Harry Bouton in Straight and Crooked Magic."

Henri, or Harry, married Inez Nourse, who played banjo with his show and helped to conduct the orchestra. They traveled throughout the United States, gradually enlarging the show. In Chicago, some time around 1920, he changed his name to Harry Blackstone. His show toured the country with some of the best tricks and illusions, and the Blackstone name soon gained prestige.

He had a farm with a large barn, at Colon, Mich., and each summer the troupe relaxed there while preparing for the new season. Blackstone's best years were in the 1930s and 1940s, touring with a full-evening show.

He retired to Los Angeles, where he died at the age of 80 on Nov. 16, 1965.

JOHN MULHOLLAND

John Mulholland, born in Chicago on June 8, 1898, was one of the few magicians ever listed as a magician in Who's Who in America.

Starting his adult life as a teacher at the Horace Mann School for Boys in New York, John became more and more interested in magic and finally succumbed to the lure of the platform. He presented his lecture on magic throughout the English-speaking world.

Editor of the Sphinx magazine for many years, Mulholland accumulated one of the finest magical libraries in the world. A magic scholar, he wrote extensively about magic and magicians. His library is now at the Players' Club in New York City.

Mulholland died on Feb. 25, 1970.

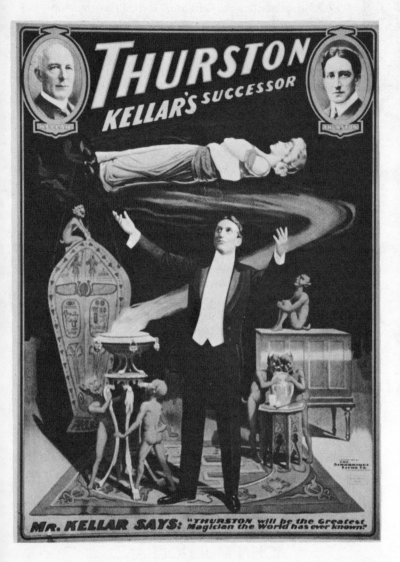

HOWARD THURSTON

Howard Thurston, born in Columbus, Ohio, on July 20, 1869, was attracted to magic by Alexander Herrmann, and started with an act of playing card manipulation. His education had been planned to prepare him for the ministry.

By 1900, he was performing with success in London, along with Houdini and T. Nelson Downs, the King of Koins. A book which is still being reprinted, *"Howard Thurston's Card Tricks, as presented in the leading theaters of the world including six consecutive months at the Palace Theater, London,* first appeared in 1901.

In the next few years, he went on a world tour, playing in India, Australia and the Orient. He returned to the United States to be chosen as Kellar's successor, with Kellar introducing him from the stage of Ford's Theater in Baltimore in May of 1908 as the heir to the Kellar throne.

The Thurston show was the most successful magic show in the United States for the next 25 years. However, with the decline of full-evening magic shows in 1935, Thurston suffered a stroke while playing in Charleston, West Virginia, late in the year. He went to Miami Beach to recuperate from his illness, but died there on April 13, 1936. He is buried in the city of his birth.

THE BLACK ART EXPOSED

ILLUSTRATED.

(NOTE: Even as recently as the early 1900s, magic or conjuring or legerdemain was, in the opinion of many uneducated people, closely akin to witchcraft. In the 15th and 16th centuries, it was not always healthy to be a magician, and many charlatans preyed upon the gullibility of the superstitious.

The Black Art Exposed, author unknown, first appeared in the United States about the turn of the century, minus any copyright. It is believed to have originated in England, where it had appeared from time to time in various editions, always without credit to the author.

It is a curious mixture of magicians' principles which are still in use today and, to us, completely unbelievable reliance upon "charms" and similar nonsense. Some of the tricks are unworkable and some could be performed only at great risk of life and limb. Fire eating, walking on a hot iron bar, blowing sparks from the mouth and similar demonstrations are not only extremely dangerous, but the methods are unreliable. The "stopping a watch" trick can cause serious damage to a good watch. Most of the chemical tricks are extremely dangerous. Some of the tricks are in extremely bad taste.

The publishers of MAGIC DIGEST present *The Black Art Exposed* as a literary magical curiosity, nothing else, with a warning that there is no guarantee by anyone, and certainly not by us, that the tricks will work. We disclaim any responsibility for any accidents that may occur should anyone be so ill-advised as to try the "secrets" of *The Black Art Exposed*.)

THE BLACK ART,

FULLY EXPOSED AND LAID BARE.

To Determine the Article Selected by the Company, the Performer Being Absent from the room at the Time of the Selection.—The effect of this trick upon the uninitiated is little short of marvelous. The performer places three articles in a row upon the table. As, for instance, a decanter, a glass, and a plate. He then requests the company to determine among themselves, in his absence, which of the articles he shall touch on his return. He leaves the room and is recalled when the decision is made. Pretending to examine the articles from various points of view, and after an apparent mental calculation, the conjuror points out the article selected by the company.

In order to accomplish this mystery, the performer simply employs a confederate, agreeing with him beforehand upon signs and signals to denote the numbers 1, 2, and 3. For example, the confederate is to pass his hand through his hair for number one; keep his hand on his watch-chain for number two; and do nothing at all for number three. Let it be understood that the articles are to be known by numbers, counting always from the *performer's* left hand. Thus, the decanter is number one, the glass number two, and the plate number three. The articles being in position, the operator leaves the room. The confederate, of course, remains with the company, who, we will suppose, select the wine-glass. The operator is recalled; and, in the course of his examination or calculation, takes an opportunity of stealing a glance at the confederate, who, with his hand on his watch-chain, signifies number two (the glass) to be the article selected. The operator may then repeat the performance, varying the effect by requesting the company to place the articles in any other position they please; the operator and his confederate always remembering to count from *the left hand*.

To Knock a Tumbler Through a Table.—This trick is very effective, and calculated to excite an immense amount of curiosity and surprise. Take an ordinary tumbler and a newspaper. Sit on a chair *behind the table*, keeping the audience in front of it. Place the tumbler on the table and cover it with the newspaper, pressing the paper closely round, so that it gradually becomes *fashioned to the form of the glass*. Then draw the paper to the edge of the table, and drop the tumbler into your lap—quickly returning the paper to the centre of the table; the stiffness of the paper will still preserve the form of the tumbler; hold *the form* with one hand, and strike a heavy blow upon it with the other; at the same moment drop the tumbler from the lap to the floor; and you will appear to have positively knocked the tumbler through the solid table. Care should be taken after the tumbler is in the lap to place the legs in such a fashion that the glass may slide gradually toward the ankles, so that the fall may not be sufficiently great to break the glass. Care should be also taken to smooth out the paper after the blow has been struck, to prevent suspicion of the fact that the *form of*

the glass was simply preserved by the stiffness of the paper. Never repeat this illusion.

To Drive one Tumbler Through Another.—This trick requires some little practice, or the result is nearly certain to be attended with considerable destruction of glass. Select two tumblers of exactly the same pattern, and considerably larger at the top than the bottom—so much so, indeed, that either tumbler will fit at least half-way into the other. Sit on a chair, so that the falling tumbler may fall softly into the lap. Hold one tumbler between the thumb and second finger of the left hand. Then play the other tumbler with the right hand several times in and out of the left-hand tumbler, and during this play contrive at the same instant to retain the right-hand tumbler between the thumb and first finger of the left hand, while the other or lower glass drops into the lap. Well done, this trick has few superiors, and it is worth any amount of practice to achieve it. It would be desirable to get a tinman to make a couple of common tumbler-shaped tin cups to practice with. It will save much expense in glass.

The Dancing Skeleton.—This is calculated to excite much astonishment, if well arranged beforehand.

Get a piece of board about the size of a large school-slate, and have it painted black. The paint should be what is known as a dead color, without gloss or brightness. Sketch out the figure of a skeleton on a piece of cardboard, and arrange it after the manner of the dancing sailors and other cardboard figures exposed for sale in the toy-shops, so that by holding the figure by the head in one hand, and pulling a string with the other, the figure will throw up its legs and arms in a very ludicrous manner.

Make the connections of the arms and legs with black string, and let the pulling string be also black. Tack the skeleton by the head to the black-board. The figure having been cut out, is of course painted black like the board.

Now to perform. Produce the board. Show only the side upon which there is nothing.

Request that the lights may be reduced about half, and take position at a little distance from the company. With a piece of chalk make one or two attempts to draw a figure; rub out your work as being unsatisfactory; turn the slate; the black figure will not be perceived; rapidly touch the edges of the cardboard figure with chalk, filling up ribs, etc., at pleasure, and taking care *that nothing moves* while the drawing is progressing. Then manipulate with the fingers before the drawing, and request it to become animated. By pulling the string below the figure it will, of course, kick up the legs and throw about the arms, to the astonishment of everybody.

A little music from the piano will greatly assist the illusion.

The Head of the Decapitated Speaking.—This illusion, performed with a table, under which two pieces of

looking-glass are placed, at an angle of forty-five degrees, concealing the body of the actor, attracted thousands to the London Polytechnic when first exhibited.

The Mystery of the Floating Head.—One of the most startling of conjurors' tricks, and one which has piqued public curiosity to the utmost, is that sensationally announced as the "Human Head Floating in the Air." Multitudes have witnessed and wondered at this performance, which seems to have defied any explanation by the uninitiated.

That the head is a gutta-percha or plaster affair, is a pet theory with those who have not seen it, but after witnessing the exhibition this idea is reluctantly discarded. In reality it *is* a human head, and the seeming absence of

THE "FLOATING HEAD" AS EXHIBITED.

any body attached thereto will be accounted for as soon as we disclose the mystery and secret of the performance.

The sides and back of the stage are hung with curtains. Near the back of the stage two mirrors are placed at right angles, the *point*, equi-distant from each side of the stage, facing the audience. The mirrors being at angles with the sides, of course reflect the curtains at the sides, and these curtains being the same in style and material, their reflection has the same appearance as the curtain at the back of the stage. The audience seeing this reflection naturally imagine they are having an unobstructed view of the back of the stage.

HOW THE "FLOATING HEAD" TRICK IS DONE.

Behind this wall of glass the conjuror's confederate takes his position, of course only that part of his person which is above the glass being visible. So the "floating

head" is really a man peeping over a glass fence. The cushion which is commonly used to apparently support the head, is suspended outside of the glass, by fine wire.

The exhibitor is always careful to keep out of the angles of the glass, otherwise he would be reflected, and the existence of the glasses disclosed to the audience. When standing at the stage "wings," or when *directly* in front of the central "point" of the mirrors, he is secure from reflection.

Our illustrations will, we think, make this explanation perfectly clear. The first shows the head as it appears to the audience; the second shows the position, behind the glass, of the individual personating the "head." In the latter picture the spectator is supposed to be looking *through* the mirrors. Thick plate glass will answer equally as well as the mirrors in exhibiting this trick.

To Place a Lighted Candle under Water, without Extinguishing it; or a Handkerchief without Wetting it.—Procure a good-sized cork, or bung; upon this place a small lighted taper; then set it afloat in a pail of water. Now, with a steady hand, invert a large drinking-glass over the light, and push it carefully down into the water. The glass being full of air prevents the water entering it. You may thus see the candle burn *under* water, and bring it up again to the surface, still alight. This experiment, simple as it is, serves to elucidate that useful contrivance called the diving-bell, being performed on the same principle.

The largest drinking-glass holds but half a pint, so that your diving-light soon goes out for want of air. As an average, a burning candle consumes as much air as a man, and he requires nearly a gallon of air every minute, so that, according to the size of the glass over the flame, you can calculate how many seconds it will remain alight; of course a large flame requires more air than a small one. For this and several other experiments, a quart bell-glass is very useful, but, being expensive, it is not found in every parlor laboratory; one is, however, easily made from a green glass pickle-bottle; get a glazier to cut off the bottom, and you have a bell-glass that Chilton would not reject. In the same manner you may put a handkerchief rolled tight together, and it will not wet.

To Place Water in a Drinking-glass Upside Down. Procure a plate, a tumbler, and a small piece of tissue or silver paper. Set the plate on a table, and pour water in it up to the first rim. Now very slightly crumple up the paper, and place it in the glass; then set it on the fire. When it is burnt out, or rather just as the last flame disappears, turn the glass quickly upside down into the water. Astonishing! the water rushes with great violence into the glass! Now you are satisfied that water can be placed in a drinking-glass upside down. Hold the glass firm, and the plate also. You can now reverse the position of the plate and glass, and thus convince the most sceptical of the truth of your pneumatic experiment. Instead of burning paper, a little brandy or spirits of wine can be ignited in the glass; the result of its combustion being invisible, the experiment is cleaner.

The Faded Rose Restored.—Take a rose that is quite faded, and throw some sulphur on a chafing-dish of hot coals; then hold the rose over the fumes of the sulphur, and it will become quite white; in this state dip it into water, put it into a box, or drawer for three or four hours, and when taken out it will be quite red again.

The Protean Liquid.—A red liquor, which, when poured into different glasses, will become yellow, blue, black, and violet, may be thus made : Infuse a few shavings of logwood in common water, and when the liquor is red, pour it into a bottle ; then take three drinking-glasses, rinse one of them with strong vinegar, throw into the second a small quantity of pounded alum, which will not be observed if the glass has been newly washed, and leave the third without any preparation. If the red liquor in the bottle be poured into the first glass, it will assume a straw-color ; if into the second, it will pass gradually from bluish-gray to black, provided it be stirred with a bit of iron, which has been privately immersed in good vinegar ; in the third glass the red liquor will assume a violet tint.

The Burned Handkerchief Restored.—Get a flat-topped stand, such as is shown at A, and make a neat pasteboard or tin cover, as is seen at C, and be sure to ornament it with various showy devices. The cover must slip

very easily over the stand. Cut a flat circular plate, B, the least bit wider than the top of A, and just large enough to slip easily into C. Here is all your appartus.

Before you show this trick, place in your pocket a piece of white rag that looks like a handkerchief. Borrow a clean white cambric handkerchief from among the audience, and just before you receive it, conceal in your hand the white rag. Have the apparatus ready on a side-table, with the movable plate laid on the stand.

Lay the handkerchief on the plate, place the cover over the handkerchief, and press it down with a smart slap.

Now take off the cover, squeezing it well so as to take up the plate as you do so ; put your hand into it as if about to pull out the handkerchief, and substitute in its stead the white rag. Lay the rag on the stand, apply a match to it, and let it burn to ashes. Replace the cover on the stand, and press it down. Then loosen the grasp of the hand and the plate will fall on the stand, completely concealing the ashes. Lift the cover gently, when the handkerchief will fall upon the plate, and may be restored unhurt to the owner.

Eatable Candle Ends.—Take a large apple, and cut out a few pieces in the shape of candle ends, round at the bottom and flat at the top, in fact, as much like a piece of candle as possible. Now cut some slips from a sweet almond, as near as you can to resemble a wick, and stick them into the imitation candle. Light them for an instant, to make the tops black, blow them out, and they are ready for the trick. One or two should be artfully placed in a snuffer-tray, or candle-stick ; you then inform your friends that during your " travels in the Russian Empire," you learned, like the Russians, to be fond of candles ; at the same time lighting your artificial candles (the almonds will readily take fire, and flame for a few seconds), pop them into your mouth, and swallow them, one after the other.

To make a Watch Stop or Go at the Word of Command.—Borrow a watch from any person in company and request of the whole to stand around you. Hold the watch up to the ear of the first in the circle and command it to go. Then demand his testimony to the fact.

Remove it to the ear of the next, and enjoin it to stop. Make the same request of that party, and so on through the entire party.

Explanation: You must take care in borrowing the watch that it be a good one and goes well ; have concealed in your hand a piece of loadstone, which, as soon as you apply it to the watch, will occasion suspension of its movements, which a subsequent shaking and withdrawing of the magnet will restore.

To Walk Upon a Hot Iron Bar.—Take half an ounce of camphor, dissolve it in two ounces of aqua vitæ, add to it one of quicksilver, one ounce of liquid storax, which is the droppings of myrrh, and prevents the camphor from firing: take also two ounces of hematis, which is red stone, to be had at the druggist's,—and when you buy it let them beat it to a powder in their great mortar, for being very hard it cannot well be reduced in a small one; add this to the ingredients already specified, and when you purpose to walk upon the bar, anoint your feet well with it, and you may then put the feat into execution without the slightest danger.

How to cut your Arm off, without hurt or Danger.—You must provide yourself with two knives, a true

one and a false one, and when you go to show this feat, put the true knife in your pocket, and then take out the false and clap it on your wrist undiscovered, and with a sponge make the knife bloody, and it will appear you have nearly severed your arm.

A knife for the nose may be made on the same principle.

To pour cold Water into a Kettle and Make it come out hot without the aid of Fire.—You give a pint of cold water to one of the company, and taking off the lid of the kettle, you request him to put it into it; you then put the lid on the kettle. Take the pint, and the exact quantity of water comes out of the kettle boiling hot.

This trick is performed in the following way: The kettle has two bottoms; boiling water has been previously conveyed into it through the nose. There is no passage for the cold water, which is put in when the lid is off; consequently, the hot water can alone be poured out.

This trick may be varied, and for the better; as the heat of the water may betray it, should the bottom of the kettle be full. You may therefore propose to change water into wine or punch.

A coffee-pot may be made on a similar plan; but a kettle is preferable, it being more likely from its size and breadth, to baffle the examination of the curious.

This trick may also be improved by an additional expense, so that whatever liquor is on either bottom may be poured out occasionally. For this purpose there must be a double passage to the nose of the kettle, and secret springs to stop either passage.

How to cut a man's Head off, and put it into a Platter, a yard from his Body.—To show this feat, you must cause a board, a cloth, and a platter to be purposely made, and in each of them must be made holes fit for a boy's neck. The board must be made of two planks, the longer and broader the better; there must be left within half a yard of the end of each plank half a hole, that both the planks being put together, there may remain two holes like the holes in a pair of stocks. There must be made likewise, a hole in the cloth; a platter, having a hole of the same size in the middle thereof, must be set directly over it; then the boy sitting or kneeling under the board; let the head only remain upon the board in the frame. To make the sight more dreadful put a little brimstone into a chafing-dish of coals, and set it before the head of the boy, who must gasp two or three times that the smoke may enter his nostrils and mouth, and the head presently will appear stark dead, and if a little blood be sprinkled on his face, the sight will appear more dreadful. (This is commonly practiced with boys instructed for that purpose). At the other end of the table where the other hole is made, another boy of the same size as the first boy must be placed, his body on the table and his head through the hole in the table, at the opposite end to where the head is, which is exhibited.

To discover any Card in a Pack by its Weight or Smell.—Desire any person in the company to draw a card from the pack, and when he has looked at it, to return it with its face downwards; then, pretending to weigh it nicely, take notice of any particular mark on the back of the card; which having done, put it among the rest of the cards, and desire the person to shuffle as he pleases; then giving you the pack, you pretend to weigh each card as before, and proceed in this manner until you have discovered the card he had.

To turn water into Wine.—Take four beer glasses, rub one of them on the inside with a piece of alum; put in the second a drop of vinegar; the third empty, and then take a mouthful of clean water and a clean rag, with ground brazil tied in it, which must lie betwixt your hind teeth and your cheek. Then take of the water out of the glass into your mouth, and return it into the glass that has the drop of vinegar in it, which will cause it to have the perfect color of sack; then turn it into your mouth again, and chew your rag of brazil, and squirt the liquor into the glass, and it will have the perfect color and smell of claret; returning the brazil into its former place, take the liquor into your mouth again, and presently squirt it into the glass you rubbed with alum, and it will have the perfect color of mulberry wine.

Magic Breath.—Put some lime-water in a tumbler; breathe upon it through a small glass tube. The fluid, which before was perfectly limpid, will gradually become white as milk. If allowed to remain at rest for a short time, real chalk will be deposited at the bottom of the tumbler.

To make a Party appear Ghastly.—This can only be done in a room. Take half a pint of spirits, and having warmed it, put a handful of salt with it into a basin, then set it on fire, and it will have the effect of making every person within its influence look hideous.

How to eat Fire.—Anoint your tongue with liquid storax, and you may put a pair of red hot tongs into your mouth, without hurting yourself, and lick them till they are cold. You may also take coals out of the fire and eat them as you would bread; dip them into brimstone powder, and the fire will seem more strange, but the sulphur puts out the coal, and if you shut your mouth close

you put out the sulphur, and so chew the coals and swallow them, which you may do without offending the body. If you put a piece of lighted charcoal into your mouth, you may suffer a pair of bellows to be blown into your mouth continually and receive no hurt; but your mouth must be quickly cleaned, otherwise it will cause a salivation. This is a very dangerous trick to be done, and those who practice it ought to use all means they can to prevent danger. I never saw one of these fire-eaters that had a good complexion.

To Dip the Hand in Water without Wetting It.—Powder the surface of a bowl of water with lycopodium; you may put your hand into it and take out a piece of money that has been previously put at the bottom of the bowl, without wetting your skin; the lycopodium so attaching itself to the latter as to keep it entirely from coming in direct contact with the water. After performing the experiment, a slight shake of the hand will rid it of the powder.

How to Shoot a Bird and bring it to Life Again.—Load your gun with the usual charge of powder, but instead of shot put half a charge of quicksilver; prime and shoot. If your piece bears ever so little near the bird, it will find itself stunned and benumbed to such a degree as to fall to the ground in a fit. As it will regain its senses in a few minutes, you may make use of the time by saying, that you are going to bring it to life again, this will astonish greatly the company; the ladies will no doubt interest themselves in favor of the bird, and intercede for its liberty. Sympathizing with their feelings for the little prisoner may be the means of some of them sympathizing with yours.

Hideous Metamorphosis.—Take a few nut-galls, bruise them to a very fine powder, which strew nicely upon a towel; then put a little brown copperas into a basin of water; this will soon dissolve and leave the water perfectly transparent. After any person has washed in this water, and wiped with the towel on which the galls have been strewed, his hands and face will immediately become black; but in a few days by washing with soap they will again become clean. This trick is too mischievous for performance.

How to Fill a Glass with Beer and Water at the same time, without mixing the two Liquids.—It is done thus :—Half fill a tumbler with beer, then take a piece of brown paper or thin card, and placing it on the top of the beer, let it get perfectly still and quiet, taking care to keep the table on which the tumbler is placed quite steady. When all vibration has ceased, take some clear spring water, and having a small phial filled with it, proceed to pour it on the card as gently as possible, and in as small a quantity as you can, recollecting at the same time, that the whole success of the experiment rests on the steadiness with which you pour the water on the card. You will by degrees perceive the water sliding from the card to the surface of the beer, and covering it like a sheet of paper, making them appear separated, one lying on the top of the other; but the steadiness of hand must be preserved until the glass is sufficiently full. You may reverse the order of the liquids if you please—i. e. by putting in water first and then the beer, the same process will give the same result.

How to Kill a Fowl and bring it to Life Again.—Take a hen or chicken, and thrust a sharp-pointed knife through the midst of the head, the joint toward the bill, that it may seem impossible for her to escape death, then use some words, and pulling out the knife, lay oats before her, and she will eat, being not at all hurt with the wound, because the brain lays so far behind the head, that it is not touched.

To light a Candle by a Glass of Water.—Privately stick a small piece of phosphorus on the edge of a glass of water, apply a candle newly blown out to it, and it will immediately be re-illuminated. The warmth of the snuff causes the phosphorus to ignite.

To Light a Candle by Smoke.—When a candle is burnt so low as to leave a tolerably large wick, blow it out, and a dense smoke, which is a compound of hydrogen and carbon, will immediately arise; then if another candle or lighted taper be applied to the utmost verge of this smoke, a very strange phenomenon will take place : the flame of the lighted candle will be conveyed to that just blown out, as if it were borne on a cloud.

To Freeze Water by Shaking It.—During very cold weather put some water into a close vessel and deposit it in a place where it will experience no commotion ; in this manner it will often acquire a degree of cold superior to that of ice, but without freezing. If the vessel however, be agitated ever so little, or if you give it a slight blow, the water will immediately freeze with singular rapidity.

Iron changed into Silver.—Dissolve mercury in marine acid, and immerse in it a bit of iron, or if this solution be rubbed over iron, it will assume a silver color.

Two cold Liquids when mixed become boiling hot.—Put into a thin phial two parts (by measure) of sulphuric acid, and add to it one part of water; on agitating or stirring them together the mixture instantly becomes hot, and acquires a temperature above that of boiling water.

The incombustible Handkerchief.—Mix the whites of eggs and alum together; then smear a handkerchief with it all over. Wash it in salt and water, and when dry fire will not consume it.

Two cold Liquids produce Fire.—Put a small quantity of aquafortis into a saucer, add a few drops of oil of turpentine, oil of caraways, or any other essential oil, and a flame will instantly be produced.

To give a person a Supernatural Appearance.—Put one part of phosphorus into six of olive oil, and digest them in a sand heat. Rub this on the face (taking care to shut the eyes) and the appearance in the dark will be supernaturally frightful; all the parts which have been rubbed appearing to be covered by a luminous lambent flame of a bluish color, whilst the eyes and mouth appear like black spots. No danger whatever attends this experiment.

The floating Needle.—Pour some water in a plate; then drop a needle lightly and carefully upon the surface, and it will float.

Luminous Writing.—Take a piece of phosphorus, and, during candle-light, write upon a whitewashed wall any sentence or word, or draw any figure according to fancy. Withdraw the candle from the room, and direct the attention of the spectators to the writing. Whatever part the phosphorus has touched will be rendered quite luminous, emitting a whitish smoke or vapor. Care must

be taken while using the phosphorus, to dip it frequently in a basin of cold water, or the repeative friction will throw it into a state of the most active combustion, to the manifest detriment of the operator.

Beautiful Transformations.—Pour half an ounce of diluted nitro-muriate of gold into an ale glass, and immerse in it a piece of very smooth charcoal. Expose the glass to the rays of the sun, in a warm place, and the charcoal will very soon be covered over with a beautiful golden coat. Take it out with forceps, dry it, and enclose it in a glass for show.

To Break a Stone with a Blow of the Fist.—Find two stones, from three to six inches long, and about half as thick; lay one flat upon the ground, on which place one end of the other, raising the reverse end to an angle of forty-five degrees, and just over the centre of the other stone, with which it must form a T, being upheld in that position by a piece of thin twig or stick an inch or an inch and a half long; if the elevated stone be now smartly struck about the centre with the little finger side of the hand, the stick will give way, and the stone will be broken to pieces. The stones must be placed, however, so as not to slip, otherwise the feat will not be effected.

Magical Teaspoons.—Put into a crucible four ounces of bismuth, and when in a state of fusion, add two ounces and a half of lead, and one ounce and a half of tin; these metals will combine, and form an alloy fusible in boiling water. Mould the alloy into bars, and take them to a silversmith to be made into teaspoons. Give one to a stranger to stir his tea with, and he will be greatly surprised to find it melt in his teacup.

To bring two separate Coins into one Hand.—Take two cents, which must be carefully placed in each hand, as thus: The right hand with the coin on the fourth and little finger, as in the illustration. Then place, at a short distance from each other, both hands open on the table, the left palm being level with the fingers of the right. By now suddenly turning the hands over, the cent from the right hand will fly, without being perceived, into the palm of the left, and make the transit appear most unaccountable to the bewildered eyes of the spectators. By placing the audience in front, and not at the side of the exhibitor, this illusion, if neatly performed, can never be detected.

To cut and tear into pieces a Handkerchief, and to make it whole again.—This feat, strange as it appears, is very simple; the performer must have a confederate, who has two handkerchiefs of the same quality, and with the same mark, one of which he throws upon the stage to perform the feat with. The performer takes care to put this handkerchief uppermost in making up a bundle, though he affect to mix them together promiscuously. The person whom he desires to draw one of the handkerchiefs, naturally takes that which comes first to hand. He desires to shake them again, to embellish the operation, but in so doing, takes care to bring the right handkerchief uppermost, and carefully fixes upon some simpleton to draw; and if he find that he is not likely to take the first that comes to hand, he prevents him from drawing by fixing upon another, under pretence of his having a more sagacious look. When the handkerchief is torn and carefully folded up, it is put under a glass upon a table placed near a partition. On that part of the table on which it is deposited is a little trap, which opens and lets it fall into a drawer. The confederate, concealed behind the curtain, passes his hand within the table, opens the trap, and substitutes the second handkerchief instead of the first; then shuts the trap, which fits so exactly the hole it closes, as to deceive the eyes of the most incredulous. If the performer be not possessed of such a table (which is absolutely necessary for other feats as well as this), he must have the second handkerchief in his pocket, and by sleight of hand change it for the pieces, which must be instantaneously concealed.

How to fire a loaded Pistol at the Hand, without hurting it.—This extraordinary illusion is performed with real powder, real bullets, and a real pistol; the instrument which effects the deception being a ramrod. This ramrod is made of polished iron, and on one end of it is very nicely fitted a tube, like a telescope tube. When the tube is off the rod, there will, of course, appear a little projection. The other end of the rod must be made to resemble this exactly. The ramrod with the tube on being in your hand, you pass the pistol round to the audience to be examined, and request one of them to put in a little powder. Then take the pistol yourself, and put in a very small piece of wadding, and ram it down; and in doing so you will leave the tube of the ramrod inside the barrel of the pistol. To allay any suspicion which might arise in the minds of your audience, you hand the ramrod to them for their inspection. The ramrod being returned to you, you hand the pistol to some person in the audience, requesting him to insert a bullet, and to mark it in such a way that he would know it again. You then take the pistol back, and put in a little more wadding. In ramming it down, the rod slips into the tube, which now forms, as it were, an inner lining to the barrel, and into which the bullet has fallen; the tube fitting tight on to the rod is now withdrawn along with it from the pistol, and the bullet is easily got into the hand by pulling off the tube from the rod, while seeking a plate to "catch the bullets;" and the marksman receiving order to fire, you let the bullet fall from your closed hand into the plate just as the pistol goes off.

A Vessel that will let Water out at the Bottom, as soon as the Mouth is uncorked.—Provide a tin vessel, two or three inches in diameter, and five or six inches in height, having a mouth about three inches in width, and in the bottom several small holes, just large enough to admit a small needle. Plunge it in water with its mouth open and full; while it remains in the water stop it very closely. You can play a trick with a person, by desiring him to uncork it; if he places it on his knee for that purpose, the moment it is uncorked the water will run through the bottom, and make him completely wet.

The Conjuror's Banquet.—In which he eats a quantity of paper shavings; afterwards draws from his mouth a barber's pole, six feet in length; then draws out several yards of different colored ribbons; then pushes out with his tongue an ounce of pins; and lastly, after well shredding the paper shavings, to show that there is nothing in them, a flight of birds come out from among them, their number *ad libitum.* This is really a first-rate experiment, and if got up carefully will excite much wonder. I shall commence by giving instructions how to make the necessary properties, commencing with the Barber's Pole. Cut some white paper into lengths, three inches wide; paste them

together, making a long length of ten or twelve feet or more; paint one side red, a strip about half an inch wide, the whole length of the paper, and at its edge; glue on at one end of the paper a piece of round wood, with a small knot on the end; then roll the paper up like a roll of ribbons. I will explain presently what to do with it. The next is to prepare your pins and ribbons. In a piece of soft paper, in as small a compass as you can, roll up a number of pins, and upon this packet roll your ribbons of different colors, making altogether a round ball, which you can conveniently slip into your mouth; then make a long paper bag similar to those of the confectioner; paint it in stripes—pink and white; in this place your birds—canaries, sparrows, or any small birds you can most conveniently procure. The process will not hurt them, if you make a few pin-holes in the bag to admit the air; you then procure some pink and white tissue paper, cut it into strips until you have a good heap, as many shreded out as would fill a small bread-basket, in which you place them; at the right hand, hid in the shavings, you have the barber's pole, the ribbons and pins, and the bag containing the birds, and by your side a glass of water, of which you pretend to drink occasionally. Thus prepared, you present yourself to the audience. Sip a little water, make two or three preliminary ahems! run your fingers through your hair, arrange your necktie, curl your moustache—if you have none it will be the greater burlesque to pretend to curl it—and then, with mock dignity, address your audience: "Ladies and gentlemen, doubtless you have witnessed the performance of many conjurors, some of them clever; but of all the professors you ever saw, none of them ever possessed such extraordinary abilities as the illustrious individual who now does you the honor of exerting himself for your amusement. My natural modesty and diffidence prevent my saying more. I shall at once commence my peformance by introducing the Conjuror's Banquet. I have some macaronies (alluding to the paper shavings.) Excuse the vulgarity, but I must refresh (takes a quantity of shavings in each hand and commences munching them as a horse would eat hay, taking a little water occasionally, smacking his lips, and seeming to enjoy the feast very much.) After having proceeded in this manner for a short time, take up among the shavings the barber's pole; place it, shavings and all, against your mouth, take hold of the little knob at the end of the pole which is rolled up like a roll of ribbons, pull it gradually out, and it presents the appearance of a barber's pole several feet in length; put this carefully on one side; commences feeding again upon your paper shavings in the same burlesque style, then take up your roll of ribbons and pins, and during the process of seeming to eat, you slip the roll of ribbons and pins into your mouth.

You must chew the shavings you place in your mouth into a hard lump, and as you supply one mouthful from the heap you hold in your hand, push the hard lump of chewed shavings out of your mouth with your tongue. Well, you have the roll of ribbons in your mouth; place your shavings again in the basket, put your finger and thumb in your mouth, taking the end of the ribbon, and pull it out of your mouth with both hands, one after the other; letting the ribbon slip through your hands as you pull it out, it will apperr a larger quantity. After one length or color is pulled out of your mouth, sip a little water, smack your lips, and again secure the end of the ribbon, pulling it out in the same manner as the previous one; continue this until you have pulled all the ribbon out of your mouth; you will now feel with your tongue the paper containing the pins; take a little more water.

saturate the paper and the pins will remain in your mouth; these you push out with your tongue, keeping the lips almost closed; spit the pins out on a small tray, one that will sound when the pins fall on it; it is more effective. The trick is now finished, excepting the flight of birds. Your bag containing them is at your right hand; you slip this in among the shavings, and commence shredding them, and during this process tear the bag open, and the birds, of course, escape. The paper being painted in pink and white stripes, cannot be observed.

A Dollar Bill Concealed in a Candle.—Ask some one to lend you a dollar bill, and to notice the number, etc. You then walk up to the screen behind which your confederate is concealed, pass the bill to him, and take a wax or composite candle. Then, turning to the audience, you ask one of them—a boy would be preferred—to step up on the platform. At your request he must cut the candle into four equal parts. You then take three of them, and say you will perform the trick by means of them, passing the fourth piece to the other end of the table, where your confederate has already rolled up the note in a very small compass, and thrust it into a hollow bit of candle, previously made ready. You take up this piece, and, concealing it in your hand, you walk up to the boy, and appear accidentally to knock one of the bits of candle out of his hand, and while you are stooping to pick it up off the floor, you change it for the bit which contains the bill. You then place it on the table, and say to the audience, "Which piece shall I take—right or left?" If they select the one which contains the note, ask the boy to cut it carefully through the middle, and to mind that he does not cut the bill. When he has made a slight incision, tell him to break it, when the note will be found in the middle. If the audience select the piece which does not contain the note, you throw it aside, and say the note will be found in the remaining piece. When this is done with tact, the audience will naturally believe that they have really had the privilege of choosing.

To Melt Iron in a Moment, and make it Run into Drops.—Bring a bar of iron to a white heat, and then apply it to a roll of sulphur. The iron will immediately melt, and run into drops.

The experiment should be performed over a basin of water, in which the drops that fall down will be quenched. These drops will be found reduced into a sort of cast-iron.

To change a Bowl of Ink into clear Water, with Gold Fish in it.—The same glass bowl as in previous trick. If your bowl has not a foot to it, it must be placed on something that will hold it high above your table. Some small fish, a white plate or saucer, a piece of black silk just fitting the inside of your bowl, a spoon of peculiar construction, so that in a hollow handle it will retain about a teaspoonful of ink, which will not run out as long as a hole near the top of the handle is kept covered or stopped. A large tumbler and two or three minnows will do for a simpler exhibition, but will, of course, not be so pleasing to the eye.

Place the black silk so as to cover the part of the bowl that is shaded; when damp it will adhere to the glass. Pour in clear water to fill the space covered by the black silk, and place the fish in the water.

Commence the trick in public thus: Holding the spoon-handle slanting up and uncovering the hole in the handle, the ink which you have placed in the handle will run into the bowl of the spoon, and the spoon being held carefully to the surface of the water, concealing the black silk, will give the spectators the impression that you fill the spoon from the glass bowl.

Pour the spoonful of ink on a white saucer, and show it round to convince the spectators it is ink. They will see it is undeniably ink, and they will conclude, if the spoon were properly lifted out of the bowl, that the glass bowl contains nothing but ink.

Borrowing a silk handkerchief, place it for a few seconds over the bowl, and feigning to be inviting fish to come to the bowl, exclaim "Change!" Then, placing your hand on the edge of the bowl near yourself, draw off the handkerchief, and with it take care to catch hold also of the black silk. The bowl when uncovered will exhibit the fish swimming about in clear water. While the spectators are surprised at the fish, return the handkerchief, having first dropped out of it the black silk on your side of the table. Decline giving any explanation, as people will not thank you for dispelling the illusion.

How to Swallow a number of Needles and Yards of Thread.—The trick is performed as follows: In the first place thread a dozen needles, put them in as small a compass as possible, and place them between the gum and the upper lip; you can speak without difficulty, and without any effort they will remain there. Let the needles be short ones, and take the end of the thread a little distance from the needles, and deposit it between the gum and the lips in such a position that you can always feel it and pull it out when required. Thus being prepared, of course unknown to your audience, you take your second dose of needles, placing them one by one on your tongue, seeming to swallow them, but depositing them on the other side of your mouth, between your gums and lip, which will effectually conceal them, notwithstanding an examination of the mouth; afterward roll up between your fingers about a yard of thread; place this in your mouth, and with your tongue conceal it between your gum and lip. Take a drink of water, make a few wry faces, then place your finger and thumb in your mouth, securing the end of the thread upon which the needles are threaded, draw it out and exhibit it, taking an early opportunity of retiring to get rid of the needles concealed in your mouth. This is a most effective trick, and easily performed. Be careful not to swallow the needles.

To Make a Bird seem as dead.—Take any bird out out of a cage, and lay it on a table; then wave a small feather over its eyes, and it will appear as dead; but directly you take the feather away it will revive again. Let it lay hold of the stem part of the feather with its feet, and it will twist and turn about just like a parrot; you may also roll it about on the table any way you like.

To Make the appearance of a Flash of Lightning when any one enters a room with a lighted Candle.—Dissolve camphor in spirits of wine, and deposit the vessel containing the solution in a very close room, where the spirit of wine must be made to evaporate by strong and speedy boiling. If any one then enters the room with a lighted candle, the air will inflame, while the combustion will be so sudden, and of so short a duration, as to occasion no danger.

To Break a Stick placed on two Glasses without breaking the Glasses.—The stick intended to be broken, must neither be thick, nor rest with any great hold on the two glasses. Both its extremities must taper to a point, and should be of as uniform a size as possible, in order that the centre of gravity may be more easily known. The stick must be placed resting on the edges of the glasses, which ought to be perfectly level, that the stick may remain horizontal, and not inclined to one side more than another. Care must also be taken that the points only shall rest lightly on the edge of each glass. If a speedy and smart blow, but proportioned, as far as can be judged, to the size of the stick and the distance of the glasses, be then given to it in the middle, it will break in two, without either of the glasses being injured.

To Set a Combustible body on fire by the contact of Water.—Fill a saucer with water, and let fall into it a piece of potassium the size of a pepper corn, which is about two grains. The potassium will instantly burst into flame, with a slight explosion, and burn vividly on the surface of the water, darting at the same time from one side of the vessel to the other, with great violence, in the form of a beautiful red-hot fire-ball.

To Eat a Dish of Paper Shavings, and Draw them out of your Mouth like an Atlantic Cable.—*Preparation.* Procure three or four yards of the thinnest tissue paper of various colors. Cut these up in strips of half an inch or three-quarters of an inch breadth, and join them. They will form a continuous strip of many feet in length. Roll this up carefully in a flat coil, as ribbons are rolled up. Let it make a coil about as large as the top of an egg-cup or an old-fashioned hunting-watch. Leave out of the innermost coil about an inch or more of that end of the paper, so that you can easily commence unwinding it from the centre of the coil.

Procure a large dish or basketful of paper-shavings, which can be obtained at little cost from any bookbinder's or stationer's. Shaken out it will appear to be a large

quantity. As you wish it to appear that you have eaten a good portion of them, you can squeeze the remainder close together, and then there will appear to be few left, and that your appetite has reason to be satisfied.

Commence the trick by proclaiming you have a voracious appetite, so that you can make a meal off paper-shavings. Bend down over the plate, and take up handful after handful, pretend to munch them in your mouth, and make a face as if swallowing them, and as you take up another handful, put out those previously in your mouth, and put them aside. Having gone on with this as long as the spectators seem amused by it; at last, with your left hand, slip the prepared ball of tissue paper into your mouth, managing to place towards your teeth the end you wish to catch hold of with your right hand, for pulling the strip out from your mouth. You will take care also not to open your teeth too widely, lest the whole coil or ball should come out all at once.

Having got hold of the end, draw it slowly and gently forward. It will unroll to a length of twenty yards or more in a continuous strip, much to the amusement of the spectators.

When it has come to the end, you may remark : "I suppose we have come to a fault, as there is a 'solution of continuity here, just as the strongest cables break off,' so we must wait to pick up the end again, and go on next year, when the Great Eastern again goes out with its next Atlantic Cable."

To Produce from a Silk Handkerchief Bonbons, Candies Nuts, etc.—*Preparation.* Have packages of various candies, wrapped up in bags of the thinnest tissue paper, and place them on your table rather sheltered from observation. Have also a plate or two on your table.

Memorandum.—It will be always desirable to have the table removed two or three yards at least from the spectators, and of a height that they cannot see the surface of it while sitting down in front of it.

Commence the trick by borrowing a silk handkerchief, or any large handkerchief. After turning it about, throw it out on the table, so as to fall over one of these packages.

Having carefully observed where the bag lies, place your left hand so as to take up the bag while catching hold of the middle of the handkerchief.

Taking the handkerchief up by nearly the centre, the edges of it will fall around and conceal the bag; make some pretended wavings of your wand or right hand over the handkerchief, and say, "Now, handkerchief, you must supply my friends with some bon-bons." Squeeze with your right hand the lower part of the bag which is under the handkerchief; the bag will burst, and you can shake out into a plate its contents.

Asking some one to distribute them among your young friends, you can throw the handkerchief (as it were carelessly) over another bag, from which you can in the same way produce a liberal supply of some other sweetmeats, or macaroon biscuits, etc., all of which will be duly appreciated by the juveniles, and they will applaud as long as you choose to continue this sweet trick.

To keep a Stone in Perpetual Motion.—Put very small fillings of iron into aquafortis, and let them remain there until the water takes off the iron requisite, which it will do in seven or eight hours. Then take the water and put it into a phial an inch wide, with a large mouth, and put in a stone of *lapis calaminaris*, and stop it up close ; the stone will then keep in perpetual motion.

To make a Card jump out of the Pack and run on the Table.—Take a pack of Cards, and let any one draw any card they please; put it into the pack, so that you may know where to find it at pleasure. Put a small piece of wax under your thumb-nail, to which fasten a hair, and the other end of the hair to the card; spread the cards open on the table, and desire the one chosen to jump out, which you may readily cause to do by means of the hair.

How to tell a Person any Card he Thinks of, and to Convey it into a Nut.—Take a nut, in which burn a hole with a hot bodkin, and with a needle break and extract the kernel. Write the name of a card on a piece of thin paper, and roll it up hard, and put it in the nut ; stop the hole with wax, which rub over with a little dust, that the puncture may not be perceived, then let some one draw a card ; you must take care it be that which is written on the paper ; desire him to break the nut, in which he will find the name of the card he has drawn.

To Make a Cone or Pyramid move upon a table without springs or any other Artificial Means.—Roll up a piece of paper, or any other light substance, and put a lady beetle, or some such small insect, privately under it ; then, as the animal will naturally endeavor to free itself from its captivity, it will move the cone towards the edge of the table, and as soon as it comes there, will immediately return, for fear of falling ; and by thus moving to and fro, will occasion much sport to those who are unacquainted with the cause.

How to make an Egg, apparently of itself, leave the centre of the Room and traverse to a Saucer of Water placed in the Corner.—This is not adapted for public exhibition, as the process is tedious, but it is no less wonderful. Blow the yolk out of an egg, and insert a leech within the shell, securing the end by sticking on a piece of tissue paper. Place the egg and leech in the centre of the room, and the saucer in the other end. In the course of time—it may be hours—the natural instinct of the leech leads it to the water, and by its efforts causes the egg to move to the edge of the saucer containing the water.

To Eat cotton Wool and blow Fire and Sparks out of your Mouth.—Obtain some cotton wool, such as the jewelers use to pack their jewelry; get a piece of old linen and burn it, damping it out when it is burnt black and reduced to tinder. If you don't understand, ask your grandparents how they used to make tinder to obtain a light previous to the invention of lucifer matches. Put a light to the tinder; it will not flame, but smolder. Fold it lightly in a piece of the wool, just as large as you can conceal in the palm of your hand, commencing eating in the same manner as in the Barber's Pole Trick, with the shavings. When you have satisfied yourself, and while feeding yourself with the wool, slip in the small piece of wool containing the lighted tinder; blow, and smoke and sparks will issue from your mouth, to the astonishment, of the lookers-on. A very good system to practice many of these tricks, is to stand before a looking-glass.

To Make a peg that will exactly fit three different kinds of Holes.—Let one of the holes be circular, another square, and the third oval; then it is evident that any cylindrical body of a proper size may be made to pass through the first hole perpendicularly, and if its length be just equal to its diameter, it may be passed horizontally through the second or square hole; also, if the breadth of the oval be made equal to the diameter of the base of the cylinder, and its longest diameter of any length whatever, the cylinder being put in obliquely, will fill it as exactly as any of the former.

Magic Money.—This conjuring trick is performed thus: —Procure two quarters and a half-eagle; conceal one of the quarters in the *right* hand; lay the other quarter and the half-eagle on a table, in full view of the audience; now ask for two handkerchiefs; then take the gold-piece up, and pretend to roll it in one of the handkerchiefs; but, in lieu thereof, roll up the quarter, which you had concealed, and retain the gold coin; give the handkerchief to one of the company to hold; now take the quarter off the table, and pretend to roll that up in the second handkerchief; but put up the half-eagle instead; give this handkerchief to another person, and beg him to "hold it tight," while you utter, "Presto! Fly!" On opening the handkerchiefs the money will appear to have changed places.

The Magic Knife.—This trick, which is at once simple and clever, has not before been published. Ask one of your audience for a pocket-knife, and stick two small square pieces of white paper on each side. Give the knife to your audience to be examined, and then take it in the left hand, palm upward. Let the handle of the knife be clasped between the thumb and forefinger, and the blade extended outward from you; the handle will then lie on the palm of the hand toward you. With practice you will be able, by a rapid turn of the wrist, to pass the knife from one side of the hand to the other, always keeping the same side of the blade upward, while to your audience, it will appear that you reverse it at every turn. Wipe the bits of paper off one side, turn the knife as directed, pass your fingers again across the blade, leading your audience to believe that you have wiped them off the second side also. Both sides of the blade will now appear to be perfectly clean, but in fact you have only removed the two pieces off one side. By rapidly turning the knife you may cause the bits of paper to appear and disappear at command. All that is required is a little dexterity in the turn of the wrist, which may be acquired by practice.

To bring Colored Ribbons from your Mouth.—Heap a quantity of finely carded wool upon a plate, which place before you. At the bottom of this lint, and concealed from the company, you should have several narrow strips of colored ribbons, wound tightly into one roll, so as to occupy but little space. Now begin to appear to eat the lint by putting a handful in your mouth. The first handful can easily be removed and returned to the plate, unobserved, while the second is being "crammed in." In doing this care should be taken not to use all the lint, but to leave sufficient to conceal the roll. At the last handful, take up the roll and push it into your mouth, without any lint; then appear to have had enough, and look in a very distressed state as if you were full to suffocation; then put your hands up to your mouth, get hold of the end of the ribbon, and draw hand over hand, yards of ribbon, as if from your stomach. The slower this is done, the better the effect. When one ribbon is off the roll, your tongue will assist you in pushing another end ready for the hand. You will find you need not wet or damage the ribbons in the least. This is a trick which is frequently performed by one of the cleverest conjurors of the day.

A Cheap way of being Generous.—You take a little common white or beeswax, and stick it on your thumb. Then, speaking to a bystander, you show him a dime, and tell him you will put the same into his hand; press it down on the palm of his hand with your waxed thumb, talking to him the while, and looking him in the face. Suddenly take away your thumb, and the coin will adhere to it; then close his hand, and he will be under the impression that he holds the dime, as the sensation caused by the pressing still remains. You may tell him he is at liberty to keep the dime; but on opening his hand to look at it, he will find, to his astonishment, that it is gone.

To Make Fire Bottles.—The phosphoric fire bottles may be prepared in the following manner: Take a small phial of very thin glass, heat it gradually in a ladleful of sand, and introduce into it a few grains of phosphorus; let the phial be then left undisturbed for a few minutes, and proceed in this manner till the phial is full. Another method of preparing this phosphoric bottle, consists in heating two parts of phosphorus and one of lime, placed in layers, in a loosely stopped phial for about half an hour; or put a little phosphorus into a small phial, heat the phial in a ladleful of sand, and when the phosphorus is melted, turn it round, so that the phosphorus may adhere to the sides of the phial, and then cork it closely. To use this bottle, take a common brimstone match, introduce its point into the bottle, so as to cause a minute quantity of its contents to adhere to it. If the match be rubbed on a common bottle cork, it will instantly take fire. Care should be taken not to use the same match a second time immediately, or while it is hot, as it would infallibly set fire to the phosphorus in the bottle.

Artificial Thunder.—Mix two drachms of the filings of iron with one ounce of concentrated spirit of vitriol, in a strong bottle that holds about a quarter of a pint; stop it close, and in a few moments shake the bottle; then, taking out the cork, put a lighted candle near its mouth, which should be a little inclined, and you will soon observe an inflammation arise from the bottle attended with a loud explosion.

To guard against the danger of the bottle bursting, the best way would be to bury it in the ground, and apply the light to the mouth by means of a taper fastened to the end of a long stick.

The Magic Flask.—Take a glass bottle; put in it some volatile alkali, in which has been disolved copper filings, which will produce a blue color. Give this flask to some one to cork up, while indulging in some pleasantry, and then call the attention of the company to the liquid, when, to their astonishment, they find the color has disappeared as soon as it was corked. You can cause it to reappear by simply taking out the stopper, and this change will appear equally astonishing.

How to let Twenty Gentlemen draw twenty Cards, and to Make One Card Every Man's Card.—Take a pack of cards: let any gentleman draw a card and put it in the pack again, but be sure you know where to find it again; then shuffle the cards, and let another gentleman draw a card, but be sure you let him draw the same card as the other gentleman drew, and continue till ten or twelve, or as many as you may think fit, have drawn; then let another gentleman draw another card, and put them into the pack, and shuffle them till you have brought the cards together; then showing the last card to the company, the other will show the trick; by this means many other feats may be done.

How to Double Your Pocket Money.—The only preparation is to have four cents concealed in your left palm.

Commence the trick by calling forward one of the spectators, and let him bring up his hat with him.

Then borrow five cents, or have them ready to produce from your own pocket should there be any delay.

Request your friend, while he places them one by one on a small plate or saucer, to count them audibly, so that the company may hear their number correctly. Inquire, "How many are there?" He will answer, "Five." Take up the saucer and pour them into your left hand, (where the other four are already concealed.) Then say, "Stay, I will place these in your hat, and you must raise it above your head, for all to see that nothing is added subsequently to them." You will have placed these nine cents in his hat unsuspected by him.

Borrow five cents more. Appear to throw those five into your left hand, but really retaining them in your right hand, which is to fall by your side as if empty.

Afterwards get rid of four of the five cents into your pocket, retaining only one in your right palm.

Hold up your closed left hand, and say, while blowing on it: "Pass, cents, from my left hand into the hat. Now, sir, be kind enough to see if they have come into your possession. Please to count them aloud while placing them in the saucer." He will be surprised, as well as the spectators, to find that the cents in his hat have become nine.

You may then put on a rather offended look, and say: "Ah, sir! ah! I did not think you would do so! You have taken one out, I fear." Approaching your right hand to his sleeve, shake the sleeve, and let the one cent, which you have in your own hand, drop audibly into the saucer. It will raise a laugh against the holder of the hat. You can say: "Excuse me, I only made it appear that you had

taken one. However, you see that the original money is now doubled."

To Catch Money from the Air.—The following trick, which tells wonderfully well when skillfully performed, is a great favorite with one of our best known conjurors. So far as we are aware, it has not before been published. Have in readiness any number of silver coins—say thirty-four; place all of them in the left hand, with the exception of four, which you must palm into the right hand. Then, obtaining a hat from the audience, you quietly put the left hand with the silver inside; and whilst playfully asking if it is a new hat, or with some such remark for the purpose of diverting attention, loose the silver, and at the same time take hold of the brim with the left hand, and hold it still, so as not to shake the silver. Now address the audience, and inform them that you are going to "catch money from the air." Ask some person to name any number of coins up to ten—say eight. In the same way you go on asking various persons, and adding the numbers aloud till the total number named is nearly thirty; then looking round as though some one had spoken another number, and knowing that you have only thirty-four coins, you must appear to have heard the number called, which, with what has already been given, will make thirty-four; say the last number you added made twenty-eight, then, as though you had heard some one say six, and twenty-eight and six make thirty-four, "thank you, I think we have sufficient." Then with the four coins palmed in your right hand, make a catch at the air, when they will chink. Look at them, and pretend to throw them into the hat, but instead of doing so palm them again; but in order to satisfy your audience that you really threw them into the hat, you must, when in the act of palming, hit the brim of the hat with the wrist of the right hand, which will make the coins in the hat chink as if they had just fallen from the right hand. Having repeated this process several times, say: "I suppose we have sufficient," empty them out on a plate, and let one of the audience count them. It will be found that there are only thirty, but the number which you were to catch was thirty-four. You will therefore say: "Well, we are four short; I must catch just four—neither more nor less." Then, still having four coins palmed in your right hand, you catch again, and open your hands, saying to the audience: "Here they are."

Curious Watch Trick.—To tell at what hour a Person will rise in the Morning.—By means of this trick, if a person will tell you the hour at which he means to dine, you can tell him the hour at which he means to get up next morning. First ask a person to think of the hour he intends rising on the following morning. When he has done so, bid him place his finger on the hour, on the dial of your watch, at which he intends dining. Then—having requested him to remember the hour which he first thought—you mentally add twelve to the hour upon which he has placed his finger, and request him to retrograde, counting the hours you mention, whatever that may be, but that he is to commence counting with the hour he thought of from the hour he points at. For example: suppose he thought of rising at eight, and places his finger on twelve as the hour at which he means to dine, you desire him to count backwards twenty-four hours; beginning at twelve he counts eight, that being the hour he thought of rising, eleven he calls nine, ten he calls ten—(mentally, but not aloud)—and so on until he has counted twenty-four, at which point he will stop, which will be eight, and he will probably be surprised to find it is the hour he thought of rising at.

To Produce a Cannon Ball from a Hat.—This is a very old trick, though it still finds favor with most of the conjurors of the present day. You borrow a hat, and on taking it into your hands you ask a number of questions about it, or say it would be a pity for you to spoil so nice a hat, or make some such remark. This, however, is only a ruse for the purpose of diverting attention. Then, passing round to the back of your table—(where, by the way, you have arranged on pegs a large wooden "cannon ball," or a cabbage, or a bundle of dolls, trinkets, etc., loosely tied together, so that they may be easily disengaged)—you wipe, in passing, one or other of these articles off the pegs—where they must be very slightly suspended—into the hat so rapidly as not to be observed.

Returning to the gentleman from whom you received the hat, you say to him : "You are aware, sir, that your hat was not empty when you gave it to me," at the same time emptying the contents in front of the audience. Supposing you have, in the first instance, introduced the dolls and trinkets, you may repeat the trick by wiping the "cannon ball," or one of the other articles, into the hat, and again advancing towards the gentleman from whom you received it, say : "Here is your hat ; thank you sir." Then, just as you are about to give it to him, say : "Bless me, what have we here ?" and turning the hat upside down, the large cannon-ball will fall out.

An Aviary in a Hat.—This excellent but well-known trick requires the assistance of a confederate. A hat is borrowed from one of the audience, and turned round and round to show there is nothing in it. It is then laid on the operator's table, behind a vase or some other bulky article ; after which, as if a new idea had occurred to you, perform some other trick, during which the confederate removes the borrowed hat, substituting one previously prepared. This substituted hat is filled with small pigeons, placed in a bag with a whalebone or elastic mouth, which fits the inside of the hat. The bag containing the birds is covered with a piece of cloth, with a slit in the top. The operator, taking up the hat, puts his hand through the slit, and takes out the birds, one by one till all are free. The hat is then placed on the table, for the ostensible purpose of cleaning it before handing it back, and the confederate again changes the hats, having in the interim fitted the borrowed hat with a bag similar to the other, and also filled with pigeons. This having been done, you call out to your confederate, and request him, so that all your audience may hear, "Take the gentleman's hat away, and clean it." He takes it up, and peeps into it, saying : "You have not let all the birds away ;" upon which, to the surprise and amusement of the spectators, you produce another lot of birds as before. In brushing the hat previous to restoring it to the owner, the bag must be adroitly removed.

To See a Future Husband.—On Midsummer-eve, just after sunset, three, five, or seven young women are to go into a garden, in which there is no other person, and each to gather a sprig of red sage, and then, going into a room by themselves, set a stool in the middle of the room, and on it a clean basin full of rose-water, in which the sprigs of sage are to be put, and, tying a line across the room, on one side of the stool, each woman is to hang on it a clean white handkerchief; then all are to sit down in a row, on the opposite side of the stool, as far distant as the room will admit, not speaking a single word the whole time, whatever they see, and in a few minutes after twelve, each one's future husband will take her sprig out of the rose-water, and sprinkle her handkerchief with it.

On St. Agnes' night, 21st of January, take a row of pins, and pull out every one, one after another, saying a paternoster on sticking a pin in your sleeve, and you will dream of him you will marry.

A bit of the bride-cake thrice drawn through the wedding-ring, and laid under the head of an unmarried woman, will make her dream of her future husband. The same is practiced in the North with a piece of the groaning cheese.

To Know what fortune your future Husband will have.—Take a walnut, a hazle-nut, and nutmeg; grate them together, and mix them with butter and sugar, and make them up into small pills, of which exactly nine must be taken on going to bed; and according to your dreams, so will be the state of the person you will marry. If a gentleman, of riches; if a clergyman, of white linen; if a lawyer, of darkness; if a tradesman, of odd noises and tumults; if a soldier or sailor, of thunder and lightning; if a servant, of rain.

To Give Eggs a variegated Appearance.—Cut up a couple of handfuls of different colored rags into small strips, mix them together indiscriminately, and completely envelope the egg in them; then tie the whole in a piece of cloth and boil them for three or four hours.

The wet Sleeve.—Go out, one or more, to a south running spring or rivulet, where "three laird's lands meet," and dip your left shirt-sleeve. Go to bed in sight of a fire, and hang your wet sleeve before it to dry. Lie awake; and some time near midnight an apparition, having the exact figure of the grand object in question, will come and turn the sleeve, as if to dry the other side of it.

To Produce beautiful Fireworks in miniature.—Put half a drachm of solid phosphorus into a large pint Florence flask—holding it slanting, that the phosphorus may not break the glass. Pour upon it a gill and a half of water, and place the whole over a tea-kettle lamp, or any common tin lamp, filled with spirit of wine. Light the wick, which should be almost half an inch from the flask; and as soon as the water is heated, streams of fire will issue from the water by starts, resembling sky-rockets; some particles will adhere to the sides of the glass, representing stars, and will frequently display brilliant rays. These appearances will continue at times till the water begins to simmer, when immediately a curious aurora borealis begins, and gradually ascends, till it collects to a pointed flame; when it has continued half a minute, blow out the flame of the lamp, and the point that was formed will rush down, forming beautiful illuminated clouds of fire, rolling over each other for some time, which, disappearing, a splendid hemisphere of stars presents itself; after waiting a minute or two, light the lamp again, and nearly the same phenomenon will be displayed as from the beginning. Let the repetition of lighting and blowing out the lamp be made for three or four times at least, that the stars may be increased. After the third or fourth time of blowing out the lamp, in a few minutes after the internal surface of the flask is dry, many of the stars will shoot with great splendor, from side to side, and some of them will fire off with brilliant rays; these appearances will continue several minutes. What remains in the flask will serve for the same experiment several times, and without adding any more water. Care should be taken, after the operation is over, to lay the flask and water in a cool, secure place.

To Construct and Inflate a small Balloon.—It is an interesting and amusing experiment to inflate a small balloon made of gold-beater's skin, (using a little gum arabic to close any holes or fissures) filling it from a bladder or jar, and tying a thread round the mouth of it to prevent the escape of the gas. When fully blown, attach a fanciful car of colored paper, or very thin pasteboard to it, and let it float in a large room; it will soon gain the ceiling, where it will remain for any length of time; if it be let off in the open air, it will ascend out of sight. This experiment may be varied, by putting small grains of shot into the car, in order to ascertain the difference between the weight of hydrogon gas and atmospheric air.

The Enchanted Cock.—Bring a cock into a room with both your hands close to his wings, and hold them tight; put him on a table, and point his beak down as straight as possible; then let any one draw a line with a piece of chalk directly from his beak, and all the noise you can possibly make will not disturb him for some time, from the seeming lethargy which that position you have laid him in has effected.

The Oriental Ball Trick.—This trick, as practiced by the Eastern juggler who visited England some time ago with the famous Oriental Troupe, is particularly effective. Procure three balls of wood, the size of billiard balls, each having a small hole drilled completely through it, the hole the size of an ordinary black-lead pencil.

Procure also two pieces of white tape, each ten feet long. Double each tape exactly in half, so that they become only five feet long. Insert the folded end into one of the balls; pull it through about an inch; then open the double tape, which of course becomes a loop; into which

loop insert about an inch of the folded end of the other piece of tape; then carefully draw the first tape back into the ball, and it will be found that the joint of the two tapes *in the ball* is not only very firm, but completely hidden. Then thread the *other ends* of one tape into one of the other balls, and slide the ball along the tape until it reaches the first ball. Do the same with the other ball on the other tape. Thus all the balls will be threaded on the tape, the centre ball containing the tape connections. All this is prepared beforehand. When the trick is performed, show the three balls on the tapes, and ask two persons to hold the ends of the tapes, allowing the balls to swing loosely in the centre. Show that there is no trick about it by sliding the two outer balls to and fro upon the tape. To make it more wonderful (but really to accomplish the trick), ask each person to drop *one end* of their respective tapes, so that the balls may be tied on. Make a single tie of the two lengths, and give each person an end, *but not the end he held before.* Now request the assistants to pull gradually, and as the tapes become strained, strike two or three smart blows with the hand, or a stick, upon the balls, and they will fall to the ground uninjured, while, to the astonishment of everyone, the tapes remain unbroken. The tape used should be of the best linen, and about three-quarters of an inch wide.

An Excellent Card Trick.—Place all the diamonds of the pack, except the court cards, in a row on the table. Place also a few *common* spades and hearts, or clubs, between some of the diamonds, as, for example, three of hearts, five of diamonds, nine of clubs, six of diamonds, four of spades, nine of diamonds, &c. Take care to lay all the cards in the same direction—that is, with the tops of the cards all one way. This is easy enough as regards

the spades, clubs, and hearts—and really as easy as regards the diamonds—for on close inspection it will be seen that the margin between the point of the diamond and the edge of the card is much smaller at one end of the card than the other. Place the narrow margins at the top, and the trick is ready.

Request one or two of the company to invert any of the cards in your absence. They will naturally turn a diamond, never suspecting the difference of margin; the change of spades, &c., being too apparent a matter. On your return you at once detect the changed card or cards. Should any one discover the trick, defy the *detector* to tell which card is turned during his absence. When he leaves the room turn a spade or heart *completely round,* leaving it exactly as it was before; then summon the would-be-conjuror, whose perplexity will afford considerable amusement.

The Ring and Stick.—This trick is very puzzling, and requires but little preparation or practice.

Get two brass curtain rings; keep one of them in the coat sleeve, offer the other to the company for examination—procure a light walking-stick, and secretly slip the ring from the sleeve upon the stick, covering it well with the left hand. Hold the stick in the centre with the ring concealed, and invite two persons to hold the ends of the stick. While engaging the attention by some apparent necessity for having the stick either higher or lower—a little higher at one end, a little lower at the other, etc., etc.—give the stick a smart tap with the examined ring in your right hand, and withdraw the left hand rapidly, making the ring on the stick spin violently.

It will appear that the ring in the right hand has passed miraculously upon the stick; how, no one can tell, the ring being solid, and the stick guarded at both ends. The

right-hand ring must be secreted in the sleeve or pocket after the effect is produced; but no great haste is required, as every one will be too intent upon examining the ring on the stick to watch the operator.

The Hat Puzzle.—Request any person to mark upon the wall the exact height of an ordinary silk hat, supposing the hat to be placed on its crown on the floor. Exhibit the hat before its height is marked, and it is curious to observe how entirely different are the ideas of half a dozen persons upon the subject—the greater number marking high enough for two or three hats.

The Restored Handkerchief.—A hat, a newspaper, a handkerchief, a pair of scissors, and a plate, are required to carry out this illusion. Place a hat on the table at the back of the room, that is, *away* from the audience, but in sight of them. Borrow a handkerchief, and dexterously substitute another in its place. This is easy enough to do. Proceed as follows:—

Secrete a common handkerchief between the lower edge of the coat and waistcoat, the lower button of the coat being fastened, that the handkerchief may not fall. Having obtained a lady's handkerchief, holding it in the left hand, turn sharply round, and, in the act of turning, draw the concealed handkerchief from the coat, and pass the borrowed handkerchief from the left to the right hand, so that the two handkerchiefs are brought together. Pretend to look for some mark in the borrowed handkerchief, but *really* be crushing the borrowed handkerchief into small compass, and spreading out the false one.

Then lay it *on the edge* of the hat, exposing well the false article, and dropping the real one into the hat, at the same time bidding the company observe that the handkerchief never leaves their sight. Then fetch a pair of scissors, or borrow a pen-knife. Take the false handkerchief and cut out the middle. Ask some one to hold the middle tightly in his hand; some one else to hold the edges in the same manner. Leave the room to fetch a plate, taking the hat away at the same time. Lay the real handkerchief flat between two pages of a newspaper, fold the paper and return with both paper and plate to the company. Now set fire to the edges of the destroyed handkerchief; let the fire burn itself out in the plate. Spread the paper out on the table, all but the last fold, which conceals the other handkerchief. Place the cut centre on the paper; empty the ashes from the plate upon the centre; fold up the paper and crush it as much as possible, so that the folds or creases may not betray anything. Lastly, pick the paper to pieces until the restored handkerchief is gradually developed; pull it out, and throw the paper all into the fire. A little practice will render this illusion very startling in its effect. Care must be taken, in borrowing the handkerchief, to secure one as much like the *property handkerchief* as possible.

Excellent Trick with Shilling-pieces.—In a plate the operator has twenty-four shillings. He holds the plate in the left hand, having another eight shillings in the hand or fingers, covered by the plate. He asks one of the company to count the pieces one by one on the plate, first pouring the twenty-four pieces into his hands. He counts twenty-four. Then he takes the plate in the right hand, quickly pouring the pieces into the left hand, and thus mixing the concealed eight pieces with the rest, making thirty-two in all. He asks the same person to hold the pieces in one hand and the plate in the other; then he desires him to drop several pieces on the plate. When eight have fallen, the operator takes them away. The person holding the balance believes himself now to have only sixteen pieces. The operator takes the eight pieces in a pile, and rolls them up in a piece of newspaper, which should be torn from a crumpled paper especially placed beforehand. Having folded the eight pieces in paper, he announces that he will make them disappear from the paper, and appear in the hand of the person holding the plate and coins. At this moment the operator discovers that the wrapping has burst, and, returning to the crumpled paper, rids himself secretly of the package altogether, leaving it, of course, in the mass of paper, while he tears off another portion, and pretends to re-wrap the coins. He then commands the money to disappear, shows that it has obeyed; and upon the gentleman holding the coins counting them one by one on the plate, he will, of course, discover that there are twenty-four, as in the first instance. The operator must remove the unused newspaper before any one thinks to examine it? or, at all events, remove the package containing the eight shillings.

A Rope Trick.—Procure a rope the size of a clothes' line, and about twelve or fifteen feet long.

Ask some one to tie your wrists together with a handkerchief; then get him to draw the rope through the arms, and hold the two ends tightly. Bid him stand as far away as the double ropes will permit. The performer is now to drop the rope from his arms, without untying the handkerchief.

To accomplish it, he must pull tightly against the person holding the ends of the rope.

This enables him to draw the rope well in *between* the wrists, until, on slacking the rope, the fingers can easily reach it and draw it *through* the handkerchief, until suff-

cient is through to permit one hand to slip through the noose of rope which is formed by this last movement. A slight pull from the assistant causes the rope to fall free of the hands and arms.

An Impossibility.—Request any one to stand with his back *against* the wall—the heels being close to the wall; drop a handkerchief at his feet, and defy him to pick it up without moving his feet.

To Make a Cane or Poker stand in the middle of the Room.—Get two black pins, and a piece of black silk thread about a yard long. Tie a pin on each end, and fasten the pins into the cloth of the trousers under each knee; thus the walking about is not interfered with, and the line hangs loosely between the knees. Sit down at some distance from the company, and spread the knees to tighten the silk. Take the stick or poker, and rest it against the silk, and it will remain stationary, even at a great angle. The operator should pretend to make magnetic passes with the hands, as though the effect were due to magnetic influence.

The Trick of the Inexhaustible Bottle.—This is so well known, that it requires but little description. It is an ordinary-looking bottle from which, after having been proved to be perfectly empty, many kinds of wines and spirits are produced in apparently inexhaustible varieties and quantities.

The bottle is made inside with four tubes, into each of which, by means of a small funnel, different sorts of liquors are poured. By keeping the fingers over the apertures on the outside of the bottle, the different liquids are retained in the bottle ; but the instant the fingers are removed, the air rushes in, and allows whatever is in that particular tube to escape. Care must be observed, in pouring out, that the head of the bottle be kept down in the wine-glass, to avoid showing that the liquid flows but in a small stream. The glass should be thick at the bottom, holding but a small quantity, and yet appearing to contain much more.

The Dice Trick.—To perform this trick satisfactorily you must try to impress your audience with the idea that the dice actually dissolves, and goes through the hat.

For the performance a hat is required, which you may borrow from one of the company.

Removing the cover, the true and false dice are placed together in the hat.

You then state that you are going to take the dice out of the hat; but this you do not do in reality, as you take only the false dice out, leaving the true dice in.

The "Twenty Cent" Trick.—Borrow twenty cents from the company, which display on a plate, having previously prepared five cents in your *left hand*, which you keep concealed. Then take the cents from the plate in the right hand, and mixing them with the concealed five, give them to one of the company to hold. Ask the possessor to return five to you, which he will do, supposing he then retains only fifteen, although, in reality, he of course has twenty. Now have another cent palmed in your right hand, so that when giving the five cents to another person to hold, you may mix it with that sum, and place the *six* cents in his hand. You may now ask him, as before, to return *one;* when you take it remind him he has only four, and you must now proceed with the most marvelous part of your illusion. Taking the one cent you have just received in the right hand, *palm* it, and pretend to place it in the left. Then, striking the left hand with a rod, bid it fly into the closed hand of the person holding five, or, as he supposes, the *four* cents. On unclosing the hand, the cent will of course appear to have been transferred thither, and great amazement will result. Now, taking the five cents, make a more dexterous pass into the left hand, whence you bid them fly into the closed hand of the person holding the supposed fifteen, and whom you now ask to return you the full sum of twenty cents, much to his own wonder and that of the company. If executed with care and dexterity, no illusion can be more effective.

To Make an egg stand on one end on a table or Looking-Glass.—To make an egg stand on end on any polished surface seems very extraordinary, yet is to be done even on a looking-glass. Now, from the form of an egg, nothing is more liable to roll, and on nothing more than a looking-glass. To accomplish this trick, let the performer take an egg in his hand, and while he keeps talking and staring in the faces of his audience, give it two or three hearty shakes; this will break the yolk, which will sink to one end, and consequently make it more heavy, by which, when it is settled, you may make it, with a steady hand, stand upon the glass. This would be impossible while it continued in its proper state.

The Magic Cups.—Procure two tin cups without handles, quite plain, straight sides. With the bottoms sunk a quarter of an inch. On the bottoms spread some glue, and completely cover the glue with some kind of bird seed, only so as not to be seen when standing in an ordinary position. Have ready a bag filled with the same kind of seed as you used in covering the bottoms. Put the cups on the table; also two hats. Put one cup then into the bag, appear to fill it, and take it out turned bottom up-wards, when it will look as if it had been filled. Put it in that position under one hat; in doing so turn it over. Then take the other empty cup, put that under the other hat; and, in doing so, turn that over, which of course must be invisible to the audience. Then remove the hat, and the cups will appear to have changed places.

The Bogle Bodkin.—Take a hollow bodkin, (or if you prefer it a dagger) so that the blade may slip into the handle as soon as the blade is turned upward. Seem to thrust it into your forehead, (or if a dagger, into your bosom,) then after showing some appearance of pain, pull away your hand suddenly, holding the point downward, and it will fall out, and appear not to have been thrust into the haft; but immediately afterward, throw the bodkin or dagger into your lap or pocket, and pull out another plain one like it which will completely deceive the spectators.

To Put a Ring through one's Cheek.—Have two rings exactly alike, one of which has a notch which admits your cheek. When you have exhibited the perfect ring, you change it for the other, and privately slip the notch over one side of your mouth; in the meantime, you slip the whole ring on your stick, hiding it with your hand; then desire some one to hold the end of the stick, whip the ring out of your cheek, and smite with it instantly upon the stick, concealing it, and whirling the other ring which you hold in your hand over around about the stick. The celebrated Chinese ring trick, of linking from seven to nine rings together, is done on the same principle as the above, that is, one of the rings is split, all the others are solid, and are examined by the company; two or three are made solid by linking, and by means of the split ring they can all be joined in various ways.

ACKNOWLEDGEMENTS

Jay Marshall's technical editing of this book has been invaluable. Jay's knowledge of magic is overwhelming, and his recall is one of the great tricks of all time. Jay and his wife, Frances Ireland Marshall, are not only two of the best-informed people in magic but two of the nicest.

Allan Carr, who designed MAGIC DIGEST, took hundreds of snapshots of my hands, and his wife translated the photographs into the line drawings that illustrate the various tricks. Allan is an avid amateur magician whose liking for the hobby made him give this assignment extra-special attention.

Milt Klein, president of Digest Books, Inc., had wanted for years to publish a magic book. When he saw the first draft of this one, he went all-out for it. It was his idea, and I think it's a great one, to include sample pages of representative magic catalogues.

Rosalyn Adler, who worked with me on the production of the Magic Ranch television series and many other show business projects, and who is one of my favorite people of all time, is now a staff member of Digest Books. Her contributions to MAGIC DIGEST start with her getting me together with Milt Klein for a previous book, *Gambler's Digest,* and go on from there.

Sheldon Factor, certainly one of the most competent and conscientious production men in the field of publishing, has nursed the book from first draft to completion, giving me the assurance throughout that the book was in good hands.

Chuck Hartigan, who brought Follett Publishing Co. into the picture, and Bob Follett, who saw MAGIC DIGEST's possibilities, deserve my gratitude and have it.

So many people have contributed over the years to my knowledge and appreciation of magic that it would be impossible to list all of them. Those I recall with special fondness, some no longer living, are:

David Abbott, Allan Ackerman, Max Adali, Don Alan, Ted Annemann, Theo Bamberg, Joe Berg, McDonald Birch, J. Elder Blackledge, Harry Blackstone, Paul Braden, Glenn Bunnell, Eddie Clever, Clarke Crandall, Dorny, Bruce Elliott, Art Felsman, King Felton, Neil Foster, Fox, Karrell Fox, A.C. Gilbert, U.F. "Gen" Grant, the Gwynnes, Richard Himber, Max Holden, Jean Hugard, Bill Hyer, Laurie Ireland, Clifford Jurgenson, the Larsens, Ed Marlo, Ed McLaughlin, Joe Mercedes, Orville Meyer, John Mulholland, C. A. George Newmann, Johnny Platt, Rajah Raboid, Dr. Harlan Tarbell, J. G. Thompson, Jr., Jimmy Thompson, C. R. "Bud" Tracy, Vic Torsberg, and Dai Vernon.

It is almost impossible to give credit for all of the tricks included in MAGIC DIGEST. Over the years, as a trick is adapted to a performer's particular style and abilities, he forgets where the basic idea originated. Also, little "twists" are added that originated with someone else. And anyone who does magic over a lengthy period contributes his own variations that make the trick, in his mind, his baby.

An additional problem is that magicians "swap" tricks. One performer thinks of a trick as being the creation of the man who showed him how to do it when, in reality, that performer may have gotten the trick from somebody else.

Tricks are often claimed, in all sincerity, by more than one originator, operating independently of each other. I've sometimes come up with what I thought was a revolutionary new idea, only to be told by an old timer that it was first done by Kellar or Herrmann the Great. Kellar and Herrmann undoubtedly learned to their surprise that some of what they considered their originations were first performed by Robert Houdin or in ancient India.

A new trick is almost never completely original. One of the finest close-up sleight-of-hand tricks to come along in many years was Dr. Sack's dice routine, first published in a magazine. It depended on the "paddle move," one of the oldest manipulations in magic, and the fact that the top and bottom of a dice (or die) will always total 7. Mock Sad Ali had been doing the paddle move with a single die 50 years previously and many dice tricks had depended on the mathematical arrangement of dice spots. However, Sack, by doing a routine with a pair of dice instead of one, made an ordinary trick a superior one.

Ted Annemann came up with a marvelous trick, Pseudo-Psychometry. It was based upon secretly marked envelopes, which had been used in mental magic for years. I added the twist to it of letting a spectator grab a bunch of envelopes from a box of envelopes, which seemed to preclude the possibility of marked envelopes. In truth, every envelope in the box was marked, running in sets of five, so that when the spectator counted off five envelopes into my hand, there were bound to be envelopes marked from 1 to 5. I did not include this twist in the MAGIC DIGEST version because the performer must rearrange the pile of 5 envelopes in 1-to-5 order before passing them out. Then I added another twist, the use of dowsing rods, which adds a great impact. Ted cheerfully admitted that his trick was based on an old dodge —and I just as readily admit that mine is based on his.

Most of the new tricks that achieve popularity every year are based upon principles that are as old as time. In many cases, nothing new is added. The tricks have simply been forgotten and somebody is smart enough to revive them.

Since the basic secrets of magic are limited in number, most tricks are adaptations of those secrets to new articles and new plots. Analyze what happens in most tricks. Something appears from nowhere or vanishes. Two objects are magically transposed. Something is destroyed and then restored. The magician "divines" something of which he is unaware. One solid object apparently goes through another solid object. The law of gravity is defied. That's just about it.

That magicians can use such a limited number of principles in so many different ways and make their tricks seem new and fresh is to their everlasting credit. A good magician uses as much imagination as skill to make his tricks interesting to an audience.

So if we are to "credit" tricks, the only safe way to do it is to credit all tricks to the magic fraternity at large, which I hereby do.